PRINCIPLES OF MULTICULTURAL COUNSELING AND THERAPY

COUNSELING AND PSYCHOTHERAPY
INVESTIGATING PRACTICE FROM SCIENTIFIC, HISTORICAL,
AND CULTURAL PERSPECTIVES

Editor, Bruce E. Wampold, University of Wisconsin

This innovative new series is devoted to grasping the vast complexities of the practice of counseling and psychotherapy. As a set of healing practices delivered in a context shaped by health delivery systems and the attitudes and values of consumers, practitioners, and researchers, counseling and psychotherapy must be examined critically. By understanding the historical and cultural context of counseling and psychotherapy and by examining the extant research, these critical inquiries seek a deeper, richer understanding of what is a remarkably effective endeavor.

Published

Counseling and Therapy with Clients Who Abuse Alcohol or Other Drugs
Cynthia E. Glidden-Tracy

The Great Psychotherapy Debate
Bruce Wampold

The Psychology of Working: Implications for Career Development, Counseling, and Public Policy
David Blustein

Neuropsychotherapy: How the Neurosciences Inform Effective Psychotherapy
Klaus Grawe

Forthcoming

The Pharmacology and Treatment of Substance Abuse: Evidence and Outcomes Based Perspective
Lee Cohen, Frank Collins, Alice Young, Dennis McChargue

Making Treatment Count: Using Outcomes to Inform and Manage Therapy
Michael Lambert, Jeb Brown, Scott Miller, Bruce Wampold

The Handbook of Therapeutic Assessment
Stephen E. Finn

IDM Supervision: An Integrated Developmental Model for Supervising Counselors and Therapists, Third Edition
Cal Stoltenberg and Brian McNeill

The Great Psychotherapy Debate, Revised Edition
Bruce Wampold

Casebook for Multicultural Counseling
Miguel E. Gallardo and Brian W. McNeill

Culture and the Therapeutic Process: A Guide for Mental Health Professionals
Mark M. Leach and Jamie Aten

Principles of Multicultural Counseling and Therapy
Uwe P. Gielen, Juris G. Draguns, and Jefferson M. Fish

PRINCIPLES OF MULTICULTURAL COUNSELING AND THERAPY

Uwe P. Gielen, Juris G. Draguns, Jefferson M. Fish

EDITORS

Routledge
Taylor & Francis Group
New York   London

Chapter 10 reproduced with permission from Sage Publications India Pvt. Ltd.

Routledge
Taylor & Francis Group
270 Madison Avenue
New York, NY 10016

Routledge
Taylor & Francis Group
2 Park Square
Milton Park, Abingdon
Oxon OX14 4RN

© 2008 by Taylor & Francis Group, LLC
Routledge is an imprint of Taylor & Francis Group, an Informa business

Printed in the United States of America on acid-free paper
10 9 8 7 6 5 4 3 2 1

International Standard Book Number-13: 978-0-8058-6204-1 (Softcover) 978-0-8058-6205-8 (0)

Library of Congress Cataloging-in-Publication Data

Principles of multicultural counseling and therapy / edited by Uwe P. Gielen, Juris G. Draguns, Jefferson M. Fish.
    p. ; cm.
Includes bibliographical references and indexes.
ISBN 978-0-8058-6205-8 (hardbound : alk. paper) -- ISBN 978-0-8058-6204-1 (pbk. : alk. paper)
    1. Psychiatry, Transcultural. 2. Cross-cultural counseling. I. Gielen, Uwe P. (Uwe Peter), 1940- II. Draguns, Juris G., 1932- III. Fish, Jefferson M.
    [DNLM: 1. Counseling--methods. 2. Cross-Cultural Comparison. 3. Cultural Diversity. 4. Psychotherapy--methods. WM 55 P957 2008]

RC455.4.E8P748 2008
616.89--dc22

2008010895

Visit the Taylor & Francis Web site at
http://www.taylorandfrancis.com

and the Routledge Web site at
http://www.routledge.com

This book is dedicated to the memory of Pittu Laungani, a dear friend and multicultural counselor who walked the road between East and West.

Contents

Foreword

It is a pleasure to write the foreword for a book devoted to cross-cultural counseling—a topic that is intrinsically fascinating—and this task is especially enjoyable because the editors have pulled together such a prominent and distinguished group of luminaries to contribute chapters. These authors include, among many others, Juris Draguns, Jefferson Fish, Uwe Gielen, Judy Kuriansky, Jeffrey Rubin, Michael Stevens, and Junko Tanaka-Matsumi; all of these individuals are icons in the world of cross-cultural psychology. In addition, I have kicked around enough to know many of the contributors on a first-name basis, and I cherish their friendship.

The world of those most passionately invested in international and cross-cultural psychology is relatively small, and one of the most gratifying aspects of working in this arena is participating in international meetings with many of the authors in this book. A number of us attended the International Congress of Psychology in Beijing in 2004 and the International Association of Applied Psychology meeting in Athens in 2006, and we'll be meeting up once again in Berlin next year for the 2008 International Congress of Psychology. The time I've spent with colleagues in these international venues makes up some of my favorite professional memories, and I'm certain I will cherish these memories—and these friends—all the more as I age.

Although this book can be read from chapter by chapter, cover to cover, I suspect many readers will find it just as rewarding to pick out pages at random and mine them for the rich ore they contain. For example, I was unfamiliar with the hot/cold classification of diseases in Latin America before reading Linda Sussman's chapter on the role of culture in illness interpretation and therapy—but who better than an anthropologist to educate us about such matters. For this chapter, like so many others, I found myself eager to follow up with the helpful and carefully selected suggested readings. Likewise, I was intrigued by Jefferson Fish's thoughtful discussion of race and challenged by the provocative ethics cases provided in Michael Stevens's chapter.

It is clear that these authors care deeply about cross-cultural psychology, and I found myself thinking what superb professors they must be. Their passion comes across in every page of this book, and I suspect it must come across in the classroom as well. I wonder if their students realize how lucky they are.

This text is replete with case examples and clinical anecdotes, and these are what the reader may remember the longest. However, there are also specific tools that many practitioners may find useful. Judy Kuriansky is one of the most prolific—and best traveled—figures in contemporary cross-cultural psychology, and the "toolbox" she has prepared grew out of her experience with thousands of clients in hundreds of groups across dozens of countries. I can't wait to try out many of the tools Judy is promoting.

A foreword is supposed to be brief, but it is hard for me to avoid being effusive about this splendid contribution to the cross-cultural counseling literature. Those of us who take time to read the book and adapt it to our own professional situations likely will be better therapists and counselors—at the very least, we'll better understand the beauty, fascination, complexity, and challenges associated with life in a multicultural world.

Danny Wedding, PhD, MPH
Saint Louis

Series Foreword

This series is devoted to understanding the complexities of the practice of counseling and psychotherapy. As a set of healing practices, delivered in a context molded by health delivery systems and the attitudes and values of consumers, practitioners, and researchers, counseling and psychotherapy must be examined critically. Volumes in this series discuss counseling and psychotherapy from empirical, historical, anthropological, and theoretical perspectives. These critical inquiries avoid making assumptions about the nature of counseling and psychotherapy and seek a deeper understanding of the bases of what is a remarkably effective endeavor.

In the current era of globalization, counseling and psychotherapy are being employed predominantly in contexts that involve cultural issues. The culturally encapsulated delivery of psychological services is rare, if it ever existed, and institutions, therapists, and systems of care must adapt to cultural complexity so that services are acceptable and effective. Simple admonitions to be culturally sensitive or aware of one's own biases and privilege/ oppression are insufficient—needed is a deep understanding of the manner in which culture affects well-being and distress as well as healing. And this is exactly what Uwe Gielen, Juris Draguns, and Jeff Fish provide in *Principles of Multicultural Counseling and Therapy*. This edited volume, which is immersed in anthropology, cultural studies, and cross-cultural psychiatry and psychology, places the concepts of well-being and distress in cultural context and then builds the principles of service delivery from a multicultural perspective that considers biological, psychological, and social perspectives. The models, which are applicable to a variety of contexts, are then illustrated with practices across the globe. Finally, the difficult issues, such as the tension between Western and indigenous healing practices, are discussed.

Preface

There is more to counseling and therapy than exists in the United States. With widespread migration and culture contact in an era of globalization, and thousands of cultures around the world, no individual can begin to comprehend them all. What are counselors and therapists to do? We believe that an understanding of general principles can help to clarify and bring intellectual structure to this wide-ranging diversity.

As its title indicates, this volume introduces some basic cultural concepts and principles that people in the helping professions (individual, marital, family, and other therapists; educational, vocational, guidance, and pastoral counselors; social workers; persons training for positions in human resources; school psychologists; psychiatrists; and others) need to understand in order to practice successfully in the modern multicultural world. The various chapters included in the volume explore the role of culture in defining, interpreting, and managing interpersonal situations that center on clients' distress and confusion, and professional efforts to ameliorate their predicament.

Books on multicultural counseling and therapy often attempt to guide professionals from mainstream American or European cultural backgrounds who are confronted with the task of counseling culturally distinct clients, usually from African American, Latino, Asian American, Native American, Middle Eastern, North African, and other backgrounds. In contrast, the present volume focuses on the *general* nature of cultural influences in the context of counseling and therapeutic encounters. Furthermore, we are adopting a worldwide approach rather than restricting ourselves to interactions between a "mainstream" counselor or therapist and clients from specific American or European minority group backgrounds. We believe that such a broader, more internationally oriented approach will lead readers to a deeper understanding of cultural principles that govern a broad variety of counseling and therapeutic situations around the globe. To better understand the general assumptions underlying the contents of this book, it may prove useful to briefly indicate its origins within a historical framework.

Modern forms of psychotherapy and counseling originated in Europe at the end of the 19th and the beginning of the 20th centuries. They subsequently evolved in Europe and North America throughout the 20th century. But while the underlying theories of pioneering psychologists and psychiatrists were shaped by the broader context of Western culture, culture as a pervasive force remained largely invisible to their Western eyes. It is only during the last few decades that, given the ubiquitous forces of globalization and the worldwide spread of psychology, culture and cultural diversity have been recognized as central to the practice of counseling and psychological healing. In response to these developments, a variety of volumes covering various approaches to multicultural counseling have appeared in recent years. Given that a good many such texts are now available, the question arises: What does our volume add to the extant literature? In what ways does it offer new frameworks and information? To answer these questions, let us review briefly the origins of this book.

Principles of Multicultural Counseling and Therapy is a descendant of the editors' earlier volume, *Handbook of Culture, Therapy, and Healing*. Soon after its appearance in 2004, a number of enthusiastic readers as well as Steven Rutter from Lawrence Erlbaum Associates let us know that this volume filled a void by focusing on the role of culture in therapy from a worldwide perspective and by emphasizing principles and concepts rather than American minority groups. However, some professors indicated that, as a handbook, it was too lengthy, too advanced, and too expensive for course assignment. Consequently, we designed the present volume to respond to these concerns by being more concise and teachable and by introducing brief case studies and examples where appropriate. It also covers a variety of applied topics not dealt with in the original handbook. In classes on multicultural counseling and other forms of psychosocial intervention, this book may profitably be assigned together with other reading materials reviewing interventions with specific cultural groups.

We believe that students of counseling and therapy will best understand the pervasive role of culture in their professional endeavors by being exposed to a truly global perspective. This means that our book focuses not only on modern Western practices of counseling but also on a broad variety of related topics: shamanism, the practices of indigenous healers, historical considerations, the role of cultural expectations in medical healing, Buddhist conceptions of mental health and meditation, interactions between body and mind, counseling refugees and immigrants from other nations, and other pertinent topics. We believe that this broad perspective is both unique and essential.

Throughout the volume, it is assumed that culture influences pervasively the following:

- What we experience as distressing and disorienting; how we label our distress; to what sources and to whom we attribute the distress; whether we believe that invisible beings and forces are part of the origins of disorientation and distress and their treatment
- To whom, if anyone, we communicate our suffering; whom we consult in the hope of alleviating our distress; whom we regard as appropriate healers, therapists, and counselors; what we expect from them and how we experience our interactions with them; whom we regard as appropriate participants in the counseling and healing process
- Whether healing and counseling take place publicly or privately; what we consider to be a successful outcome or cure; how our bodies react to the encounters with healers; whether we choose to continue a given treatment; whether we take our pills or throw them away; and many other health-related and well-being–related actions, beliefs, and feelings

In this context, it frequently proves useful to consider mental and physical health as intertwined and dependent on each other.

In brief, we argue that counseling, therapy, and healing cannot be understood unless the role of culture and cultural context in therapeutic interactions is thoroughly examined. By learning how psychological interventions operate in other cultures, we also learn how our interventions are pervaded with our own cultural assumptions and expectations that may—or may not—diverge from or even clash with those of our clients.

A crucial benefit of studying multicultural psychology is a gain in the therapist's self-awareness. Both therapist and client are bound to benefit from such a gain because a counselor's "cultural encapsulation" inevitably leads to divergent expectations between counselor and client about the nature and goal of the therapeutic encounter, misdiagnosis of the client's concerns, mutual misunderstandings, missed nonverbal cues, client feelings of being misunderstood, and other dangers to the therapeutic alliance and outcome. Such difficulties often lead clients to discontinue their treatment prematurely—a frustrating experience for counselor and client alike.

Our decision to adopt a global perspective was shaped in part by our formative experiences. Uwe P. Gielen, a specialist in culture and developmental psychology, grew up as an internal refugee in Germany, immigrated to the United States, has done research and fieldwork on several continents, has edited/coedited/coauthored numerous volumes focusing on cross-cultural and international psychology, and is interested in global psychology. Jefferson M. Fish, a specialist in culture and therapy, has served as a Fulbright scholar and visiting professor in Brazil, where he trained clinical psychologists to function as therapists in cultural settings quite different from those prevailing in his native New York and where he accompanied his anthropologist wife on fieldwork with the Krikati Indians. Juris G. Draguns, a specialist in culture, psychopathology, and cross-cultural counseling, was born in Latvia, attended high school in Germany, immigrated to the United States, and has held visiting appointments at universities located on four continents. Thus, an awareness of the importance of cultural factors in counseling and healing has come to us as a result of personal experience and has become an integral part of our subjective outlook and our professional modus operandi.

Principles of Multicultural Counseling and Therapy is organized into an introductory chapter and five parts. The introductory chapter outlines the concept of culture and its implications in the context of psychological healing and counseling. Part 1 (chapters 2–6) provides background knowledge and broad psychological and anthropological perspectives conducive to a better understanding of healing and counseling situations. Part 2 (chapters 7–9) introduces a variety of models of multicultural counseling, and Part 3 (chapters 10–13) focuses on the practice of multicultural counseling in diverse cultural settings. Part 4 (chapters 14–15) discusses both indigenous and Western healing and counseling activities and their possible integration. Finally, Part 5 (chapters 16–17) reviews some academic findings and resources of potential use to multicultural counselors and therapists.

Acknowledgments

We gratefully acknowledge the invaluable assistance of several people, whose contributions to the book were critical in bringing it to fruition. We thank Steven Rutter from Lawrence Erlbaum Associates for suggesting the idea behind this book to us, and Dana Bliss and Nicole Buchman for helping to bring the book to completion. Bruce Wampold recommended several additional contributors to the volume and reviewed a number of chapters. Renée Goodstein, Jennifer Lancaster, Melba Mathurin, Michael Parker, Bernard Polnariev, Michael Schulman, and Michael D. Welsh-Balliett each reviewed one or more chapters and provided many helpful suggestions to the authors. We thank Nathan Abookire and Peter David Gonzales for their help with typing and the production of chapter manuscripts. We also express our appreciation to the University Seminars at Columbia University for financial assistance in preparing the manuscript for publication. Material drawn from this work was presented to the University Seminar on Ethics, Moral Education, and Society. Finally, the Institute for International and Cross-Cultural Psychology at St. Francis College provided much appreciated institutional support during the lengthy editing process.

Uwe P. Gielen
Juris G. Draguns
Jefferson M. Fish

Principles of Multicultural Counseling and Therapy
An Introduction

Uwe P. Gielen, Juris G. Draguns, Jefferson M. Fish

Contents

Culture hides much more than it reveals and strangely enough what it hides, it hides most effectively from its own participants. Years of study have convinced me that the real job is not to understand foreign cultures but to understand our own.

—**Edward T. Hall,** *The Silent Language*

Providing advice and guidance to the confused and perplexed, supporting sufferers emotionally, socially, and spiritually, and attempting to heal those broken in spirit, mind, and body have been human endeavors for thousands of years. Over the years, a broad variety of healers and counselors such as shamans, medicine men and women, medical doctors, herbalists, priests, priestesses, monks, nuns, father confessors, exorcists, mesmerists, phrenologists, faith healers, diviners, astrologers, and, more recently, psychologists, psychiatrists, social workers, counselors, and psychotherapists have offered their services to those in need of help. In past times, healers and sufferers frequently shared a common worldview that helped to support joint expectations about the nature of their bond, the meaningfulness of the healing and counseling efforts, and the means and ultimate goals of their efforts. Today, however, this is less and less the case.

Because many modern societies are steadily becoming more diverse, multicultural, and complex in nature, they are in need of counselors, psychotherapists, social workers, and healers who are able to interact effectively with clients from a broad variety of cultural, ethnic, social, political, and religious backgrounds. Today's mental health specialists are frequently asked to counsel members of various subcultures and minority groups, immigrants, refugees, foreign students, ever more diverse members of "the" majority culture, and bicultural/multicultural persons who may bring to the therapeutic encounter a bewildering variety of life experiences and cultural beliefs that at times diverge sharply from those of the therapist.

This situation requires a special type of "psychocultural mobility" from mental health specialists who not only must be able to think in terms of a variety of cognitive, sociocultural, and theoretical perspectives but also must acquire the ability to decide which perspective is most appropriate for which situation. Self-knowledge as well as knowledge of other cultures, a positive attitude toward new experiences, multilinguistic skills, and the ability to perceive general human problems and dilemmas beneath the seemingly exotic cultural garb of some of one's clients are all characteristic of a good multicultural counselor-therapist. These abilities should be accompanied by feelings of compassion with underdogs and the lonely, anxious, unhappy, angry, and confused, as well as the ability to communicate with, and put at ease, clients with different physical characteristics, personalities, belief systems, and life experiences. A good multicultural therapist is mentally flexible, eschews ethnocentric beliefs in the unique superiority of his or her culture, religion, and lifestyle, is able to see his or her culture(s) "in (multi)perspective," senses some of the client's unvoiced expectations and hesitations, and both experiences and displays warmth and care toward a broad range of people. In short, the therapist should be able to embrace the old adage "Nothing human is foreign to me," although, in truth, nobody can fully live up to the ideal implied in this saying.

Given these complex demands, our book is designed to familiarize mental health professionals and their students with recent social scientific thinking on the role of culture in the broader context of therapeutic and counseling interventions. Furthermore, because globalization is a pervasive tendency of our times, we believe that a global perspective that considers American minority groups as well as international cultural currents will prove most helpful in practicing multicultural therapy and counseling. Of course, reading books cannot replace a counselor's actual immersion in foreign cultures and languages, but it can sensitize her or him and expand her or his cultural horizon. After all, few Western counselors and therapists will ever observe the manifestations of despair of an alienated young Salish Indian in Canada or the complex experiences of educated, modern women walking behind a veil through the streets of Kuwait City. Reading this book cannot replace actual experience, but it can provide a reflective introduction to a broad range of human situations and therapeutic encounters.

The Concept of Culture

In the modern social sciences, the concept of culture has frequently been used as a master term to refer to that part of the environment that has been created by humans. Culture is simultaneously physical, behavioral, and mental in nature, and it exists both outside and inside of us. In the words of the anthropologists Kroeber and Kluckhohn (1952),

> Culture consists of patterns, explicit and implicit, of and for behavior acquired and transmitted by symbols, constituting the distinctive achievement of human groups, including their embodiments in artifacts; the essential core of culture consists of traditional ideas and especially their attached values; culture systems may, on the one hand, be considered as products of action, on the other as conditioning elements of further action. (p. 181)

Cultures are composed of complex, functional yet at times contradictory systems made up of socially patterned expectations; coordinated social roles; scripted action sequences; historical, explanatory, and emotionally pleasing narratives; verbal and nonverbal communication systems; and shared values, norms, attitudes, images, metaphors, and goals. Taken together, they help the members of a society to solve the problems associated with living and, more generally, to survive. Thus, healing systems have evolved everywhere in order to help individuals deal with physical and emotional distress in the service of adaptation and survival. As Sussman points out in this volume, a number of shared components can be discerned in healing and medical systems around the world, despite the great diversity of specific medical beliefs and practices found throughout the world. The components include illness classification systems, etiological beliefs, treatment practices, expectations about illnesses and treatment outcomes, designated healing specialists, norms regarding treatment seeking and illness management, and norms regarding consultations with healing specialists. This list can be expanded to include healing systems that deal with individuals who may be physically sick, mentally-behaviorally "sick," or spiritually "sick" or who present some combination of these complaints. In modern societies, mental health systems have partially diverged from medical systems, although many parallels and much overlap exist between them.

Sussman's chapter also reminds us that anthropologists have discussed the concept of culture for a much longer time period than psychologists have. Anthropologists tend to endorse more complex and cross-culturally informed conceptions of culture than many therapists and counselors who have only during the last few decades begun to critically examine the pervasive impact of culture upon their professional activities. Consequently, it behooves mental health specialists to learn from cultural and medical anthropologists in order to form a broader perspective and reduce the danger of professional tunnel vision (see also the two chapters by Fish in this regard).

It is important to point out that especially in modern multicultural societies, individuals internalize only selected aspects of the culture(s) that surrounds them. Furthermore, individuals may be members of several cultures and subcultures at once. A Chinese American student born in New York City, for instance, may speak Cantonese with her parents, English with her teachers, and Cantonese or Mandarin "Chinese-English" with some of her friends although she may be able to recognize only a few Chinese characters. She may have internalized some aspects of Chinese beliefs about the importance of *hsiao* or "filial piety" (felt obligations toward her parents) yet may also endorse seemingly contradictory beliefs about the desirability of behavioral and emotional autonomy as an adolescent. The latter would probably reflect the combined influences of many of her peers, the mass media, and even her developmental psychology textbook. She may resent some of the external and internal pressures that come with being a member of a high-achieving "model minority" yet be secretly proud of it. Perhaps she deeply appreciates her Chinese heritage yet rejects various aspects of it as old-fashioned, unjust, outdated, or just plain irrelevant. In a similar vein, she may have internalized—whether consciously or not—many aspects of American mainstream culture but object to others. Should she choose to enter therapy, it is likely that her bicultural identity and her complex feelings about it will become an important focus of discussion. After all, there is nothing simple about a bicultural identity such as hers, which can be simultaneously puzzling, enriching, constraining, and liberating.

It is likely that a bicultural Chinese counselor-therapist would intuitively recognize some of these complexities and ambivalent feelings but that a monocultural, non–East Asian mental health specialist would find it difficult to fully enter her frame of mind. Multicultural counseling and therapy are not for the faint of heart: They demand all the skills and emotional requirements inherent in the mental health professions, plus an additional layer of complexities having to do with highly diverse cultural expectations, experiences, modes of communication, and ways of being-in-the-world.

The notion of "internalized culture" underlines that individuals are not carbon copies of their surrounding society. While they are pervasively influenced by it, their personalities, behavioral patterns, thoughts, emotions, and identities reflect simultaneously biological, psychological, and sociocultural influences (Hirsch, this volume). Many individuals, moreover, will believe that supernatural beings and forces rather than the visible members of their group have created and/or are in charge of their bodies, minds, and souls (e.g., Jilek & Draguns; Sussman, both in this volume). Others will display physical symptoms that have an underlying physical substratum yet hold a symbolic significance.

As the quote by Edward Hall at the beginning of this chapter indicates, culture does much of its work outside of our sphere of awareness. We are most likely to become aware of our cultural assumptions when they are violated or when we are plunged into cultural settings different from those that we are used to. Cultural awareness thrives on cultural comparisons and emotion-provoking contradictions. However, the rich variety of existing cultural norms throughout the world does not obligate us to accept cultural relativism in its entirety (Kuriansky, this volume; Tanaka-Matsumi, this volume). In counseling situations, for instance, counselor and client may share many perspectives and beliefs, yet their encounter may still be derailed by seemingly small differences in behavioral expectations. There is wisdom in the remark of the proverbial Vermont farmer who announced, "People is mostly alike, but what differences there is, is mighty important."

Social scientists discussing the cross-cultural variability of human behavior have adopted a variety of theoretical positions. Cultural relativists such as Fish (this volume) emphasize that an enormous variety of beliefs and behavior can be observed across societies. In contrast, universalists are more concerned with discovering similar psychological processes beneath the rich tapestry of culturally patterned behavior. Psychoanalytic scholars such as Rubin (this volume) postulate that certain personality patterns, ego-defense mechanisms, thought processes, and basic motives can be found around the world. In this volume, both relativists and universalists are given a voice in order to fully represent the range of positions regarding this central issue. In other words, contributors to this volume deal with both the universal psychological processes that purportedly underlie forms of intervention that appear quite different and some of the more culture-specific manifestations of healing and counseling.

Other cross-cultural researchers have focused on a number of value dimensions along which cultures and subcultures can be ordered. These include Hofstede's five value dimensions (see Draguns, this volume) as well as the important "context dimension" that distinguishes between the poles of high-context cultures (e.g., traditional Japanese small-town culture) and low-context cultures (e.g., modern American culture, especially within or around metropolitan urban centers).

Members of low-context cultures are taught to communicate their thoughts and emotions explicitly and to believe in general principles that can be used to create meaning and order in the sociomoral fabric of society (e.g., liberty, justice, and the pursuit of happiness). In contrast, communication in high-context cultures tends to be indirect, implicit, context-dependent, unspoken, and nonverbal. Such communication patterns are especially likely to occur in relatively homogeneous and collectivistic cultures in which tacit understandings are widely shared. As modern cultures become more heterogeneous in terms of ethnicity and lifestyle, high-context communication patterns become more dysfunctional and are difficult to sustain. This holds especially true when members of different subcultures attempt to convey intricate emotional meanings and subtle social expectations to each other.

The distinction between low-context and high-context cultures frequently proves important for understanding certain cross-cultural misunderstandings in counseling/therapeutic situations. Therapists and counselors from a low-context cultural background, for instance, may find it difficult to "read" clients who matured in a high-context culture. They want their clients to spell out what bothers them so that they can jointly get down to work. The clients, however, may expect that a good counselor "doesn't need to be told," that she/he should be empathic and thus able to understand the client's feelings and expectations through a kind of emotional osmosis. They may think: If she is unable to understand my unspoken meanings and messages, why does she call herself a therapist? In such situations, both therapist and client will easily feel disappointed without being fully aware of the cultural origins of their frustration. Premature termination of therapy by the client is not an uncommon outcome in such situations.

Ethnic, Racial, Religious, and Gender Identities in a Multicultural World

It has been said that every person is in some ways like all other persons (shared human nature), in some ways like some other persons (shared group characteristics), and in some ways like no other person (a unique individual; Kluckhohn, Murray, & Schneider, 1953). By way of analogy, we may postulate that a person's subjective identity includes the person's awareness that she/he is like all (or almost all) others ("I am a human being with human perceptions, thoughts, and feelings rather than an animal, plant, lifeless object, ghost, or demon"), like some others ("I am a married Mayan woman and housewife, different from the racially and culturally mixed *Ladinos*, a Mayan-speaking rather than Spanish-speaking minority group member, and an inhabitant of Guatemala"), and like no others ("I am a unique person with a specific name and a self inhabiting a unique body"). The special emphasis of this volume is on various culturally shaped group identities together with the associations, thoughts, images, linguistic markers, historical narratives, and feelings that persons associate with their ethnic, racial, religious, and political identities. Especially in collectivistic societies, such group identities form the very core of a person's subjective and symbolic location in time and sociocultural space.

Cultures offer their members a variety of identities that at times are mandatory and at times optional. Thus, gender identities are usually mandatory, although persons of the same biological sex are allowed to fill these identities out with somewhat different content. Similarly, racial identities in America were until recently considered immutable and unavoidable: "One drop of black blood" automatically turned a person into a Negro and thus a severely disadvantaged person who, furthermore, was thought by most Whites to have certain (predominantly unfavorable) mental and behavioral characteristics. In contrast, in Brazil, people have adopted more than 100 labels for persons of different "racial" visible (biological) makeup (Fish, this volume). Thus, racial identities are socially constructed, vary in complex ways across cultural boundaries, are generally based on misleading biological theories, and are frequently embedded in sociocultural and socioeconomic hierarchies from which individuals cannot easily escape.

The advent of modern forms of cultural pluralism in Canada, Australia, South Africa, the United States, and parts of western Europe has softened or altered the outlines of some identities, making them more malleable, negotiable, and at times even optional. Ethnic identities in particular have been redefined in a variety of ways in the United States and elsewhere. Whereas for earlier generations the ethnic identities of (White) immigrant families were expected to be melted down in the course of two generations, today many Americans are proudly displaying hyphenated ethnic identities, although they may have lost much of their linguistic and cultural heritage. At the same time, because of increasing intermarriage among persons of different ethnic, religious, and "racial" backgrounds, we find among the younger generations many persons with complex and amalgamated ethnic-linguistic-religious-racial identities. Around the world the hybridization of cultures is steadily afoot and is creating an increasing number of individuals with complex and mixed cultural identities.

New ethnic identities and "super-identities" are continually being created, although they frequently include contradictory conceptions and misleading implications of biological/racial origins. Cultural categories also frequently differ from census categories, creating further confusion. The category of "Hispanic," for instance, was originally created by the American Census Bureau as a racial category, reflecting American folk beliefs, to refer to persons of Latin American origin—although Hispanics are extremely diverse in physical appearance (and the nearly 200 million people in Brazil speak Portuguese, not Spanish). Subsequently, the census categories changed to assert that Hispanics were an ethnic group that could be of "any race"—creating the paradox of a race that could be of any race.

Vast numbers of Mexicans and Central Americans have a much greater percentage of New World ancestry than do Native Americans; however, they cannot classify themselves as "Indians" because they are not members of an official list of recognized tribes in the United States. Forty-two percent of self-classified Hispanics choose "Other" as their race—demonstrating that the category does not culturally fit individuals it is meant to classify. Furthermore, "Other" has become the fastest-growing census category (United States Department of Agriculture, 2006)—suggesting that the ways the census classifies Americans do not correspond to the ways Americans classify themselves.

To cite another example of incoherence, the label "Asian American" has traditionally referred to people of East Asian origin while tacitly excluding other Asian immigrants such as Russians from Siberia, Turks from Anatolia, Uzbeks from Central Asia, Kurds from Iraq, Jews from Israel, and many more. More recently, the "Asian American" label appears to be expanding to include South Asian immigrants—both directly from India, Pakistan, Bangladesh, and Sri Lanka and indirectly from the Caribbean and other parts of the world—and their descendants. A "Desi" minority group cultural identity appears to be forming, as a parallel to the Hispanic/Latino one, so that the children of Muslim Pakistani immigrants and Hindu Indian immigrants view themselves (and are viewed by other Americans) as members of the same ethnic group even while their countries of origin are poised in a nuclear standoff.

Ethnic and racial identities, then, refer to a person's subjective internalization of one or more culturally constructed labels that may include contradictory ideas yet also evoke powerful emotions conducive to serious intergroup conflicts as well as unsatisfying interactions between client and counselor-therapist.

All of us carry a variety of identities that are differentially activated in different contexts. The salience of identities, moreover, may change over time. In psychotherapy, for instance, the divergent ethnic identities of therapist and client may be of considerable importance in the beginning stages but (temporarily) fade away once a successful therapeutic alliance has been created.

In a related vein, African American clients may surreptitiously test a White therapist early in therapy, to see whether she or he is reasonably free of prejudice and shows some understanding of and sensitivity to African American culture and issues of minority group membership. American Blacks who do not trace their origins to slavery in the United States may react quite differently from those who do. Here is the voice of a college student of West Indian origin who criticizes a recent trend in the United States to label many dark-skinned persons such as herself "African American":

> I really dislike the label "African American." After all, I have never been in Africa nor have any members of my family been there during the last six generations. I am a Trinidadian ["with a green card"], not an African American. I have some East Indian relatives and know more about Hindu customs than about anything African. I would rather be called Black than African-something-or-other.

As the quote indicates, ethnic-racial identities—like other identities—are frequently contested while evoking strong and at times conflictual emotions. Likewise, two persons applying the same identity label to themselves may nevertheless link the label to quite varied thoughts, feelings, and images of what the label should mean both to themselves and to others. To use a musical analogy, we may think of identities as providing a cultural theme that is followed by an endless string of more or less harmonious individual variations. Identities, then, are both culturally and individually constructed, interact with a person's other identities, emerge and submerge in specific situations, are more or less fluid in character, and are "filled out" with rich conscious and unconscious content. Given that cultural identities constitute the bridge between a person's individual personality and his or her sociocultural environment, mental health interventions frequently lead to redefinitions and restructuring of a person's identities.

While in the United States racial labels and identities form the center of many multicultural discussions, in European countries such as France or England questions of race frequently take a backseat to religious-ethnic considerations (as well as those of social class). Given the resurgence of Islamic identities throughout the Middle East and North Africa, widespread political tensions between these regions and the West, and the failure of many European countries to fully integrate North African and Middle Eastern immigrants into their societies, religious identifications have served to accentuate existing economic, cultural, and political gaps between the members of the European host societies and the members of immigrant families. Multicultural counselors in these societies must be specially prepared to handle religious issues arising in therapeutic encounters with insight and sensitivity. This is not easy to do because modern psychology and other social sciences tend to encourage secular, scientistic, and relativistic conceptions of human nature. Many mental health specialists may find it difficult to empathize with and to intuitively understand those clients who cast their personal struggles, core identity, and existence in terms of a personal or collective journey toward salvation. The task is made even more challenging when the client's religious belief system and identity are foreign to the counselor. At the same time, European mainstream counselors must also remember that many other immigrants from Muslim nations subscribe to more or less secular beliefs. In addition, immigrants from Middle Eastern countries include Christians, Jews, Baha'is, Druze, and so on. In the United States, the majority of persons of Arab origin are Christians. Religious and ethnic identities, then, often interact in ways that may at first seem surprising to an uninformed outsider-therapist yet feel natural to the client in question.

Therapeutic situations are inevitably influenced by the family constellations and gender identities of the participants in the encounter. Because both family systems and gender roles have rapidly changed over the past few decades, and because in many countries, old certainties have given way to more fluid, tolerant, but also confusing ways of defining oneself both as a family member and as a woman or man (or occasionally as something in between), it is crucial that mental health specialists are familiar with the broad range of family systems and associated gender roles found around the world (see Roopnarine & Gielen, 2005, for examples).

Gender identities are lodged very deeply in a person's psyche and emerge in their earliest though still fluid forms between the ages of 2 to 3. They act as linkages between mostly unconscious early childhood influences; the heightened, more reflective, and more sexualized forms of awareness emerging in adolescence; and the memory traces of the various encounters with potential or actual romantic partners as well as other persons of both sexes. To these are added images, metaphors, and narratives encountered through exposure to literature, music, and the mass media, the client's sometimes painful self-assessment of oneself as a woman or man, and her or his gender-linked expectations, hopes, and fears about the future. The expectations, hopes, and fears often act as self-fulfilling prophecies because they tend to induce behavior in accordance with them.

Because cultural influences are everywhere intertwined with a person's evolving sense of gender identity from infancy through adulthood, mental health specialists must possess a thorough and developmentally informed understanding of gender roles, gender differences, and sexuality together with their manifestations in different cultures. A certain skepticism about the prevailing and often competing gender-oriented ideologies is, at least in our opinion, advisable as well. Especially in multicultural situations, this may keep us from inadvertently indoctrinating or misleading those of our clients whose understanding of family and/or gender-linked role responsibilities diverges sharply from our own. After all, our primary job is to help our clients to live more easily and productively with themselves and significant others, rather than trying to convert them to our way of life and thinking.

Some Basic Ingredients of Therapy, Counseling, and Healing

The terms *psychotherapeia*, *psychotherapy*, and *psychotherapeutics* appeared for the first time in the second half of the 19th century in western Europe. Walter Cooper Dendy (1853), for instance, used the term *psychotherapeia* to refer to "the helpful influence of a healer's mind upon that of a sufferer" (Jackson, 1999, p. 9). The term is based on a combination of the Greek words respectively for "soul" (*psyche*) and "tending to, attending to, or medically treating" (*therapeia*). Implicit in the term is the ancient Greek idea that physicians, priests, and philosophers, each in their own way, are expected to treat the various "sicknesses of the soul" through care, consolation, moral counsel and education, admonition, confession, symbolic purification, remission of sins, suggestion, clarification, and the dispelling of ignorance about one's true nature as a human being.

In various combinations and under different names, many of these activities continue to serve as the basic ingredients of modern psychotherapy and counseling. Others, such as confession and remission of sins, have been pushed into the background by the forces of secularization but nevertheless form the unacknowledged basis from which modern therapy and counseling evolved.

Across time and space, healing, counseling, and psychotherapeutic situations have typically included the following (see also Frank & Frank, 1991):

- A demoralized, suffering, and/or confused person or group of persons seeking relief from mental, spiritual, and physical distress.
- A socially recognized healer, therapist, or counselor who is expected to act as a mental health expert and guide.
- A worldview that is shared (to various degrees) by healer and client.
- A culturally constituted belief system that defines what is desirable, admissible, forbidden, or even thinkable in therapy and counseling, as well as the boundaries of the healer-client relationship and the goals of their encounter.

- The healer's attempts to explain the origins of the client's distress in culturally convincing terms ("assessment and diagnosis"). The healer's explanation may postulate physical, behavioral, mental, and/or spiritual-religious-magical forms of causation together with conceptually coordinated prescriptions and suggestions for the amelioration of the client's distress.
- The healer-sufferer relationship as the fulcrum around which much of the helping effort revolves.
- A series of contacts over time that are defined as therapeutic in nature.
- Audiences that at various points in time are either physically present or merely imagined. The symbolically present audiences may include supernatural beings as well as persons.
- The mostly latent presence of other healers, therapists, and counselors who may be asked to join in the therapeutic effort ("referral") or who may serve as potential alternatives ("healer shopping").

Within the general framework espoused here, it is recognized that many forms of modern counseling and psychotherapeutic intervention are deeply embedded in the traditional healing arts. Prince (1980) was able to discern a number of universal components of psychotherapy in interventions practiced across cultures in all of the world's regions. These features include a worldview shared by the healer and the sufferer, the ability to provide a culturally meaningful explanation of distress or dysfunction, and the exercise of social influence through suggestion and other means. Overshadowing these external features, however, Prince highlighted the mobilization of the sufferer's endogenous self-healing or self-corrective mechanisms, often in the form of altered states of consciousness, as the most important and universally valid ingredient of psychotherapy. In other words, the healer will be successful only if his or her symbolic actions find resonance in the sufferer's heart-mind, meet his or her implicit and explicit expectations, mobilize hope, and link up with already existing coping mechanisms and resources. Culture is the medium in and through which this social influence process occurs.

In his scholarly volume *Care of the Psyche: A History of Psychological Healing*, the medical historian Stanley W. Jackson (1999) has traced essential elements of psychological healing in the Western tradition from antiquity to modern times. According to Jackson, "talking cures" have traditionally included an emphasis on the healer–sufferer relationship; an authoritative and attentive healer; and his or her use of reward or punishment, suggestion and persuasion, explanation, interpretation, and guidance. The healer offers consolation and comfort to the sufferer and provides support for the client's efforts "to get things out." Confession, confiding, and changes in the client's self-understanding and self-observation have also been essential features of successful psychotherapeutic interventions over the centuries. It should be added that many of these therapeutic processes can also be found in non-Western healing encounters, although cultural influences and explanations typically determine which of these elements are assigned primary importance and which of them are relegated to the tacit background for the encounter between healer and sufferer.

It has long been recognized that the nature of the healer–sufferer or counselor–client relationship tends to be a crucial ingredient in successful healing and counseling (Jackson, 1999). Modern research on the effectiveness of psychotherapy bears this out; it demonstrates that clients respond above all to the quality of their relationship with the therapist rather than to the specific psychotherapeutic techniques and methods that he/she employs (Wampold, 2001). Carl G. Jung (1970) recognized this many years ago:

> One can easily see what it means to the patient when he can confide his experience to an understanding and sympathetic doctor. His conscious mind finds in the doctor a moral support against the unmanageable affect of his traumatic complex. No longer does he stand alone in his battle with these elemental powers, but some one whom he trusts reaches out a hand, lending him moral strength to combat the tyranny of uncontrolled emotion. . . . For myself, I would . . . call it his [the doctor's] human interest and personal devotion. These are the property of no method, nor can they ever become one; they are moral qualities which are of the greatest importance in all methods of psychotherapy. (pp. 132–133)

Nevertheless, a cross-cultural examination of healing shows that many relationships between native healers and their clients have either a remote or an emotionally mixed quality and that they, furthermore, are frequently of brief duration (Jilek & Draguns, this volume). Ladakhi shamans in northwest India, for instance, may shout at their patients, try to intimidate them, and even hit them. The patients usually take this in their stride because their semi-Buddhist cultural beliefs tell them that the powerful *lha* (spirits, deities) occupying the body of the shaman may act in a capricious fashion (Gielen, personal observations, 1980–81). Among the Yoruba of western Africa, the *Babalwo* or traditional doctor-diviner does not even know the patient's problem during his divination session (few problems of confidentiality here!).

Instead, he performs certain rituals in order to determine whether the super-natural agencies at work are prepared to release their hold on the sufferer. In a similar vein, the interactions between Mexican spiritualist healers and their patients are quite impersonal in nature (Spires-Robin & McGarrahan, 1995). The healer's spiritual authenticity and therefore her healing power are revealed through her state of trance rather than through her ability to con-sciously empathize with her patient. From a psychodynamic point of view, the healer's unconscious is at work here whereas modern forms of psychotherapy emphasize conscious and ego-syntonic insight and guidance.

Carl Rogers's emphasis on the therapist's ability to empathize with his clients and to adopt his frame of reference is irrelevant in many traditional healing rituals that are instead based on the healer's authoritative and direct instructions and his or her ability to marshal the assistance of invisible spiri-tual beings and powers, perform culturally validated ritual procedures, and invoke the presence of community members to whom the patient is "re-bound" over the course of the healer's ritualistic activities. Traditional healing is often public in nature because its implicit or explicit goal is the reintegration of the patient into the community (Jilek & Draguns, this volume). At its best, such holistic healing achieves simultaneously the patient's inner psychological (re-) integration, her (re-) integration into society, and her (re-) integration into the society's symbolic-religious universe. Person, society, and culture are made whole again, which is the original meaning of the term *healing*. However, in spite of the potentially positive contributions of indigenous healers, there exists a paucity of rigorous research studies evaluating the ability of indig-enous healers to reduce physical and emotional distress in their clientele. It should be added that neither romantic glorifications of such healers nor negative descriptions of shamans as psychopathologically impaired charla-tans are conducive to an objective assessment of their strengths, weaknesses, and therapeutic efficacy (Jilek & Draguns, this volume).

Ecological and Ethical Perspectives on Counseling and Healing

Whereas most forms of modern psychotherapy and counseling are based on individualistic models of personality change, in many situations more broadly conceived models of communal change may prove of greater value than an exclusive or predominant focus on holding counseling sessions with individual clients. Jilek and Draguns (this volume), for instance, discuss the deliberate revival and transformation of Salish guardian spirit ceremonials by indigenous healers. The rituals were designed to counteract multiple social and psychiatric problems besetting Salish Indian communities in western Canada and the United States. The authors' findings underline the therapeutic importance of shared rituals in communities that strengthen their cohesiveness, improve family relations, combat generalized patterns of demoralization and anomie, and reduce antisocial behavior. Jilek and Draguns's chapter also supports the notion that cooperation of psychiatrists/psychotherapists/counselors with both native healers and indigenous authority figures may be of crucial importance in many non-Western sociocultural settings (for recent African examples, see Wessells & Monteiro, 2004). This holds true especially when modern mental health professionals are separated from their clients by a cultural gulf and by their clients' feelings of skepticism or mistrust.

The more general lesson here is that an exclusive focus on individualistic forms of psychotherapy and counseling tends to be of limited value in combating widespread and destructive economic, political, social, and cultural forces (Denham, this volume; Wohl, 2000). This holds true both for indigenous healing in small non-Western societies such as the Salish Indians in Canada and for psychosocial interventions in modern large-scale school systems in the United States and elsewhere. Following this line of reasoning, multicultural psychologists and mental health specialists such as Coleman and Lindwall (this volume) have moved toward adopting a systems-oriented, ecological perspective that supports expanding the scope of multicultural guidance and school counseling programs. They argue forcefully that school counselors need to prepare their students for competing effectively in the global economy while helping to reduce existing achievement gaps that reflect pervasive racial and class disparities. Altogether, they ask the multicultural school counseling profession to adopt a more activist stand in order to increase its impact among the young. In their view, the counseling profession needs to place its individualistic activities in a broader political and societal context while making good on those democratic values that society claims to hold dear but which it often violates in practice. One can see in this approach a certain similarity to the social systems perspective and politically oriented style of intervention that community psychologists have developed over the years.

From their early beginnings, counseling, therapeutic, and healing activities have been suffused with ethical values, considerations, and dilemmas. A concern with values is inherent in the enterprise of counseling and therapy and cannot be avoided in the name of science. In various Western countries, the response of professional mental health associations to the repeated occurrence of moral dilemmas has been to develop codes of ethics that the association members are expected to abide by. In some non-Western nations such as Kuwait, however, no professional codes of conduct have as yet been developed for counselors, and so they tend to informally adopt applicable portions of those Western codes they are familiar with (Gielen & Al-Khawajah, this volume). It remains an open question whether a universally acceptable professional-ethical code for mental health professionals will soon be developed—and whether such a development would be desirable from a culture-sensitive point of view (Pettifor, 2007).

Are the existing professional guidelines and ethical codes in the United States and elsewhere in the Western world satisfactory? Stevens (this volume) does not think so. For instance, he observes that the approach of the American Psychological Association (APA) to ethical practice remains "conservative, hierarchical, and self-serving." An excessive concern for informed consent, proper record keeping, transfer, and termination can easily interfere with timely and effective intervention in emergency situations, with serving effectively international and culturally varied populations unfamiliar with the rather legalistic approach of American middle-class professionals, and with helping groups that prefer a more measured, collectivistically oriented style of decision making. In addition, by placing the therapists' avoidance of lawsuits and compliance with legal authority above their commitment to their clients' welfare, the American system creates contradictions in the ethical basis of therapy itself.

Healers, Therapists, and Counselors

Shamans and Other Traditional Healers

Most known foraging (hunting and gathering) societies—a form of society that was universal until about 12,000 years ago—were or are familiar with the institution of shamanism. A foraging society typically consists of a band of a few dozen to a few hundred kinfolk. Foragers have few possessions, because they move around in pursuit of game and edible plants, and their small numbers do not allow for much role specialization. Shamanism is typically a part-time pursuit and includes activities that large-scale industrialized societies divide among medicine and religion, as well as counseling and therapy. There even exist some tantalizing paintings in the caves of southern France suggesting that, approximately 15,000 to 17,000 years ago, ancestors of modern Europeans may already have been guided by the magical practices and spiritual experiences of shamans who, dressed as animals, may have danced themselves into altered states of consciousness (Curtis, 2006).

In small-scale foraging societies, among nomadic pastoralists, and in many traditional agricultural village societies, shamans, so-called witch doctors, medicine men, and medicine women function as medical healers, spiritual healers, priests and priestesses, counselors, therapists, and psychiatrists, often all at once. Although in modern industrialized societies these roles are commonly occupied by practitioners separated from each other by title, professional training, and worldview, shamans inhabit a unitary world in which body, mind, and soul are seen as inhabited and ruled by primordial and frequently invisible forces and beings responsible for life and death, health and disease, and well-being and emotional-physical distress (Vitebsky, 1995).

Shamans serve as intermediaries between the world of potent invisible beings and the visible but less powerful world of humans and animals. Frequently these invisible beings are believed to erect obstacles and to send disease and distress to humans who have disobeyed or displeased them. Entering a state of intentional trance, the shaman becomes a mouthpiece for the offended spirits or (s)he battles with them for the lost soul of the "dis"-eased patient—all under the threat of visionary physical dismemberment (which may be interpreted as a symbol of temporary ego-fragmentation). It is certainly not easy to be a shaman, and becoming one is typically accompanied by physical and mental suffering, illness, disorientation, frenzied acting out, speaking in tongues, hallucinating, falling ill, and being threatened by the many aggressive spirits populating the shaman's unconscious. At the same time, the shaman's inner development and career are guided by supportive tutelary spirits that may be seen as ego-ideals and protectors against the onslaught of ego-alien demonic apparitions.

Shamans are the intellectual predecessors of contemporary counseling and therapy, although some of us might find it difficult to recognize ourselves in the frenzied shouting and gesticulation of a Peruvian shaman experiencing vivid visions under the influence of *ayahuasca*, a plant-derived hallucinogenic drug (see Winkelman & Roberts, 2008, for research on the use of hallucinogenic substances in psychotherapy). Our modern rationalistic training as counselors and therapists keeps us from making use of altered states of consciousness in this striking way (Timothy Leary to the contrary notwithstanding). The path of the shaman leads to frequent but reasonably controlled encounters with what Jungians view as archetypal forces of the netherworld, in contrast to students in the modern helping professions who are expected to abide by the rationalistic models of science. Shamans are forcefully called by supernatural beings to assume their role as healers, and useful traits for this calling are a vivid imagination/high self-hypnotizability, a trained ability to experience altered states of consciousness at will, perhaps a sense of showmanship, and reasonable psychological stability. In contrast, mental health specialists choose their profession voluntarily, are schooled in more sober, bookish, and restrained training models, and have their professional conduct constrained by a network of laws, codes of conduct, and oversight and enforcement entities. Culturally shaped expectations as well as individual belief systems, however, are central to determining who is more effective in alleviating the distress of their clients. Frequently it is the client's strength of faith together with the nature of her expectations that determine the success or failure of a healing encounter.

As societies became larger, more complex, and increasingly literate, and as increased role differentiation evolved as a consequence of the introduction of agriculture and the rise of cities, the various functions that had been united in the person of the shaman or native healer were taken over in separate ways by priests, medical doctors, and, eventually, philosophers. In this context, religion, medicine, and philosophy can be viewed as the seeds that over time would flourish to create a garden of psychology, psychiatry, therapy, counseling, and the various helping professions.

Therapists and Counselors

In traditional cultures, healers tended to address the gamut of human dysfunction. In the modern era, this holistic orientation to healing has been increasingly compromised and strained, if not irretrievably lost. Fragmentation and specialization have supplanted undifferentiated unity—as subdisciplines within and outside medicine, psychology, counseling, nursing, social work, and religious ministry complement each other's services and often minister to, and even compete for, the same clients.

In philosophy, René Descartes drew a sharp line between the body and the mind. In the ensuing centuries, the secularization of Western civilization largely banished spiritual problems from the purview of scientifically based biomedical and psychological interventions, thereby extending separation of church and state to the individual on the intrapsychic plane. In her chapter in this volume, Michele Hirsch further develops some aspects of this theme.

In response to this compartmentalization of human experience, counseling and therapy came into being. The field can provisionally be defined as "a method of working with patients/clients to assist them to modify, change, or reduce factors that interfere with effective living" (Fabrikant, 1984, p. 184). The advent of psychotherapy as a specific modality of the treatment of human distress can be traced to the last decades of the 19th century. As the founder of psychoanalysis, Sigmund Freud is widely regarded as a pivotal figure in this development, although no single person can be identified as its inventor, inaugurator, or first known practitioner (Ellenberger, 1970). Instead, the beginning of psychotherapy can be viewed as the outgrowth of the prevailing zeitgeist, which placed emphasis on introspection, individualism, and the extension of scientific practices to mental and subjective phenomena. Therapy originated at a time when the authority of traditional beliefs and religious leaders was gradually undermined by constant sociocultural change and the concomitant rise of science.

At the same time that spiritual concerns were marginalized from and medical concerns played a diminished role in Western therapy and counseling—in contrast to traditional healing—a broad range of approaches proliferated, dealing with an ever wider range of thoughts, feelings, and behavior. Here are three examples, in the order in which they developed. Psychoanalysis and related approaches have their roots in psychiatry and medicine, with a view of psychopathology as generated by conscious and unconscious mental and brain states and a disease model of problem behavior as symptomatic of underlying causes that need to be treated (cf. Rubin, this volume). Behavioral and cognitive approaches are mainly associated with psychology, with a view of normal and abnormal behavior as produced by and capable of being changed by the same psychological processes, and with a reliance on experimental evidence of treatment efficacy (cf. Tanaka-Matsumi, this volume). Family systems approaches have grown up mainly in social work, with a view of abnormal behavior as produced by problematic interactional patterns and malfunctioning hierarchies in the family and larger social contexts, and with a particular interest in the poor, immigrants, and different cultures. While practitioners from all the counseling and therapy professions can be found in all of these approaches (and others), the conceptual and disciplinary origins of each form of counseling or therapy have an ongoing effect on the treatment subculture that has developed.

The similarity of training around the globe leads to an international sharing of these worldviews. Thus, psychoanalysts from North America, Latin America, Europe, Asia, and Africa share with one another more of a common outlook regarding therapy than they do with behavioral, cognitive, or systemic therapists from their own country. At the same time, all of these approaches have to be adapted to local conditions; and when the therapist is not native to the culture, the use of cultural consultants (within or outside of the session) can help.

For example, one of us (Jefferson Fish) was the therapist for a depressed woman in Brazil whose husband had left her. She needed to work and had two possible career directions that were equally acceptable to her. The first choice would have been a much better one in the United States, but the therapist did not act on that assumption. Instead, he invited one of his supervisees (who was a licensed psychologist with a private practice) to sit in on a couple of sessions. It turned out that the second option was by far the better one in Brazil, and the woman was counseled accordingly.

Most mental health professionals have been exposed to a variety of theoretical approaches to counseling and therapy. It is clear that not every approach is equally acceptable and convincing to professionals of different cultural backgrounds. Freudian forms of psychoanalysis including its Kleinian and Lacanian varieties, for instance, predominate among Argentinean therapists. By way of contrast, they would be considered unacceptable to most Chinese professionals who might note potential clashes between psychoanalysis and Confucian notions of propriety, restraint, reluctance to disclose sexual thoughts, the assuredly nonsexual nature of the mother–son relationship, and the central importance of *hsiao* (filial piety). In contrast, cognitive-behavioral approaches appear to travel more easily across cultural boundaries (cf. Gielen & Al-Khawajah; Tanaka-Matsumi, both in this volume). Other multicultural professionals, moreover, are adopting an eclectic approach while aiming at an integration of various Western and Eastern approaches and techniques (e.g., Kuriansky, this volume). Her "toolbox" approach is not only multicultural in character but also multimodal, multidimensional, and multidisciplinary.

Multicultural Counseling and Therapy Situations

Mental health professionals need to be exposed to a rich variety of multicultural situations before they can fully appreciate the cultural basis of their work. In this volume, the following types of multicultural and non-Western situations are depicted:

1. Healers and clients are both members of the same non-Western culture (e.g., Gielen & Al-Khawajah; Jilek & Draguns; Sussman, all in this volume).
2. A non-Western counselor trained in Western techniques applies them in a non-Western setting (e.g., Al-Khawajah in Kuwait; Tanaka-Matsumi in Japan, both in this volume).
3. A Western-trained Austrian immigrant psychiatrist advises the elders of a Canadian "First World" nation (a Native American group) as they re-create and transform indigenous rituals designed to reintegrate alienated young men into their society (Jilek & Draguns, this volume).
4. Western mental health specialists provide counseling (e.g., Denham, this volume) and brief psychosocial interventions (e.g., Kuriansky, this volume) to semi-Western or non-Western clients. The clients include both those suffering from traumatic reminiscences and those attending lectures, workshops, and brief training sessions.
5. A bicultural counseling psychologist straddling East and West counsels a bicultural and bi-religious couple who experience a variety of marital, cultural, religious, and psychological conflicts (Laungani, this volume).
6. An American psychotherapist discusses his integration of a Western (i.e., psychoanalytic) approach with an Eastern (i.e., Buddhist) approach (Rubin, this volume). Buddhist meditation techniques are suggested in order to improve the listening skills of psychotherapists. Kuriansky (this volume) has been aiming at an integration of Eastern and Western approaches as well in her "toolbox" approach, which includes a broad variety of techniques deriving from various cultural and theoretical traditions.
7. A team of mental health specialists from a minority group creates a culture-sensitive counseling program suitable for adolescents from a similar ethnocultural background (Koss-Chioino, Baca, & Vargas, this volume).

The variety of multicultural therapy and counseling situations analyzed in this volume reaches well beyond the prototypical situation described and criticized in several widely read multicultural counseling volumes. In these books, a (more or less) well-meaning but culturally insensitive European American counseling specialist fails to interact effectively with his or her minority group clients and students because of the counselor's cultural encapsulation, ethnocentrism, and/or implicit racism (for examples, see Sue & Sue, 2008).

Although such situations undoubtedly occur and need to be both critically analyzed and remedied, today's multicultural world presents numerous complexities not adequately addressed by such examples. Pettifor (2007, p. 322), for instance, has commented that "international students training to become counselors and psychologists feel racial discrimination when the literature and courses on diversity always place the minority person as a client and the mainstream person as the professional." In other words, the field of multicultural counseling and therapy needs to move beyond the analysis and critique of Euro-American counselor–minority group client relationships and their sociopolitical underpinnings. Instead, we need theoretical frameworks that can encompass a rich variety of culturally structured interactions between healers/therapists/counselors and their clients around the world.

Future research might, for instance, investigate situations where a mental health specialist from one minority background interacts with a client from another minority background. An example would be a middle-class Korean American counselor in Los Angeles who counsels a poor African American client. Given the sometimes contentious history between the two ethnic communities and the cultural as well as social class differences between counselor and client, we might foresee potential problems centering on issues of trust, cultural compatibility, racialized perceptions, and verbal and nonverbal styles of relating to each other. The example should also remind us that social class differences between counselor and counselee are at times more detrimental to effective counseling than ethnic or perceived racial differences. "Talking cures," after all, tend to be more acceptable to upper–middle-class rather than to working-class clients, some of whom may instead prefer physical remedies or alcohol-supported confessions and discussions with their (Australian) "mates" or buddies at the local bar.

A word or two should also be said about the multilinguistic capabilities of mental health professions as well as their basic sociocultural and geographic knowledge about immigrant and minority groups. Griner and Smith's (2006) meta-analytic review of culturally adapted mental health interventions found that when the interventions were conducted in the clients' first language, they were especially effective. Furthermore, such interventions were most promising when they were directed at relatively homogeneous groups (see also Draguns and Tanaka-Matsumi, both in this volume). A good example of such an intervention is the group therapy with Mexican American and Mexican adolescents described by Koss-Chioino, Baca, and Vargas in this volume.

More generally, the research evidence suggests that counselors striving for multicultural competence should consider learning the language (and culture) of their clients. Some Anglo counselors in the southwestern regions of the United States may learn Spanish in order to be of optimal service to their Latino(a) clients. In other situations, however, acquiring complete multilinguistic competence is simply not a realistic goal: School counselors in many New York schools, for instance, are likely to interact with immigrant students and their family members from dozens of countries. Consequently, multicultural health professionals will at times have to avail themselves of the services of interpreters (or bilingual family members), as may be seen in Denham's (this volume) analysis of interactions between English-speaking Australian professionals and their Albanian-speaking Kosovar refugee clients. Good interpreters, moreover, not only serve as preliminary cultural bridges between counselors and their clients but also introduce the counselors to many of the more subtle ingredients of the clients' cultures and modes of being-in-the-world. In these and other ways, they can serve as "culture brokers." The same holds sometimes true for bilingual children who act as interpreters between their monolingual immigrant parents and a social worker or psychologist. However, such situations entail potential complications and drawbacks because they may undermine the authority of the parents and lead to role confusion in a family that is already under pressure.

When psychotherapists meet immigrant and refugee clients, they need to inform themselves about the geographic and sociocultural background of their clients (Denham, this volume). In the United States, this is made more difficult by the fact that geography is only rarely taught in high schools and colleges. My (U. P. G.) conversations with clients of several New York–based mental health professionals have convinced me that at least some of those professionals—who after all are practicing in one of the most multiethnic cities on earth—remain quite ignorant about much of the world outside the United States. Not surprisingly, some of the clients indicated to me that they had lost confidence in their counselors or therapists whom they perceived (probably correctly) as lacking the necessary cultural knowledge to adequately grasp their situation and inner and outer conflicts.

The lesson arising from such reports is clear: Competent multicultural health professionals need to acquire broad sociocultural and geographic knowledge about the world at large. Some of this can be done in surprisingly pleasant ways: Traveling abroad; watching foreign movies; reading novels by non-Western writers, travelogues, and world histories; attending multicultural events; participating in culturally diverse family celebrations, religious ceremonies, festivals, and so on; interacting with foreign students and colleagues; making friends with persons from culturally varied backgrounds; sampling foreign cuisine; and conducting research together with overseas colleagues are all activities that can be fun while enriching and educating us about the endless variety of human cultures and their achievements. In time we also learn the important truth that persons from similar cultural backgrounds may differ widely in their personalities and outlook on life. Such awareness is helpful in undercutting our natural and difficult-to-avoid tendency to engage in cultural stereotyping. Ironically, such stereotyping is also at times an unwitting reaction to encountering discussions about the purported cultural characteristics of various ethnic groups in the scientific literature.

Organization and Contents of This Book

This book explores the interaction between cultural belief systems and the practice of counseling, therapy, and healing in a multicultural and global context. Part 1, Conceptual Foundations and Ethical Considerations, lays the basis for the remainder of the volume by introducing several broadly conceived conceptual frameworks and by examining a number of fundamental issues in multicultural counseling.

In her broadly conceived chapter, "The Role of Culture in Illness Interpretation and Therapy," the anthropologist Linda Sussman presents the perspective of medical anthropology. It emphasizes both the shared features of healing systems around the world and the infinite variety of existing illness definitions, interpretations, and management procedures. Furthermore, within complex societies, a variety of therapeutic systems typically coexist. Because many illnesses include both somatic and behavioral syndromes, her systematic and cross-culturally informed approach to the health-seeking process is also applicable to interventions focused on mental health.

Jefferson M. Fish's first chapter, "Theoretical Issues, Principles, and Themes Relevant to Multicultural Counseling and Therapy," draws a basic distinction between the *etic* perspective of the scientific observer and the *emic*, meaning-imbued perspectives of the people under observation. He subsequently introduces six themes and commonalities that can help us understand better how psychotherapy, counseling, and healing are practiced across cultures. The themes include the impact of social structures, economic forces, and power relationships on therapy, the role of cultural meaning systems in problem behavior and their solutions, the rise of interactional perspectives and systems theory in the social sciences, the role of expectancy in both producing and changing behavior, and the cross-cultural applicability of general psychological principles of learning and cognition. Jefferson M. Fish is also the author of the following chapter, "A Multicultural Counselor's Guide to Race." In it, he outlines modern biological and anthropological understandings of race that frequently are at variance with popular ideas about human biological variation. Because questions of race and racial identification can become emotionally charged topics in therapy and counseling, it is imperative that mental health professionals acquire up-to-date scientific information about these issues.

Recent research on psychoneuroimmunology has shown convincingly that body and mind are intimately linked. In her chapter titled "Healing the Body and Mind: An Overview of Biopsychosocial Foundations and Applications," Michele S. Hirsch outlines some of the basic findings of health psychology and then connects those to healing practices found around the world. More specifically, she discusses the positive role that expectancies, social support, mindfulness, and emotional disclosure through writing can have upon both body and mind.

Mental health professionals are frequently enjoined to do no harm and to enhance the welfare of the public. In order to meet this mandate, psychologists, counselors, social workers, and others have developed professional ethical codes. In his chapter, "Professional Ethics in Multicultural and International Context," Michael J. Stevens asks how such codes and, more generally, a concern for ethical principles and moral integrity can be developed and supported among mental health specialists around the world. In this context, he compares several professional codes and guidelines and also reviews recent discussions centering on a "Universal Declaration of Ethical Principles for Psychologists." Finally, he introduces a social constructionist approach to ethical decision making that emphasizes collaborative interaction and dialogue when solving moral dilemmas in multicultural and international practice.

Part 2, Models of Multicultural Counseling, presents three ways of thinking about the practice of multicultural counseling. In her chapter, "Functional Approaches to Evidence-Based Practice in Multicultural Counseling and Therapy," the Japanese psychologist Junko Tanaka-Matsumi introduces an innovative effort to integrate multicultural perspectives with functional approaches to cognitive-behavioral therapy. Cognitive-behavioral therapists have been at the forefront of those who are interested in providing evidence for the scientific efficacy and clinical effectiveness of their preferred treatment approaches. In this context, Tanaka-Matsumi reviews some of the literature on psychotherapy outcome research and notes that increasingly both therapists and researchers are emphasizing the importance of cultural adaptations of empirically supported therapies. One important long-term goal is to train multicultural mental health specialists who are able to combine universally applicable principles of behavior change with culturally specific treatment modalities.

In their chapter, "Multiculturalism and School Counseling: Creating Relevant Comprehensive Guidance and Counseling Programs," Hardin L. K. Coleman and Jennifer J. Lindwall outline their vision of how the profession of school counseling can respond more effectively to the twin pressures of globalization and pervasive achievement gaps between students of different racial-ethnic and social class backgrounds. Adopting an ecological approach, they suggest a new way of integrating culturally responsive counseling into comprehensive school guidance and counseling programs. They make specific suggestions about how culturally responsive components can be built into the very foundation of counseling programs together with more effective delivery and management systems and improved accountability. Their model, they argue, reaches beyond the common conceptions of multicultural competence that focus on the counselor's multicultural awareness, knowledge, and skills.

Joan D. Koss-Chioino, Louise Baca, and Luis A. Varga have developed a new form of culture-sensitive therapy for Latinos/Latinas, which they introduce in their chapter titled "Group Therapy With Mexican American and Mexican Adolescents: Focus on Culture." As part of their intervention, the therapeutic team created a "fourth lifespace" (neither home nor school nor the streets) that would allow the troubled youths to explore identity problems, develop an improved sense of self-efficacy, practice new styles of interpersonal communication, and confront difficult issues such as drug use, high-risk sexual behavior, family problems, economic pressures, and ethnic discrimination and oppression. The authors also report the results of a preliminary outcome study that point to a decrease in the youths' educational problems together with improved interactions in their families, although there were no significant changes on some other behavioral indicators.

The four chapters included in Part 3, The Practice of Multicultural Counseling, suggest that multicultural interventions are now taking place in countries as varied as Malaysia, Kuwait, China, Serbia, Israel, and Australia. It is entirely appropriate that the initial chapter in this section has been written by Pittu Laungani, to whom this volume is dedicated. Of Indian descent but residing in London prior to his death in early 2007, Laungani was especially interested in counseling bicultural Asian clients for whom he developed a special empathy based, in part, on his own experience. In his chapter, "A Clash of Cultures: A Case Study," he discusses the cultural, religious, social, and familial conflicts that had begun to seriously undermine the marriage between a Muslim architect from Malaysia and his Confucian-Chinese wife from Taiwan. As the case study unfolds, we learn about the religious-ethnic differences and family pressures that threaten to pull their relationship apart, together with their increasingly successful efforts to accept and respect the differences in light of their mutual appreciation and love.

The article "The Practice of Counseling in Kuwait: An Interview With Jasem M. al-Khawajah" takes a different path from the other chapters. In it, al-Khawajah discusses the application of cognitive-behavioral counseling techniques in the Arab-Islamic milieu of Kuwaiti society. His clients include men and women experiencing difficulties in their marriages together with those suffering from PTSD, depression, anxiety, and sexual difficulties. Although many traditional Kuwaitis continue to see counseling in a negative light, the practice of counseling in Kuwait has made considerable progress in recent years, and especially so after the Iraqi occupation of 1990–91 when counselors helped many Kuwaitis to come to terms with their traumatic experiences and memories. Like Tanaka-Matsumi in Japan (see chapter 7), al-Khawajah believes that the cognitive-behavioral approach to counseling and therapy shows much promise in non-Western settings especially when general principles of behavior and thought modification are applied in a culturally sensitive way.

For several decades now the American psychologist Judy Kuriansky has applied her counseling skills in a broad variety of cultural settings around the world. In response to this broad range of experiences, she has developed an integrated set of psychosocial exercises and techniques, which she describes in her chapter, "A Clinical Toolbox for Cross-Cultural Counseling and Training." Many of her exercises involve relatively simple, nonverbal, short-term group activities designed to overcome linguistic and cultural barriers. Her clinical toolbox includes a variety of "mix and match" modules that can be combined with each other—or with activities and strategies not included in the toolbox—depending on the purpose of the intervention as well as the characteristics of the groups in question.

In recent decades mental health professionals have been increasingly asked to provide emotional, clinical, and practical support for refugees. One of them is Geoff Denham, who in his chapter "Rethinking Counseling in Refugee Work: Post-traumatic What?" discusses his experiences with torture/trauma survivors from Kosovo who were residing in the refugee camp of Bandiana Safehaven, Australia. His chapter makes a distinct contribution to the development of a more integrated theory of multicultural counseling with trauma survivors while also helping prospective trauma counselors to understand more clearly the emotional and cognitive demands they will have to face in their difficult work ahead. Such work goes well beyond a detailed understanding of DSM-IV-based psychiatric categories such as "Post-traumatic Stress Disorder," which tend to omit many features that are most salient to torture-trauma survivors: their accounts of suffering, flight, and upheaval and their efforts to derive meaning from their experiences at both the individual and collective levels.

A major purpose of this volume is to broaden our understanding of mental health–oriented interventions by reflecting in a cohesive manner on both Western and non-Western healing traditions. In this vein, the contributions included in Part 4—Psychological Healing and Counseling: Indigenous, Western, or Both?—focus on several indigenous Asian and North American healing traditions and ask what we as mental health counselors can learn from them.

In their chapter, "Interventions by Traditional Healers: Their Impact and Relevance Within Their Cultures and Beyond," Wolfgang G. Jilek and Juris G. Draguns provide a concise discussion of the functions and modes of operation of native healers. Their account is theoretically sophisticated, empirically based, laced with specific examples, and appreciative of the healers' contributions to the welfare of their respective societies. Using as examples the Salish Indian Spirit Dance Ceremonial of British Columbia, Canada, and the Lao Hmong Shamanic Healing Ceremonials for opium addicts residing in a refugee camp in Thailand, the authors point to convincing evidence that such collectively based rituals can be effective in reducing drug addiction and other forms of dysfunctional behavior, especially among culturally disoriented male adolescents and young men.

The flow of information about cross-cultural counseling has been mostly from West to East, as may be seen in several of the chapters mentioned previously. The American psychologist Jeffrey B. Rubin, however, aims at a more seamless integration of Eastern and Western perspectives. In his chapter, "Deepening Listening: The Marriage of Buddha and Freud," he outlines how Buddhist meditation practices can help Western psychotherapists to become more nonjudgmental and receptive to both their own inner world and that of their clients. That is especially important in multicultural situations where unvoiced cultural assumptions, beliefs, and projections can easily derail the therapeutic encounter. Buddhism, however, has so far not developed a distinct theory about the language and logic of the unconscious. For Rubin, then, an ideal marriage between East and West means the integration of Buddhist Vipassana insight-oriented meditation practices with a psychoanalytically based understanding of the nature of (originally unconscious) primary process thinking that is said to rule much of our imaginative and emotional worlds.

The book concludes with Part 5, Academic Findings and Resources for Multicultural Counseling, which consists of a reflective chapter by Juris G.

Draguns and a working bibliography. Draguns has been a pioneer in the transcultural investigation of psychopathology and psychotherapy for several decades, and so he is ideally suited to assess the state of the art in these fields from a broad, historically informed perspective. In his chapter, "What Have We Learned About the Interplay of Culture With Counseling and Psychotherapy?" he introduces the reader to the clinical and multiculturally oriented contributions of a number of pioneers and innovators, such as Emil Kraepelin, Wolfgang Pfeiffer, Tobie Nathan, Bin Kimura, Karl Peltzer, Alba Nyda Rivera-Ramos, Karen Seeley, Pittu Laungani, and Alan Roland. This is quite an impressive multicultural and multinational crew in itself! Draguns then asks what else we need to know in order to arrive at a more comprehensive and integrative understanding of the role of culture in the psychotherapeutic enterprise. In this context he introduces the reader to several new approaches and research questions that could open new vistas on the multicultural dimensions of the psychotherapeutic experience.

The final contribution to the volume is titled "Principles of Multicultural Counseling and Therapy: A Selective Bibliography." Here the editors introduce the reader to a broad range of books and journals that span 19 separate areas within the broader field of multicultural intervention. The volumes and journals cover both the various areas discussed in the present book and related topics such as multicultural therapy and counseling with special populations, multicultural family therapy, psychopathology across cultures, transcultural psychiatry, assessment issues, and a broad range of healing traditions around the world.

Concluding Remarks

As the reader reviews the contributions to this volume, (s)he will encounter a broad variety of healers, therapists, cross-cultural counseling situations, and culture-oriented concepts. These include native healers in Madagascar, Brazilian racial classification systems, Mexican American adolescents "in trouble," American school counselors confronted with racial and social class inequities, Kuwaiti couples on the verge of divorce, Australian mental health specialists offering mental (and physical) health services to refugees from Kosovo, Salish Indian elders attempting to save their youth from anomie and rootlessness, an American psychoanalyst extolling the advantages of Buddhist meditation, a Western counseling specialist inviting Chinese medical doctors and others to "open up," a bicultural Japanese therapist advocating the integration of multicultural and cognitive-behavioral forms of therapy, and so much more. The 21st century has arrived in all its multicultural complexity in this book.

The new century is shaping up as the century of global encounters: Cultures from all corners of the world intermingle and sometimes clash with each other; Chinese and Indian ways of life are becoming more influential while the global dominance of European ways of life is partially receding; streams of immigrants, refugees, tourists, corporate executives, workers, athletes, students, pilgrims, soldiers, criminals, and the occasional terrorist are flowing between continents and countries; mosques, Hindu shrines, and Buddhist retreat centers are being erected in places where they had never been seen before; more and more people from different parts of the world are interacting electronically with each other; and people everywhere are attempting to learn how to navigate more skillfully through the ever changing global maze.

We as professors and supervisors have the inescapable duty to prepare our students for this world-in-the-making and to transcend our ethnocentric viewpoints in psychology (Marsella, 2007). If counseling and clinical psychology as well as the other mental health professions are to remain relevant and vital in the new century, we must teach our students how to familiarize themselves with the ways of intercultural communication and problem solving so that they can employ them in their future professional practice. We must prepare our students for a world that does not yet exist but that is nevertheless evolving in front of our not-always-seeing eyes and our not-always-feeling hearts.

Seen in this light, the contributions to this volume reflect a broader commitment to develop a global psychology ready to gradually shed its cultural encapsulation in predominantly Western traditions. The ultimate goal is to arrive at a psychology capable of understanding human beings everywhere (Stevens & Gielen, 2007). Although we are far from having reached this ambitious goal, it is crucial that we keep moving toward it. We invite our readers to join us on our journey toward this distant destination.

References

Curtis, G. (2006). *The cave painters: Probing the mysteries of the world's first artists.* New York: Knopf.

Dendy, W. C. (1853). Psychotherapeia, or the remedial influence of the mind. *Journal of Psychological Medicine and Mental Pathology, 6,* 268–274.

Ellenberger, H. F. (1970). *The discovery of the unconscious: The history and evolution of dynamic psychiatry.* New York: Basic Books.

Fabrikant, B. (1984). Psychotherapy. In R. Corsini (Ed.), *Encyclopedia of psychology* (Vol. 3, pp. 184–186). New York: Wiley.

Frank, J. D., & Frank, J. B. (1991). *Persuasion and healing: A comparative study of psychotherapy* (3rd rev. ed.). Baltimore, MD: John Hopkins University Press.

Griner, D., & Smith, T. B. (2006). Culturally adapted mental health intervention: A meta-analytic review. *Psychotherapy: Theory, Research, Practice, Training, 43,* 531–549.

Hall, E. T. (1959). *The silent language.* New York: Doubleday.

Jackson, S. W. (1999). *Care of the psyche: A history of psychological healing.* New Haven, CT: Yale University Press.

Jung, C. G. (1970). The therapeutic value of abreaction. In G. Adler, M. Fordham, H. Read, & W. McGurire (Eds.), *The collected works of C. G. Jung* (Vol. 16, pp. 129–138). Princeton, NJ: Princeton University Press.

Kluckhohn, C., Murray, H. A., & Schneider, D. M. (Eds.). (1953). *Personality in nature, society, and culture* (2nd ed.). New York: Alfred A. Knopf.

Kroeber, A. L., & Kluckhohn, C. (1952). Culture: A critical review of concepts and definitions. *Papers of the Peabody Museum of Archaeology and Ethnology, 47*(1). Cambridge, MA: Harvard University.

Marsella, A. J. (2007). Education and training for a global psychology: Foundations, issues, and actions. In M. J. Stevens & U. P. Gielen (Eds.), *Toward a global psychology: Theory, research, intervention, and pedagogy* (pp. 333–361). Mahwah, NJ: Lawrence Erlbaum Associates.

Pettifor, J. L. (2007). Toward a global professionalization of psychology. In M. J. Stevens & U. P. Gielen (Eds.), *Toward a global psychology: Theory, research, intervention, and pedagogy* (pp. 299–331). Mahwah, NJ: Lawrence Erlbaum Associates.

Prince, R. H. (1980). Variations in psychotherapeutic practice. In H. C. Triandis & J. G. Draguns (Eds.), *Handbook of cross-cultural psychology. Volume 6: Psychopathology* (pp. 291–350). Boston: Allyn & Bacon.

Roopnarine, J., & Gielen, U. P. (Eds.). (2005). *Families in global perspective.* Boston: Allyn & Bacon.

Spires-Robin, R., & McGarrahan, P. (1995). The healing practices of Mexican spiritualism. In L. L. Adler & B. R. Mukherji (Eds.), *Spirit versus scalpel: Traditional healing and modern psychotherapy* (pp. 121–135). Westport, CT: Bergin & Garvey.

Stevens, M. J., & Gielen, U. P. (Eds.). (2007). *Toward a global psychology: Theory, research, intervention, and pedagogy.* Mahwah, NJ: Lawrence Erlbaum Associates.

Sue, D. W., & Sue, D. (2008). *Counseling the culturally diverse: Theory and practice* (5th ed.). New York: Wiley.

United States Department of Agriculture. (2006). Race and ethnicity in rural America: Appendix. Retrieved December 20, 2006, from http://www.ers.usda.gov/Briefing/RaceAndEthnic/appendix.htm

Vitebsky, P. (1995). *The shaman: Voyages of the soul, trance, ecstasy, and healing from Siberia to the Amazon.* Boston: Little, Brown.

Wampold, B. E. (2001). *The great psychotherapy debate: Models, methods, and findings.* Mahwah, NJ: Lawrence Erlbaum Associates.

Wessells, M. G., & Monteiro, C. (2004). Healing the wounds following protracted conflict in Angola: A community-based approach to assisting war-affected children. In U. P. Gielen, J. M. Fish, & J. G. Draguns (Eds.), *Handbook of culture, therapy, and healing* (pp. 321–341). Mahwah, NJ: Lawrence Erlbaum Associates.

Winkelman, M. J., & Roberts, T. B. (Ed.). (2008). *Psychedelic medicine: New evidence for hallucinogenic substances as treatment*. Westport, NJ: Praeger.

Wohl, J. (2000). Psychotherapy and cultural diversity. In J. F. Aponte & J. Wohl (Eds.), *Psychological intervention and cultural diversity* (pp. 75–91). Boston: Allyn & Bacon.

Suggested Readings

Frank, J. D., & Frank, J. B. (1991). *Persuasion and healing: A comparative study of psychotherapy* (3rd rev. ed.). Baltimore, MD: John Hopkins University Press.

This classic comparative study views psychotherapy as a specialized form of persuasion and places it in a broadly conceived, cross-culturally informed framework.

Gielen, U. P., Fish, J. M., & Draguns, J. G. (Eds.). (2004). *Handbook of culture, therapy, and healing*. Mahwah, NJ: Lawrence Erlbaum Associates.

Taken together, the chapters in this volume provide a broad overview of Western and non-Western traditions as these span the divides among psychosocial, medical, and religious approaches to therapy and healing.

Jackson, S. W. (1999). *Care of the psyche: A history of psychosocial healing*. New Haven, CT: Yale University Press.

A medical historian reviews in rich detail the history of Western thinking on healer–patient relationships and the nature of psychological healing.

Leong, T. L., & Savickas, M. L. (2007). International perspectives on counseling psychology. Special Issue, *Applied Psychology: An International Review*, 56(1).

The contributors to this special issue describe the current status and prospects of counseling psychology in 12 countries located around the world.

Pedersen, P. B., Draguns, J. G., Lonner, W. J., & Trimble, J. E. (Eds.). (2007). *Counseling across cultures* (6th ed.). Thousand Oaks, CA: Sage.

Ever since its first edition appeared in 1976, this book has been recognized as a pioneering and major contribution to the area of multicultural counseling. It complements the present volume in a variety of ways.

Ponterotto, J. G., Casas, M., Suzuki, L. A., & Alexander, C. M. (Eds.). (2001). *Handbook of multicultural counseling* (2nd ed.). Thousand Oaks, CA: Sage.

The many chapters in this standard handbook present many facets of multicultural counseling as seen through the eyes of a group of predominantly North American scholars.

Stevens, M. J., & Gielen, U. P. (Eds.). (2007). *Toward a global psychology: Theory, research, intervention, and pedagogy*. Mahwah, NJ: Lawrence Erlbaum Associates.
This volume provides an overview of the conceptual models, research methodologies, interventions, and pedagogical approaches that are most appropriate to transnational settings. Several chapters on intervention, the global professionalization of psychology, and appropriate psychological training for a global world are especially pertinent to the present book.

Vitebsky, P. (1995). *The shaman: Voyages of the soul, trance, ecstasy, and healing from Siberia to the Amazon*. Boston: Little, Brown.
The knowledgeable author provides a concise, informative, non-partisan, richly illustrated overview of shamanism around the world.

Part I

Conceptual Foundations and Ethical Considerations

2

The Role of Culture in Illness Interpretation and Therapy

Linda K. Sussman

Contents

Introduction

The importance of culture in illness definition and management has become increasingly recognized with the ever-increasing ethnic diversity—or multicultural character—of our own population and rapid advances in medical technology that constantly confront us with new options, often leading us to reexamine our expectations, goals, values, and definitions. Through the process of enculturation, individuals learn how to view the world, experience it, and behave in it. All human societies experience illness, and each culture has devised its own ways of dealing with it. Medical systems are integral parts of the sociocultural systems in which they occur. Beliefs and practices related to illness and healing are inextricably linked to other components of the culture, such as social organization, religion, the economic system, and values.

Despite the fact that the content of medical systems varies greatly across cultures, there are several characteristics and components that are common across all medical systems. I briefly describe some of these common attributes. Then, drawing largely on my own work in Madagascar, Mauritius, and the United States, I discuss the impact of three sociocultural factors—medical beliefs, social structure and organization, and cultural values and history—on illness definition, interpretation, and management among the lay population. Because the biomedical system itself is a culturally derived system, I include examples of how the different perspectives of medical specialists and patients may result in diverse perceptions of illness and conflicting treatment goals and evaluation.

Medical Systems in Cross-Cultural Perspective

What is culture, anthropologically speaking? An excellent description was written by C. Helman in his book for health care professionals, *Culture, Health and Illness.*

> Culture is a set of guidelines (both explicit and implicit) which individuals inherit as members of a particular society, and which tells them how to *view* the world, how to experience it emotionally, and how to *behave* in it in relation to other people, to supernatural forces or gods, and to the natural environment.... To some extent, culture can be seen as an inherited "lens," through which the individual perceives and understands the world that he inhabits, and learns how to live within it. Growing up within any society is a form of *en*culturation, whereby the individual slowly acquires the cultural "lens" of that society. Without such a shared perception of the world, both the cohesion and continuity of any human group would be impossible.
>
> One aspect of this "cultural lens" is the division of the world, and the people within it, into different *categories*.... For example ... "kinsfolk" or "strangers," "normal" or "abnormal," "mad" or "bad," "healthy" or

"ill." And all cultures have elaborate ways of moving people from one social category into another (such as from "ill person" to "healthy person"), and also of confining people—sometimes against their will—to the categories into which they have been put (such as "mad," "disabled" or "elderly"). (Helman, 1994, pp. 2–3)

Shared Elements of Medical Systems

Beliefs and practices related to illness reflect the "cultural lens" through which members of the society view the world. They do not exist as isolated "folk beliefs," "folk remedies," or "superstitions" removed from the wider cultural context. Within a society, the "medical system" is a cultural system just like the religious, political, and economic systems. It is composed of all the health knowledge, beliefs, skills, and practices of members of the group. It "includes the ways in which people have become recognized as 'ill,' the ways that they present this illness to other people, the attributes of those they present their illness to, and the ways that the illness is dealt with" (Helman, 1994, p. 7) as well as "patterns of belief about the causes of illness; norms governing choice and evaluation of treatment; socially-legitimated statuses, roles, power relations, interaction settings, and institutions" (Kleinman, 1980, p. 24). Most complex societies are composed of members of ethnic and religious minorities, including recent immigrants from other cultures. Each group may possess its own cultural beliefs, norms, and practices, whereas individual members of the group may become acculturated to varying extents to the culture of the larger society.

Despite the great diversity of medical beliefs and practices throughout the world, a number of components have been found to be common to all. These include the following:

1. Conceptual components
   - An *illness classification system*, composed of labels for various symptoms and illnesses (nosology)
   - A system of beliefs concerning the possible causes of illness (etiology)
   - A means of attributing cause and labels (diagnosis) to specific episodes
   - A set of appropriate treatments for specific illnesses
   - *Expectations* regarding course of the illness and treatment outcome (prognosis)
2. Personnel
   - *Healing specialists*—individuals who:
     - Possess specialized knowledge or power

- Are usually respected members of the community
- Have a set of paraphernalia and methods for diagnosis and treatment that set them apart from other members of the community

3. Behavioral components
   - Norms regarding treatment seeking and illness management:
     - Criteria for defining oneself as "ill" and labeling others as "sick"
     - Culturally appropriate sick role behavior
     - Expectations regarding the identities of those responsible for making health care decisions and caring for the sick
   - Norms regarding consultations with healing specialists:
     - Appropriate content (e.g., physical symptoms; feelings, social relations, or moral dilemmas; context in which symptoms developed)
     - Modes of interaction (e.g., formal questions/answers, patient narratives, physical examinations, ritual ceremony)
     - Role of healing specialist (e.g., expert, authority, counselor, advisor)
     - Nature of specialist advice
     - Identification of individuals who may or should attend consultations
     - Location of consultation
     - Method and amount of payment (e.g., cash, livestock, food; mandatory or voluntary; payment for each consultation or after a cure has been effected)

Within a society, there are laymen and there are healing specialists who adhere to a particular therapeutic system. In most societies today, a number of different therapeutic systems coexist although one system may dominate. This is called "medical pluralism." The United States is an example of a society with a plural medical system in which biomedicine dominates but coexists with other systems, such as chiropractic and osteopathy, Chinese medicine and acupuncture, along with faith healing, herbalism, homeopathy, naturopathy, and healing traditions of ethnic minorities.

In societies with plural medical systems and a polyethnic population, the situation may be fairly complex. The theories and practices of each healing system (e.g., of biomedicine, chiropractic, and homeopathy) differ to varying extents from each other as do the medical beliefs and practices of lay members of ethnic groups. Of particular importance is the finding that several different therapeutic systems may be used by an individual either for different illnesses or for a single illness with little or no perceived ideological conflict (e.g., Bailey, 1991; Clark, 1970; Counts & Counts, 1989; Crandon-Malamud, 1991; Etkin, Ross, & Muazzamu, 1990; O'Connor, 1995; Press, 1969; Reeve, 2000; Scott, 1974; Snow, 1974, 1977; Sussman, 1980, 1981, 1983, 1988, 1992b; Trotter & Chavira, 1981; Woods, 1977).

The Health-Seeking Process—The Lay Perspective

> The customary view is that professionals organize health care for lay people. But typically lay people activate their health care by deciding when and whom to consult, whether or not to comply, when to switch between treatment alternatives, whether care is effective, and whether they are satisfied with its quality. In this sense, the popular sector functions as the chief source and most immediate determinant of care. (Kleinman, 1980, p. 51)

Among laymen, most illness beliefs and health-seeking behavior patterns are not formally learned in school but, starting in childhood, are "picked up" piecemeal from experience, observation, and teaching within the household and social group. They continue to be learned and modified over one's lifetime as experiences with illness accumulate. The amount and sources of knowledge may vary considerably among cultural and subcultural groups (see, e.g., Agee, 2000).

Illness is first experienced by individuals, their households, and their families, and it is usually within this context that illnesses are managed, with or without the advice or help of a healing specialist. In fact, most illness episodes in Western and non-Western societies are treated within the lay sector with no recourse to specialists (Kleinman, Eisenberg, & Good, 1978; Zola, 1972). Kleinman (1980), for example, found that in two districts of Taipei, 93% of all illness episodes in a 1-month period were first treated in the family, and 73% of all episodes were treated exclusively in the family. Cross-culturally most illnesses and conditions requiring special care are recognized, interpreted, and managed by a lay "therapy management group" (Janzen 1978, 1987), the composition of which varies from culture to culture (e.g., the individual patient, nuclear family, mother and grandmother, paternal kin, extended family). This group may obtain advice and suggestions from others in its "therapeutic network," composed of culturally appropriate informal and formal sources of advice and care.

The health-seeking process is a decision-making process engaged in by lay individuals (Chrisman, 1977; Gibbs, 1988; Kleinman, 1980; Mechanic,

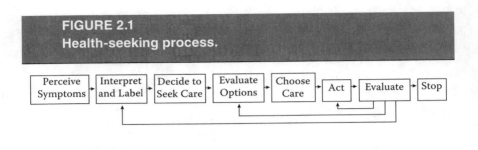

**FIGURE 2.1
Health-seeking process.**

1962, 1968, 1982; Sussman, 1992a; Sussman, Robins, & Earls, 1987). It includes (a) decisions about the need for care and associated role changes; (b) choices concerning the source of care; and (c) ongoing health maintenance decisions. It is a dynamic process and may be conceptualized as involving the following steps (Figure 2.1; Sussman, 1992a):

1. The presence of symptoms or other physical, psychological, emotional, or behavioral changes
2. Perceive and attend to those symptoms or changes
3. Interpret and label them
4. Decide to treat (or not)
5. Delineate and evaluate the options, including self-treatment and no treatment
6. Choose treatment or source of care
7. Act upon choice and treat or seek care
8. Evaluate the outcome, and then either:
9. (a) Continue the same treatment or source of care, with ongoing evaluation (steps 8–9) or
   (b) Cease current treatment/care and
       (i)   Cease treatment seeking or
       (ii) Delineate/evaluate other care options and choose care (steps 5–9) or
       (iii) Reinterpret and relabel symptoms or changes (steps 3–9)

For acute or self-limiting illnesses, this process may be relatively short and uncomplicated. For chronic and recurring illness and for psychological, emotional, and behavioral symptoms, it may be quite complex and represent a lifetime of trying different sources of care, modifying treatment regimens, and evaluating outcomes.

Context of the Health-Seeking Process

The health-seeking and health-maintenance process is shaped by the inter-action of individual, social, cultural, and societal factors (Sussman, 1992a). These are represented by four concentric circles in Figure 2.2. The inner cir-cle represents the *Individual*, who is embedded in a *Social Group*, which is embedded in the *Culture* of the (minority) group, which in turn is embedded in the *Society*, which represents the social, political, and economic realities of the society at large. It is important to realize that although these levels are separated conceptually, they are, in fact, inextricably linked and there is constant interaction and feedback among all levels.

FIGURE 2.2
Context of the health-seeking process.

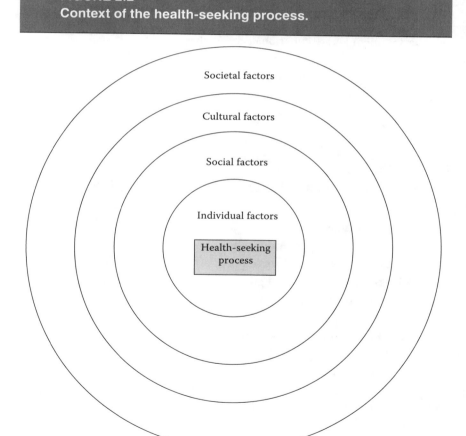

Societal factors

Cultural factors

Social factors

Individual factors

Health-seeking process

A major emphasis of this model is that individuals reflect the layers of influence that surround them. Learning and development are ongoing, and changes in one level of the model may result in changes in other levels. Changes, for example, in a nation's health care policy may lead to changes in patient behavior; alternatively, changes in patient choices and expectations may lead to changes in physician behavior or health care policy.

Individual factors may include health status, personal resources, knowledge, and experience. *Social factors* refer to the composition of groups of kin and friends, their rights and obligations, frequency of contact with them, and the nature of the relationships. *Societal factors* (sometimes referred to as *structural factors*) particularly relevant to health care and illness management include the health care system itself (distribution, cost, quality, and policies), the economic system (distribution and abundance of resources, insurance coverage, and social welfare policies), and demographics (including educational attainment and occupational status, the geographic distribution of the groups, and local neighborhood resources). Although all of the factors are clearly important and intertwined, in this chapter I focus on *cultural factors*. These include shared group norms of thought and behavior, values, and preferences, as well as shared history.

Sociocultural Factors Affecting Illness Definition, Interpretation, and Management

In this section I discuss how (a) medical belief systems, (b) social structure and organization, and (c) cultural values and history shape illness definition, interpretation, and management. These provide the lens through which patients and families of different cultural groups perceive and interpret symptoms and illness and the context in which they decide whether to seek care, choose sources of care, develop treatment goals and expectations, evaluate treatment, and decide whether to continue, cease, change, or supplement care.

Medical Belief Systems

Medical belief systems provide individuals with a coherent explanatory framework in which to view illness. This framework guides the interpretation of symptoms, decisions to seek care, decisions about where to seek care, and evaluation of treatment outcomes. It also shapes the ways in which

symptoms are presented to physicians, therapists, and other healing specialists. In speaking about the lay belief system of African Americans who had
been socialized in the rural South and maintained kin ties to the South,
Snow, for example, notes that

> It is a coherent medical system and not a ragtag collection of isolated
> superstitions. If the underlying premises are accepted, it makes just as
> much sense to the believer as the principles of orthodox medicine do to
> the graduate of an accredited medical school. (1974, p. 83)

In all medical classification systems, symptoms are generally attributed
to causes on which treatment is based. Although medical belief systems may
differ considerably from culture to culture, two themes that exist in many
systems are (a) the belief in multiple causes of illness and (b) the belief that
illness reflects and is caused by some type of imbalance or disharmony. These
themes are highly prevalent worldwide and among ethnic groups in the
United States.

Multicausal Belief Systems   The concept that illness may be caused by multiple factors is found in many medical belief systems throughout the world.
By this I do not mean that illness may be caused by germs or exposure or
heredity, et cetera, but that different categories of factors may cause illness
and that different types of treatment or healers are effective in treating different causes.

Among the most widespread is the belief that illness (and other forms of
misfortune) may be caused by either *natural* or *unnatural* (or *supernatural*)
factors and agents. This has been reported in Africa (e.g., Etkin et al., 1990;
Janzen, 1978; Janzen & Prins, 1981; Ngubane, 1977; Sussman, 1981, 1983,
1992b) and Asia (e.g., Beals, 1976; Carstairs, 1955; Kleinman, 1980; Topley,
1976), as well as among many groups in the New World (e.g., Bailey, 1991;
Brodwin, 1996; Clark, 1970; Heyer, 1981; Hill, 1973, 1976; Scott, 1974;
Shutler, 1977; Snow, 1974, 1977, 1978, 1993; Staiano, 1981; Young, 1981).

Natural illnesses may result from constitutional weaknesses or exposure to
forces of nature such as cold air, germs, or impurities in air, food, and water.
In many cultures they are viewed as part of the world as God, the creator,
intended it to be. God is, thus, viewed as part of the natural world or as the
creator, and source, of the natural world. In fact, in several cultures, "natural"
illnesses are referred to as "illnesses of God" (e.g., Brodwin, 1996; Janzen,
1978; Sussman, 1981, 1983, 1988, 1992b).

Unnatural and/or *supernatural illnesses* often represent some sort of upset in the natural order and frequently result from impaired social relations. The most common causes of these illnesses are witchcraft and sorcery. These illnesses are, thus, frequently caused by some malign human intervention calling upon supernatural resources. Among some groups, divine retribution (such as punishment by the ancestors or saints) for improper behavior toward other people, deceased ancestors, or other spiritual beings may be included in this category. Possession by various types of spirits, often not the fault of the victim, would also fall under this category.

In Mauritius and Madagascar there are multicausal belief systems— actually quite similar to each other in many respects. In Mauritius, both Creoles of African origin and Indo-Mauritians believe in two major types of illness: "illnesses of God" (*malade Bondieu*), which are naturally caused, and illness caused by sorcery (Table 2.1; Sussman, 1981, 1983). In addition, most Mauritians believe in another form of illness, "fright," that results when an individual sees a dead soul. Most Indo-Mauritians and a minority of Creoles also believe that illness may result from punishment by saints or gods, usually for not fulfilling a promise or a vow to a Hindu deity. In southwest Madagascar, the Mahafaly believe that there are "illnesses of God" (*arety Zanahary*), again naturally caused; "illnesses of man" caused by sorcery (man); "illnesses of spirits" usually resulting in spirit possession; and "illnesses of the ancestors," caused by displeased ancestors (Table 2.1; Sussman, 1992b). In both systems, one may be punished by illness if one does not behave in ways demanded by the gods, ancestors, and social group.

TABLE 2.1
Categories of Illness Recognized in Southwest Madagascar and Mauritius

Location	Illness Category	Cause of Illness
Mauritius	Illness of God	Natural
	Sorcery	Human enemies
	Fright	Seeing dead souls
	Illness of Saints	Displeased saints/deities
SW Madagascar	Illness of God	Natural
	Illness of Man	Sorcery by human enemies
	Illness of Spirits	Spirit possession/attack
	Illness of the Ancestors	Displeased ancestors

Belief Systems Based on the Concept of Balance   Another widespread theme in medical belief systems is the concept of balance, in which health is viewed as a manifestation of proper balance or harmony and ill health as a result of imbalance or disharmony. This is found in such diverse regions as Latin America, North America, Asia, and Africa (e.g., Beckerleg, 1994; Greenwood, 1981; Harwood, 1971; Helman, 1994; Kleinman, 1980; Lang, 1989, 1990; Luecke, 1993; Ngubane, 1977; Shutler, 1977; Topley, 1976; Young, 1981). In some belief systems the balance required for health involves mainly physical and behavioral factors, whereas in others optimal health is maintained only when there is balance, order, or harmony in the physical, social, and spiritual, or moral, spheres of life. Traditional Chinese medicine and Indian Ayurveda are examples of such systems. A number of belief systems in Asia, North Africa, and Latin America emphasizing the role of balance in health classify illnesses, conditions, foods, and medicines into categories of *hot* and *cold*.

Hot/Cold Theories   The hot/cold systems of disease etiology and classification found in Latin America are largely derived from the humoral theory of disease, developed in the fifth century B.C. by Hippocrates and elaborated by Galen in the second century A.D. According to this theory, health was viewed as a state of balance among four humors: blood, phlegm, black bile, and yellow bile. Health was manifest in a warm, moist body. Illness, on the other hand, was manifest in an excessively dry, wet, hot, or cold body that was caused by humoral imbalance (Harwood, 1971).

The Spanish and Portuguese later carried this theory to the New World in the 16th and 17th centuries (Helman, 1994), and variations of it were incorporated into Latin American medical practices and beliefs and persist today (e.g., Clark, 1970; Harwood, 1971; Young, 1981). Harwood (1971) found that this system is firmly rooted among New York City Puerto Ricans. Illnesses are grouped into *hot* and *cold*, and foods and medicines are categorized as *hot*, *cold*, or *cool*. Cold illnesses are treated with hot medicines and foods, and hot illnesses with cool medicines and foods. This system, however, exhibits considerable vitality because new medicines and foods are being incorporated into the system according to their effects on the body. Penicillin, for example, is classified as hot because it can cause symptoms such as rash or diarrhea, which are hot. Drugs that may cause effects such as muscular spasms, however, would be classified as cold.

The Influence of Medical Beliefs on Illness Management—Some Examples   Clearly medical belief systems are of utmost importance in decision making regarding health and illness management, and they influence all of the steps in the health-seeking and health-maintenance process shown in Figure 2.1. Some of the most relevant questions to explore are listed in Table 2.2 and discussed as follows.

Symptom Perception and Interpretation   Perceptions and interpretations of symptoms are shaped by beliefs about their etiology, treatability, and curability. First to consider is *whether the person views the symptoms as abnormal* and as requiring any treatment at all. For example, in many regions of the world diarrhea is quite common in infants and children. Although oral rehydration therapy is inexpensive and widely available, its use is rejected by many for diverse reasons. Mull and Mull (1988) found that some rural Pakistani mothers viewed diarrhea in their infants as normal and not requiring treatment; some believed that it would be dangerous to try to stop it because the "heat" in it could be trapped and spread to the brain, causing fever. Also, it is important to remember that what is viewed as normal for one age or gender group may not be normal for others.

TABLE 2.2
How Medical Beliefs Shape Health Behavior—Some Important Questions to Ask

1. Symptom perception and interpretation:	Does the patient view the symptoms as abnormal?
	What does the patient believe are the possible causes of the symptoms?
	Can an individual conceptually be "ill" in the absence of symptoms?
2. Treatment options and choices:	Who can effectively treat this illness?
	Have healers from different healing systems been consulted?
	If so, what were the diagnosis, treatment, and results?
3. Treatment expectations, goals, evaluation, and adherence:	Does the treatment conflict with the patient's concept of the illness and its appropriate care?
	What effect does the patient expect from the treatment?
	What are the treatment goals of the patient?
	What criteria are being used to evaluate treatment?
	What is the expected role of physicians/counselors/healers?
	What is thought to be appropriate behavior on the part of the physician/counselor/healer?

Biomedically defined psychological or emotional disorders may not be viewed by lay individuals as abnormal or in need of medical treatment, especially if the symptoms are mild. It is important to explore *what the individual believes are the possible causes of the symptoms.* For example, analysis of data from a national psychiatric epidemiological household survey indicated that African Americans were less likely to seek medical care for mild symptoms of depression than Whites, but they sought care with equal frequency if they experienced severe symptoms (Sussman et al., 1987). Although a number of factors may be involved in this lack of treatment seeking, two possibly important factors might be that mild depressive symptoms could be viewed as normal among African Americans if individuals are experiencing difficulties in their lives, and that it might not seem appropriate to see a medical doctor or other health care professional about such symptoms (feelings and emotions), although others in one's social group might be consulted.

What about instances in which an asymptomatic individual has been medically diagnosed as having a disease? The question to consider under these circumstances is *whether a person can conceptually be "sick" in the absence of symptoms.* Such distinctions between lay and clinical views have been addressed in sociology and anthropology through the concepts of disease, illness (Eisenberg, 1977; Mechanic, 1962), and sickness (Young, 1982). Whereas *disease* is a biologically defined pathological bodily state, *illness* refers to an individual's experience of a disvalued change of state that may include symptoms or disease. *Sick* is a socially bestowed label and culturally defined role assigned to individuals. Given these definitions, an individual can have a disease but not have an illness and not be sick. Conversely, an individual can have an illness and be sick but not have a disease.

Treatment Options and Choices   Next to consider is *who or what healing system the person believes can effectively treat the illness.* In the example from Pakistan, some respondents believed the diarrhea was caused by imbalances requiring traditional treatment with cold substances rather than with hot biomedical medicines (Mull & Mull, 1988). In Madagascar, each type of illness requires a different type of healer (Table 2.3). Moreover, specific symptoms do not necessarily correlate with particular causes, and divination (performed either by a male relative or by a diviner) is the primary means of determining cause (Sussman, 1992b; Sussman & Sussman, 1977). Illnesses resulting from angered ancestors or caused by spirit possession, for example, will not respond to biomedical treatment. The former can be cured only by appeasing the ancestors in a ritual conducted by the head of the lineage.

TABLE 2.3
Categories of Illness That Can Be Diagnosed or Treated by Each Type of Healer in Southwest Madagascar and Mauritius

	Southwest Madagascar			
Healer	Illness of God	Illness of Man (Sorcery)	Illness of Spirits	Illness of the Ancestors
Biomedical practitioner	X			
Herbalist	X			
Home treatment	X			
Medicine man		X	X	
Healer possessed by a spirit			X	
Lineage head				X
	Mauritius			
Healer	Illness of God	Sorcery	Fright	Saints
Biomedical practitioner	X			
Herbalist	X			
Home treatment	X			
Specialized healer	X			
Catholic priest	X	X	X	X
Hindu priest		X	X	X
Tamil priest		X	X	X
Sorcerer		X	X	X

Spirit possession may be manifest by many different symptoms but often involves changes in behavior or mood, general malaise and recurrent somatic symptoms such as headache and faintness, or sudden symptoms such as partial paralysis or mutism. Spirit possession may be diagnosed by a diviner or medicine man, and some types of spirits may be appeased and then exorcised by medicine men during rituals that could take place over several weeks. Such rituals may be quite costly as they involve not only the hiring of the medicine man but also frequently the hiring of musicians and payment for food for visiting members of the extended family. Therefore, during healing rituals of this type, social support is clearly demonstrated for the sick family member, creating an atmosphere conducive to healing those in emotional and psychological distress as well as easing social discord.

Possession by other types of spirits must be positively diagnosed and treated by a healer possessed by a similar spirit. In these cases, the spirit is not exorcised but is appeased by the patient and patient's family who are instructed by the spirit about the types of gifts it desires and the taboos that must be observed. The spirit will then remain with the patient but no longer cause symptoms. The terms of the "cure" are worked out by the spirit possessing the patient (while the patient is in a trance) and the spirit that possesses the healer (while the healer is in a trance). The spirits then instruct those present at the healing ceremony about what the patient and family are required to do (Sussman, 1992b).

Individuals in societies with plural medical systems may utilize more than one type of healing system either for a particular illness episode or over a lifetime for different illness episodes. To a great extent, although not exclusively, decisions regarding the type of care to seek are guided by medical beliefs. One pattern of utilization that has been reported in many societies involves the use of different types of care for illnesses with different causes. This has been termed *compartmentalization*. This is illustrated by the medical beliefs and appropriate treatment resources on Madagascar and on Mauritius (Table 2.3).

A second pattern is one in which health care options are positioned in what is called a *hierarchy of resort* (Schwartz, 1969) with options being sought in a particular order, according to culturally based criteria. Different types of care are, thus, sought consecutively until, hopefully, the desired outcome is achieved. This pattern of utilization is consistent with medical systems in which it is believed that illness may have many causes and that there is a cure for every illness if the right practitioner can be found (e.g., Beals, 1976; Snow, 1974; Staiano, 1981). This also applied to Mauritius (Sussman, 1981, 1983), where responses of an illness to particular treatments are utilized to make further diagnostic judgments. Treatments appropriate for "natural" illnesses are usually sought first. If the illness is not cured by such treatment, this may provide grounds for suspecting it to be an "unnatural" illness (also see, e.g., Ngubane, 1977; Snow, 1977; Staiano, 1981; Sussman, 1992b; Yoder, 1981). In such societies, there is a tendency to reject notions concerning the chronicity or incurability of particular diseases.

A third pattern of health care utilization involves the *concurrent* or *complementary* use of two or more systems of care. For example, an individual may consult both a physician and an *espiritista*. Or a patient may consult a physician and follow the biomedical regimen while also taking herbal remedies prepared at home. One reason for this might be to counteract presumed ill effects of one of the treatments: if a physician prescribes a "hot" medication, a patient may at the same time take a "cool" herbal tea to counteract the heat. A common variation of this pattern, especially among those with chronic diseases, is to alternate care between two systems. For example, on Mauritius it is very common for individuals with chronic illnesses requiring ongoing medication, such as diabetes and hypertension, to alternate between taking physician-prescribed medication and herbalist-prescribed remedies or home-grown remedies in order to rest the body from strong biomedical medicines and their side effects (Sussman, 1980, 1988).

Complementary treatment from two distinct therapeutic systems may also be sought in order to address multiple causes of an illness—such as an underlying supernatural cause and a resultant physical cause. For example, in Mauritius, individuals may consult sorcerers to remove magical objects from their bodies resulting from sorcery against them and simultaneously consult biomedical physicians to heal the physical injury caused by the magical objects. A typical case involved a woman diagnosed by a physician as having severe bleeding ulcers that were not responding well to treatment. A sorcerer was consulted who diagnosed the underlying cause as a magical thorn inserted into her stomach through sorcery. He was employed to remove the thorn and conduct a ritual to prevent further magical insertions, thereby enabling biomedical treatment to be effective.

Treatment Expectations, Goals, Evaluation, and Adherence   Finally, medical beliefs shape treatment expectations, goals, evaluation, and adherence. Here it is important to determine whether the actual *treatment is congruent or conflicts with the person's concept of the illness, its appropriate care, and its cure.* Lay concepts of a particular disease may differ significantly from specialist concepts. Nevertheless, it is the lay concepts that shape patient treatment expectations, goals, and evaluation and in large part determine whether particular treatment recommendations "make sense" to patients. Unless the underlying assumptions of patients concerning the disease are understood by healing specialists, patients and healers may be operating within different conceptual systems. They may be using the same words but speaking different languages. Once again, the example of diarrhea in Pakistan serves to exemplify this issue. Many of the mothers viewed diarrhea as a "hot" illness requiring treatment by "cold" foods, herbs, and remedies. Most Western medicines, however, were classified as "hot" and therefore biomedical recommendations to use oral rehydration therapy were rejected as inappropriate (Mull & Mull, 1988).

Treatment Expectations and Goals   Beliefs about the cause of an illness and its natural progression largely determine expected outcomes of treatment and influence decisions regarding care. If it is believed that an illness is the result of divine retribution or witchcraft, expectations from biomedical treatment may, for example, be quite low because it logically follows that medical treatment will have little effect. Likewise, if sorcery is the underlying cause of an illness, then biomedicine could not work until the sorcerer is dealt with first. Important questions to ask are *what effect does the person expect from the treatment* and *what are the overall short- and long-term goals of treatment from the patient's perspective?*

Treatment goals, closely linked to expectations, also reflect medical beliefs. In situations where patient and physician are from different sociocultural backgrounds, distinctions between physician and patient goals may be considerable (e.g., Raymond & D'Eramo-Melkus, 1993). In the United States, there is frequently conflict between the treatment goals of patients and physicians. For example, Hopper and Schechtman (1985) found that among low-income, predominantly African American individuals under medical care for diabetes, the phrase "treatment will help" meant to the overwhelming majority that treatment would make them feel better or decrease the frequency or severity of symptoms; only 4 to 5% viewed "helping" as lowering or controlling blood sugar levels—which was the goal of the physician.

Snow (1974) describes an example of how differing concepts of "stroke" held by a physician and an African American woman were related to conflicting treatment goals and led to the rejection of medical treatment. Characteristics of the blood are significant in many medical systems (Helman, 1994; Snow, 1977). This is reflected in the many different ways in which blood is described in medical systems throughout the world: high vs. low blood; thick vs. thin blood; hot vs. cold blood; living vs. sleeping blood; impure vs. pure blood; dirty vs. clean blood; new vs. used blood; good vs. bad blood. Moreover, among some groups, blood is not believed to be regenerative, which could certainly lead to a reluctance by patients to part with their blood for testing.

The woman described by Snow (1974) had had a light stroke and was recuperating at home, sitting up in bed. She believed that stroke was caused by "high blood," or too much blood that boiled up and gave her "blood on the brains" (p. 92). Sitting up, she thought, would make the blood go back down more quickly. She had thrown away the medication prescribed by a physician because he had told her that she would have to take it all her life. Because she believed "high blood" to be a temporary condition, her reaction was, "Now that don't make no sense" (p. 92) and she was considering a home remedy to bring the high blood down.

Throughout human history and across cultures, medical systems have focused predominantly on curing illness and reducing pain. Chronic illness represents a special and, to many laypeople around the world, a rather peculiar case of illness in that the goal of biomedical treatment is not a cure but rather lifelong management. This is not necessarily accepted by laymen in many cultures as a treatment goal. For example, in Mauritius it was generally presumed that there should be a cure for every illness—one just had to find the right kind of healer who possessed the right kind of knowledge or power to cure it. Moreover, Mauritians generally expected biomedicine to cure ailments quite quickly—within weeks—but tended to allow other types of healers, especially religious healers and sorcerers, several months. It is, therefore, important to be specific when discussing treatment goals to ensure that practitioner and patient (and family) understand and agree about the effects that are expected from treatment as well as timelines within which these effects may occur. Both short-term and long-term goals and effects need to be addressed. When dealing with psychological, emotional, or behavioral problems, it is especially important to understand how the patient and family interpret the problem and its possible causes and discuss their treatment expectations and goals. Some diagnoses may have considerable stigma attached to them in some cultural groups and, as noted earlier, members of some groups may not be willing to accept a diagnosis that has no permanent cure and that would "label" those diagnosed with the disease for the rest of their lives.

Treatment Evaluation and Adherence to Prescribed Regimens   Although treatment evaluation may at first appear to be a straightforward appraisal of "Does it work?" it is also a culturally based process (Etkin, 1988). "Does it work?" may not mean the same thing to different people or to patients and their physicians. Treatment is evaluated according to its effectiveness in meeting treatment goals, its perceived necessity and importance vis-à-vis treatment expectations, and its logic vis-à-vis the medical belief system of the patient.

Patients, who are active in managing illness but may have treatment goals different from those of the physician, will in many cases alter the treatment regimen to fit their needs, lifestyles, and goals without informing the physician. Roberson (1992) found this to be the case among rural African Americans with chronic illnesses. She notes that although many of the individuals she studied would be seen by their physicians as noncompliant, they, in fact, "saw themselves as managing their chronic illnesses and treatment regimens effectively" (p. 24).

Prescribed regimens may be totally rejected as senseless, ineffective, or objectionable, or may be altered according to the expectations, goals, and beliefs of patients and their therapy management groups. One criterion frequently utilized to evaluate treatment is the presence or absence of side effects. Biomedical medication is viewed as quite powerful by patients around the world—perhaps too powerful or potent to be taken over the long term. However, herbal and other traditional remedies are seen as acceptable and useful for long-term treatment. This has been reported, for example, by Puerto Rican patients with diabetes (Quatromoni et al., 1994) and by Mauritians with hypertension and diabetes (Sussman, 1983).

Similar attitudes have been reported toward asthma medication among patients in the United States. For example, in a health education project for African American children with asthma, 54% of the children's parents believed upon enrollment in the program that long-term medication may be harmful for children, and 52% agreed that asthma medications make children jumpy or nervous (Sussman, 1992c, 1997). In this project, pulmonary specialists, general practitioners, and patients tended to hold disparate views of asthma and its care (Sussman, 1997), with specialists and patients differing the most and general practitioners falling between these two groups. Among specialists, asthma was seen as a chronic illness requiring ongoing management, treatment, and monitoring. The goal of treatment was to prevent the onset of symptoms by keeping the airways open and not inflamed. Often several medications were prescribed for daily use, several times per day, and routine checkups were to be performed four times per year. In general, medications were believed to cause no major side effects and pose no danger. Alternatively, in addition to parental concerns about the long-term use of medication and its side effects, a high percentage of parents (59%) had rather low expectations from medical treatment and did not think that much could be done to prevent asthma symptoms from occurring despite medical care. It was generally accepted that people with asthma will at least occasionally wheeze and have attacks requiring acute care. The goal of treatment from the parents' perspectives was in most cases to stop symptoms when they occurred and then to cut back or stop use of medication whenever possible. This contrasts significantly from the specialists' goal of preventing symptoms altogether through the daily use of medications. Patients with chronic diseases, and particularly those who have had such diseases in their families over generations, experience the diseases over long periods of time and observe their changing treatment by physicians. Many will note that today doctors tell you to do this, last year they told you to do that, and next year they will tell you to do something else! The view within science and medicine is that, through research, theories are constantly being tested and refined, bringing us ever closer to the truth. However, patients and families who have experienced these diseases over generations frequently hesitate to follow prescribed regimens by the letter as treatment guidelines change and last year's "truth" becomes replaced with this year's "truth" and "facts" (see also O'Connor, 1995).

In addition to evaluating explanations of illness and the actual effectiveness of a specific treatment, patients and their families also evaluate treatment and medical encounters according to whether they meet prevailing cultural norms of interaction and expectations regarding the role of healing specialists. It is, therefore, important to ask, *What role does the patient expect the healer/physician to play?* and *What is thought to be appropriate behavior on the part of the healer/physician?* For example, Clark notes that Mexican Americans, "who expect a curer to be warm, friendly, and interested in all aspects of the patient's life find it difficult to trust a doctor who is impersonal and 'clinical' in his manner. Nor do they accept his authority to 'give orders.' He may suggest or counsel, but an authoritarian or dictatorial approach on his part is resented and rejected. His behavior, culturally sanctioned in his own society, is often interpreted by Spanish-speaking patients as discourtesy if not outright boorishness" (Clark, 1970, pp. 230–231). Similarly, O'Connor (1995) demonstrates how physician behavior perceived to be coercive and authoritarian by Hmong patients and their families may contribute to decisions to refuse treatment, even for severe illness. "Though some of the younger men in the family felt that the evaluation itself could do no harm, the older men (and in general the majority of the decision-making body) felt that pursuit of the evaluation would involve a significant risk of being coerced into the transplant itself: 'since … they are the doctor[s], right; so they say things; scare us, right?; … to make [us] decide to say yes.' … Family members decided instead to remove him from the hospital against medical advice, and to take him home for family-based care" (O'Connor, 1995, p. 96). O'Connor notes that the family strongly disliked the "intense pressure for rapid and compliant decisions" (p. 96). This behavior was seen as coercive and served to intensify feelings of distrust. The family also felt uneasy about acting on the opinions of the resident who was quite young because "the Hmong strongly associate wisdom with age and experience" (p. 96).

In summary, most lay medical belief systems reflect an eclectic approach to health and healing. A wide array of causes are recognized, and a number of diverse types of healing specialists are accepted as legitimate. Individuals working within the system are pragmatic, base their judgments and evaluation on empirical observations (made, of course, through their cultural "lens"), and may utilize, simultaneously or sequentially, a diversity of healing specialists and remedies representing different theories and ideologies (e.g., Beals, 1976; Clark, 1970; Etkin et al., 1990; Reeve, 2000; Sussman, 1981,

1983, 1988; Trotter & Chavira, 1981). Medical belief systems, while internally coherent, are not closed and static. They are, rather, open and changing. New elements—theories of causation, illness categories, illness labels, and forms of treatment—may be and are incorporated into them, but they are incorporated in forms congruent with the underlying values and principles of the system as a whole.

Social Structure and Organization: Decision Makers and Caregivers

> People in Sal si Puedes do not act as isolated individuals in medical situations. In illness as well as in other aspects of life, they are members of a group of relatives and compadres. Illness is not merely a biological disorder of the individual organism—it is a social crisis and period of readjustment for an entire group of people. (Clark, 1970, p. 203)
>
> The authority of the family group also supersedes that of the professional medical workers. Opinions of doctors and nurses certainly influence family decisions, but they are not accepted as absolute fact. (Clark, 1970, p. 205)

Social structure and organization play significant roles in illness interpretation and management. It is overwhelmingly within the context of the family and household that illness is recognized and managed throughout the world. The conditions of individuals are assessed and individuals are labeled by the social group as "sick," thereby assigning individuals to the "sick role" and granting them the culturally defined rights, privileges, and obligations of that role. The lay "therapy management group" (Janzen, 1978, 1987) makes decisions regarding the seeking of care and the following of particular treatment regimens, and specific individuals are delegated the task of caring for sick members of the group. Social structure and organization provide the means of implementing cultural beliefs, norms, and values through the delineation of those individuals responsible for the various aspects of illness management. In some cultures, it is the ill individual who is predominantly responsible for making decisions regarding treatment seeking and care, whereas in others the authority of the family or social group may supersede that of the individual and of the healer.

Across cultures there is great diversity in the ways in which peoples organize themselves into groups and in the roles and statuses of individuals within those groups. In the United States, we tend to assume that individual patients, as long as they are physically and mentally able, are in charge of their illness management. In the case of children, we assume that the parent(s) or guardian(s) are responsible for management decisions. However, worldwide, this is not necessarily the case, and family groups and responsibilities extend well beyond the household and nuclear family. For example, regarding a Hmong patient and family in Pennsylvania, O'Connor (1995) states:

> The self is collectively developed and conceived, within the structure and mutual obligations of multigenerational family relations and clan affiliation. In traditional Hmong terms, there is no equivalent to the willful, self-interested, and individuated self that is so deeply ingrained and idealized in contemporary American culture. The consent form that Mr. L. would have to sign for transport and evaluation for liver transplant could indeed be signed by him. But the act of consent that could occasion this signature had, in fact, little to do with him personally. Within his cultural framework, momentous decisions can only be made collectively, by a meeting of all relevant family members. Each family member has the right and duty to express his or her thoughts on the matter, and the opinions and concerns of all then form the basis of a general discussion.
>
> The decision-making process includes consideration of effects of actions upon individual members and upon the entire family network.... In the end it is the male family elder (or elders) who brings together all of the sentiments expressed and comes to a decision by which everyone will abide. The person whom the decision will most directly affect (as seen from the individualist American perspective, or as encoded in the bioethical principle of patient autonomy) does not have private rights in such matters that can override an elder's decision. (p. 85)

The potential complexity of the decision-making process can be seen from the following example from southwest Madagascar. In this culture, nuclear families are grouped into extended kin groups based upon biological relationship through males. An adult male will typically live in a household with his wife (wives) and unmarried children. This same adult male, if his father is deceased and if he is the eldest male child, may head a kin group composed of his wife (wives), his children, his unmarried sisters and their resident children, his mother, his widowed paternal aunts, his younger brothers and their wives and children, etc. This male is furthermore a member of a larger, patrilineal lineage, whose head is the eldest male in the most senior generation, traced back through males. The head of the lineage is the ritual leader for the lineage and, ultimately, is responsible for making important decisions about lineage members. Although minor daily health care decisions are usually left to individual female and, then, male heads of household, those regarding more serious illness or expensive treatment options may be made by the head of the extended kin group or even by the head of the lineage. To make matters more complicated, although males, and the heads of their extended kin groups, are usually responsible for their wives' well-being, in cases of serious illness, the woman's father and possibly the head of her patrilineal lineage must be notified and brought into the decision-making process because they, ultimately, are responsible for her although they may live in distant villages.

Social structure and organization, therefore, determine to a great extent *the identity of those individuals who have the authority to make health care decisions* as well as of those responsible for covering the costs of treatment (see Table 2.4). Furthermore, health care decision-makers frequently turn to an array of individuals for advice in times of illness. The identities of formal and informal sources of health care advice ("therapeutic networks") are also influenced by cultural norms and may consist of parents and other relatives, friends, other health care professionals such as pharmacists and nurses, priests and ministers, other knowledgeable community members, as well as popular literature. Even for patients of the majority culture in the United States, biomedical practitioners may be only one of several sources of advice concerning health and illness management. Then, after a decision has been made to seek care and follow a particular treatment regimen, *the identity of those who will assume the responsibility for care is largely determined by cultural norms and the roles and statuses of individuals within the group.*

Cultural Values and History

Medical beliefs and social orders reflect a larger system of cultural values. Moreover, the history of a cultural group and of a minority group vis-à-vis the majority may play significant roles in the development of cultural values and health care norms and beliefs.

TABLE 2.4 How Social Structure and Organization Shape Health Behavior—Some Important Questions to Ask	
1. Decision makers	Who is responsible for making decisions about illness management—e.g., source of care, treatment goals? Who is responsible for evaluating practitioners and treatment outcomes?
2. Caregivers	Who is responsible for caring for the sick individual?

Values Related to Gender, Generation, and Birth Order   Decisions about care may be reflective of the role, status, rights, and obligations of the sick individual within the family or social group. In some cultures there is a preference for offspring of one gender. Among some peoples, this may be exhibited as a mild preference; among others it may be quite marked (e.g., Miller, 1981), as substantial benefits may hinge upon the gender of a child. In some groups, such as the Mahafaly of Southwest Madagascar, the rights and status of a woman may depend upon both bearing a son and having that son survive into adulthood. Such preferences may influence treatment seeking, illness management, and even decisions regarding access to resources (see, e.g., Miller, 1981; Williams, Baumslag, & Jelliffe, 1994). Although in some cultures these practices may not be normative, cultural values may nevertheless lead to differential care of sons and daughters, especially when resources are scarce. Similarly, these values, linked to differential status of men and women, may play a part in decisions regarding the care given to and resources expended on adult members of various subgroups (Williams et al., 1994).

The status and roles of members of different generations or of siblings occupying particular positions in the birth order may also have an impact on decisions regarding illness management. Where elders are highly respected and hold positions of high status, many economic and human resources may be expended to maintain their health. Likewise, children holding a specific place in the birth order, often first sons, may be given preferential treatment. However, if productivity and full functioning of the elderly in the society are valued, health conditions obviating the ability to play a productive role in society may lead to the acceptance of death as superior to life-maintenance efforts.

Cultural values, therefore, may strongly influence decisions regarding the seeking of care as well as treatment goals. A number of questions to consider are listed in Table 2.5. In order to understand the decision-making process, *it is important to be aware of the status, role, rights, and obligations of the patient in the family* (Table 2.5). Moreover, within the context of therapy, counseling, and recommendations concerning changes in lifestyle, it is especially relevant *to understand the behavioral norms for patients given their age, sex, and generation within the family,* because behavioral expectations are based on cultural values that may not concur with Western majority values embedded in the medical system. These may include views on such diverse topics as individualism, autonomy, expression of emotion, conflict resolution, ideal body types, and appearance.

TABLE 2.5
How Cultural Values and History Shape Health
Behavior—Some Important Questions to Ask

What are the role, status, rights, and obligations of the patient in the family?

What are the behavioral norms for the patient, given the individual's age, sex, and generation within the family?

Do treatment goals or procedures conflict with specific values or norms of the cultural group?

What are the attitudes of the patient and other family members toward the majority culture, its values, behavioral norms, and institutions?

As products of the majority culture, are the medical system and its practitioners viewed by the patient or family members as representing values and attitudes that devalue the beliefs and practices of other cultures?

Does the patient/family exhibit distrust of the medical system and its practitioners as a result of past experience, and can a dialogue be initiated to address patient/family concerns and build trust?

Affirmation or Rejection of Ethnic Identity   Medical beliefs and practices may be utilized by individuals or nations to declare something about themselves (e.g., Bailey, 1991; Beckerleg, 1994; Carrier, 1989; Crandon-Malamud, 1991; Shutler, 1977). Peoples may affirm pride in their cultural heritage by endorsing traditional healing practices and consuming particular foods. Alternatively, rejection of traditional beliefs and practices and acceptance and use of those of the majority culture may reflect a desire to demonstrate one's level of acculturation to the majority culture (e.g., Western culture), one's education, one's status, or one's acceptance into mainstream society. Within immigrant families, members of different generations may view the new country of residence and majority culture differently. This may be reflected in diverse levels of acceptance and rejection of the norms and values of the majority culture and the culture of origin among members of the same family (see, e.g., Suárez-Orozco, 1997). Another issue faced by members of minority groups is that of "double consciousness and double self-identity" described as the desire or attempt to be American while retaining one's ethnic identity and not being viewed as "White" (Kumanyika, Morssink, & Agurs, 1992). This may result in ambivalence toward treatment regimens and programs and alternation between adherence and nonadherence.

Medical beliefs and practices are integral parts of the cultural heritage of patients. They frequently reflect deep-seated moral and social values, worldviews, and religious beliefs that transcend specific beliefs about human anatomy, physiology, and pathology. However, one must refrain from stereotyping individuals based on their apparent ethnic background because some individuals may, through their medical beliefs and practices, be attempting to assert their *dis*similarity from others from their ethnic background. It is, therefore, important *to gain an understanding of the attitudes of the patient and other family members toward the values, behavioral norms, and institutions of the majority culture and culture of origin* (Table 2.5).

History of a Group   The history of a group may be particularly relevant to current medical beliefs, patterns of health seeking, and attitudes toward particular types of healing specialists. Healing systems are products of the culture in which they develop. It is important to ask, therefore, *whether members of minority cultural groups may view the medical system and its practitioners as representing values and attitudes of the majority culture that devalue the beliefs and practices of other cultures* (see Table 2.5). For example, the ancestors of present-day African Americans were forcefully removed from their homelands, social groups, and cultural resources, and until quite recently were denied access to medical care available to Whites. Consequently, they had to develop their own unique system of medical beliefs and treatment methods based on diverse medical systems from Africa and available knowledge and resources in their new environment (Bailey, 1991; Jordon, 1979; Snow, 1974, 1977; Spector, 1979). These developed over time and, although resulting in response to conditions not of their own making, came to be parts of African American culture.

Likewise, slaves received the least desirable foods and found ways to survive on them, preserve them, and make them palatable. Particular food items and dishes then also became part of African American cultural traditions. They may serve as markers of membership in the group and could also be viewed as symbolizing the history and strife of the group. Culturally insensitive attempts by White middle-class health care professionals to alter diet and patterns of use of biomedical care may quite understandably be viewed by some African Americans as debasing their cultural traditions and blaming these traditions, originally developed as adaptive responses to White oppression, for their current health states.

Native American groups, similarly, experienced extensive oppression at the hands of Whites settling their homelands. In speaking of the causes and development of diabetes among tribe members, the Dakota, for example, tend to view the disease not only as the result of specific dietary practices and physical conditions (e.g., obesity) of individuals, but also within the social and historical perspective of the tribe, of Native Americans in general, and of their interactions with Whites (Lang, 1989, 1990). Diabetes is seen as a new illness that has been brought to them by the White man. As for African Americans, attempts by biomedical practitioners, representatives of White society, both to implicate diet in the development of disease and to change the diet, originally imposed on them by Whites but now an integral part of current traditions, may not be well accepted by Native Americans. Dietary changes are rarely followed by Dakota individuals with diabetes; in fact, they are viewed as yet "another 'imposition' on Indian people by a non-Indian world" (Lang, 1989, p. 320).

Diet is so intimately intertwined with religion, politics, social structure, and centuries of history that medical advice that appears to place blame on the victims for their illness because of poor diet and obesity are unlikely to succeed. As Lang (1989) states, food reflects one's orientation, "community solidarity vis-à-vis other Dakota communities of the region, Dakota identity vis-à-vis other Native American groups,... and Indian identity vis-à-vis white society. Foods likewise provide a means by which Dakota make connections with an idealized past" (pp. 319–320).

The history of interactions of a group with the society and, in particular, with biomedicine lives on through generations. This is clearly demonstrated in a study by Agee (2000) comparing the passing on of knowledge about menopause among African American and Euro-American women and decisions regarding treatment seeking and the use of hormone replacement therapy (HRT). In speaking of the African American women in her sample, she states that "many expressed that their collective history as African American women shaped important aspects of their contemporary identity as well as their interactions with the health care system" (p. 80). Most of the African American women, even those who had consulted physicians about menopause, chose not to use HRT, and about two-thirds of those interviewed "intimated a distrust of the medical system that informed their decisions about HRT. Women framed this distrust by talking about the history of medical mistreatment of African Americans in the area.... This history includes the inhumane treatment of African Americans in the basement of the local hospital during segregation.... Even after desegregation of the hospital, similar treatment of African Americans continued" (p. 89). Such mistreatment was actually witnessed by some of the women both before and after desegregation and is part of their personal experience as well as family experience through the generations. Agee states that "for African American women aware of biomedical practices that have attempted to limit their power and their knowledge of their bodies, being wary of biomedicine and other institutions built on knowledge/power relations informed by racist ideologies is essential to survival" (p. 90). Likewise, knowledge and experience within the social/ family group with previous bias in psychiatric diagnosis, in which African

Americans were more likely than Whites to be diagnosed as psychotic and institutionalized, may well make African Americans hesitant to seek care for psychological, emotional, or behavioral problems from biomedical health care professionals. Negative experiences in the past, whether they happened to the individual, a family member, or a close friend, do not just exist as isolated memories, but rather become part of one's experience that shapes attitudes, preferences, and decisions. It is, therefore, important *to explore whether the patient/family seems to distrust the medical system as a result of past experience with it and whether ways can be found to open communication between practitioners, patients, and families about their concerns* (see Table 2.5).

Summary

Four major themes have been emphasized throughout this chapter.

1. Medical belief systems are coherent, logical systems of beliefs, practices, norms, and values. What are frequently termed "folk beliefs" are not isolated beliefs and practices, holdovers from different times and places. Although the importance of culture in shaping medical beliefs and practices of other groups is being increasingly acknowledged in biomedicine today, the fact that biomedicine itself is a product of the culture in which it has developed is seldom addressed. Moreover, there is a disturbing trend toward blaming the "culture" of minority groups for the high prevalence, morbidity, and mortality rates of various diseases among these groups. In a way, a form of "cultural" determinism is replacing, or joining, "biological" determinism in explaining epidemiological data. This then sometimes leads to the misguided goal of wishing to "educate culture out of people." Hopefully, I have conveyed and substantiated the fact that culture is not just an isolated factor that affects illness interpretation and management, but rather that it shapes it and guides it. We view, define, and manage illness according to our cultural framework— our cultural lens. Therapy is developed and its effectiveness is evaluated within our cultural framework, and decisions and the identities of those who make decisions are congruent with cultural values. For example, do we pursue life for life's sake? Does there come a time to die because one is of no use to society or a burden to one's family? Is a boy more valued than a girl and thus more likely to receive medical care? Culture permeates our view of reality: reality is culturally constructed.

2. People who are ill, along with individuals in their social group, are active: They use their own knowledge and experience and seek that of others in attempts to make sense of illness and to find relief and cure. Although they may not consistently or completely follow treatment regimens advised by biomedical practitioners, and hence may be labeled as "nonadherent" or "negligent," they are most likely doing things—other things—and may consider themselves and be considered by others in their group to be responsibly managing their illness.

3. Lay medical belief systems are open and dynamic, constantly changing, adapting to new conditions, incorporating new elements, and even modifying old elements as long as they do not directly require rejection of beliefs and values underlying the system. New elements tend to be integrated into medical systems in forms congruent with the existing system; they rarely completely replace existing elements. Moreover, most permit, and many encourage, individuals to be pragmatic and eclectic in their quests for cure.

4. There is so much variation between individuals within groups and so many factors (individual, social, economic, and political as well as cultural) that may influence illness management that oversimplified characterization of cultural groups, or stereotyping, is misleading and counterproductive. Therefore, in this chapter I have striven to convey an appreciation for the many "lenses" through which illness may be viewed and an understanding of the multiple sociocultural issues and processes that may shape and underlie individual health decisions and illness management practices. The questions listed in Tables 2.3 to 2.5 are included as guides in helping to explore how beliefs and values may be guiding illness management decisions of patients and families and to identify possible areas of miscommunication and/or disagreement that may need to be addressed.

References

Agee, E. (2000). Menopause and the transmission of women's knowledge: African American and White women's perspectives. *Medical Anthropology Quarterly,* 14, 73–95.

Bailey, E. (1991). *Urban African American health care.* Lanham, MD: University Press of America.

Beals, A. R. (1976). Strategies of resort to curers in South India. In C. Leslie (Ed.), *Asian medical systems: A comparative study* (pp. 184–200). Berkeley: University of California Press.

Beckerleg, S. (1994). Medical pluralism and Islam in Swahili communities in Kenya. *Medical Anthropology Quarterly, 8*(3), 299–313.

Brodwin, P. (1996). *Medicine and morality in Haiti: The contest for healing power.* Cambridge, England: Cambridge University Press.

Carrier, A. H. (1989). The place of Western medicine in Ponam theories of health and illness. In S. Frankel & G. Lewis (Eds.), *A continuing trial of treatment: Medical pluralism in Papua New Guinea* (pp. 155–181). Dordrecht: Kluwer.

Carstairs, G. M. (1955). Medicine and faith in rural Rajasthan. In B. D. Paul (Ed.), *Health, culture, and community: Case studies of public reactions to health programs* (pp. 107–134). New York: Russell Sage Foundation.

Chrisman, N. J. (1977). The health seeking process: an approach to the natural history of illness. *Culture, Medicine & Psychiatry, 1*(4), 351–377.

Clark, M. (1970). *Health in the Mexican-American culture: A community study* (2nd ed.). Berkeley: University of California Press.

Crandon-Malamud, L. (1991). *From the fat of our souls: Social change, political process, and medical pluralism in Bolivia.* Berkeley: University of California Press.

Eisenberg, L. (1977). Disease and illness: Distinctions between professional and popular ideas of sickness. *Culture, Medicine & Psychiatry, 1*, 9–23.

Etkin, N. L. (1988). Cultural constructions of efficacy. In S. van der Geest & R. Whyte (Eds.), *The context of medicines in developing countries* (pp. 299–326). Dordrecht: Kluwer Academic.

Etkin, N. L., Ross, P. J., & Muazzamu, I. (1990). The indigenization of pharmaceuticals: Therapeutic transitions in rural Hausaland. *Social Science and Medicine, 30*(8), 919–928.

Gibbs, T. (1988). Health-seeking behavior of elderly Blacks. In J. S. Jackson (Ed.), *The Black American elderly* (pp. 282–291). New York: Springer.

Greenwood, B. (1981). Cold or spirits? Choice and ambiguity in Morocco's pluralistic medical system. *Social Science and Medicine, 15B*, 219–235.

Harrison, F. V. (1998). Introduction: Race and racism. *American Anthropologist, 100*(3), 609–631.

Harwood, A. (1971). Hot-cold theory of disease: Implications for treatment of Puerto Rican patients. *Journal of American Medical Association, 216*, 1153–1158.

Helman, C. G. (1994). *Culture, health and illness: An introduction for health professionals* (3rd ed.). Oxford: Butterworth-Heinemann.

Heyer, K. W. (1981). *Rootwork: Psychosocial aspects of malign magical and illness beliefs in a South Carolina Sea Island community.* Unpublished doctoral dissertation, University of Connecticut.

Hill, C. E. (1973). Black healing practices in the rural South. *Journal of Popular Culture, 6*, 849–853.

Hill, C. E. (1976). A folk medical belief system in the rural South: Some practical considerations. *Southern Medicine, 16*, 11–17.

Hopper, S. V., & Schechtman, K. B. (1985). Factors associated with diabetic control and utilization patterns in a low-income, older adult population. *Patient Education & Counseling, 7*, 275–288.

Janzen, J. M. (1978). *The quest for therapy in Lower Zaire.* Berkeley: University of California Press.

Janzen, J. M. (1987). Therapy management: Concept, reality, process. *Medical Anthropology Quarterly (NS), 1*(1), 68–84.

Janzen, J., & Prins, G. (Eds.). (1981). Causality and classification in African medicine and health. Special issue, *Social Science & Medicine, 15B*(3).

Jordon, J. W. (1979). The roots and practice of voodoo medicine in America. *Urban Health, 8*, 38–41.

Kleinman, A. (1980). *Patients and healers in the context of culture.* Berkeley: University of California Press.

Kleinman, A., Eisenberg, L., & Good, B. (1978). Culture, illness, and care: Clinical lessons from anthropologic and cross-cultural research. *Annals of Internal Medicine, 88*, 251–258.

Kumanyika, S. K., Morssink, C., & Agurs, T. (1992). Models for dietary and weight change in African-American women: Identifying cultural components. *Ethnicity & Disease, 2*(2), 166–175.

Lang, G. C. (1989). "Making sense" about diabetes: Dakota narratives of illness. *Medical Anthropology, 11*, 305–327.

Lang, G. C. (1990). Talking about a new illness with the Dakota: Reflections on diabetes, food and culture. In R. H. Winthrop (Ed.), *Culture and the anthropological tradition: Essays in honor of Robert F. Spencer* (pp. 283–318). Lanham, MD: University Press of America.

Luecke, R. (Ed.). (1993). *A new dawn in Guatemala: Toward a worldwide health vision.* Prospect Heights, IL: Waveland Press.

Mechanic, D. (1962). The concept of illness behavior. *Journal of Chronic Diseases, 15*, 189–194.

Mechanic, D. (1968). *Medical sociology: A selective view.* New York: The Free Press.

Mechanic, D. (Ed.). (1982). *Symptoms, illness behavior and help-seeking.* New York: Prodist.

Miller, B. D. (1981). *The endangered sex: Neglect of female children in rural North India.* Ithaca, NY: Cornell University Press.

Mull, J. D., & Mull, D. S. (1988). Mothers' concept of childhood diarrhoea in rural Pakistan: What ORT program planners should know. *Social Science & Medicine, 27*, 53–67.

Ngubane, H. (1977). *Body and mind in Zulu medicine: An ethnography of health and disease in Nyuswa-Zulu thought and practice.* London: Academic Press.

O'Connor, B. B. (1995). *Healing traditions: Alternative medicine and the health professions.* Philadelphia: University of Pennsylvania Press.

Page, H. E., & Thomas, B. (1994). White public space and the construction of White privilege in U.S. health care: Fresh concepts and a new model of analysis. *Medical Anthropology Quarterly, 8*(1), 109–116.

Park, K. (1996). Use and abuse of race and culture: Black-Korean tension in America. *American Anthropologist, 98*(3), 492–505.

Quatromoni, P. A., Milbauer, M., Posner, B. M., Carballeira, N. P., Brunt, M., & Chipkin, S. R. (1994). Use of focus groups to explore nutrition practices and health beliefs of urban Caribbean Latinos with diabetes. *Diabetes Care, 17*(8), 869–873.

Raymond, N. R., & D'Eramo-Melkus, G. (1993). Non-insulin-dependent diabetes and obesity in the Black and Hispanic population: Culturally sensitive management. *Diabetes Educator, 19*(4), 313–317.

Reeve, M.-E. (2000). Concepts of illness and treatment practice in a caboclo community of the Lower Amazon. *Medical Anthropology Quarterly, 14*, 96–108.

Roberson, M. H. B. (1992). The meaning of compliance: Patient perspectives. *Qualitative Health Research, 2*, 7–26.

Schwartz, L. R. (1969). The hierarchy of resort in curative practices: The Admiralty Islands, Melanesia. *Journal of Health and Social Behavior, 10*, 201–209.

Scott, C. S. (1974). Health and healing practices among five ethnic groups in Miami, Florida. *Public Health Report, 89*, 524–532.

Shutler, M. E. (1977). Disease and curing in a Yaqui community. In E. H. Spicer (Ed.), *Ethnic medicine in the Southwest* (pp. 169–237). Tucson: University of Arizona Press.

Smedley, A. (1993). *Race in North America: Origin and evolution of a worldview.* Boulder: Westview Press.

Smedley, A. (1998). "Race" and the construction of human identity. *American Anthropologist, 100*(3), 690–702.

Snow, L. F. (1974). Folk medical beliefs and their implications for care of patients. *Annals of Internal Medicine, 81*, 82–96.

Snow, L. F. (1977). Popular medicine in a Black neighborhood. In E. H. Spicer (Ed.), *Ethnic medicine in the Southwest* (pp. 19–95). Tucson: University of Arizona Press.

Snow, L. F. (1978). Sorcerers, saints and charlatans: Black folk healers in urban America. *Culture, Medicine & Psychiatry, 2*, 60–106.

Snow, L. F. (1993). *Walking over medicine.* Boulder: Westview Press.

Spector, R. (1979). *Cultural diversity in health and illness.* New York: Appleton-Century Crofts.

Staiano, K. V. (1981). Alternative therapeutic systems in Belize: A semiotic framework. *Social Science & Medicine, 15B*(3), 317–332.

Suárez-Orozco, M. M. (1997). The cultural psychology of immigration. In A. Ugalde & G. Cárdenas (Eds.), Health and social services among international labor migrants: A comparative perspective (pp. 131–149). Austin, TX: CMAS Books, University of Texas Press.

Sussman, L. K. (1980). Herbal medicine on Mauritius. *Journal of Ethnopharmacology, 2*(3), 259–278.

Sussman, L. K. (1981). Unity in diversity in a polyethnic society: The maintenance of medical pluralism on Mauritius. *Social Science & Medicine, 15B*, 247–260.

Sussman, L. K. (1983). *Medical pluralism on Mauritius: A study of medical beliefs and practices in a polyethnic society.* Unpublished doctoral dissertation, Washington University, St. Louis.

Sussman, L. K. (1988). The use of herbal and biomedical pharmaceuticals on Mauritius. In S. van der Geest & R. Whyte (Eds.), *The context of medicines in developing countries* (pp. 199–216). Dordrecht: Kluwer Academic.

Sussman, L. K. (1992a). Discussion: Critical assessment of models. In D. M. Becker, D. R. Hill, J. S. Jackson, D. M. Levine, F. A. Stillman, & S. M. Weiss (Eds.), *Health behavior research in minority populations: Access, design, and implementation* (pp. 145–149). National Institute of Health Publication, No. 92-2965.

Sussman, L. K. (1992b). *Medical beliefs and practices among the Mahafaly of Southwest Madagascar.* Sixth International Congress on Traditional and Folk Medicine. Austin, TX, December.

Sussman, L. K. (1992c). *Hard-to-reach and resistant populations: Misguided concepts in health-related interventions and research.* Annual meeting of the American Anthropological Association. San Francisco, December. (Abstract)

Sussman, L. K. (1997). *Asthma among Block Americans: Diverse perspectives.* Joint annual meeting of the Society for Applied Anthropology and the Society for Medical Anthropology. Seattle, March. (Abstract)

Sussman, L. K., Robins, L. N., & Earls, F. (1987). Treatment-seeking for depression by Black and White Americans. *Social Science & Medicine, 24*(3), 187–196.

Sussman, R. W., & Sussman, L. K. (1977). Divination among the Sakalava of Madagascar. In J. Long (Ed.), *Extrasensory ecology* (pp. 271–291). New York: Scarecrow Press.

Topley, M. (1976). Chinese traditional etiology and methods of cure in Hong Kong. In C. Leslie (Ed.), *Asian medical systems: A comparative study* (pp. 243–264). Berkeley: University of California Press.

Trotter, R. T., & Chavira, J. A. (1981). *Curanderismo: Mexican American folk healing.* Athens, GA: University of Georgia Press.

Williams, C. D., Baumslag, N., & Jelliffe, D. B. (1994). *Mother and child health: Delivering the services* (3rd ed.). New York: Oxford University Press.

Yoder, S. (1981). Knowledge of illness and medicine among Cokwe of Zaire. *Social Science & Medicine, 15B*, 237–246.

Young, A. (1982). The anthropologies of illness and sickness. *Annual Review of Anthropology, 11*, 257–285.

Young, J. C. (1981). *Medical choice in a Mexican village.* New Brunswick, NJ: Rutgers University Press.

Zola, E. (1972). Studying the decision to see a doctor. *Advances in Psychosomatic Medicine, 8*, 216–236.

Suggested Readings

Fadiman, A. (1997). *The spirit catches you and you fall down: A Hmong child, her American doctors, and the collision of two cultures.* New York: Farrar, Straus and Giroux.

Based on a detailed, long-term case study, this is the compassionately told story of a Hmong child diagnosed with epilepsy, her family, her doctors, and the divergent cultures and views of Western biomedicine and Hmong culture.

Galanti, G-A. (2004). *Caring for patients from different cultures: Case studies from American hospitals* (3rd ed.). Philadelphia: University of Pennsylvania Press.

This is a concise, highly readable, very informative collection of case studies of conflicts, miscommunications, and misunderstandings arising from cultural differences among patients, families, and health care providers. The material presented covers a wide range of topics. Commentary is provided throughout and summarized in the final chapter. Lists of suggested readings are categorized by both ethnic group and topic.

Helman, C. G. (2000). *Culture, health and illness: An introduction for health professionals* (4th ed.). Oxford: Butterworth-Heinemann.

This is an excellent, readable overview of medical anthropology with emphasis on how a cross-cultural perspective can contribute to understanding and dealing with physical and mental health and illness around the world. It includes numerous examples and case studies as well as clinical questionnaires and suggested readings for each chapter.

Kleinman, A. (1980). *Patients and healers in the context of culture: An exploration of the borderland between anthropology, medicine, and psychiatry.* Berkeley: University of California Press.

In this book, Kleinman, a psychiatrist trained in anthropology and engaged in cross-cultural research, develops a conceptual framework for examining relationships among culture, medicine, and psychiatry. He emphasizes the importance of a cross-cultural approach to the study of medicine, psychiatry, health, illness, and healing and illustrates the cultural construction of illness experience and behavior with examples from his own research in Taiwan and the United States.

O'Connor, B. B. (1995). *Healing traditions: Alternative medicine and the health professions.* Philadelphia: University of Pennsylvania Press.

In this book, O'Connor addresses topics concerning the relationships among health beliefs, values, and health care decisions and also concerning the use of multiple healing systems by patients. These are discussed largely within the context of two studies: a case study of a Hmong refugee patient and the American biomedical system; and a study of the use of alternative therapies for HIV/AIDS in the United States.

Rosman, A., & Rubel, P. G. (1989). *The tapestry of culture: An introduction to cultural anthropology* (3rd ed.). New York: Random House.

This is a very readable, clearly written, concise introduction to basic concepts and theories in cultural anthropology, with ethnographic examples provided throughout.

3

Theoretical Issues, Principles, and Themes Relevant to Multicultural Counseling and Therapy[1]

Jefferson M. Fish

Contents

Let us imagine how a modern university hospital might look to anthropologists from Mars studying healing shrines in an industrialized society. They would learn that the local medical school is reputed to be a site of amazing cures... certain areas were open to the public and other areas... were reserved exclusively for the performance of arcane healing rituals.... These special-purpose rooms contain spectacular machines.... Those who tend and control these machines speak a special language that is unintelligible to the layperson and prominently display on their person healing amulets and charms.... The operating rooms are the holy of holies.... So jealously guarded are the mysteries of the operating room that patients are rendered unconscious before they are allowed to enter them.

In evaluating the reports of the cures that occur in such a shrine, anthropologists might be as impressed with the features that mobilize the patient's expectant faith as with the staff's rationale for the treatments administered.

—**Jerome D. Frank and Julia B. Frank**, *Persuasion and Healing*
(**1991, pp. 108–109**)

Process and Content

Does Psychology Have Any Content?

A cross-cultural perspective requires us to ask fundamental questions about the nature of psychology. In this case, in order to discuss theoretical issues, principles, and themes relevant to multicultural counseling and therapy, we must first make a distinction between psychological processes and psychological content in order to clarify the subject matter under discussion.

If psychology is the science of behavior, then—at least with regard to our own species—it aims at making generalizations about the behavior of all human beings. For this reason, the anthropologist George Peter Murdock suggested that it is the function of psychology to describe behavioral processes and of anthropology to describe the cultural conditions under which those processes lead to different forms of behavior (Murdock, 1972). Another way of putting this would be to say that psychology describes the processes, and anthropology fills in the content.

Issues of culture need to be taken into account, however, even when studying such presumably universal human processes as perception, cognition, or learning. For example, in the course of formal education, children learn to think in different ways; and psychologists can study those thought processes.

But in cultures that have no schools—the condition of all of our species for the first 95% of its existence, and the condition of much of the world today—people are not exposed to or instructed in such thought processes, and therefore never acquire them (Ogbu, 2002). For example, "arithmetic reasoning" is not a concept easily applied to cultures that count "one, two, many." Still, once culture is taken into account by considering the varied conditions under which human psychological processes develop differentially, it becomes possible to make important generalizations about such processes.

The Recapitulation Fallacy

Once we move from process to content, though, the possibility of making any significant generalizations would seem to evaporate.[2] Although Freud (and later Jung, on a grander scale with his archetypes) postulated universal content, such as the Oedipus complex and dream symbols, such assertions foundered on the inability to explain how humans acquired such content (quite apart from issues of verifiability and accuracy). Freud's reliance on recapitulation theory, in which the stages of psychological development were seen as corresponding to stages in human history, was essentially Lamarckian, and has been shown to be false by modern genetics (Fish, 1996a; Gould, 1981, 1987). In other words, even if many generations of men did actually rise up to kill their fathers in the distant past, such acts would have had no effect on the genes they passed on to their children, and could not, therefore, have led to the creation of the Oedipus complex.

The recapitulation fallacy is sometimes seen in a new guise in modern biologized explanations for patterns of behavior that can more parsimoniously be understood as having arisen through social circumstances. Thus, personality traits like altruism, or social customs, like the Inuit abandoning sick elders to die, are explained by persuasive stories of how genes for altruism or elder abandonment proliferate through natural selection. However, the same stories can easily be modified to show how people learn and pass on the information that it is advantageous to treat others nicely—or to abandon even esteemed others when group survival is at stake—without postulating the existence of genes to accomplish the task. Cultural transmission has the advantage over genetic transmission of being much more rapid and of allowing different groups to develop quite opposite patterns of behavior in adaptation to very different environments.

B. F. Skinner (1974) has suggested that there is a parallel between the way in which the environment selects the behavior of individual organisms (through reinforcement) and the way in which natural selection operates at the species level. Thus, if one wished to postulate genetic explanations for patterns of behavior, one could refer to the genes that presumably underlie the social learning process. In other words, postulating genes for the general process of social learning requires fewer assumptions than postulating genes—via speculative evolutionary explanations—for a series of specific forms of social behavior.[3]

Furthermore, therapy is a recently invented Western institution, about 100 years old, whereas anatomically modern humans have been around for about 200,000 years—190,000 of which were spent as hunters and gatherers. Thus, any distinctively human psychological content that might exist would be adapted to forms of social interaction far removed from managed care and the 50-minute hour.

Dealing With Unacceptable Difference

Although all cultures deal with physical handicaps, illness, deviant behavior, and other abnormalities, counseling, therapy, and healing rituals constitute only one of five different ways of dealing with people who are temporarily or enduringly different. Societies may (a) kill, injure, imprison, or otherwise punish such people; (b) isolate them—for example, by creating leper colonies; (c) deliberately ignore them or their abnormalities; (d) reward or attempt to capitalize on their "infirmity"—for example, by viewing epilepsy as an ability to contact the spirit world; and/or (e) attempt to assist them, or ameliorate or cure their "illness."

All of these options are exercised by the world's cultures; and Western societies implement all five. Furthermore, these interventions may be combined, and different groups of people may even differ as to which is or are intended. For example, would group homes for mentally retarded adults be classified as (b), (c), or (e)—or as two or all three of these possibilities? The retarded adults, their families, the staff of the group home, the agency employing them, and neighbors—to mention some of the principal groups—might all have differing views as to what is being accomplished and why.

In the situation of the "involuntary commitment" of the "mentally ill," the case is even more complicated, in that what is referred to as "counseling, therapy, and healing rituals" (e) sometimes may actually represent (a) punishment—in disguise (Szasz, 1970, 1974)—not to mention (b) or (c). For this reason, although this chapter, and indeed this book, is ostensibly about the fifth alternative, we should remain alert to other less acknowledged cross-cultural similarities in dealing with unacceptable difference.

Ethnocentrism

In addition to avoiding the postulation of a biological basis for cross-cultural similarities in counseling, therapy, and healing rituals, we also have to avoid the fallacy of ethnocentrism. Ethnocentrism—in which people mistakenly view their own shared cultural perspective as reflecting objective reality—is the cultural counterpart of egocentrism—in which an individual mistakenly views his or her own individual psychological perspective as objectively accurate.

Etics and Emics

Ethnocentric bias is unavoidable because all adults, including mental health professionals, were enculturated long before they were in a position to consider theoretical issues in the social sciences. For this reason, and so as to minimize otherwise unavoidable ethnocentric bias, anthropologists make use of the distinction between *etics* and *emics* (Harris, 1980, 1999). These concepts were first introduced by the linguist Kenneth Pike (1954, 1967), and are derived from the endings of the linguistic terms phon*etics* and phon*emics*.

Definitions and Applications

Phonetics is the study of the actual physical sounds of speech as the vocal apparatus produces them, so its principles and findings apply universally to all languages. Phonemics is the study of the units of meaning (phonemes) that are associated with particular ranges of sounds in a given language. Thus, phonemes vary from one language to another. For example, English divides the range of vowel sounds in the words *sit* and *seat* into two phonemes, whereas French has only one.

In a similar way, etics deals with objective information that is physically observable, or with conceptual abstractions that can be applied to all cultures; etic descriptions are made from the perspective of a scientific observer, and can be used in the construction of scientific theories. Emics, on the other hand, deals with meanings within a given culture; emic descriptions are formulated from the perspective of participants within a culture (Harris, 1999). As a result, one can make etic comparisons or generalizations across many cultures, but emic comparisons must be limited to a small number of cultures whose features can be examined in fine-grained detail.

For example, "the number of males and females in the United States" is etic, but "the number of men and women in the United States" is emic, because age, or undergoing a social ritual, or other variable factors might determine who qualifies for manhood or womanhood in different cultures. In other words, one can make etic comparisons between the number of males and females in different cultural groups, but not emic comparisons between the number of men and women in different groups, because the cultural meanings of *man* and *woman* vary. Here is another example: "The protein content of a group's diet" is etic, but which plants and animals they consider food is emic. Furthermore, the same or cognate linguistic term can have different meanings in different cultures. For example, the avocado is a vegetable in the United States and a fruit (*fruta*) in Brazil—indicating that the cognates *fruit* and *fruta* have different emic meanings in English and Portuguese[4] (Fish, 1995b).

Thus, the search for cross-cultural commonalties in therapy and healing is a search for etically grounded generalizations based on shared conditions of life and human circumstances. Can such generalizations be made without falling into the recapitulation trap, or otherwise postulating biological causes, or ethnocentrically treating American (or Western) emic categories as if they were universal? (Cross-cultural psychologists recognize that it is possible to operationally define a particular concept [e.g., borderline personality disorder] that comes from a particular culture [e.g., the United States today] in such a way that it can be imposed on other cultures of which it is not a part for the purposes of gathering comparative data. Such a concept is referred to as an "imposed etic" [Berry, 1969].)

Many sociocultural anthropologists are either skeptical about the existence of important cross-cultural etic generalizations or feel their time can be spent more productively in activities other than seeking them out. They pursue an emic strategy, and attempt to understand each culture from within. In the case of therapy, one can describe the emic world of another culture, what behavior its members view as worthy of change and why, what they do to change it and why, and how they understand the varying outcomes of their efforts. Such emic descriptions give us a glimpse of a significant aspect of another cultural world—but are not intended to generalize beyond that world. Even the culture next door might view apparently similar undesired circumstances quite differently, might do quite different things to improve the situation, or might do similar things for very different reasons.

Consider the example of shamanism, which has many features in common with therapy (Dobkin de Rios, 2002; Krippner, 2003; Money, 2001). Many traditional cultures have healing rituals that are dramatic (or appear so to Western eyes) and in which the suffering individual undergoes physically and/or emotionally stressful treatments and expresses intense emotion. What are we to make of this "cross-cultural commonality"?

We want to avoid the fallacy of viewing American culture or Western culture as reality, and therefore inaccurately viewing ethnocentric emic explanations as universal. For example, if we were to view the intense emotional experience as some sort of abreaction or expression of repressed material we would be passing off an unverifiable Western (psychoanalytic) explanation as a universal one (similar to the group's own explanation in terms of "spirits" or other unverifiable elements).

On the other hand, as is discussed further in this chapter, one might make sense of the process in terms of response expectancies (Kirsch, 1990, 1999; Weinberger & Eig, 1999) and placebo effects (Fish, 1973; Frank, 1961, 1973; Frank & Frank, 1991; Kirsch, 1990, 1999; Pentony, 1981). Here, the observable credibility of the ritual—strengthened by its emotional intensity—can be explained in terms of experimentally documented psychological processes to produce a generalized explanation for positive psychological change. (Even in this case, one would have to confirm the operation of these principles in cultures very different from those found in industrialized societies. For example, this cross-cultural verification has been accomplished for color categorization [Berlin & Kay, 1969]. Unfortunately, however, this is not yet the case for the great majority of what are considered to be experimentally well-established psychological processes or principles.)

Issues in Making Generalizations

Because we have narrowed our focus to etics, one might ask why it is that we would want to make universal generalizations about therapy principles. One goal might be to identify and categorize procedures in other cultures that seem strange to us, and to try to understand how and why they are reported to work. For example, we might want to make use of elements that work in other cultures in our own therapy. In contrast, we might want to know which of our therapeutic approaches might work best in other cultures— especially non-Western ones—or we might want to try to figure out how we could modify our therapeutic procedures so that they can be of use in those other cultures. (Naturally, plants or other substances unknown to Western medicine that are used as part of healing rituals might well have important pharmacological effects, and are also worthy of investigation. But the discussion in this chapter is limited to psychological "treatments." Also, although our focus is on therapies we should not forget that other cultures may divide healers into different categories from those we are accustomed to—e.g., an herbalist, who makes medicines, a diviner who makes diagnoses and/or predicts the future, and a healer who treats people; or a *bruxa* who casts spells and a *curandero* who heals [Torrey, 1986]).

These kinds of questions would suggest that our interests encourage us to limit the scope of our etic generalizations in several ways. If we want to apply principles from other cultures—especially nonliterate ones—to our own, then we are likely to look in their "therapies" for the operation of general principles of social influence that have been established by Western science. This is because the alien cultural specifics would likely seem irrelevant or misleading to Western clinicians; and because of this they would be unlikely to attempt to understand how exotic-appearing elements function in order to seek out new general principles of social influence. It is interesting to observe that the search for new drugs among the medicines of non-Western healers is an acceptable scientific enterprise, but the psychological counterpart to that search has only been rarely pursued. (Rubin [2004] and Tanaka–Matsumi [2004] are two such examples.) Psychologists' assumption that there is nothing to discover would seem to imply that, at least in this area, psychology is more ethnocentric than medicine, and that both disciplines share a folk belief that the study of biological determinants of behavior is somehow more scientific than the study of social determinants of behavior.

If instead we want to promote the cultural diffusion of most of our "therapies," then we would primarily be interested in dealing with nation-states that have a system of higher education, including formal training in Western medicine and psychology. This is because such therapies are so saturated with decades of formal training, and are so much a part of the fabric of highly differentiated professional role relationships in complex societies, that they would be inaccessible to nonliterate members of simpler cultures—such as hunter-gatherers. In fact, for non-Westerners, the process of undergoing the extensive training necessary to become a therapist can be understood as a de facto voluntary acculturation to Western values and habits of thought. (Of course, even hunter-gatherers might happily incorporate elements of Western therapies without accepting—or even understanding—the complex cultural systems of which they are a part. For example, they might perform their healing rituals with the sick person lying on a couch instead of on a mat. Western therapists might not view this change as a great success, despite the satisfaction of the group that adopts the practice. This adoption of therapeutic elements out of their cultural context is comparable to the use of techniques from simpler cultures by Western therapists, especially New Age therapists [McGuire, 1988]. Here, as well, Western therapists are quite happy to appropriate elements from other cultures' healing systems, but may be less concerned with shamans' reactions concerning the inappropriateness of their use.)

In other words, our desire to spread Western "scientific" ways of understanding and changing behavior predominates over the desire to learn from non-Western ones. Rather, the desire to learn from those approaches is secondary, and involves their etic "translation" into already discovered general principles of psychology that are supposed to apply to all humans. This is in contrast to the strategies of either stopping at their emic description in a particular culture or trying to generalize discoveries from that culture into new general principles.

There is nothing inherently wrong with such an approach, as long as its Western bias is understood. It does mean, however, that the search for "theoretical issues, principles, and themes relevant to multicultural counseling and therapy" has to be viewed as occurring in the context of current global transformations. These include the end of the Cold War and colonialism, the information revolution and instantaneous worldwide communication, increased global trade and international travel, and the increased importance of multinational corporations and other transnational institutions—all of which accompany the diffusion of Western values and cultural forms. Cross-cultural psychologists are increasingly taking such factors into account, usually under the rubric of "globalization" (Arnett, 2002, 2007).

Six Commonalties in Search of a Theory[5]

In considering cross-cultural commonalties relevant to multicultural counseling and therapy, I was able to identify six themes as unifying (if not necessarily universal) elements that bring some etic order to an otherwise bewildering range of cultural practices. These include (a) current global trends, (b and c) social science principles, (d) the interactional perspective, and (e and f) psychological principles and processes. In a sense, the first theme describes the current global conditions that create the context for the other five conceptual themes.

Industrialization and Globalization

The first theme, which was just alluded to, is changes in culture as a result of industrialization and globalization. This includes the spread of Western cultural forms, including medicine and therapy—with some cultural diffusion in the other direction as well, as can be seen in this book (Appadurai, 2000; Giddens, 2000).

Consider the global spread of American fast-food restaurant chains. (I like this analogy between food for the body and food for the soul—especially because the diffusion of brief therapy, with which I am involved, can be seen as a counterpart to the diffusion of fast food. I should mention in passing that brief therapy might have a special appeal for non-Western cultures that transcends its lower cost. That is, people in these cultures may be less willing to share intimate personal details with an impersonal therapist. Thus, brief therapy's focus on results both minimizes embarrassing personal disclosures and also shortens the loss of face involved in consulting a therapist for one's personal problems. In any event, in comparing brief therapy to fast food, I would like to view it as more of a low-fat, nutritionally sound salad bar than a dispensary of psychic bacon double cheeseburgers.)

Fast-food chains did not exist in my postwar New York City childhood; and before they displaced French *bistros*, they displaced American luncheonettes. The education of women, their mobilization in the workforce, demographic increases in the numbers of two-career families, the high divorce rate, single-parent families, and adults living alone, along with the shortage of time for housework (including cooking), and the lengthening workweek (leaving harried parents less time to prepare meals—not to mention increasing their vulnerability to children's demands for advertised freebies), are some of the social forces that have led to the success of the fast-food formula in both the United States and France.

Thus, the spread of this American social form can be seen as part of worldwide economic transformations that occurred first in the United States, rather than simply as American cultural imperialism. To the extent to which these forces are at work elsewhere, as growing middle classes around the world become part of a global economy, they become a partial explanation for the spread of fast-food chains to developing countries as well. And the same forces that are pressing for fast food for increasing numbers of the world's people are pressing for fast therapy to assuage their discontents.

Naturally, the American import has to be adapted to local cultural conditions in order to succeed. For example, Brazilians are concerned about dirt—corresponding to Americans' preoccupation with germs—and don't like to touch their food, which they consider dirty. Thus, when the Subway chain came to Brazil, they found that they had to wrap their sandwiches to protect their customers' hands; and Brazilians eat their fast-food french fries with toothpicks for the same reason. Some Brazilian supermarkets—another imported institution—even provide gloves of plastic film so that customers don't have to touch the produce. On the other hand, a Brazilian, unlike an American, will readily take a bite out of someone else's partially eaten sandwich or piece of fruit—indicating that the Brazilian folk concept of dirt (*sujeira*) is different from the American folk concept of germs.

In the same way, when American therapies are exported to Brazil, they undergo similar cultural adaptations. For example, I supervised and lectured on behavior therapy—viewed as an up-to-date scientific import—to Brazilian clinical psychologists in the mid-1970s. In doing so, I discovered that, when therapists taught parents to reward their children for desired behavior, they had them use blue token reinforcers for boys and pink ones for girls. This color-coding of the tokens exemplified the importance of acknowledging the greater sex role differentiation in Brazilian culture than in American culture.

Here is another example. During the same period, Brazil's first token economy—an import of American psychology's scientific technology—was set up in a Brazilian spiritist hospital. I have written elsewhere about "Brazilian dual consciousness (the official bureaucratic way of doing things versus the informal ... way of getting things done)" (Fish, 1996a, pp. 208–209). In this case, Brazilian psychiatric inpatients were getting their prosocial behaviors conditioned by a token economy (official science) at the same time that they were receiving guidance from mediums about overcoming the causes of their distress in the spirit world (going around the rules and making use of powerful unofficial contacts).

These two intellectual worlds seemingly operated on parallel tracks without causing cognitive dissonance for the participants. For example, the token economy did not appear to disturb the spirits, nor did the psychologists investigate the impact of the spirits on the response to token reinforcers. In fact, the hospital itself was spiritist only in an unofficial sense. Its formal stance was that patients were free to consult spiritual advisors of their choice, so the spiritist component of treatment could be treated officially as a demographic coincidence—based on patients' religious preferences—rather than medical policy. Thus, although the rules of the game of the token economy were the same as in the United States, the cultural context within which the game was played, and to which it was adapted, transformed it significantly.[6]

Industrialization and globalization are also relevant to the social context of problems and healing. In the developed world, they raise issues of overcoming the alienation found in individualistic cultures. This leads to a willingness to adopt a variety of alternative worldviews stressing holism and connectedness as a way to overcome the shortcomings of individualism

(McGuire, 1988). In addition, participants in a mobile workforce, who also lack an extended kin network, may find that participation in religious, healing, or therapeutic organizations is a way of mobilizing group support in a lonely world. Meanwhile, around the planet but especially in traditional cultures, the rapid rate of change and disruption of traditional role relationships brought about by globalization has both created many personal problems and increased openness to Western therapies—at least among educated, affluent, and Westernized elites who participate in the global economy.

Finally, it should be pointed out that cultural diffusion often takes place in a complex back-and-forth pattern. For example, African Americans have adopted hairstyles they consider "African," which have then been imitated by African elites because they consider them American. In a similar manner, any cultural elements that Western therapies adapt from non-Western culture areas can diffuse back to those areas as part of an imported Western therapeutic package. For example, I have argued elsewhere (Fish 1995a, 1995c) that solution-focused therapy (de Shazer, 1982, 1984, 1985, 1988, 1989, 1991, 1994; de Shazer et al., 1986; Fish, 1996b, 1997) is a Western therapy with significant East Asian influences (especially regarding acausal thinking) that shows signs of gaining acceptance in that region.

Social Structure, Economics, and Power

The second theme is that problem behavior is often created by (and helped by taking into account) social structure and economic and power relations in the larger society and its institutions.

To begin with, there are the gross inequalities of wealth and power that, although pronounced in the developed world, are extreme elsewhere. Studies of happiness have shown that "once people are able to afford life's necessities, increasing levels of affluence matter surprisingly little" (Myers & Diener, 1995, p. 13). It is true that cultures differ in how happy their people are, as well as in how important personal happiness is thought to be; and the definition of "life's necessities" is cultural and varies from place to place. Nevertheless, it is also true that in poor countries the majority of people lack what they consider to be basic necessities. As a result, any benefits they might receive if therapy were made available to them pale in comparison to their greater needs for food, clothing, shelter, personal safety, and rudimentary health care and education.

Tom Lehrer (1959) spoke of a physician who "became a specialist, specializing in diseases of the rich" (track 6). That pretty much describes the case of therapy—not to mention medicine—in much of the world. In Brazil, for example, where the need for public health measures is obvious, the rural poor receive virtually no services, some of the urban poor have the option of waiting on long lines for many hours to get perfunctory health care of poor quality, and the rich indulge themselves with cosmetic surgery and psychoanalysis.

Popular culture recognizes these differences in treatment—as in the following joke from the era when sex therapy (Masters & Johnson, 1970) arrived in Brazil:

> A man comes for his first appointment to a sex therapy clinic. While he is in the waiting room, he sees a beautiful young woman escort another man to her treatment room. A while later, an ugly old woman escorts a second man to her room. After the door closes, he asks the secretary to explain the difference. She says, pointing toward the second door, "He's with the national health plan."

Power relations also come into play in problems arising from politics at work (e.g., getting an ulcer from office politics, or getting depressed after being fired), or politics within the family (e.g., conflict between the parents leading them to discipline their children inconsistently, resulting in behavior problems), or conflicts between the demands of family and work (e.g., anxiety over having to choose between keeping one's job and staying married). When power relations are central, therapy can be seen as resembling diplomacy; and the best emotional outcomes result from an explicitly or implicitly negotiated "treaty," which the opposing parties see as preferable to continued conflict.

When thinking in terms of social structure and power, it is also important to recognize that therapy is an institution whose practice is encouraged, channeled, constrained, and impeded by other social institutions. These include—with variations from country to country—various levels of government; legislatures and the licensing, malpractice, and other therapy-related laws they produce; the courts; insurance companies or other economic parties to therapeutic arrangements; the structure and curricula of university-based and other training programs; and the formal and informal organization of service delivery settings, such as schools, clinics, and mental hospitals.

Cultural Factors

The third theme is the understanding that problem behavior and its solutions are expressive of culturally determined patterns of normative and deviant behavior (e.g., Westerners view a consistent self as more important for psychological well-being than East Asians; Suh, 2002) and of beliefs about how behavior changes.

We need to remember that beliefs that are considered exotic and magical in the West are ordinary and practical to those who hold them. The decision in another culture to undergo a dramatic and dangerous healing ritual to rid oneself of evil illness-causing spirits is essentially the same as the decision in our own culture to undergo a dramatic and dangerous operation to rid oneself of a brain tumor.

This practicality can be seen among the Krikati Indians of central Brazil. A tribe of several hundred hunter-gatherer-horticulturists, their life is organized around complex social ceremonies—rather than procuring harvests, game, or healing through supernatural means. They recognize that neighboring tribes are more adept at healing than they, and they make pragmatic use of shamans passing through their village, as they do of Western medicine when it is available. When left to their own devices, they have an experimental attitude toward seeing what works. Two examples of their treatments are a man with vertical scratches on his forehead to treat headaches, and a woman who boiled a bulbous (i.e., swollen in appearance) plant root to see if the liquid would help her son's swollen glands.

The Interactional Perspective

The fourth theme, the contribution of systems theory (Fish, 1992; Hoffman, 1981; Nichols & Schwartz, 2006; Watzlawick, Weakland, & Fisch, 1974), is the ability to view the problem behavior of an individual as part of a larger interactive social matrix. Systems theory is not so much a psychological theory as an attempt to understand and change behavior at the interactional level, rather than solely at the individual level. Thus, people's problems can be understood as embedded in interactional networks consisting of repetitive sequences of behavior among various individuals. Alterations in those sequences can then lead to non-problem behavior, and restructuring hierarchical relationships can relieve conflicting demands on triangulated third parties (Haley, 1963, 1973, 1980, 1984, 1987; Madanes, 1981, 1984; Minuchin, 1974; Minuchin & Fishman, 1981; Palazzoli et al. 1978; Papp, 1983).

Although the work system and other social groups (in cultures that have them) can create and perpetuate difficulties, it is the family—however it may be defined and constituted—that is the center of the most important affect-laden interactions.[7] (Although this may be even more true in traditional cultures than in the industrialized West, the family may also, in some cultures, be so central as to exclude an outsider—like a therapist—from a position of influence on important matters. This suggests that there is a limit to the cultural variability across which therapies can be transported, even if a culturally sensitive attempt is made to adapt them.)

Consider the case of a couple whose child has behavior problems resulting from inconsistent discipline. Let us suppose that the father and mother cannot agree on how to act because the mother's mother is pressuring her to bring up her child in one way, whereas the father's mother is pressuring him in a different direction. In the United States, to change the child's problematic American behavior, a family therapist would most likely pursue a strategy of getting the parents to exclude the grandparents from child-rearing decisions, so that they could then agree on and implement a mutually acceptable plan of action. In some Asian cultures, in contrast, to change child behavior considered unacceptable, a family therapist might try to get the grandparents to agree among themselves, so they could communicate a consistent message to the parents who could then implement it. Thus, different cultural norms would lead to different strategies for different behavior; but in both cases the transformation from a hierarchy that is dysfunctional (as judged by the norms of its own culture) to an internally consistent one can be seen to lead to the resolution of the child's culturally unacceptable behavior.

As this example illustrates, although the systemic approach opens up new possibilities for therapeutic interventions, it also raises theoretical, clinical, and ethical issues that go beyond those usually considered in individual treatment.

Expectancy and Placebo

The fifth theme is the role of expectancy in both producing and changing behavior. This applies especially to expectancies regarding involuntary behavior. Thus, the anticipatory fear of becoming afraid triggers anxiety, whereas confidence that one will not be fearful decreases it. Similarly, pessimism about not being able to overcome sadness makes one more unhappy, whereas confidence that the sadness will end has the opposite effect.

In response expectancies, we have a psychological means for understanding and making therapeutic use of the placebo effect, hypnosis, and other means of persuasion and expectancy alteration (Fish, 1973; Frank, 1961, 1973; Frank & Frank, 1991; Kirsch, 1990, 1999; Pentony, 1981). The power of expectancy to alter behavior (especially "involuntary" behavior) helps us to understand why different psychological therapies—and even ones based on mutually contradictory rationales—can have positive effects, as can various forms of shamanism and religious healing.[8]

For example, some Brazilian social scientist friends and I accompanied my anthropologist wife, Dolores Newton, to an Umbanda spiritist meeting in São Paulo in the mid-1970s. (Believers consult spiritist mediums for help with personal and physical problems, as they might a therapist or physician.) During these religious services, which include extended periods of dancing to percussive rhythms, participants are possessed by spirits from Brazil's past—either of old slaves or of Indians. Because this was a night when the Indian spirits were going to make their presence felt, and my wife's specialty is Brazilian Indians and other native peoples of the New World, our friends wanted to get her reaction to the experience. After it was over, they asked her if the trance behavior of the participants reminded her of that of Brazilian Indians. She said that it did not, but that it did resemble that of North American Indians as portrayed in Westerns.

Such observations support the etic generalization that the kinds of religious healing that take place under such circumstances result from the culturally specific beliefs and expectancies of the participants, as well as from the emotional persuasiveness of the experience—which is also culturally specific. This is in contrast to the otherworldly forces to which the participants themselves attribute change (and to equally unverifiable psychoanalytic explanations such as the expression of repressed impulses while in an altered state of consciousness). For example, Torrey (1986) emphasizes the importance of the shared worldview of the patient and healer, the personal qualities of the healer, and the client's sense of mastery as important elements along with the patient's expectations. It is easy to understand how the first three influence those expectations. In addition, we may be interested in the interactions among expectancies, the placebo effect, and various physiological processes (e.g., Hirsch, 2004).

Naturally, from within a given culture, emic explanations are still preferred. One of my Brazilian students asked, "We understand what you are saying about expectancy—but ... what if spirits really do exist?" In a similar way, an American might ask, "We understand what you are saying about expectancy—but ... what if unconscious impulses really do exist?"

Learning and Cognition

The sixth theme is that general psychological principles of learning and cognition apply cross-culturally to changing behavior, even though the cultural content may vary dramatically. Thus, principles of reinforcement, extinction, shaping, and modeling can be presumed to apply across cultures (though, as mentioned previously, this generality needs to be empirically confirmed)—and may be seen to operate in a variety of therapeutic or healing circumstances. For example, assuming that a fear is culturally inappropriate, gradually and persistently approaching the feared object—as opposed to avoiding it—will help to overcome the fear. However, what that fear might be, and who and what it might take to get the fearful person to participate, are examples of culturally variable content. Even here, though, the altered expectancy ("I won't be afraid of X") that results from successfully approaching the feared object plays an important role as well (Kirsch, 1990; Schoenberger, 1999).

In the same way, cognitive therapists (e.g., Beck, 1976; Ellis, 1984) have argued that getting people to change culturally inappropriate upsetting cognitions will lead to their becoming less upset. Once again, though, the content of those cognitions and the rhetorical means needed to change them—as well as the social role of the rhetorician and the culturally appropriate context for persuasion—vary widely. (Thomas Szasz [1974, 1978] and Jerome Frank [Frank & Frank, 1991] have discussed in great detail the pervasive role of rhetoric and persuasion in psychotherapy. In addition, an important part of the reason that cognitive change has its effect is that new beliefs alter individuals' expectancies regarding their own behavior [Kirsch, 1990, 1999].)

In summary, then, this chapter attempted to make a number of cross-cultural generalizations about therapy and healing. In order to do so, and to avoid a number of theoretical and ethnocentric pitfalls, it was necessary to explore a number of issues concerning process and content, and etics and emics. Once relevant distinctions were made, six themes were identified that bring into focus significant commonalties among the otherwise diverse and changing practices of therapy and healing around the world. These commonalties can be seen in part as reflecting the global homogenization of cultures. And they suggest the need for empirical verification of the cross-cultural generality of basic psychological processes—especially because the cultural variability against which these processes must be evaluated is rapidly diminishing.

Notes

1. I would like to thank Dolores Newton for her helpful suggestions.

2. A controversial book that might take exception to this statement is Donald Brown's *Human Universals* (1991). Many of Brown's proposed universals can be disputed, and others—his "near universals"—might less charitably be called "nonuniversals." Even if one were to accept many of his proposed

universals, however, they are at such a level of generality—for example, the use of language or the existence kin categories—as to be irrelevant to counseling and therapy.

3. Naturally, if any specific genes are discovered that have specifiable effects on behavior, that would be another story.

4. Because most of my cross-cultural experience, including most of my cross-cultural clinical experience, has been in Brazil, most of the examples presented in this chapter are Brazilian ones. Those interested in additional discussion of therapy-related topics in a Brazilian context can find them in *Culture and Therapy: An Integrative Approach* (Fish 1996a).

5. With apologies to Pirandello (1922/1958).

6. An imperfect ethnocentric analogy that occurs to me (imperfect because Brazilians take their soccer very seriously) would be of a major league baseball game with wild parties going on in the dugouts, and the batter, with lipstick on his face, blowing kisses to the fans between pitches. Perhaps it is this dual consciousness, along with the lack of a firm separation between work and play, that led Charles De Gaulle to remark haughtily that *Brésil n'est pas un pays sérieux* (Brazil is not a serious country). Brazilians, on the other hand, view Americans and their inability to simultaneously hold conflicting ideas or go around irrational rules as rigid, inflexible, and lacking in creativity.

7. An important exception to this generalization is the large and increasing number of homeless children in many countries who grow up among and can be said to be raised by homeless peers. In those cases where social institutions intervene to help these children (as opposed to imprisoning or killing them), the pattern seems to be to remove them from the streets or to provide services for them despite their homelessness. I am not aware of programs of systemic therapy aimed at improving the child-rearing function of informally constituted groups of street children.

8. Therapy researchers (e.g., Lambert, 1992; Lambert & Bergin, 1994; Wampold, 2001) also point to shared relationship elements in diverse treatments, such as therapist empathy and warmth, as well as to individual characteristics of the therapist (Beutler, Machado, & Neufeld, 1994; Wampold, 2001) as explanations for the positive effects of diverse treatments. It seems reasonable to me, at least, that much of the therapeutic impact of the relationship or therapist characteristics can be explained by their effects on client expectancies.

References

Appadurai, A. (Ed.). (2000). *Globalization*. Durham, NC: Duke University Press.

Arnett, J. J. (2002). The psychology of globalization. *American Psychologist, 57*(10), 774–783.

Arnett, J. J. (2007). *Adolescence and emerging adulthood: A cultural approach* (3rd ed.). Upper Saddle River, NJ: Prentice Hall.

Beck, A. T. (1976). *Cognitive therapy and the emotional disorders*. New York: International Universities Press.

Berlin, B., & Kay, P. (1969). *Basic color terms*. Berkeley: University of California Press.

Berry, J. W. (1969). On cross-cultural comparability. *International Journal of Psychology, 4*, 119–128.

Beutler, L. E., Machado, P., & Neufeld, S. (1994). Therapist variables. In A. E. Bergin & S. L. Garfield (Eds.), *Handbook of psychotherapy and behavior change* (4th ed., pp. 229–269). New York: Wiley.

Brown, D. E. (1991). *Human universals*. New York: McGraw Hill.

de Shazer, S. (1982). *Patterns of brief family therapy*. New York: Guilford Press.

de Shazer, S. (1984). The death of resistance. *Family Process, 23*, 11–21.

de Shazer, S. (1985). *Keys to solution in brief therapy*. New York: Norton.

de Shazer, S. (1988). *Clues: Investigating solutions in brief therapy*. New York: Norton.

de Shazer, S. (1989). Resistance revisited. *Contemporary Family Therapy, 11*(4), 227–233.

de Shazer, S. (1991). *Putting difference to work*. New York: Norton.

de Shazer, S. (1994). *Words were originally magic*. New York: Norton.

de Shazer, S., Berg, I. K., Lipchik, E., Nunnally, E., Molnar, A., Gingerich, W., et al. (1986). Brief therapy: Focused solution development. *Family Process, 25*, 207–221.

Dobkin de Rios, M. (2002). What we can learn from shamanic healing: Brief psychotherapy with Latino immigrant clients. *American Journal of Public Health, 92*(10), 1576–1581.

Ellis, A. (1984). *Reason and emotion in psychoherapy* (rev. ed.). New York: Birch Lane Press.

Fish, J. M. (1973). *Placebo therapy*. San Francisco: Jossey-Bass.

Fish, J. M. (1992). Discontinuous change. *Behavior and Social Issues, 2*(1), 59–70.

Fish, J. M. (1995a). Does problem behavior just happen? Does it matter? *Behavior and Social Issues, 5*(1), 3–12.

Fish, J. M. (1995b). Mixed blood. *Psychology Today, 28*(6), 55–61, 76, 80.

Fish, J. M. (1995c). Solution-focused therapy in global perspective. *World Psychology, 1*(2), 43–67.

Fish, J. M. (1996a). *Culture and therapy: An integrative approach*. New York: Jason Aronson.

Fish, J. M. (1996b). Prevention, solution focused therapy, and the illusion of mental disorders. *Applied and Preventive Psychology, 5*, 37–40.

Fish, J. M. (1997). Paradox for complainants? Strategic thoughts about solution-focused therapy. *Journal of Systemic Therapies, 16*(3), 266–273.

Frank, J. D. (1961). *Persuasion and healing: A comparative study of psychotherapy*. Baltimore: Johns Hopkins.

Frank, J. D. (1973). *Persuasion and healing: A comparative study of psychotherapy* (2nd ed.). Baltimore: Johns Hopkins.

Frank, J. D., & Frank, J. B. (1991). *Persuasion and healing: A comparative study of psychotherapy* (3rd ed.). Baltimore: Johns Hopkins.

Giddens, A. (2000). *Runaway world: How globalization is reshaping our lives.* New York: Routledge.

Gould, S. J. (1981). *The mismeasure of man.* New York: Norton.

Gould, S. J. (1987). Freud's phylogenetic fantasy. *Natural History, 96*(12), 10–19.

Haley, J. (1963). *Strategies of psychotherapy.* New York: Grune & Stratton.

Haley, J. (1973). *Uncommon therapy: The psychiatric techniques of Milton H. Erickson, M. D.* New York: Norton.

Haley, J. (1980). *Leaving home.* New York: McGraw-Hill.

Haley, J. (1984). *Ordeal therapy: Unusual ways to change behavior.* San Francisco: Jossey-Bass.

Haley, J. (1987). *Problem solving therapy* (2nd ed.). San Francisco: Jossey-Bass.

Harris, M. (1980). *Cultural materialism: The struggle for a science of culture.* New York: Vintage Books.

Harris, M. (1999). *Theories of culture in postmodern times.* Walnut Creek, CA: AltaMira Press.

Hirsch, M. (2004). A biopsychosocial perspective on cross-cultural healing. In U. P. Gielen, J. M. Fish, & J. G. Draguns (Eds.), *Handbook of culture, therapy, and healing* (pp. 83–99). Mahwah, NJ: Erlbaum.

Hoffman, L. (1981). *Foundations of family therapy.* New York: Basic Books.

Kirsch, I. (1990). *Changing expectations: A key to effective psychotherapy.* Pacific Grove, CA: Brooks/Cole.

Kirsch, I. (Ed.). (1999). *How expectancies shape experience.* Washington, DC: American Psychological Association.

Krippner, S. (2003). What psychologists might learn from the study of shamans and shamanism. *Psychological Hypnosis, 12*(1), 5–10.

Lambert, M. J. (1992). Psychotherapy outcome research: Implications for integrative and eclectic therapists. In J. C. Norcross & M. R. Goldfried (Eds.), *Handbook of psychotherapy integration* (pp. 94–129). New York: Basic Books.

Lambert, M. J., & Bergin, A. E. (1994). The effectiveness of psychotherapy. In A. E. Bergin & S. L. Garfield (Eds.), *Handbook of psychotherapy and behavior change* (4th ed., pp. 143–189). New York: Wiley.

Lehrer, T. (1959). In Old Mexico. *On An evening wasted with Tom Lehrer* [33 rpm record]. Cambridge, MA: Tom Lehrer, TL 202.

Madanes, C. (1981). *Strategic family therapy.* San Francisco: Jossey-Bass.

Madanes, C. (1984). *Behind the one-way mirror: Advances in the practice of strategic therapy.* San Francisco: Jossey-Bass.

Masters, W. H., & Johnson, V. E. (1970). *Human sexual inadequacy.* Boston: Little, Brown & Co.

McGuire, M. B. (1988). *Ritual healing in suburban America.* New Brunswick, NJ: Rutgers University Press.

Minuchin, S. (1974). *Families and family therapy.* Cambridge, MA: Harvard University Press.

Minuchin, S., & Fishman, H. C. (1981). *Family therapy techniques.* Cambridge, MA: Harvard University Press.

Money, M. (2001). Shamanism as a healing paradigm for complementary therapy. *Complementary Therapies in Nursing and Midwifery, 7*(3), 126–131.

Murdock, G. P. (1972). Anthropology's mythology. The Huxley memorial lecture, 1971. *Proceedings of the Royal Anthropological Institute of Great Britain and Ireland for 1971.*

Myers, D. G., & Diener, E. (1995). Who is happy? *Psychological Science, 6*(1), 10–19.

Nichols, M. P., & Schwartz, R. C. (2006). *Family therapy: Concepts and methods* (7th ed.). Boston: Allyn & Bacon.

Ogbu, J. U. (2002). Cultural amplifiers of intelligence: IQ and minority status in cross-cultural perspective. In J. M. Fish (Ed.), *Race and intelligence: Separating science from myth*. Mahwah, NJ: Erlbaum.

Palazzoli, M. S., Boscolo, L., Cecchin, G., & Prata, G. (1978). *Paradox and counter-paradox*. New York: Jason Aronson.

Papp, P. (1983). *The process of change*. New York: Guilford Press.

Pentony, P. (1981). *Models of influence in psychotherapy*. New York: Macmillan.

Pike, K. (1954). *Language in relation to a unified theory of the structure of human behavior* (Vol. 1). Glendale: Summer Institute of Linguistics.

Pike, K. L. (1967). *Language in relation to a unified theory of the structure of human behavior*. The Hague: Mouton.

Pirandello, L. (1958). Six characters in search of an author. In E. Bentley (Ed. & Trans.), *Naked masks: Five plays by Luigi Pirandello* (pp. 211–276). New York: Dutton.

Rubin, J. B. (2004). Psychoanalysis and Buddhism. In U. P. Gielen, J. M. Fish, & J. G. Draguns (Eds.), *Handbook of culture, therapy, and healing* (pp. 253–276). Mahwah, NJ: Erlbaum.

Schoenberger, N. E. (1999). Expectancy and fear. In I. Kirsch (Ed.), *How expectancies shape experience* (pp. 125–144). Washington, DC: American Psychological Association.

Skinner, B. F. (1974). *About behaviorism*. New York: Knopf.

Suh, E. M. (2002). Culture, identity consistency, and subjective well-being. *Journal of Personality and Social Psychology, 83*(6), 1378–1391.

Szasz, T. S. (1970). *The manufacture of madness: A comparative study of the Inquisition and the mental health movement*. New York: Harper & Row.

Szasz, T. S. (1974). *The myth of mental illness: Foundations of a theory of personal conduct*. New York: Harper & Row.

Szasz, T. S. (1978). *The myth of psychotherapy: Mental healing as religion, rhetoric, and repression*. Garden City, NY: Doubleday Anchor.

Tanaka-Matsumi, J. (2004). Japanese forms of psychotherapy: Naikan therapy and Morita therapy. In U. P. Gielen, J. M. Fish, & J. G. Draguns (Eds.), *Handbook of culture, therapy, and healing* (pp. 277–291). Mahwah, NJ: Erlbaum.

Torrey, E. F. (1986). *Witchdoctors and psychiatrists: The common roots of psychotherapy and its future*. New York: Harper & Row.

Wampold, B. E. (2001). *The great psychotherapy debate: Models, methods, and findings*. Mahwah, NJ: Erlbaum.

Watzlawick, P., Weakland, J. H., & Fisch, R. (1974). *Change: Principles of problem formation and problem resolution*. New York: Norton.

Weinberger, J., & Eig, A. (1999). Expectancies: The ignored common factor in psychotherapy. In I. Kirsch (Ed.), *How expectancies shape experience* (pp. 357–382). Washington, DC: American Psychological Association.

Suggested Readings

Arnett, J. J. (2002). The psychology of globalization. *American Psychologist, 57*(10), 774–783.

This article introduces psychologists to the many effects of globalization on human behavior and its development in cultures around the world.

Fish, J. M. (1996). *Culture and therapy: An integrative approach.* New York: Jason Aronson.

The perspective of the book is the binocular vision of the therapist as subject and object, of viewing oneself both as an individual and as a representative of one's culture, as both an insider in one's culture and an outsider in another culture, as both the recipient of environmental influences and an influencer of the environment, as both the therapist and client of one's own self-therapy, and as both teacher and student, supervisor and therapist, in evolving one's own theoretical orientation.

Frank, J. D., & Frank, J. B. (1991). *Persuasion and healing: A comparative study of psychotherapy* (3rd ed.). Baltimore: Johns Hopkins.

This book looks at the relationship between the healer/therapist and patient/client, and the ways the former makes use of rhetorical devices to help the latter overcome demoralization. The authors view this as the central process in Western counseling and therapy, as well as in other forms of healing in other cultures.

McGoldrick, M., Giordano, J., & Garcia-Preto, N. (Eds.). (2005). *Ethnicity and family therapy* (3rd ed.). New York: Guilford.

This book contains useful information to inform culturally sensitive practice with families and individuals from over 40 different ethnic groups in the United States.

Pentony, P. (1981). *Models of influence in psychotherapy.* New York: Macmillan.

This book examines a variety of approaches to therapy and argues that they implement one of three models of interpersonal influence: a placebo model, a resocialization model, or a contextual model.

4

A Multicultural Counselor's Guide to Race

Jefferson M. Fish

Contents

Despite all the interest in cross-racial counseling, counselors and therapists are by training remarkably uninformed about the subject of race. In part, this is a natural instance of the difficulty in obtaining information which clashes with a society's dominant ideology. However, there is a subcultural conflict as well, which impedes communication in this area. It is the mutual incoherence of the scholasticisms of psychology and anthropology (Fish, 2002a).

This chapter is my attempt to communicate an understanding of the topic of race in the hope that counselors will, when they think in terms of their own race and that of their clients, do so more lucidly and respond in a more sophisticated and sensitive manner.[1]

Race and "Blood"

Perhaps I can best begin the discussion by describing a hypothetical example I have used in my teaching. Whatever race may be, I have said, let us consider a hypothetical mating between one person who has only genes for "Whiteness" and another of the opposite sex who has only genes for "Blackness." What proportion of "Blackness" genes will the offspring have? My students invariably give the correct answer of one-half. Then, suppose one of these offspring mated with someone who has only "Whiteness" genes—what percentage of "Blackness" genes will the children of this union have? Nearly all students give the incorrect answer of one-fourth.

It is easy to see why they would make such an error. Despite their knowledge of elementary genetics, they are culturally American. As such, when thinking about race, they do so in terms of American folk concepts: Someone with one Black parent has one-half Black blood; someone with one Black grandparent has one-quarter Black blood. But American culture is not biology and genes are not blood. When I point out to the students that the correct answer is a range, from zero to one-half, depending on which of the "mixed" person's genes happen by chance to be involved, it helps in understanding that biological variation and the social concept of race are quite different.[2]

Biological Variation

I will first discuss biological variation so as to provide a basis for contrasting it with the social classification of race, a concept of greater interest to therapists. First, let us review some definitions.

A species consists of those organisms that can mate together and produce fertile offspring. Thus, gorillas, chimpanzees, and humans are three distinct species. Two kinds of borderline cases exist. First, horses and donkeys are separate species because, although they can mate, the offspring which they produce—mules—are sterile. Second, there are examples of species spread out over great distances, such that those at point A can breed with those at point B; those at point B can breed with those at point C; but those at point C cannot breed with those at point A.

The complex chemicals which control heredity are called genes, and occur together in groups called chromosomes. Humans have 46 chromosomes (23 pairs), which are made up of about 20,000 to 25,000 genes. The members of each pair of chromosomes are similar, but not identical. In reproduction, a sperm or ovum contains one member from each of the twenty-three pairs; and which member is included in a particular germ cell is determined independently for each pair. Because, in a given mating, any conceivable sperm might mate with any conceivable ovum, there are $2^{23} \times 2^{23} = 2^{46}$ possible arrangements of chromosomes which might occur in the offspring of given parents. This astronomical figure, however, assumes that the chromosomes in each pair retain their integrity before separating into two groups of 23. On the contrary, through a process known as crossing over, they exchange unpredictable amounts of genetic material with each other before separating into germ cells. Hence, the figure of 2^{46} is but an infinitesimal estimate of the number of possible offspring that could be produced from the mating of two humans. It is for this reason that it is safe to say that—with the exception of identical twins—although we are all members of the same species, each of us is genetically unique.

The relationship between an individual's genes, or genotype, and their physical expression, or phenotype, is a complex one. The phenotype produced depends, to differing degrees in different instances, on genetic factors, environmental factors, and complex interactions among them. Thus, a man with brown hair (his phenotype) may or may not carry genes for blond hair. The important point is that the hair color of his offspring will be determined by the genes which he and his mating partner carry, and not by the color of his hair. Two phenotypically brown-haired people may, and often do, produce blond offspring. (An explanation of this phenomenon would lead us into a discussion of dominance, penetrance, and polygenetic determination—topics whose treatment is not necessary for the present discussion.)

Breeding Populations

With this brief background it is possible to explain the closest biological concept to race, that of a breeding population.[3] A breeding population consists of members of a species which breed among themselves more frequently than they do with other members of the species. As a result, the breeding population comes to differ from other populations of the species in the frequencies of certain genes. In general, this distinctiveness arises through the mechanisms of mutation, natural selection, and genetic drift.

Mutations, or changes in genetic material, occur infrequently. Because their phenotypic expressions are most often disadvantageous, they tend not to show up in populations where they occur (e.g., death occurs before the organism expressing the mutation has a chance to reproduce). When they are neutral—conferring neither a reproductive advantage nor disadvantage—they may continue on through the generations. If two groups do not interbreed, perhaps as a result of physical distance between them, then the appearance and survival over many generations of different mutations in each group may occur.

Those rare mutations which are adaptive—which increase the chances of survival to reproductive age, or increase the likelihood of producing more offspring who will breed successfully—will, over the course of generations, spread to ever larger percentages of the population where they occur. The increase in the frequency of adaptive genes is called natural selection.

It is important to remember that populations contain variations in both genotypes and phenotypes for any given trait, and that what is adaptive in one environment may be maladaptive in another.

Archaeological evidence indicates that our earliest ancestors evolved in Africa and then spread out through the rest of the world. As they migrated into Europe, Asia, and the New World,[4] they encountered widely varying physical environments (Marks, 1995). It appears—though it is not certain, because skeletal remains give only limited clues about the skin that once covered them—that many of the features which are regarded by our culture as racial signs had adaptive value. Thus, dark skins may have been selected for where they served a protective function against the tropical sun, whereas light skins may have been selected for in cold regions, where people wore clothes, because they were helpful in maximally utilizing sunlight for the production of vitamin D. This would explain the parallel evolution (independent selection for similar forms in similar environments) of skin color around the world. Indigenous peoples of tropical Africa and South America have dark skins, whereas groups in northern North America and northern Europe have much lighter skins. Even within Africa, the Bushmen of southern Africa have lighter skins than their neighbors to the north.

By contrast, the additional (epicanthic) fold of skin which many Asians have on their eyelids appears to have been adaptive as extra protection for the eye against the extreme cold of northern Asia. Unlike skin color, this trait seems in no way maladaptive in other climates; and so it can be seen among the indigenous peoples of North and South America who are descendants of Asians.

Whereas some of the physical traits that were probably selected for in particular climates are regarded by our culture as racial signs, other equally obvious physical traits (which were most likely also the result of natural selection) are not so regarded. A case in point would be body shape. The smaller the surface area of an object of given mass (i.e., the more like a ball), the more slowly it loses heat; and the larger the surface area (i.e., like the pipes of an old-fashioned radiator), the more rapidly it loses heat. Thus, it is likely that the rounded bodies of peoples like the Inuit in northern North America were selected for as heat conservers, whereas the elongated bodies of African groups like the Masai were selected for as heat dispersers. The relevant point to understand is that our culturally specific categories for the racial classification of people arbitrarily include certain dimensions (e.g., light vs. dark skin) and exclude others (e.g., round vs. elongated bodies). In other words, we Americans think of "rounded" people and "elongated" people as two kinds of Whites or two kinds of Blacks. But there is no biological reason why we should not instead think of light-skinned people and dark-skinned people as two kinds of "roundeds" or two kinds of "elongateds." The choice of skin color as a basis for classification is an arbitrary and cultural one.

A key factor which makes natural selection possible, and which thereby protects the survival of a species, is genetic diversity within the species. As environments change, certain low frequency traits may become highly adaptive and thus more widespread in successive generations. A famous example concerns a species of English moth whose light coloring served as camouflage against light tree bark and protected it against predatory birds. With the coming of the Industrial Revolution, soot from the factories darkened the bark and provided a contrasting background, which made the moths easy prey. As a result, the previously rare darkly colored moths of the same species rapidly spread while their lighter-colored brethren were decimated. Within a few years, the color of the species appeared to have changed miraculously.

This is the essence of natural selection: genetic diversity plus the selective pressure of the environment. It is not a process of "survival of the fittest" in which members of a species slug it out against each other, like teams of sportsmen at elite private schools or like cutthroat businessmen in an unregulated marketplace—though Darwin's contemporaries may have viewed it in this way. Nor is evolution a process whereby mankind struggles heroically ever onward toward perfection (this is known as the Teleological Fallacy). Species appear to reflect their Creator's intelligent design in their harmonious adaptation to the environment because the inharmoniously maladapted brethren of their ancestors died off before reproducing, leaving the survivors to define themselves as the model of perfection. Members of a species who are well adapted in one environment would have a poor chance of survival in another. When the entire range of genetic variability is insufficient to adapt, the species itself becomes "inharmonious" and dies out.

Although mutations and natural selection are dramatic explanations of ways in which different human breeding populations come to differ from one another in the frequencies of certain genes, genetic drift provides both a humbler explanation and one which may account for a larger proportion of such differences. Genetic drift refers to accidental changes in gene frequencies. When some members of a tribe break away and migrate or when disaster strikes a population (e.g., an earthquake or a volcano), it is virtually impossible for such events not to affect gene frequencies. Just by chance, the people who move away or who survive the calamity are bound to differ in the frequencies of various genes from those who do not. Even physical separation over many generations will eventually lead two equivalent populations to differ in the frequency of genes—as people with some genotypes in each group reproduce more than their counterparts in the other. Assuming that the genes which accidentally increase in frequency have no effect on survival to reproductive age, their higher frequencies will be maintained as the population increases in size.

With this background, we can compare the biological concept of breeding population with the concept of race. First of all, breeding populations are merely statistical subgroups of species, which may be defined in whatever way is useful for research purposes. For example, one might wish to examine populations characterized by 99% inbreeding over 20 generations (there are no such human populations) or one might investigate populations characterized by 51% inbreeding over 2 generations (there are millions of such human groups). Second, it is important to remember that all breeding populations belong to a given species. Humans from anywhere in the world, regardless of physical appearance, are capable of producing fertile offspring with other humans from anywhere else. Finally, even when a group qualifies as a breeding population according to some statistical criterion, it can merge with other groups and cease being a breeding population in a single generation. Modern transportation has increased gene flow around the world, so that the number of breeding populations according to any given statistical criterion is rapidly declining.

It is easy to see that the biological concept of breeding population is different from the social concept of race to which we are accustomed. In particular, social judgments of race are largely based on physical traits, such as skin color. Clearly, one cannot tell a person's breeding population from phenotypic information. Neither, however, can a person's breeding population be determined by a knowledge of genotype. Suppose, for example, that 20% of the members of a particular race have the gene R, whereas 40% of other humans have the gene. The fact that a given individual does or does not carry the gene is of no help in deciding whether or not the person belongs to the breeding population in question.

Given the distinction between a breeding population and the social classification of race, it is worthwhile pointing out that neither Whites nor Blacks constitutes a breeding population. Whites are not a worldwide breeding population, because Whites in America breed with Blacks in America more frequently than they do with Whites in Australia or Russia (i.e., Whites do not breed among themselves more frequently than with others). And Blacks are not a worldwide breeding population, because Blacks in America breed with Whites in America more frequently than they do with Blacks in Ghana or Tanzania. In contrast to Blacks and Whites, residents of an isolated small town are a good example of a breeding population because they do breed among themselves more frequently than with others.

Given that Blacks and Whites aren't breading populations, what can we say about their physical appearance? First, we can say that they aren't at the opposite ends of a single racial continuum. If this were so, then characteristics considered by our culture to be racial would vary together: A "totally White" person would have a white skin, straight blond hair, blue eyes, narrow nose, and thin lips; a "totally Black" person would have dark brown skin and eyes, tight curly black hair, broad nose, and thick lips; and people in between would have, to a correlated degree, skin, hair, and eyes of intermediate color, loosely curly hair, noses of medium width, and lips of medium thickness. Anyone who takes a look around can see that this is not the case. These features vary independently. It is not only perfectly possible to have a person with dark brown skin, straight dark hair, narrow nose and thin lips, but in another culture (northeastern Brazil) which has a different social conception of race, there is actually a specific term to designate people who look like this.

Clines

Just as cartographers color a map of the world according to the height of the terrain, it is possible to color a map of the world according to the mean value of some biological feature of the inhabitants. Thus, it is possible to create a world map of average skin color, or of average hair form or nose breadth (actually, the ratio of breadth to length), or of an average index of lip thickness (evertedness), or of the average proportion of people with a given chemical in their blood, or of any other characteristic which is supposed to be an index of race.

If Blacks and Whites really were different biological entities, then these maps should coincide. In fact, they do not. What happens is much more interesting. Not only do the different features vary independently, but they do so gradually and in different directions along lines known as clines. The reason for this finding is easy to understand. Suppose that several breeding populations are situated along a line, where the members of A have some contact (including sexual contact) with those of B, B with C, and so forth. If the population of A has a high frequency of some gene that is absent in the other populations, then it is likely that some of the offspring of their contacts with B will carry the gene. Because A and B are separate breeding populations, the frequency of the gene among the members of B will never reach its level among A. Some of the carriers in B will transmit it to the offspring of their matings with people of C, though the frequency of the gene among the members of C will never reach its level among B, and so forth. In this way, over many generations, the trait will spread out in declining frequencies the further one is from A.

The hodgepodge of clines, running every which way all over the globe, does not suggest that humans consist of a small number of distinct entities which developed separately. Rather, the data are more what one would expect from a species in which different groups migrated to all corners of the earth in differing numbers and at different times, splitting apart, becoming isolated, merging with new groups, and generally combining and recombining in myriad ways across time and space. The model of evolution which best explains human variation is not that of a branching tree, but rather a tangled lattice.

Folk Taxonomies

The social classification of race, which plays such an important part in our everyday lives, is a strikingly different conceptual domain from biological variation. It is what anthropologists refer to as a folk taxonomy, that is, a culturally (as opposed to scientifically) based system of categories. For example, in the American folk classification of edible plants, the avocado is a vegetable:

People eat it with oil and vinegar in a salad. In Brazil, the avocado is a fruit: People eat it with lemon juice and sugar for dessert. Although the botanical classification of the avocado is invariant across cultures, its folk classification does vary.

Just as edible plants are biological organisms which are categorized in different places according to differing pseudobiological plant classifications, so human beings are biological organisms which are categorized in different places according to differing pseudobiological racial classifications.

American "Races"

The American system of the social classification of race is based on the concept of "blood," or the racial classification of one's parents. It is a system according to which various groups in society are ranked according to their racial status; when parents come from different groups, their children are classified as belonging to the lower status group. For this reason, the system has been called one of hypo-descent (Harris, 1964). Thus, all children of couples with one parent classified as White and one parent classified as Black—regardless of the physical appearance of the children or their parents—would traditionally be classified as Black.[5] If some of the children had straight blond hair, blue eyes, white skin, narrow nose, and thin lips, they would still "really" be Black. If, on growing up, they associated primarily with Whites, and never let on about the racial classification of their parents, they would be said to be "passing" for White—that is, pretending dishonestly to belong to a higher status racial category.[6]

It is true that the words *mulatto, quadroon,* and *octoroon* exist in our vocabulary, but given the short genealogies and high mobility of our nation of immigrants, they are rarely used in classifying people today. The only term I have heard used in conversation—and that very infrequently—was mulatto, used by Whites in referring to a child of a Black–White marriage. Those who used the term had no knowledge of the racial classification of the child's grandparents (e.g., the Black parent might have been a mulatto, thereby making the child a quadroon) and were employing it as a shorthand way of saying something about the parents—that one was Black and the other White—while ostensibly speaking about the child. It was not used to imply—and could not have been so used in our racial system—that the child was neither Black nor White, but belonged to some third category. The closest that one can come to this status in America is to be considered Black by Whites and White by Blacks.

It is possible that the rankings of groups of intermediate racial status may vary regionally, so that people of Latin American descent have higher status in areas where they are scarce, and people of Native American ancestry have higher status where there are few of them. Hence, it is possible that a child who had one parent from each of these groups might be classified as an Indian in South Dakota and as a Hispanic in New York City. Such regional variations emphasize once again that race is a social label rather than a biological attribute.

New immigrant groups sometimes challenge American racial categories and go through a period of adjustment while negotiating with the larger society over what to call themselves. Thus, Cape Verdeans found they had to choose between being White and being Black, and immigrants from India have had to choose among White, Black, and Asian.

In addition, as the American population becomes increasingly diverse, with ever more marriages producing offspring that are hard to classify, it is possible that a new "multiracial" or "multicultural" category will emerge. A child whose four grandparents are Black, White, Asian, and Latin American stretches the American system of racial classification beyond its limits. The fact that categories have to be invented or changed to accommodate to social realities highlights once again the fact that race is a social rather than biological concept.

Brazilian Tipos

In contrast to our racial system based on ancestry, Brazil's system of racial *tipos* (which varies regionally, and is most elaborate in northeast Brazil) is based on physical appearance, as modified to some extent by social status. Detailed discussions of this system can be found in Harris (1964, 1970) and Degler (1971).

Because the American racial system is based on ancestry, all children of a given marriage receive the same racial classification. In a marriage between an African American and a European American, this means that all children are regarded as Black (or mixed), despite the usual genetic outcome of a range of phenotypes. In Brazil, however, each child is classified according to its physical appearance. Because large families abound, it would not be unusual for a couple in the city of Salvador, Bahia, to have children of a half-dozen different racial *tipos*.

Brazilians and Americans, because of a lack of familiarity with each other's cultures, are often not aware that their racial systems are different.

Because Portuguese and English often use cognate terms, communication on the already sensitive topic of race often becomes bewildering. For example, in Brazil a *mulato* is someone with tight curly black hair and light tan to brown skin, who probably—but not necessarily—has dark eyes, thick lips, and a broad nose. A *moreno* is someone who looks similar, except without tight curly hair and with a slightly lighter range of possible skin and hair colors. *Mulato* is a darker and less prestigious racial classification than *moreno*. A marriage between a *moreno* and a *morena* might well produce a *branco* (White) or *mulato* child, or even both.

This result, of parents producing children with a higher or lower racial classification than either of them, is impossible in the American system of hypo-descent.[7]

One informant[8] from northern Brazil explained to me that a certain person was a *mulata* and not a *preta* (Black) because she "doesn't have that really kinky hair and black skin that Africans have." The fascinating aspect of this report is that both my informant and I knew that the woman in question was the daughter of African immigrants to Brazil. Hence she was one of the few Brazilian citizens of whom it could be said with conviction that she was of 100% African ancestry. Not only was the racial *tipo* assigned without regard to ancestry, but the folk explanation of its origin was offered (by a college-educated informant) in disregard of evidence to the contrary. In this respect, neither Brazilian nor American stereotypes take into account the breadth of physical variation that is to be found among Africans (Alland, 1971).

A New Yorker who would be called a *moreno* in Brazil is perplexing to his fellows in the United States because he is not easily classified. In meeting people, he must endure interrogations of the what-was-your-name-again-and-where-do-you-come-from variety, as his audience tries to decide whether he is Black, White, or Hispanic. By contrast, he is an immediately recognizable *tipo* in Brazil and creates no confusion for others there.

Two categories used in northeastern Brazil, but which are unknown in the more Europeanized south, are *sarará* and *cabo verde* (after the Cape Verde Islands, where it is common to find people who look this way). What is interesting about these *tipos* is that, because they are opposite to each other, they form a dimension in the Euro-African domain, and this dimension is independent of the Black–White dimension (Harris, 1970). That is, a ranking can be made along the Black–White dimension (with approximate equivalents offered parenthetically in American English and with some unavoidable distortions of cultural meaning necessary for this brief presentation) as follows: *louro* (blond), *branco* (white), *moreno* (in the Northeast, a kind of white), *mulato* (a kind of black), *preto* (black). However, *sarará–cabo verde* forms an independent dimension; people categorized as either *tipo* are considered to be neither Black nor White. A *sarará* is someone with light (red or blond) tight curly hair, light (blue or green) eyes, light skin, broad nose, and thick lips; a *cabo verde* has black straight hair, dark eyes, dark brown skin, narrow nose, and thin lips.

These few *tipos* should be sufficient to give the reader the flavor of the Brazilian racial system. There are many dozens of such racial terms. (I have not even referred to the Indian-White [e.g., *mameluco*] or Indian-Black [e.g., *cafuzo*] *tipos*, to avoid going into unnecessary detail.)[9]

I hope it is clear from all this that a person's race is not a biological characteristic of his or her own, but a cultural label applied by others to certain aspects of the person's physical appearance, ancestry, or social attributes. To the extent to which it is treated as a biological entity, race becomes a reified concept. The everyday process of racial classification is learned behavior; people exposed to different environments learn to categorize differently. A person may change race by moving from one place to another (e.g., from the United States to Brazil). What changes is not the individual's genes, or physical appearance, or ancestry, but the behavior of the people labeling it.

In personal terms, I must say that after having lived in Brazil I can no longer look at people and say what race they belong to. I have to know where they are from and to whom I am speaking. Even then I find that I can be more precise by qualifying my answer culturally. For example, I met a family in New York which I would describe in this way: The father was Black here and a *mulato* in Brazil; the mother was Hispanic here and a *morena* in Brazil; and their daughter was Black here, a *mulata clara* (light *mulata*) in southern Brazil and a *sarará* in northeastern Brazil.

Stereotypes

The function of social classification is to serve as a guide to action. Whether or not a given piece of beef is kosher will determine its edibility for Orthodox Jews. Whether an avocado is a fruit or a vegetable makes a difference for Brazilians and Americans regarding how it is to be prepared and during what part of a meal it is to be eaten. In a similar way, knowing whether people are Black or White fills the important social need (no matter how inaccurately) of predicting how they will behave. That is, among groups who use systems of racial classification, there are stereotypes associated with the different racial categories, which create specific expectancies regarding the behavior of each race. These stereotypes grew up for historical reasons (e.g., conditions during slavery and thereafter). Like similar phenomena elsewhere—as a therapist, diagnostic labeling comes to my mind first—racial stereotypes are notoriously resistant to change. Factors perpetuating racial stereotypes include social patterns (e.g., the distribution of power going against those groups unfavorably stereotyped), cultural patterns (e.g., children learning and relearning them from parents and peers), and psychological patterns (e.g., the resistance to extinction of intermittently reinforced responses—some people can always be found who act as the stereotypes predict—and the self-fulfilling prophesy of people conforming to negative expectations).

Because racial stereotypes function to predict behavior within a cultural setting, it follows that such stereotypes are culturally relative. This contrast can be seen between stereotypes of women's beauty and sexuality in northeastern Brazil and the United States. In the United States, blondes are considered the most attractive and sexy ("Blondes have more fun"), whereas in northeastern Brazil, blondes are seen as cold. The most beautiful women there are the *morenas*—a category we do not have, but which is in any event much closer to our concept of a brunette. In the United States, Black women are considered sensual, whereas in Brazil this stereotype is applied not to the *preta*, but to the *mulata* (another category we do not have). In northeastern Brazil, a prostitute with tan skin and straight hair might well wear a wig of tight curly hair to attract customers; in the United States, it would be more likely for a prostitute with tan skin and tight curly hair to wear a wig of straight hair for the same reason.

The Therapeutic Relationship

Given this brief introduction to biological variation, social race, and the stereotypes associated with the latter, it is possible to consider the therapeutic relationship from a new perspective. For purposes of simplicity, I will discuss the one-to-one relationship and leave it to the reader to elaborate these points for therapy of interracial marriages, of families with cross-racially adopted children, or of interracial therapy groups.

Whenever a therapist and client get together we can be confident that each categorizes the other in racial terms and draws behavioral inferences from the categories applied. More specifically, the therapist knows that he or she belongs to a given race A, that the client belongs to another race B, that As are one kind of person, that Bs are another kind of person, and that As and Bs commonly interact in a pattern P. Meanwhile, the client knows that he or she belongs to a race B', that the therapist belongs to another race A', that B's are one kind of person, that A's are another kind of person, and that B's and A's commonly interact in a pattern P'. Difficulties in communication arise from the fact that A and A' may not be the same, nor may B and B', nor P and P'.

In terms of increasing complexity (and perplexity, for the participants), the therapist and client may come from the same culture and be of the same race,[10] they may come from the same culture and be of different races, or they may come from different cultures and be of different races.

The simplest case, and the one that has characterized most therapy and counseling ever since Freud, is where the therapist and client are from the same culture and of the same race (e.g., White). In this case, issues related to race need never affect the therapeutic relationship—not because they do not exist, but because there is no occasion for them to arise or to affect the clarity of communication between therapist and client. This is a typical instance of a cultural variable appearing to be a constant in a limited cultural context. If therapist and client came from the same economic or educational background these issues too might never cause confusion. One might even suggest that a therapist who has a sociocultural background identical to that of his or her client would have the least difficulty in understanding or communicating in the therapy situation and the least likelihood of opening the client up to new vistas. By contrast, a therapist from a different background would most likely have greater difficulties in understanding and communication. As these were dealt with, differing assumptions of therapist and client would emerge and might well lead to the consideration of alternative courses of action. Naturally, the greater the difference in backgrounds, the greater would be the likelihood of misunderstandings occurring; and bad ones might even lead to the abrupt termination of therapy. Despite this risk, the potential for change in what might otherwise have been an unrecognizable direction remains an important counterbalancing benefit. This kind of thinking suggests the hypothesis of a curvilinear relationship between the amount of sociocultural difference between therapist and client and the likelihood of the client developing useful sociocultural awareness from the resulting therapy (i.e., too little difference or too much difference might be less effective than moderate difference).

It is when therapist and client are from the same culture but of different races that the complications begin. The nature of these complications depends on the culture in question; but I will limit my discussion to the American case. I will consider the example of the White therapist with a Black client for illustrative purposes, because it is the most common, but most of the same observations would apply, *mutatis mutandis*, with a Black therapist and White client, or with members of any two American racial classifications.

In this case, the therapist believes that he or she is White, that the client is Black, and that each is a member of a different race. The client holds the same beliefs. Because they share the American system of racial classification, it is unlikely that difficulties in communication will arise concerning the "biological" categories they are supposed to belong to. On the other hand, each holds stereotypes of what it means to be White, what it means to be Black, and how Whites and Blacks interact. It is unlikely that these stereotypes and expectancies are the same for both participants, because they were learned in different subcultural settings. Hence, difficulties in communication are most likely in this area.

For example, if the client is a woman whose dress and hairstyle are distinctively African American, a White male therapist might well assume that she holds militant political views and might even blame him personally for the oppression of Blacks. Such conclusions might lead him nonverbally to communicate a stance either of defensive coldness ("It's unjust of you to prejudge me like that") or of ingratiating egalitarianism ("Actually, I'm one of the good guys opposed to racism, so you don't have to be angry at me"). In fact, the woman might have chosen her hair style because she considers it attractive, and might be wearing a dashiki because it is loose-fitting and she is pregnant. In such a situation, the therapist's nonverbal stance (based on unfounded but culturally determined assumptions) would likely be disruptive of communication between him and his client.

In a similar way, many younger White therapists dress casually for sessions, at least in part because they believe that this will put their clients at ease. However, an African American client might view such dress as an expression of disrespect, and be put off rather than relaxed by it. If the therapist is not aware of subcultural differences in the importance and meaning of clothes, such undetected assumptions might also undermine the quality of the therapeutic relationship.

I will not treat separately the case of the therapist and client who are from different cultures but of the same race, because it is really dealt with in other parts of this discussion. That is, to the extent to which the two cultures have the same system of racial classification, with regard at least to race, the therapist and client are really from the same culture; and to the extent to which the two cultures have different systems, the therapist and client are by definition of different races. Hence, the only remaining case to be discussed is that of the therapist and client who are from different cultures and of different races.

Here we have extraordinary possibilities for misunderstanding. Whether or not the therapist and client recognize that they are of different races, neither claims to be a member of the race to which the other would assign him or her. Most likely, neither really understands that the other categorizes race differently, or even that racial categorization involves social as opposed to biological judgments. Needless to say, the stereotypes that each associates with various racial categories differ from those of the other. If the categories are associated with identical or cognate words, so much the worse. Should the subject of race be dealt with explicitly, friction is likely to result when they each apply their own stereotypes to a word that actually represents the other's category.

The difficulties arising in such therapy can be illustrated by the hypothetical treatment of a rich Brazilian businessman who is setting up an office of his company in the United States. Let us assume that he looks like a *mulato*, as defined earlier in this chapter, and that he is being treated by a White male therapist. Because of what Brazilians describe as the remarkable "whitening" power of money, he might think of himself as White (*branco*) and be accustomed to being treated as a member of this prestigious racial category. Because prejudice increases as one ascends the social hierarchy in Brazil (the opposite of the United States), he might well make an occasional anti-Black remark. Although such comments (e.g., regarding the incompetence of Black servants) might be made unthinkingly, if there were a motive behind them, it would most likely be one of demonstrating solidarity between himself and the therapist, as White men of importance and power. He would probably be shocked to find that the therapist regards such remarks as racist—especially because the client believes himself to be free from prejudice and is proud of coming from Brazil, the world's only racial democracy. For a Brazilian, his belief stands in stark contrast to America's obvious racism, which labels as Black many people who are not, and unjustly discriminates against them.

From the therapist's point of view, he is treating a Black Brazilian. Perhaps it would occur to him that the Black Brazilian experience might be different from the Black American experience. If so, the client's anti-Black comments might remain a question mark for him, rather than a basis for hastily concluding that his client's conflict over being Black was manifesting itself in denial, reaction formation, identification with the aggressor, or some other defensive reaction. It is unlikely that he would guess that the client made the remarks because he thought of himself as White, and even less likely that he would imagine that Brazil's system of racial classification is different from our own. Although this example may seem extreme to White American therapists with little or no cross-cultural experience, the fact of the matter is that people classified as Black in the United States are culturally heterogeneous, and not at all the single group that our system makes them out to be. For example, there is a large population of Americans born in the Caribbean area, from English-, Spanish-, French-, or Dutch-speaking backgrounds. Each island or colony developed a separate set of social and cultural patterns—including linguistic ones—in relative isolation from the others; and each created a unique breeding population from disparate elements. The mixture of isolated indigenous groups with conquerors from one area of Europe and slaves from other areas of Africa ultimately resulted in each island or country having a unique range of physical variation associated with its unique range of social and cultural variation.

It is only natural that such diversity includes differences in systems of racial classification. (Haiti and Puerto Rico, for example, have systems that are quite different from each other's, and quite different from those of Brazil and the United States.) The classification of New Yorkers living in Harlem into the categories of White, Black, and Hispanic cannot begin to do justice to the myriad ways they classify themselves and each other, not to mention the broad range of stereotypes associated with the various categories of the differing systems.

One consequence of this is that some people from the Caribbean, who are regarded by Americans as Black, think of themselves either as White or as something other than White or Black. This can lead to bizarre situations such as the equal opportunity hiring by American Whites of immigrant "Blacks"—who think of themselves as White, and whose hiring only antagonizes American-born Blacks who view them as illegitimate competitors from an alien culture. In a similar way, Hispanics in New York include both culturally American descendants of Spanish speakers and people who actually grew up in a Hispanic culture. In each of these groups there are large numbers of people whose cultural identification is Dominican, Cuban, or Puerto Rican (not to mention groups from other areas). Hence, there are at least six major groups of Hispanics who classify one another in varying ways (three countries × two races = six).

It is unclear exactly what the outer limits of the Hispanic category are (as used by most New Yorkers to make judgments on the basis of casual social contact). Certainly it includes Brazilians, who speak Portuguese. At times, I think it must extend to anyone with dark hair and/or skin who has a Spanish or unrecognizable accent (e.g., a Pakistani might not be classified as Hispanic, because his accent would probably identify him as Indian).

The point is, once again, that race is a cultural as opposed to a biological phenomenon. If we, as therapists, can recognize that the racial categories and stereotypes we apply to ourselves and to our clients are a subtle and pervasive result of our cultural training, we will have lifted from our eyes an important veil which distorts our interpersonal vision. To the extent that we succeed in doing so, we can be available to deal rationally with this aspect of the therapeutic relationship and with our clients' problems in this area.

Notes

1. For those who are interested in a more extensive treatment of the biological and cultural issues discussed in this chapter, I go into much greater detail in a chapter in my edited volume on race and intelligence (Fish, 2002b). The cultural anthropologist Audrey Smedley (1998, 2002) has given a thorough historical description of the origin and spread of the "race" concept. Additional points of view from psychologists include Betancourt and Lopez (1993) on ethnicity, and Carter and Pieterse (2005) on race.

2. To spell this out in detail, let us assume for the sake of argument that eight genes determine "race." (I am using the hypothetical number eight for illustrative purposes because of the tradition in parts of the South of classifying people according to their proportion of Black "blood" as mulatto [1/2], quadroon [1/4], or octoroon [1/8].) If one parent has the genes WWWWWWWW and the other has WWWWBBBB, then a child would receive WWWW genes from the first parent and WWWW, or WWWB, or WWBB, or WBBB, or BBBB from the second parent, resulting in a range from WWWWWWWW to WWWWBBBB.

3. Two other biological concepts, not discussed here, are subspecies and lineage. Templeton (2002) shows why *Homo sapiens* has no subspecies or lineages.

4. They were able to follow game from northeast Asia across the Bering Strait because, during the last ice age, so much water was in the form of ice that the lower sea level created a land bridge.

5. In recent years, many Americans would classify many such people as "mixed." The invention of this new category shows once again that race is a cultural classification that varies over time, and not a fixed biological entity. Because of

hypo-descent, Americans consider "mixed" people more Black than White—that is, Americans might debate whether such a person is Black or mixed, but would be unlikely to debate whether the person is White or mixed.

6. I am spelling out these details—although they are obvious to Americans—because they appear so alien to people whose systems of racial classification are different from our own.

7. It should be mentioned that Brazil does have social stratification based on "race," though it is weaker than that in the United States. On the other hand, Brazilian discrimination based on class is stronger than American racial discrimination. Perhaps as a result, Brazilians say that "money whitens." That is, the more money dark-skinned Brazilians have, the lighter the *tipos* they would use in self-classification, and the lighter the terms others would use in referring to them.

8. This term, which is neutral to anthropologists, conjures up images of stool pigeons to psychologists and other outsiders, much as our use of "subjects" sounds demeaning to nonpsychologists. This is one more example of the difficulty in communication among the social science subcultures.

9. A study by the IBGE, the Brazilian Institute of Geography and Statistics (1976/1999), the agency responsible for the census, asked people to identify their skin color (*cor*—a term synonymous, for our purposes, with *tipo*). Individuals responded with 134 different terms!

10. I am using both "culture" and "race" as admittedly inadequate shorthand forms because of the lack of vocabulary to avoid the reification of culture and the conceptual confusion associated with race. To say that nearly all Americans hold a similar pseudobiological view of what it means to be White is not to imply that there is one clearly structured and all-encompassing American culture, nearly all of which is shared by nearly all Americans.

References

Alland, A. (1971). *Human diversity*. New York: Columbia University Press.
Betancourt, H., & Lopez, S. R. (1993). The study of culture, ethnicity, and race in American psychology. *American Psychologist, 48,* 629–637.
Brazilian Institute of Geography and Statistics. (1976/1999). What color are you? In R. M. Levine & J. J. Crocitti (Eds.), *The Brazil reader: History, culture, politics* (pp. 386–390). Durham, NC: Duke University Press.

Carter, R. T., & Pieterse, A. L. (2005). Race: A social and psychological analysis of the term and its meaning. In R. T. Carter (Ed.), *Handbook of racial-cultural psychology and counseling: Theory and research* (Vol. 1, pp. 41–63). New York: Wiley.

Degler, C. N. (1971). *Neither Black nor White: Slavery and race relations in Brazil and the United States.* New York: Macmillan.

Fish, J. M. (2002a). A scientific approach to understanding race and intelligence. In J. M. Fish (Ed.), *Race and intelligence: Separating science from myth* (pp. 1–28). Mahwah, NJ: Lawrence Erlbaum Associates.

Fish, J. M. (2002b). The myth of race. In J. M. Fish (Ed.), *Race and intelligence: Separating science from myth* (pp. 113–141). Mahwah, NJ: Lawrence Erlbaum Associates.

Harris, M. (1964). *Patterns of race in the Americas.* New York: Walker.

Harris, M. (1970). Referential ambiguity in the calculus of Brazilian racial identity. *Southwestern Journal of Anthropology, 26*(1), 1–14.

Marks, J. (1995). *Human biodiversity: Genes, race, and history.* New York: Aldine de Gruyter.

Smedley, A. (1998). *Race in North America: Origin of a worldview* (2nd ed.). Boulder, CO: Westview.

Smedley, A. (2002). Science and the idea of race. In J. M. Fish (Ed.), *Race and intelligence: Separating science from myth* (pp. 145–176). Mahwah, NJ: Lawrence Erlbaum Associates.

Templeton, A. R. (2002). The genetic and evolutionary significance of human races. In J. M. Fish (Ed.), *Race and intelligence: Separating science from myth* (pp. 31–56). Mahwah, NJ: Lawrence Erlbaum Associates.

Suggested Readings and Web Sites

Fish, J. M. (Ed.). (2002c). *Race and intelligence: Separating science from myth.* Mahwah, NJ: Lawrence Erlbaum Associates.

This is a multidisciplinary book, of which parts I and II are most relevant to understanding race. In five chapters, evolutionary biology, biological anthropology, cultural anthropology, and cross-cultural psychology contribute to explaining why the human species has no biological races, comparing and contrasting the concept of "race" in different cultures, and showing how the concept of race developed in Europe and spread widely around the planet.

The following two books may be seen as complementing each other—dealing with the biological and cultural aspects of "race."

Marks, J. (1995). *Human biodiversity: Genes, race, and history.* New York: Aldine de Gruyter.

In this book, a biological anthropologist examines the history of biological views of race up to modern times. He examines the growth of scientific knowledge and the cultural context within which it developed, and discusses biologically based movements like eugenics.

Smedley, A. (1998). *Race in North America: Origin of a worldview* (2nd ed.). Boulder, CO: Westview.

In this book, a cultural anthropologist examines the history of cultural views of race up to modern times. She examines the linkage between views of race and the social institutions like slavery and segregation that formed their cultural context.

The following three Web sites contain authoritative information and striking graphics to help explain what is known about the subject referred to as "race."

Race: Are we so different? Retrieved from http://www.understandingrace.org/home.html

This Web site is the product of work by leading experts from the American Anthropological Association (AAA) and related disciplines. It contains much authoritative information, and is part of a larger project that includes a traveling museum exhibit and educational materials.

All of us are related, each of us is unique. Retrieved from http://allrelated.syr.edu/

This Web site contains a complete museum exhibit that discusses human biological variation, and explains why the human species has no races.

The National Geographic genographic project. Retrieved from https://www3.nationalgeographic.com/genographic/resources.html

This Web site has lots of useful information, especially Spencer Wells's *The Map of Us All,* http://www.nationalgeographic.com/adventure/0508/excerpt1.html?fs=www3.nationalgeographic.com&fs=plasma.nationalgeographic.com. This map traces the migration of humans out of Africa and around the planet from an analysis of tens of thousands of DNA samples from human groups around the world. (Populations that died out in the past often leave remains that can be studied by archaeologists.)

5

Healing the Body and Mind
An Overview of Biopsychosocial Foundations and Applications

Michele S. Hirsch

Contents

As a result of the rapid development of science and technology during the late 1800s and early 1900s, Western medicine embraced a biomedical model of health. Individuals' emotional state and the interpersonal relationship between them and their physician played an important role before the biomedical model of illness was adopted. Until the turn of the 20th century, before scientists possessed the technology to advance the biomedical model, doctors and physicians practiced their trade by observing their sick patients to determine what in that individual's environment might be contributing to his or her ailment. That is, biopsychosocial factors were believed to interact with one another to produce illness. Physicians diagnosed and treated their patients on an individual-by-individual basis. There was no disease model to dictate diagnosis or how the course of treatment should proceed. It was the individual *as a whole* who was considered by the treating physician.

Disease theory brought about enormous, undeniable change in Western medicine. Etiology, diagnosis, and cure became the predominant factors on which medical practitioners focused when treating physically ill patients. As the biology of diseases processes became better understood and technology to cure diseases became readily available, the need to "treat" patients in a holistic manner diminished.

As a result of the impersonal nature of health care, many individuals have become dissatisfied with the current state of affairs in Western medicine. Data (Eisenberg et al., 1993) indicate that some of these disgruntled patients are choosing alternative, or complementary, therapies in addition to, if not in place of, traditional, or Western, medicine. Subsequently, within the last 30 years, the (Western) scientific appreciation of the bidirectional relationship between our minds and our bodies has been renewed and has seen enormous growth. The numerous wellness approaches that have gained a huge following are just beginning to become more widely accepted by the medical community. As an example, the U.S. government, just 7 years ago, assembled a panel of commissioners to review and amass the latest empirical evidence on complementary and alternative health care approaches as well as to make recommendations on how best to advance this burgeoning area of health care (National Institutes of Health, 2002). However, as delineated at the end of this chapter, embracing new models of health care does not come without its obstacles. Recommendations and scientific evidence do not always readily translate into positive change.

Nevertheless, we can no longer conceptualize our personal experiences as being unconnected to our biochemistry and physiology (Ray, 2004). Certainly, as technology continues to evolve, so will our comprehension of the complex interplay between our mental and physical states and their effects on our mind–body systems. The aim of this chapter is to provide an overview, based upon our current understanding of the mind–body connection, of how the disciplines of biology, psychology, and sociology intersect in the use of several healing applications. Indeed, there are many applications that have been shown to have positive influences on the mind and body. This chapter will focus on just a few (the manipulation of expectancies, the role of social support and interpersonal relationships, mindfulness meditation, and emotional disclosure through writing) whose efficacy has been demonstrated and replicated under controlled experimental conditions.

The Mind–Body Connection: A Psychoneuroimmunological Perspective

There exist many different modalities that have been shown to provide positive effects on the mind and body with regular practice. Although the type of application may vary by culture, they possess virtually the same underlying mechanisms of how they ultimately influence our minds and bodies. At the most basic, cellular level, the field of psychoneuroimmunology has been instrumental in establishing direct links between our mental functioning and our physical health (Hirsch, 2004; Ray, 2004). That is, our physical bodies are literally affected by their psychosocial environments and vice versa.

To comprehend how our physical health can be affected by our psychology and/or our environment, a foundational understanding of the immune system is necessary. Many studies, conducted predominantly within a Western conceptualization of health and illness, focus on how the body's immune system can become compromised in the face of different types of psychosocial stressors. The following three sections provide an introduction to the immune system and how its functioning is assessed so that the reader will be able to better navigate the technical language used in the Western literature highlighting the mind–body relationship.

Basic Mechanisms of the Immune System

One of the most complex systems of the human body is the immune system. Its main function is to protect us against pathogens. Pathogens are any type of foreign or nonself microorganisms that have entered the body such as bacteria, fungi, viruses, transplanted tissues, allergens, and toxic substances. Although it is the largest immune organ, pathogens can enter the body through cuts or lesions anywhere on the skin. They may also enter the body through inhaling them in the air or through the mouth via foods we eat or liquids we drink. Although the body does have in place several mechanisms to destroy these pathogens (e.g., cilia and mucus lining the respiratory tract, gastric processes in the digestive system), some nevertheless evade these defenses. When this occurs, our immune system begins its complex and comprehensive task of activating an immune response in order to kill or inactivate the pathogen.

The immune system is akin to the circulatory system. It operates via the lymphatic system, a noncentralized group of organs that work in concert to destroy renegade and mutant cells. Organs such as the spleen, the thymus, lymph nodes, and bone marrow all play a role in the production and maintenance of highly specialized immune system cells. Although it is beyond the scope of this chapter to detail all the intricacies of the lymphatic system, Brannon and Feist (1997) provide a good review.

Before the immune system can mobilize against a pathogen, the microorganism must be recognized as foreign to the body. That is, the immune system has the daunting task of constantly discriminating between what is part of the body, or self, and what is not, or nonself. All cells of the body are coded by an array of protein molecules that function as a self marker. Foreign microorganisms also have protein molecules, but they are different than those of the body cells, thus they can be identified as nonself. Altered body cells, such as cancer cells, undergo protein changes and also become classified as nonself. Nonself proteins are called antigens. Immune system cells interact in a communication network that relays information about surrounding organisms within the body's environment. An immune response is triggered when an antigen is discovered.

Before detailing the immune response it is important to make a distinction between nonspecific immunity and acquired immunity. Nonspecific immunity is defined as the immune system's ability to respond to new antigens, ones that the body has not yet encountered. Once an antigen has been "discovered" and attacked, specific cells (T and B cells, discussed on the next page) develop a memory for that antigen. Thus, prior exposure to both illnesses and vaccines (where a harmless version of a virus is introduced) plays a role in acquired immunity. Should that antigen reappear in the body again, it is easily recognized by the memory cells and a swift attack is initiated to destroy it.

When an antigen is recognized, the immune system mobilizes and the resulting drama is termed an immune response. Highly specialized white blood cells, called leukocytes, mediate this complicated defense response. There are three classes of leukocytes: lymphocytes, monocytes, and granulocytes. Lymphocytes are categorized as B or T cells. T lymphocytes are produced in the thymus (hence the *T*) and are the major players of cell-mediated immunity. T cells have both a stimulatory effect function (helper T cells) and a restrictive effect function (suppressor T cells) on B cells. A third type of T cell is capable of producing cytotoxic cells, which play a more direct role in killing antigens. Natural killer (NK) cells, believed to be a precursor of the mature T cell not yet exposed to the target antigen, are also classified as lymphocytes. Tumor growth and metastasis are probably kept in check by NK cells. B cells carry out humoral, or circulatory, immunity. When an antigen is recognized, B lymphocytes produce plasma cells, which in turn produce antibodies (immunoglobins) that are secreted into the bloodstream. The antibodies are synthesized by different immunoglobins so that they can combine with the antigen that initiated the immune response. The major classes of immunoglobins are IgG, IgM, IgA, IgD, and IgE; each performs a slightly different function.

Bone marrow gives rise to monocytes, which only circulate in the bloodstream for about 8 to 10 hours. Upon leaving the bloodstream, they enter tissues, and mature into larger cells better able to engage in phagocytosis (destruction of cells and particulate via chemotaxis, attachment, engulfment, and/or intracellular events) called macrophages. Granulocytes are named for the presence of intracytoplasmic granules whose function is to cut through, or lyse, the cellular membrane of the target cells.

The *Neuro* in *Psychoneuroimmunology*

It is equally important to comprehend how the immune system can be influenced by psychological and social variables. Researchers believe that there are two main interrelated systems that allow for brain-immune system communication: the sympathetic-adrenomedullary (SAM) system and the hypothalamic-pituitary-adrenocortical (HPA) system. Both of these systems are activated when the body encounters sympathetic nervous system (fight or flight) arousal. More specifically, the organs detailed by the acronym SAM denote that when the sympathetic branch of the autonomic nervous system is activated, the medulla of the adrenal glands are stimulated and release catecholamines (such as adrenaline and noradrenaline). These catecholamines then stimulate the body's organs involved in stress reactions (e.g., increased heart rate, muscle tension, and blood pressure). Likewise, the organs denoted in the HPA system are activated when the pituitary gland releases hormones (i.e., adrenocorticotropic hormone [ACTH]) and endorphins (painkillers) after it is stimulated by the hypothalamus. ACTH then travels to the adrenal glands, which in turn secrete corticosteroids (anti-inflammatories).

In short, once activated, these two systems stimulate parts of the endocrine system. Thus, the endocrine system is one of the known intermediaries between psychological variables and immune system changes. It works in concert with the nervous system in sending messages to the various parts of the body. In so doing it has been referred to as a "second nervous system" (Baum et al., 1997). In fact, the nervous and endocrine systems are so intimately tied together that they have been likened as one system: the neuroendocrine environment (Ader et al., 1995).

The endocrine system consists of glands, including the pituitary, adrenals, gonads, and thyroid, which produce and then release hormones into the circulating bloodstream. Hormones are chemical messengers that help regulate organs and structures throughout the body. To accomplish this, the hormones travel in the bloodstream until they reach their destination, where they bind to the targeted organ to deliver their message. This enables communication between organs that are not in close physical proximity with one another. For example, adrenal hormones (i.e., epinephrine, cortisol) are known to affect the cardiovascular system and other endocrine organs as well as the immune system. Receptors for hormones exist within the lymph system, bone marrow, thymus, and spleen. Most recently, receptors for hormones have been found on lymphocytes, monocytes/macrophages, and granulocytes. In addition, bidirectional pathways exist between the endocrine and immune system (Ader et al., 1995). Thus, the ability for hormones to enable organ-to-organ, organ-to-immune, and immune-to-organ system interactions throughout the body is immense.

The more purely neurological aspects of immune mediation have been the recent focus of researcher's attention as well (Ader et al., 1995). There are now known bidirectional pathways between the brain and the immune system. Moreover, it has been proposed that the neocortex of the brain may be a link between psychosocial factors and immune system functioning. This is important in that the neocortex has a "central role ... in the perception and interpretation of environmental circumstances, including stressful life experiences" (Ader et al., 1995, p. 100).

Taken together, immune, neurological, endocrine, and psychological processes are highly interactive and undeniably interrelated. The following section provides a brief description of how scientists have been able to test these system interactions.

Measuring Immune System Functioning

Immunocompetence is the term used to describe optimal immune system functioning. A state of immunosuppression or immunocompromise exists when the immune system is not operating effectively. Researchers in the field of psychoneuroimmunology assess the effects of various variables on the immune system. However, the cells of the immune system organs cannot easily be accessed. In order to assess an individual's immunocompetence at any point in time, scientists can assay blood, saliva, and/or urine samples for immune system components. It has only been in the last 15 years that technology has allowed researchers to directly test assumptions about the relationship between emotional states and physical health (Salovey, Rothman, Detweiler, & Steward, 2000).

Researchers observe the cells that they have obtained and look for specific immune cell activity. How the cells are activated, their cytotoxicity, and how they transform and mobilize themselves are of interest to psychoneuroimmunology-related studies. Additional specific measures include "the ability of lymphocytes to kill invading cells (lymphocyte cytotoxicity), the ability of lymphocytes to reproduce when artificially stimulated by a chemical (mitogen), the ability of certain white blood cells to ingest foreign particles (phagocytotic activity)" (Taylor, 1999, p. 430).

Interestingly, advances in psychoneuroimmunology continue at a rapid pace with new and exciting discoveries suggesting that more and more of our immune, neurological, and endocrine systems communicate and even "share" roles. Scientists are on the brink of better understanding that specific cells that they once identified as belonging to one of the aforementioned systems actually have the ability to influence and function within and on the other systems (Jian-Lan, Yi-Hua, Yu-Ping, & Jian-Jun, 2006; Pozo & Delgado, 2004). Just 10 short years ago, researchers had evidence of a mind–body connection in terms of outcomes, yet they lacked the knowledge to explain the mechanisms by which the mind and body influenced one another (Wickramasekera, Davies, & Davies, 1996); it is exciting and encouraging that we have arrived at a place where these specific processes can now be documented and their very complex roles understood.

It is advantageous for researchers to be able to understand and document the bidirectional processes by which the systems of the mind and body operate in unison so that they can measure the direct effect(s) of moderating variables on these systems. In the effort to aggregate findings on these moderating variables, Kiecolt-Glaser, McGuire, Robles, and Glaser (2002) reviewed the psychoneuroimmunology literature since 1939. Findings from the 118 publications suggest that the immune system can be modulated by psychosocial factors such as stress, coping skills, and interpersonal relationships. Several of these variables will be discussed in the remainder of this chapter.

Healing Practices From a Cross-Cultural Perspective

In reviewing the healing process from an evolutionary standpoint, Bloom (2005) elucidates several important commonalities of the Yanomami (Brazil/Venezuela), G/wi (Botswana), and Walbiri (Australia) healing ceremonies. Primarily, he points out that "the ability to ascertain an etiology as well as some action that can be taken to treat it may be one of the most common themes all of healing ceremonies" (p. 256). Further, Bloom draws the upon the foundational processes used in healing ceremonies as he advocates their continued use in treating individuals today: "a healing process that promoted placebo effect, hope, and expectancy while empowering patients is as important today as ever" (p. 257). Perhaps even more importantly, Katz (1982) astutely notes that it is not constructive to be evaluative when different healing modalities are being compared. Instead, it is more productive that each be recognized for its strengths and weaknesses.

As a follow-up to Bloom's (2005) examination of cross-cultural healing practices, Coulehan (2005) provides a commentary wherein he reaffirms that what an illness or a bout of ill health means to the patient is often overlooked in today's medical practice but can be quite significant to the individual. Because illness has been demonstrated to be culturally constructed, the meaning an individual ascribes to an illness may evoke personal, societal, and even political meanings (see Sussman, this volume).

Coming from a different angle, Cross (2003) encourages practitioners to view culture as a resource for mental healing. He states:

> It is my assertion that culture provides many of the resources for posi-
> tive emotions and that cultural resources should be thought of as a key
> element of any strength-based approach. As practitioners, we can tap
> into the resources that culture provides and find those elements that
> promote and support positive emotions. Family events, cultural foods,
> art, music, stories, spiritual practices, ceremonies, and crafts—these are
> the outward and visible elements of culture that we know support posi-
> tive emotions. (p. 358)

Cross offers a four-quadrant model of well-being to further explain his view
on the importance of integrating culture into health care. The four quadrants
he presents are mind, body, spirit, and context. Best health is achieved when
there is a balance across the quadrants. To maximize such a balance one may
focus upon (a) cultural teachings and cognitive processes to help the mind,
(b) foods, sleep, and dance to help the body, (c) rituals and ceremonies to
help the spirit, and (d) family and cultural events to help with context. Each
of these quadrants is addressed, both directly and indirectly, in the following
sections on expectancies, social support, mindfulness, and emotional disclosure reviewed in this chapter.

Expectancies

Research on expectancies as they apply to health began in earnest in the 1960s.
Later, in the 1970s the role of expectancies was often examined within the
framework of Rotter's (1966) work on internal and external locus of control.
Strickland (1978) summarizes these studies and concludes the following:

> Another major finding emerging from this review is that congruence
> of expectancies and situations appears to enhance behavior change.
> Practical implications are that change agents such as health personnel
> will be most effective when techniques are tailored to individual expec-
> tancies. (p. 1205)

Thus, practitioners who are mindful of those for whom they are caring may
yield the best health outcomes by their actions and words. It is apparent that
the relationship the healer and patient develop plays a role in that patient's
course of healing.

Since the 1970s, expectancies have also been discussed in the literature as
being linked to classical conditioning (see Rescorla, 1988; Wickramasekera,
1980) and the placebo effect (see Fish, this volume; Kirsch, 1985; Montgomery

& Kirsch, 1996). Specifically, expectancies, operating within a classical conditioning paradigm, are believed to be mediating factors in placebo anal-
gesia. They are instrumental in the perception of stimuli. Additionally, an
individual's expectancies themselves are moderated by the meaning and
interpretations that person ascribes to their illness—or even their health.
For example, a diagnosis of cancer may yield different thoughts: "cancer is a
death sentence" versus "cancer is a warning for me to slow down and spend
more time with my family."

How an illness is interpreted by an individual, and the faith that person
has in his or her healer (see Rappaport & Rappaport, 1981), is an undeniable
aspect in the healing process. Another important factor is an individual's
perception of control over his or her own health. The belief that one has that
he or she can positively or negatively influence his or her health is a major
variable in actual positive or negative health outcomes, respectively (Ray,
2004; Scheier et al., 1989; see also Fish, this volume).

Arthur Kleinman and his colleagues have focused their research on cross-
cultural understandings of health and illness. Hahn and Kleinman (1983)
address the power of belief and expectations and conclude that "the healing
powers of beliefs and expectations, those socially given and created in a society's
ethnomedicine, constitute the vast and neglected, even stigmatized processes
referred to as the 'placebo phenomenon'" (p. 17). Kleinman, Eisenberg, and
Good (1978) underscore the importance of communication between practitioner and patient in what was termed the "cultural construction of clinical reality." Specifically, practitioners should attempt to assess patients' perspectives
and beliefs about the nature of the presenting problem and then incorporate
this information into treatment recommendations. Further, data from several
research studies in the relatively new field of positive psychology demonstrates
that optimism is related to positive health outcomes (Snyder & Lopez, 2002).

Social Support

Social support has been defined from both a structural and a functional point
of view. A structural view of social support focuses on the actual social network in question, and the functional view focuses on the emotional support
that is available within that network (Uchino, Cacioppo, & Kiecolt-Glaser,
1996). Within both of these social support frameworks, the cardiovascular, immune, and endocrine systems have all been shown to be affected by
changes in social support (Uchino et al., 1996).

The Roseto studies (Bruhn, Chandler, Miller, Wolf, & Lynn, 1966; Bruhn, Philips, & Wolf, 1972; Bruhn, Philips, & Wolf, 1982; Egolf, Lasker, Wolf, & Potvin, 1992; Wolf, 1992) are good examples of highlighting how social support, through a tight-knit community, can act to buffer the risk factors of cardiovascular disease. The Roseto community was featured in several articles over an approximate 25-year span and was of interest to researchers because, although male Roseto residents experienced the same risk factors for heart disease, namely smoking and diet, the males from Roseto died at half the rate of comparable males in an adjacent town. However, over time, intermarriage, eating out, and several other major lifestyle changes resulted in the loss of protection from coronary heart disease and related deaths (for a more detailed overview, see Hirsch, 2004).

In their review of studies on psychological variables related to surgical recovery, Kiecolt-Glaser, Page, Marucha, MacCullum, and Glaser (1998) examined the literature on postsurgical recovery within a psychoneuroimmunology context. They propose several pathways through which psychosocial variables modulate pain, wound healing, and immune system function. One of the main pathways they emphasize as being instrumental in healing is that of social support and interpersonal interactions. Citing contributions by Kulik and colleagues (Kulik & Mahler, 1989; Kulik, Mahler, & Moore, 1996), Kiecolt-Glaser and coworkers reinforce the notion that presurgical interventions require increased interpersonal interactions. Additionally, patients who utilize their social support network heal faster and report less pain than their counterparts who did not have the same access to others in their environment (e.g., Krohne & Slangen, 2005). Further, the quality of the interpersonal interactions within one's support network also seems to mediate postsurgical health outcomes (Fekete, Stephens, & Druley, 2006).

Mindfulness

Jon Kabat-Zinn (e.g., Kabat-Zinn, 1990) was a pioneer in applying mindfulness practice to counter daily stress. He adopted the method of mindfulness, defined as "an intentional focused awareness—a way of paying attention on purpose in the present moment, non-judgmentally" (Center for Mindfulness in Medicine, Healthcare, and Society, 2007)—from his Buddhist training and developed a program whereby he mainstreamed its use to counter the effects of daily stress in the everyday environment. For the first time, mindfulness was available as a complimentary intervention in Western health care. As evidenced by many empirical studies (e.g., Carlson, Speca, Patel, & Goodney, 2003; Davidson et al., 2003; Tacón, Caldera, & Ronaghan, 2004), mindfulness has become associated with successful stress reduction and improved immune system functioning (for the positive effects of Buddhist meditation on psychotherapists' ability to listen attentively and nonjudgmentally to their clients, see Rubin, this volume).

Interestingly, as with the earlier work on expectancies, locus of control is an important factor in mindfulness. To become fully engaged in the mindfulness process, individuals are asked to shift their locus of control to an internal one (Krasner, 2004). The preponderance of evidence within the health psychology literature (notably from Western countries) suggests that individuals with an internal locus of control exhibit better health outcomes than their counterparts who possess an external locus of control. This is not surprising given that an internal locus of control allows individuals to maintain a sense of control over their environment and their health. Indeed, data strongly intimate that it is the perception of control that is important (e.g., Taylor, 1983).

Social support is another integral variable related to mindfulness interventions. For example, mindfulness trainers, in essence, must develop an interpersonal relationship whereby they become "containers" to help their students hold and process the emotions and sensations that arise during their practice (Krasner, 2004). This intimate type of trusting interpersonal relationship that allows one to better access the more remote parts of one's consciousness speaks to its significance in the maintenance of our health. As a testament to the value of mindfulness interventions, the Center for Mindfulness in Medicine, Healthcare, and Society (2006) was established at the University of Massachusetts Medical School in 1979 (formerly known as the Stress Reduction Clinic founded by Kabat-Zinn).

Emotional Disclosure Through Writing

Soon after the first studies that established a connection between the mind and its influence on the immune system (e.g., Ader & Cohen, 1975) were published, Pennebaker (1982, 1997, 2004) began to explore the possibility that suppressing emotions after having suffered a psychological trauma is related to compromised immune system functioning. In one of his early studies (Pennebaker & Beall, 1986), college undergraduates were asked to write essays for four consecutive sessions. Participants were randomly assigned to either a trauma-emotion condition (participants wrote only about the emotional content of their trauma), trauma-fact condition (participants wrote only a fact-laden narrative about their trauma), trauma-combination condition (participants wrote a narrative that contained the facts of their trauma and how they felt about it), or a control group (participants wrote about a trivial topic such as the shoes they were wearing during the writing session). Nine physiological symptoms and eight moods were assessed both before and after each writing session. Additionally, visits to the campus health center were recorded at several different follow-up times over the course of a year and a half.

Overall, participants who disclosed emotional content in writing about their trauma were those who reported the highest levels of negative affect immediately after their writing session but over the long-term were those who made the least visits to the health center. To explain their results, Pennebaker and Beale (1986) provide a framework in which by not disclosing their emotions to another, individuals are increasing their susceptibility to physical stress and subsequent illness by exerting constant psychic energy in emotional suppression (which they characterize as behavioral inhibition). Thus, they argue, writing about one's trauma and its accompanied emotions is one way in which individuals are freeing themselves from the undue stress of engaging in behavioral inhibition.

Results from Pennebaker's subsequent studies (Pennebaker, Colder, & Sharp, 1990; Pennebaker, Kiecolt-Glaser, & Glaser, 1988; Petrie, Booth, & Pennebaker, 1995) have continued to bolster the evidence that disclosing emotional material is related to positive health effects. After having explored the effects of emotional disclosure of past traumatic events on health (Pennebaker & Beall, 1986), Pennebaker et al. (1990) found similar results when participants wrote about their adjustment to college life. Likewise, positive immune system changes (increased proliferation of lymphocytes) were detected and significantly fewer visits were made to the student health center by the students who wrote about their traumatic experiences than students assigned to a control condition (Pennebaker et al., 1988).

Finally, a recent meta-analysis (Frattaroli, 2006), a statistical technique that allows the researcher to combine the results of selected studies, also reinforces the positive role that emotional disclosure plays in health and psychological outcomes. Collectively, the 146 studies included in the meta-analysis indicate that moderators of successful studies tended to use participants with a health problem or participants with a history of trauma, to make sure participants were very comfortable during disclosure (e.g., by allowing them to disclose at home), to pay participants, to administer a large dose of disclosure (e.g., by requiring at least three disclosure sessions), to have participants disclose events that had yet to be fully processed (e.g., more recent events), to provide very detailed and specific disclosure instructions (e.g., directed questions), and to have relatively short follow-up periods (e.g., less than 1 month). (p. 860)

Not surprisingly, disclosing the emotional meaning of trauma through writing has been linked to health improvement in several different specific areas. Low, Stanton, and Danoff-Burg (2006) examined the effects of emotional disclosure as it related to a diagnosis of breast cancer. Women diagnosed with either Stage I or Stage II cancer were randomly assigned to one of three conditions: to write about their "deepest thoughts and feelings," to write about their positive perceptions about their cancer diagnosis, or to write about just the facts about their cancer and treatment (control group). Participants wrote for 20 minutes in four consecutive sessions. In addition to having their heart rate (HR; used as measure of autonomic activity) assessed during each writing session, they also provided information on medical visits and self-report of physical symptoms. Low et al. report that HR habituation (i.e., diminished heart rate reactivity) was greatest for the emotion-focused group of women and those women who reported greatest physical symptoms also reported the most medical appointments. Overall, their data suggest that health improvements were related to autonomic habituation to emotional disclosure.

Rheumatoid arthritis has also been shown to be affected by emotional disclosure. Kelley, Lumley, and Leisen (1997) recruited 72 participants afflicted with rheumatoid arthritis. Over four sessions, those assigned to the disclosure group were asked to verbally disclose into a tape recorder their most stressful trauma or "upheaval," past or present, while controls were asked to view a neutral stimulus and then describe it. Mood and changes in health status were also assessed. As found in other related studies on emotional disclosure, data suggest that participants in the disclosure group initially experienced greater negative mood affectivity than they experienced at follow-up (3-month average).

Obstacles to the Use of Holistic Applications

Western medicine has made great strides in its efforts to better understand and even incorporate other healing modalities into its framework. Yet, despite these efforts and the plethora of research that continues to explore and expand our knowledge of the mechanisms of the psychoneuroimmunological system that exists, there remain roadblocks to their use. Astin, Soeken, Sierpina, and Clarridge (2006) discuss several of these based upon their survey findings from physicians. Physicians were asked to complete survey questionnaires that assessed whether or not they actively incorporate mind–body techniques into their practice and their beliefs about the efficacy of various techniques. Perhaps not surprisingly, more than 85% of the respondents reported that they do not employ mind–body methods due to insufficient insurance reimbursement.

Likewise, patients too are sensitive to factors that affect their health care. Bloom (2005) explains that patient dissatisfaction, as assessed in many studies, stems from the lack of interpersonal contact with their practitioners. Given the established importance of expectancies and social support in the healing process, traditional Western medicine falls short in its effort to help others. Western biomedical practices indeed attempt to treat the "problem" (i.e., viruses, bacteria, cancer, etc.), but they fail at treating the *person.*

A Hopeful Future

The benefits of conceptualizing illness from a biopsychosocial perspective, as opposed to a biomedical one, extend beyond the boundaries of its prevention and the maintenance of health. For example, Sussman (2001), in her review of Magnusson's (1988, 1989; Magnusson & Stattin, 1998) holistic model of development, gives a thorough review of how incorporating "the reciprocal and holistic interactions that transpire between biological, psychological, and social-contextual processes" (p. 164) has resulted in gains that deepen our understanding of the development of antisocial behavior. Levenstein (2002) properly notes that there has been a dramatic decline in the literature that once highlighted psychosomatic connections to peptic ulcer and ulcerative colitis due to a movement toward "physiological reductionism." However, she maintains that a biopsychosocial model of understanding these gastrointestinal problems is warranted on the grounds of recent research findings. Stress and its psychophysiological and behavioral mediators have been shown to play a role in the course of these chronic conditions.

Acknowledging and understanding that individuals interpret their health and illness based upon the social context within which they operate is of utmost importance. The key to proper implementation of different healing methodologies is that the patient/client believes (via expectancies and social support) that the healer has the ability to guide him or her back toward health. It is therefore encouraging that more and more medical school and residency programs now teach their students about the mind–body connection. Cultural sensitivity is essential in this realm. The aforementioned initiative by the U.S. government to further explore and have practitioners utilize effective mind–body applications (National Institutes of Health, 2002) also adds to the hopeful future of a more holistic approach to health.

This chapter represents just a fraction of what has been published on the topic of healing as it is influenced by the intersection of one's biological, psychological, and social systems. Our immune, hormone, endocrine systems, social support networks, and ability to psychologically process and be mindful of events that we experience have inextricable effects on one another. In the end, the message to be taken from the plethora of empirical findings is that our conceptualization of healing still requires a shift from "someone's *body* is ill" to a more holistic–whole individual approach.

References

Ader, R., & Cohen, N. (1975). Behaviorally conditioned immunosuppression. *Psychosomatic Medicine, 37,* 333–340.

Ader, R., & Cohen, N., & Felten, D. (1995). Psychoneuroimmunology: Interactions between the nervous system and the immune system. *The Lancet, 345,* 99–103.

Astin, J., Soeken, K., Sierpina, V. S., & Clarridge, B. R. (2006). Barriers to the integration of psychosocial factors in medicine: Results of a national survey of physicians. *Journal of the American Board of Family Medicine, 19,* 557–565.

Baum, A., Gatchel, R. J., & Krantz, D. S. (1997). *An introduction to health psychology* (3rd ed.). New York: McGraw-Hill.

Bloom, M. V. (2005). Origins of healing: An evolutionary perspective of healing practices. *Families, Systems, and Health, 23,* 251–260.

Brannon, L., & Feist, J. (1997). *Health psychology: An introduction to behavior and health* (3rd ed.). Pacific Grove, CA: Brooks/Cole.

Bruhn, J. G., Chandler, B., Miller, M. C., Wolf, S., & Lynn, T. N. (1966). Social aspects of coronary heart disease in two adjacent, ethnically different communities. *American Journal of Public Health: Nations Health, 56,* 1493–1506.

Bruhn, J. G., Philips, B. U., & Wolf, S. (1972). Social readjustment and illness patterns: Comparisons between first, second and third generation Italian-Americans living in the same community. *Journal of Psychosomatic Medicine, 16,* 387–394.

Bruhn, J. G., Philips, B. U., & Wolf, S. (1982). Lessons from Roseto 20 years later: A community study of heart disease. *Southern Medical Journal, 75,* 575–580.

Carlson, L. E., Speca, M., Patel, K. D., & Goodney, E. (2003). Mindfulness-based stress reduction in relation to quality of life, mood, symptoms of stress, and immune parameters in breast and prostate cancer outpatients. *Psychosomatic Medicine, 65,* 571–581.

Center for Mindfulness in Medicine, Healthcare, and Society. (n.d.). Retrieved February 5, 2007, from http://www.umassmed.edu/cfm/history.aspx

Center for Mindfulness in Medicine, Healthcare, and Society. (n.d.). Retrieved October 10, 2006, from http://www.umassmed.edu/cfm/index.aspx

Coulehan, J. (2005). Empathy and narrativity: A commentary on "Origins of Healing: An Evolutionary Perspective of the Healing Process." *Families, Systems, and Health, 23,* 261–265.

Cross, T. L. (2003). Culture as a resource for mental health. *Cultural Diversity and Ethnic Minority Psychology, 9,* 354–359.

Davidson, R., Kabat-Zinn, J., Schumacher, J., Rosenkranz, M., Muller, D., Santorelli, S. F., et al. (2003). Alterations in brain and immune function produced by mindfulness. *Psychosomatic Medicine, 65,* 564–570.

Egolf, B., Lasker, J., Wolf, S., & Potvin, L. (1992). The Roseto effect: A 50-year comparison of mortality rates. *American Journal of Public Health, 82,* 1089–1092.

Eisenberg, D. M., Kessler, R. C., Foster, C. Norlock, F. E., Clakins, D. R., & Delbanco, T. L. (1993). Unconventional medicine in the United States—Prevalence, costs, and patterns of use. *New England Journal of Medicine, 328,* 246–252.

Fekete, E. M., Stephens, M. A. P., & Druley, J. A. (2006). Effects of spousal control and support on older adults' recovery from knee surgery. *Journal of Family Psychology, 20,* 302–310.

Frattaroli, J. (2006). Experimental disclosure and its moderators: A meta-analysis. *Psychological Bulletin, 132,* 823–865.

Hahn, R., & Kleinman, A. (1983). Belief as pathogen belief as medicine: "Voodoo death" and the "placebo phenomenon" in anthropological perspective. *Medical Anthropology Quarterly, 14,* 3–19.

Hirsch, M. S. (2004). A biopsychosocial perspective on cross-cultural healing. In U. P. Gielen, J. Fish, & J. G. Draguns (Eds.), *Handbook of culture, therapy, and healing* (pp. 83–99). Mahwah, NJ: Lawrence Erlbaum Associates.

Jian-Lan, J., Yi-Hua, Q., Yu-Ping, P., & Jian-Jun, W. (2006). Immunoregulatory role of endogenous catecholemines synthesized by immune cells. *Acta Physiologica Sinica, 58,* 309–317.

Kabat-Zinn, J. (1990). *Full catastrophe living: Using the wisdom of your body and mind to face stress, pain and illness.* New York: Dell.

Katz, R. (1982). Utilizing traditional healing systems. *American Psychologist, 37,* 715–716.

Kelley, J. E., Lumley, M. A., & Leisen, J. C. C. (1997). Health effects of emotional disclosure in rheumatoid arthritis patients. *Health Psychology, 16,* 331–340.

Kiecolt-Glaser, J. K., McGuire, L., Robles, T. F., & Glaser, R. (2002). Psychoneuroimmunology and psychosomatic medicine: Back to the future. *Psychosomatic Medicine, 64,* 15–28.

Kiecolt-Glaser, J. K., Page, G. G., Marucha, P. T., MacCullum, R. C., & Glaser, R. (1998). Psychological influences on surgical recovery: Perspectives from psychoneuroimmunology. *American Psychologist, 53,* 1209–1218.

Kirsch, I. (1985). Response expectancy as a determinant of experience and behavior. *American Psychologist, 40,* 1189–1202.

Kleinman, A., Eisenberg, L., & Good, B. (1978). Culture, illness, and care: Clinical lessons from anthropologic and cross-cultural research. *Annals of Internal Medicine, 88,* 251–258.

Krasner, M. (2004). Mindfulness-based interventions: A coming of age? *Families, Systems, & Health, 22,* 207–212.

Krohne, H. W., & Slangen, K. E. (2005). Influence of support on adaptation to surgery. *Health Psychology, 24,* 101–105.

Kulik, J. A., & Mahler, H. I. (1989). Social support and recovery from surgery. *Health Psychology, 8,* 221–238.

Kulik, J. A., Mahler, H. I., & Moore, P. J. (1996). Social comparison and affiliation under threat: Effects on recovery from major surgery. *Journal of Personality and Social Psychology, 71,* 967–979.

Levenstein, S. (2002). Psychosocial factors in peptic ulcer and inflammatory bowel disease. *Journal of Consulting and Clinical Psychology, 70,* 739–750.

Low, C. A., Stanton, A. L., & Danoff-Burg. (2006). Expressive disclosure and benefit finding among breast cancer patients: Mechanisms for positive health effects. *Health Psychology, 25,* 181–189.

Magnusson, D. (1988). Individual development from an interactional perspective. In D. Magnusson (Ed.), *Paths through life* (Vol. 1). Hillsdale, NJ: Erlbaum.

Magnusson, D. (1999). Holistic interactionism: A perspective for research on personality development. In L. A. Pervin & O. P. John (Eds.), *Handbook of personality: Theory and research* (2nd ed.). New York: Guilford.

Magnusson, D., & Stattin, H. (1998). Person-context interaction theories. In W. Damon & R. M. Lerner (Eds.), *Handbook of child psychology. Volume 1: Theoretical models of human development.* New York: Wiley.

Montgomery, G. H., & Kirsch, I. (1996). Classical conditioning and the placebo effect. *Pain, 72,* 107–113.

National Institutes of Health. (2002). *White House Commission on Complementary and Alternative Medicine Policy, Final Report* (NIH Publication 03-5411). Washington, DC: U.S. Government Printing Office.

Pennebaker, J. W. (1982). *The psychology of physical symptoms.* New York: Springer-Verlag.

Pennebaker, J. W. (1997). *The healing power of expressing emotions.* New York: Guilford.

Pennebaker, J. W. (2004). *Writing to heal.* Oakland, CA: New Harbinger.

Pennebaker, J. W., & Beall, S. K. (1986). Confronting a traumatic event: Toward an understanding of inhibition and disease. *Journal of Abnormal Psychology, 95,* 274–281.

Pennebaker, J. W., Colder, M., & Sharp, L. K. (1990). Accelerating the coping process. *Journal of Personality and Social Psychology, 58,* 528–537.

Pennebaker, J. W., Kiecolt-Glaser, J., & Glaser, R. (1988). Disclosure of traumas and immune function: Health implications for psychotherapy. *Journal of Consulting and Clinical Psychology, 56,* 239–245.

Petrie, K., Booth, R., & Pennebaker, J. W. (1995). Disclosure of traumas and immune response to a hepatitis B vaccination program. *Journal of Consulting and Clinical Psychology, 63,* 787–792.

Pozo, D., & Delgado, M. (2004). The many faces of VIP in neuroimmunology: A cytokine rather than a peptide? *The FASEB Journal, 18,* 1325–1334.

Rappaport, H., & Rappaport, M. (1981). The integration of scientific and traditional healing. *American Psychologist, 36,* 774–781.

Ray, O. (2004). How the mind hurts and heals the body. *American Psychologist, 59,* 29–40.

Rescorla, R. A. (1988). Pavlovian conditioning: It's not what you think it is. *American Psychologist, 43,* 151–160.

Rotter, J. B. (1966). Generalized expectancies for internal versus external control of reinforcement. *Psychological Monographs, 80*(1, Whole No. 609).

Salovey, P., Rothman, A. J., Detweiler, J. B., & Steward, W. T. (2000). Emotional states and physical health. *American Psychologist, 55,* 110–121.

Scheier, M. F., Matthews, K. A., Owens, J. F., Magovern, G. J., Sr., Lefebvre, R. C., Abbott, R. A., et al. (1989). Dispositional optimism and recovery from coronary artery bypass surgery: The beneficial effects on physical and psychological well-being. *Journal of Personality and Social Psychology, 57,* 1024–1040.

Snyder, C. R., & Lopez, S. J. (2002). *Handbook of positive psychology.* New York: Oxford University Press.

Strickland, B. R. (1978). Internal-external expectancies and health-related behaviors. *Journal of Consulting and Clinical Psychology, 46,* 1192–1211.

Sussman, E. J. (2001). Mind-body interaction and development: Biology, behavior and context. *European Psychologist, 6,* 163–171.

Tacón, A. M., Caldera, Y. M., & Ronaghan, C. (2004). Mindfulness-based stress reduction in women with brain cancer. *Families, Systems, & Health, 22,* 193–203.

Taylor, S. E. (1983). Adjustment to threatening events: A theory of cognitive adaptation. *American Psychologist, 38,* 1161–1173.

Taylor, S. E. (1999). *Health psychology* (4th ed.). Boston: McGraw-Hill.

Uchino, B. N., Cacioppo, J. T., & Kiecolt-Glaser, J. K. (1996). The relationship between social support and physiological processes: A review with emphasis on underlying mechanisms. *Psychological Bulletin, 119,* 488–531.

Wickramasekera, I. (1980). A conditioned response model of the placebo effect: Predictions from the model. *Biofeedback and Self-Regulation, 5,* 5–18.

Wickramasekera, I., Davies, T. E., & Davies, S. M. (1996). Applied psychophysiology: A bridge between the biomedical model and the biopsychosocial model in family medicine. *Professional Psychology: Research and Practice, 27,* 221–233.

Wolf, S. (1992). Predictors of myocardial infarction over a span of 30 years in Roseto, Pennsylvania. *Integrated Physiological Behavior Science, 27,* 246–257.

Suggested Readings

Ader, R. (2005). On the clinical relevance of psychoneuroimmunology. In K. Vedhara & M. Irwin (Eds.), *Introduction to human psychoneuroimmunology* (pp. 343–349).Oxford: Oxford University Press.

Reading on the applied nature of psychoneuroimmunology. (NB: The edited book itself is a wonderful resource with theoretical, empirical, and practical issues concerning psychoneuroimmunology.)

Germer, C. K., Siegel, R. D., & Fulton, P. R. (Eds.). (2005). *Mindfulness and psychotherapy*. New York: Guilford.

This volume is designed for the practitioner who wishes to introduce mindfulness techniques into his or her practice.

Grawe, K. (2006). *Neuropsychotherapy: How the neurosciences inform effective psychotherapy*. Mahwah, NJ: Lawrence Erlbaum Associates.

Kabat-Zinn, J. (1994). *Wherever you go, there you are: Mindfulness meditation in everyday life*. New York: Hyperion.

An introduction to mindfulness meditation and its applications.

Lepore, S. J. J., & Smyth, J. M. (Eds.). (2002). *The writing cure: How expressive writing promotes health and emotional well-being*. Washington, DC: American Psychological Association.

Edited book with chapters written by experts from various areas discussing the positive health effects of emotional disclosure through writing. Specific topics such as cancer, stress, memory, children's narrative, and late life-span issues are addressed.

Pennebaker, J. W. (1997). *Opening up: The healing power of expressing emotions*. New York: Guilford Press.

Written for the layperson, Pennebaker's book divulges over a decade's worth of research in an easy-to-read and easy-to-understand format. Useful as a bibliotherapy resource.

Pressman, S. D., & Cohen, S. (2005). Does positive affect influence health? *Psychological Bulletin, 131*, 925–971.

Review of the sparse literature on positive affect. Both the pros and cons of positive affect as it can affect health are discussed.

6

Professional Ethics in Multicultural and International Context

Michael J. Stevens

It [a code of ethics] should be a grand statement of overarching principles that earn the respect of the public by reflecting the profession's moral integrity. (Bersoff, 2003, p. 1)

Contents

Introduction

Psychologists, counselors, and social workers operate in richly diverse and rapidly changing environments. The ambiguities and complexities of contemporary professional practice require ethical principles, based on values, to ensure that these professionals do no harm. Moreover, practitioners are challenged increasingly to enhance the welfare of the public, a public that has become more varied in culture and international in scope. One response to this challenge is the collaboration of the American Psychological Association's (APA) Ethics Office, Office of International Affairs, and Science and Practice Directorates to develop educational materials on the ethical issues pertaining to research and intervention in response to disasters and emergencies.

Regrettably, the call for ethical principles to guide multicultural and international practice is offset by standards of conduct geared toward avoiding disciplinary action and litigation. Such protectionism is exemplified by the APA's guidelines for outreach programs at its 2006 meeting in New Orleans, a city recovering from Hurricane Katrina. These guidelines spell out familiar cautions: "Any kind of direct service provision, no matter how brief, can raise ethical issues of informed consent, record keeping, transfer and termination" (Jordan, 2006). Members are advised to limit their community assistance to educational presentations and not undertake activities that could be construed as professional service. The specter of being in violation of ethical and legal mandates appears to trump the need and opportunity for more comprehensive, socially responsible service, in this instance, to a vulnerable public comprised largely of lower-income African Americans. The APA's approach to ethical practice, like that of other professional associations, remains conservative, hierarchical, and self-serving. Ironically, although they are expected to provide culturally competent services, ambiguous ethical principles coupled with rigid standards of conduct often hamper practitioners when working with diverse populations, especially those in nontraditional settings who are confronting extraordinary life circumstances. Internationally, the disconnect between ideal and real practice is even greater (e.g., tsunami relief, the interrogation of military detainees) and can leave practitioners feeling confused, frustrated, and hesitant to work internationally where their knowledge and skills are needed. Social service professionals are hand-tied as they seek to fulfill their duty to improve lives while adhering to standards that support the status quo (Pack-Brown & Williams, 2003; Pedersen, 2002; Pettifor, 2001, 2005; Prilleltensky, 1997; Sue & Sue, 2003). Professional associations are at a crossroad: The growing demand for effective multicultural and international interventions requires that ethical principles and standards evolve in order to facilitate the competencies of multicultural and international practitioners. Multicultural and international competence is a necessary but insufficient condition for ethical practice in today's world.

I begin this chapter by examining the relationship between values and professional ethics as well as the ethical values of master therapists. I then evaluate components of the most recent versions of ethics codes of the APA, American Counseling Association, and National Association of Social Workers that bear on multicultural and international practice. I review the guidance that each code offers to practitioners who work with culturally diverse persons and/or in international settings. I highlight how the wording of ethics codes either facilitates or impedes effective multicultural and international practice. I also report progress on the *Universal Declaration of Ethical Principles for Psychologists* (Gauthier, 2005), a draft document that presents a common framework to guide scientific and applied work worldwide.

Next, I summarize the prevailing models of ethical decision making and describe an alternative approach built upon the tenets of social constructionism. Social constructionism in ethical decision making is well suited to the ethical ambiguities and conflicts of multicultural and international practice because it places considerable weight on universal values, collaborative interaction, contextual factors, and language. I end the chapter with two case examples that illustrate how social constructionism can guide the resolution of ethical dilemmas frequently encountered in multicultural and international practice.

Values and Ethics

Ethics codes tend to steer clear of such concepts as goodness, rectitude, and morality (Tjeltveit, 2000). Not only does the role of morality in secular, pluralistic societies stir debate, but the social service professions have taken a dim, if not hostile, view toward morality as well. McFall (1991) advocated for a professional practice based entirely on empirically based science. Yet, science cannot guide practice goals that are worthwhile or methods that are appropriate in multicultural and international contexts. The founders of various schools of psychotherapy also posited adverse outcomes from cleaving to moral values (e.g., intrapunitive superego, conditions of worth, irrational beliefs). Yet, these claims are themselves tied to moral convictions.

Ethical principles and standards of conduct are tacit statements about behavior governed by values. Ethics codes obtain from normative values. Normative values are constructed through everyday interactions within a community that occur repeatedly over generations. Over time, established interactional patterns become distilled and symbolized in language, and reflect a community's history, religion, and culture. In turn, a community's values charter new norms of social interaction, including the discourse that characterizes professional relationships. Insisting on moral neutrality places practitioners and recipients of their services at a disadvantage. That is, the values that underlie ethical practice remain implicit, inaccessible, unexamined, and unavailable when resolving dilemmas that arise in the ambiguous, novel, and complex circumstances of multicultural and international practice. The advance of multiculturalism and globalization reminds social service professionals that values permeate virtually all aspects of practice and that dialogue is essential in refining the moral foundation of ethical views and reasoning (Tjeltveit, 2000).

According to Paul Pedersen (2002), professional ethics are guided by relativism ("To each his or her own"), absolutism ("Mine is best"), or dynamic universalism ("We are both the same yet different"). Relativism attempts to understand values and their culture-bound expression, and abstains from judgments of right or wrong because values rest on cultural tradition. Absolutism maintains that there is one moral compass expressed similarly across cultures, no matter how different; ethical action is based on uniformly applied principles. Universalism holds that, although core values may be shared by different cultures (e.g., nonmaleficence, beneficence, justice, fidelity, responsibility), they are manifested in culturally specific ways. Universalism in multicultural and international practice requires an understanding of underlying similarities and observable differences, that is, the ability to enter with openness and respect into another culture while remaining cognizant of one's values and their potential impact (Frame & Williams, 2005). Accordingly, universalism gives practitioners a foundation upon which to tailor ethical principles to distinct multicultural and international challenges. It encourages practitioners not only to operate within existing ethical principles, but also to frame those principles in ways that are congruent with the multicultural and/or international realities in which they are applied (Pack-Brown & Williams, 2003).

As an approach to professional ethics, universalism resonates with virtue ethics. Virtue ethics take a moral view of professional activity and respect the cultural expression of generally held values (Meara, Schmidt, & Day, 1996). Virtue ethics demand the exercise of professional judgment as an antidote to insensitive, formulaic prescriptions for conduct. Thus, consideration must always be given to how general ethical principles are interpreted and applied.

The preceding suggests that ethics codes be applied flexibly to serve a diverse public well. This view dovetails with research showing that 77% of senior psychologists believed that standards of conduct should be broken in favor of values if it would benefit clients (Pope & Bajt, 1988). In a qualitative study of master practitioners in psychology, social work, and psychiatry representing different therapeutic traditions, Jennings, Sovereign, Bottorff, Mussell, and Vye (2005) identified nine values on which these experts rely, which the authors clustered into two categories: building and maintaining interpersonal attachments (relational connections, beneficence, autonomy, and nonmaleficence) and building and maintaining expertise (competence, humility, openness to complexity and ambiguity, and self-awareness). The four values nested within interpersonal attachments highlight a respect for clients. Deference to the worldview of another culture strengthens the professional relationship, makes available additional services, empowers the client or community, and, presumably, avoids inflicting harm. However, implementing values in diverse cultural contexts can challenge or violate professional norms that define, for instance, confidential and dual relationships and bartering and accepting gifts for services rendered. The four values associated with building and maintaining expertise underscore a vision of competence that grows rather than remains stagnant and is mutually determined rather than hierarchically imposed. Eschewing an attitude of omniscience, continually seeking new knowledge and skills, appreciating the intricacies of working with culturally diverse populations, and recognizing when personal issues intrude into professional practice promote multicultural and international competence. Perhaps it is in the interpersonal realm, in which multicultural and international practice occurs, where universalism or virtue ethics conflict with restrictive standards of conduct. Such conflicts must be resolved through value-oriented decision making (Pack-Brown & Williams, 2003).

Codes of Ethics

Ethics codes serve to educate practitioners about appropriate professional conduct, ensure professional accountability, and enhance the effectiveness of teaching, research, practice, and public service (Herlihy & Watson, 2003; Kocet, 2006; Pack-Brown & Williams, 2003; Pedersen, 2002). Ethics codes have been severely criticized for failing to address many issues related to appropriate multicultural practice (Freud & Krug, 2002; Herlihy & Watson, 2003; Pack-Brown & Williams, 2003; Pedersen, 2002; Pettifor, 2001, 2005; Sue & Sue, 2003). Moreover, there is no published literature evaluating the relevance of ethics codes to international practice. Some of the criticisms have been strident; others are more muted. All are timely and underscore a commitment to eliminate poor or harmful multicultural and international practice (e.g., revictimization through professional insensitivity or intolerance).

Recently, many ethics codes have been revised. Thus, it is important to reevaluate the most recent iteration of these codes as to the guidance they provide for working with diverse persons in nontraditional settings. Rather than find fault, I examine the contributions of each code to ethical multicultural and international practice, identifying former weaknesses that have been modified and principles and standards that direct international work. Because an exhaustive analysis of ethics codes is not possible here, I focus on the guidance that each code offers in its general statements and principles and in its standards of conduct that subsume competence, the professional relationship, confidentiality, and assessment and diagnosis.

American Psychological Association

The *Ethical Principles of Psychologists and Code of Conduct* (American Psychological Association, 2002) consists of an introduction, preamble, five general principles, and 10 sets of ethical standards (see Table 6.1).

General Statements and Principles

The APA's code contains an expanded introduction that covers activities related to public service, policy development, and social intervention. Though vague, the code establishes that psychology has a key societal role and by implication is a multidisciplinary partner in serving the public. The introduction notes that qualifiers (e.g., *reasonably*, *potentially*) have been added throughout in order to encourage professional judgment and avoid rigid application of the code to novel or changing circumstances. The introduction allows psychologists "to consider other materials or guidelines that have been adopted or endorsed by scientific and professional psychological organizations and

TABLE 6.1
Ethical Principles of Psychologists and Code of Conduct (APA, 2002)

Introduction and Applicability

Preamble

General Principles

   Principle A: Beneficence and Maleficence

   Principle B: Fidelity and Responsibility

   Principle C: Integrity

   Principle D: Justice

   Principle E: Respect for People's Rights and Dignity

Ethical Standards

1. Resolving Ethical Issues
2. Competence
3. Human Relations
4. Privacy and Confidentiality
5. Advertising and Other Public Statements
6. Record Keeping and Fees
7. Education and Training
8. Research and Publication
9. Assessment
10. Therapy

the dictates of their own conscience" (American Psychological Association, 2002, p. 2). This passage acknowledges that the 1992 code was inadequate to the demands of multicultural and international practice; it invites psychologists to draw upon a wider array of resources in making ethical decisions generally, not merely in instances of conflict between the code and the law. It also states that psychologists may trust in moral values when resolving ethical dilemmas, although it does not condone responsible disobedience when ethical and legal standards preclude what is best for clients.

Principle D on justice is new and calls on psychologists not to engage in or condone unjust practices. However, Principle E on respect for people's rights and dignity contains language that accentuates the individual over the community, mirroring a subtle ethnocentrism that permeates the code. For example, Principle E asserts that, "Psychologists respect . . . the rights of individuals to privacy, confidentiality, and self-determination" (American Psychological Association, 2002, p. 4), wording which overlooks evidence of cultural variation within these domains. Likewise, it is *people's*, rather than *peoples'*, rights and dignity that the code inspires psychologists to respect; the placement of the apostrophe conveys insensitivity to entire groups (the principle on respect for the dignity of persons and peoples in the ethics code of the New Zealand Psychological Society [2002] is the only known principle to formalize group rights). Ironically, Principle E later reminds psychologists "to protect the rights and welfare of persons and *communities* [italics added for emphasis]" (American Psychological Association, 2002, p. 4), an exhortation also set forth in the preamble.

Competence

Section 2.01b expects psychologists to remedy deficiencies in competence when an understanding of age, gender, race, ethnicity, national origin, religion, sexual orientation, disability, socioeconomic status, and/or culture is essential to effective service. Yet, Section 3.01 on *unfair* discrimination implies that there are occasions when psychologists may discriminate fairly on the basis of sociodemographic variables. The ambiguous language of this standard contrasts with the clarity of two overarching principles: Principle A on beneficence and nonmaleficence and Principle E on respect for people's rights and dignity.

Sections 2.01d and 2.02 on the boundaries of competence and on providing services in emergencies are new to the 2002 code. Consistent with Principle D, which presses for universal access to psychological services, psychologists may offer such services when they are not available or are interrupted following natural and human-inspired disasters. Although psychologists with closely aligned training are permitted to serve the public, the code waives this requirement in emergencies. Some view this exception as the APA's tolerance of inferior services and noncompliance with its general stance toward competent practice (Pedersen, 2002; Sue & Sue, 2003). Although not directly stated, this standard presumes that competencies can be transferred to diverse contexts, but warns that psychologists must exert sensitivity and conclude their work quickly if unable to remedy deficiencies in specific knowledge and skills. It allows psychologists to intervene in domestic and international disasters that cry out for humanitarian assistance. Regrettably, legal constraints prevent psychologists from fulfilling their moral obligation to help those in need, as in the case of citizens suffering the effects of Hurricane Katrina. The introduction to the APA code places psychologists, regardless of their competence to provide emergency services, in an ethical bind by supporting their moral conviction to assist those in need while discouraging them from practicing where they are not licensed.

Professional Relationships

A significant update to the APA's code appears in Section 3.05a, which defines multiple relationships for the first time: "Multiple relationships that would not reasonably be expected to cause impairment or risk exploitation or harm are not unethical" (American Psychological Association, 2002, p. 6). Although this standard grants more freedom to determine the appropriateness of multiple relationships, the double negative phrasing argues tentatively for their ethical legitimacy. A more strongly worded standard would acknowledge that multiple relationships are normative in many cultures and countries, and view psychologists who enter such relationships as having exerted sound ethical judgment. Similarly, in Section 6.06 on bartering, a tradition in cultures whose economy is less dependent on money, the exchange of goods or services for psychological services is no longer considered as having inherent potential to damage the professional relationship. Although the code authorizes psychologists to use professional judgment, its case for bartering is weak, again indicating limited appreciation of the economic realities of multicultural and international practice. Gift giving is common in many Asian communities, where it is a means of showing respect and gratitude and of cementing a relationship. Refusing a gift is viewed as an insult. Although psychologists generally refrain from accepting gifts, the

APA standards give little assistance in knowing how to balance concern for the integrity of the professional relationship against appreciation of the cultural meaning that gift giving has for the client. Section 10.02 would not preclude establishing an unorthodox professional relationship with a culturally diverse couple or family provided that the psychologist clarifies the relationship, roles, and services. However, this standard does not delineate the accommodations needed to ensure a trusting professional relationship with couples and families in multicultural or international contexts. Only by creatively interpreting the standard's ambiguity can a weak case be made for its multicultural and international applicability.

Confidentiality

Sections 3.10 on informed consent, 9.03c on informed consent in assessments, and 10.01 on informed consent to therapy, and all of Section 4 on privacy and confidentiality, suggest that more than one person can give consent and that informed consent documents should be couched in comprehensible language, with the aid of an interpreter if necessary. However, these standards reflect a mainly individualistic worldview and nowhere cite alternative cultural constructions of consent, privacy, and confidentiality (e.g., marriage counseling with a Middle Eastern couple may preclude meeting alone with the wife, unless her husband consents and is informed later of what transpired). Not surprisingly, these standards are highly legalistic, given the need for compatibility between the code and state laws, most of which define consent, confidentiality, and privacy in unambiguous and conventional ways.

Assessment and Diagnosis

Section 9 contains several new or modified standards that evince greater sensitivity in multicultural and international assessment. Sections 9.02b and 9.02c require psychologists to administer measures whose psychometric properties have been established for the population being tested and to employ methods that are compatible with respondents' preferred language. Though laudable, these standards, like most of Section 9, do not make plain the need for instruments that are properly translated, validated, and standardized for multicultural and international use. Culture is mentioned once in Section 9.06, in which the current code expects psychologists to interpret test results from the perspective of culture and language, and to report any related limitations to the veracity of their interpretation. Section 9.10 now authorizes psychologists to take reasonable steps to share assessment findings with a respondent's designated representative, although it is unclear whether this standard would permit psychologists to disclose test results to a culturally diverse person's family.

Overall, the *Ethical Principles of Psychologists and Code of Conduct* (American Psychological Association, 2002) appears situated in the European American tradition of individualism and legalism. The general principles combine a somewhat stronger commitment to multiculturalism with an insufficient appreciation of the centrality of group identity and the meaning conveyed by language. Regrettably, the general principles no longer include social responsibility, wherein psychologists were to mitigate human suffering and advance the welfare of communities. Although the standards of conduct acknowledge the diverse nature of contemporary professional practice, they contain inconsistencies and offer little guidance for multicultural and international work. Their strength lies in a more accommodating position on multiple relationships, but their application often leaves psychologists to their own devices. The code is especially deficient in addressing international issues, such as practicing across national borders, collaborating with governments and nongovernmental organizations (NGOs), and adopting nontraditional work roles.

American Counseling Association

The *Code of Ethics* (American Counseling Association, 2005) consists of a preamble, statement of purpose, eight sections each with an aspirational introduction followed by standards of conduct, and a glossary of terms (see Table 6.2).

General Statements and Principles

The preamble of the code holds that counselors recognize diversity and "embrace a cross-cultural approach in support of . . . people within their social and cultural contexts" (p. 3). Compared to the 1995 code and ethics codes of other social service professions, the preamble reflects a more collectivistic worldview, replacing *each individual* with *people* (like the APA's code, the ACA's reliance on the singular fails to recognize entire groups), accentuating the diverse contexts in which people are situated and underscoring a dialogic approach to improving their quality of life. The preamble also invites counselors to serve in multiple capacities, foreshadowing later provisions that permit nontraditional roles.

TABLE 6.2 Code of Ethics (ACA, 2005)
Preamble
Purpose
Section A: The Counseling Relationship
Section B: Confidentiality, Privileged Communication, and Privacy
Section C: Professional Responsibility
Section D: Relationships with Other Professionals
Section E: Evaluation, Assessment, and Interpretation
Section F: Supervision, Training, and Teaching
Section G: Research and Publication
Section H: Resolving Ethical Issues
Glossary of Terms

The introduction to Section A contains two aspirational statements. Beyond understanding the cultures of those whom they serve, Section A advises counselors "to explore their own cultural identities and how these affect their values and beliefs about the counseling process" (American Counseling Association, 2005, p. 4). These statements unite a core ethical principle with two dimensions of multicultural competence: awareness of the client's worldview and the counselor's values and biases (Herlihy & Watson, 2003; Sue & Sue, 2003). Section B asserts the importance of discussing confidentiality with sensitivity and skill in order to establish trust with culturally diverse persons. Section C legitimizes advocacy as a professional activity through which to remove barriers and improve lives, although the relevance of advocacy in serving marginalized and disadvantaged populations is not made explicit. The code encourages multidisciplinary collaboration in Section D, indirectly supporting what counselors in international practice have long known: Intervening appropriately in multiply determined phenomena-in-context demands the perspective and cooperation of allied professionals (Stevens & Gielen, 2007). Finally, Section E makes cultural sensitivity in the use of assessment devices paramount and inseparable from the welfare of those who are assessed.

Competence

Sections C.2.a on boundaries of competence and C.2.f on continuing education expect counselors to refine the awareness, sensitivity, and skills needed to serve diverse populations. Although these standards demand more than the 1995 commitment to become culturally competent, they do not define the boundaries of multicultural and international competence with precision. Counselors are thrust into a paradox: Do no harm by operating within existing competencies, but stretch the boundaries of competence to serve diverse populations in need (e.g., working in tandem with an indigenous healer to relieve a client's somatic symptoms of depression; Herlihy & Watson, 2003; Pettifor, 2005). However, Section A.1.c charges counselors to work with clients to devise interventions that are compatible with their circumstances, implying autonomy when adapting their practice to diverse populations and settings. Section A.1.d also supports multicultural competence by recognizing cultural variations in social support and permitting counselors to determine with their clients the appropriateness of involving family and community members in treatment.

Professional Relationships

Section A.2.c vaguely directs counselors to modify informed consent procedures when these threaten to undermine the professional relationship by conflicting with cultural traditions. Although prohibited from developing nonprofessional relationships, Section A.5.d affirms that nonprofessional *interactions* with clients are acceptable and may yield beneficial outcomes. This standard empowers counselors who seek latitude to incorporate local expectations and customs into their practice. It lists examples of nonprofessional interaction, such as attending a ceremony or buying a product. It also guides counselors in determining beforehand whether or not to initiate a nonprofessional interaction. Conversely, any unintentional harm caused by a nonprofessional interaction must be remedied.

In keeping with competent multicultural practice, Section A.6.a sanctions advocacy at the individual, group, institutional, and societal level in order to remove barriers to well-being and growth. For example, Section D.1.h gives counselors options for changing workplace policies that may be harmful (e.g., the lack of translation services for non-English speakers). Without saying so, these standards seek to correct environmental conditions that diminish the lives of marginalized persons and frame nontraditional roles (e.g., social change agent) as cultural adaptations which fit the intent of the code, although they caution against impaired professional judgment, conflict of interest, and risk to clients. Consider the actions of a counselor who works at a mental health center that serves the immigrant community to which she belongs. At an annual review, the counselor is chastised for partnering with local leaders, some of whom are clients, to organize a civic group that plans to lobby the city and state for tax breaks for start-up businesses. Although the counselor believes that economic independence can lead to adaptation and empowerment, she is concerned that her professional judgment may have been clouded. Similarly, Sections A.10.d on bartering and A.10.e on receiving gifts clearly state that these practices have a place in multicultural and international work, but that counselors must discuss their concerns about the integrity of the professional relationship.

In a nod to international work, Sections A.12.e and A.12.f mandate counselors to consult experts and comply with applicable laws when using technology across national borders. In accommodating those whose primary language is not English, Sections A.12.g on technology and informed consent and A.12.h on the World Wide Web oblige counselors to confer with clients about cultural and/or linguistic traditions that might impact service delivery and offer means for translation, if feasible. Sections D.1.b on forming relationships and D.1.c on interdisciplinary teamwork stress the value of collegial interaction with experts in allied fields.

Strangely, Section C5 reads, "Counselors do not discriminate ... in a manner that has a negative impact" (American Counseling Association, 2005, p. 10), implying that there may be neutral or even positive consequences to discrimination.

Confidentiality

Section B.1.a argues strongly for dialogue with clients on decisions to disclose confidential information given different cultural meanings ascribed to privacy. Although the standard does not endorse a violation of mainstream practice, it implies that counselors and clients have relative autonomy in constructing a balance between professional integrity and cultural values. However, Section B.5.b recommends generic sensitivity to the diversity of families (e.g., corporal punishment, supervision of children) while obligating counselors to uphold the legal rights and responsibilities of parents and guardians.

Assessment and Diagnosis

Examples abound of the misapplication of psychometric measures, constructed and standardized on mostly homogeneous groups, with culturally diverse populations having limited proficiency in English (Herlihy & Watson, 2003; Sue & Sue, 2003). Section E.1.a stipulates that assessment should yield reliable and valid quantitative or qualitative data, an improvement over the 1995 version, which implied the superiority of "objective" approaches to assessment. Sometimes, accuracy in assessment with culturally diverse persons necessitates the use of subjective, nonlinear methods, as with West Africans who communicate in richly symbolic narratives. In parallel fashion, Sections E.6.c, E.8, and E.9.a obligate counselors to evaluate the suitability of assessment techniques and tools for diverse populations, interpret test results in light of contextual factors, and communicate any reservations about cultural misapplication. However, these generic cautions leave clients at the mercy of counselors' idiosyncratic biases and suggest that culturally inappropriate assessment may be tolerated as long as it is reported. Researchers in the developing world often hire undergraduates majoring in English to translate instruments that were constructed, normed, and validated in the United States. These translations neither conform to standard procedures (e.g., transliteration, back translation) nor are they evaluated for equivalence. A U.S. counselor involved in such a test-translation project recognizes that local resources and need preclude scientific rigor, yet worries about the future application of a psychometrically unsound measure.

Sections E.5.b and E.5.d provide equally nebulous instructions to consider sociodemographic factors when diagnosing and to refrain from diagnosing if it might cause harm. These standards do not inform counselors about how to infuse diversity into the medical model that undergirds diagnosis, which poses further risk to already vulnerable clients (e.g., recapitulating inequality in the professional relationship, construing symptoms as pathological rather than as adaptive compromises; Herlihy & Watson, 2003; Pedersen, 2002; Pettifor, 2005; Sue & Sue, 2003).

Like the APA's standard 1.02 on resolving ethical dilemmas, the *Code of Ethics* (American Counseling Association, 2005) does not permit responsible disobedience when counselors determine they must deviate from ethical and legal standards that place clients at risk (see Section H.1.b). Notwithstanding this limitation and occasional inconsistencies and generalities, the code has advanced substantially since 1995 in guiding multicultural and international practice (Kocet, 2006). It reveals an appreciation of collectivistic as well as individualistic worldviews, emphasizes collaborative solutions to ethical ambiguities and conflicts, and speaks in the active voice when prescribing culturally sensitive and competent conduct. The code allows a reasonable amount of flexibility to establish culturally appropriate parameters of practice without being excessively vague. Finally, though incomplete, the code contains several standards with clear international applications.

Code of Ethics of the National Association of Social Workers

The *Code of Ethics of the National Association of Social Workers* (National Association of Social Workers, 1996) consists of a preamble, six values and derivative principles, and six standards of conduct (see Table 6.3).

General Statements and Principles

The preamble identifies the profession's historic focus on the person-in-context and defines the term "client" as inclusive of groups and communities. The mission of social work is social justice, specifically eradicating oppression and advancing well-being in culturally sensitive ways via traditional and unorthodox means (e.g., community organizing, political action). The preamble

---

TABLE 6.3
Code of Ethics of the National Association of Social Workers (NASW, 1996)

Preamble

Ethical Principles

    Value: Service

        Principle: Social workers' primary goal is to help people in need and to address social problems.

    Value: Social Justice

        Principle: Social workers challenge social injustice.

    Value: Dignity and Worth of the Person

        Principle: Social workers respect the inherent dignity and worth of the person.

    Value: Importance of Human Relationships

        Principle: Social workers recognize the central importance of human relationships.

    Value: Integrity

        Principle: Social workers behave in a trustworthy manner.

    Value: Competence

        Principle: Social workers practice within their areas of competence and develop and enhance their professional expertise.

Standards

1.   Social Workers' Ethical Responsibilities to Clients

2.   Social Workers' Ethical Responsibilities to Colleagues

3.   Social Workers' Ethical Responsibilities in Practice Settings

4.   Social Workers' Ethical Responsibilities as Professionals

5.   Social Workers' Ethical Responsibilities to the Social Work Profession

6.   Social Workers' Ethical Responsibilities to the Broader Society

deliberately links social work to values, from which obtain ethical principles and standards of conduct (Freud & Krug, 2002). The preamble cautions that the code is not prescriptive, given the nuances of multicultural and international practice. Instead, it invites social workers to apply moral reasoning and various resources in collaborating with clients on ethical solutions. It raises the possibility of civil disobedience when laws conflict with humanitarian values; however, Section 1.01 advises social workers that legal conformity may supersede loyalty to clients.

Almost all values and principles communicate a perspectival view of the client, broadly conceived. The value of service elevates assisting those in need and remedying social ills to preeminent status. The value of social justice challenges social workers to act with and on behalf of vulnerable individuals and groups to overcome conditions that impede health and fulfillment. Valuing the dignity and worth of the person acknowledges the importance of diversity and of strengthening the capacity for diverse populations to meet their own needs. Valuing the importance of human relationships inspires partnership in the helping process. Surprisingly, the value and principle of competence neglect to exhort social workers to expand their multicultural and international expertise.

Competence

Section 1.03b permits hiring an interpreter or translator when clients are illiterate or unable to comprehend the primary language used in a professional setting. Section 1.05 expects social workers to be generally sensitive and competent, aware of the strengths within all cultures and the oppressive forces within society. Section 1.10 addresses cultural sensitivity concerning touch, but offers no details. Although recognizing the value of interdisciplinary treatment teams, Section 2.03a fails to promote interdisciplinary collaboration when working with culturally diverse persons and communities. Section 1.05 requires social workers to become educated about cultural diversity; yet, this directive is not repeated in Section 3.08 on continuing education and staff development or in Section 4.01 on keeping current on emerging practices. Most social workers have completed coursework in multicultural counseling. After years of practice, they may be unwilling to invest in further multicultural training because they only occasionally serve culturally diverse clients. When such a client enters treatment, a social worker may erroneously conclude on the basis of the above standards that cultural sensitivity and general empathy are sufficient to ensure competent intervention.

Professional Relationships

Section 1.06a takes the unusual position that social workers may terminate professional relationships to protect the interests of clients, although it does not specify the criteria which must be met in such decisions. Section 1.06c grants social workers autonomy to draw culturally appropriate boundaries in cases of multiple relationships with clients, but fails to identify the parameters of or a process for establishing such boundaries (Freud & Krug, 2002). Section 1.13b allows bartering when congruent with local practice norms, essential to the provision of service, and negotiated freely at the behest of clients; nowhere, however, are cultural considerations mentioned or strategies delineated for their negotiation. Consistent with its commitment to social justice, Section 6 denotes ways that social workers may discharge their obligation to society, including the international community. Section 6.01 urges advocacy to promote human and societal welfare, namely values and institutions favorable to social justice at home and abroad. Section 6.03 calls for social workers to volunteer in emergencies, but fails to define the ethical and legal constraints in doing so. Section 6.04 outlines courses of social and political action for improving social conditions and ensuring equal access for disadvantaged and oppressed populations. Sections 6.04c and 6.04d address eliminating "isms" along with promoting respect for diversity in the United States and globally via support for institutions, policies, and legislation. However, these standards leave social workers at a loss in circumstances that evoke civil disobedience (e.g., is it morally justifiable to agitate unskilled workers to strike illegally so that they can earn a living wage and work in safe conditions?) (Freud & Krug, 2002).

Confidentiality

Contrary to the multicultural sensitivity and competence of the preamble and the code's values and principles, Section 1.07 offers no guidance on resolving difficult confidentiality issues that often arise in multicultural and international practice (Sadeghi, Fischer, & House, 2003). Take the case of an international exchange student who discloses homicidal ideation toward his academic advisor by whom he feels humiliated. Given the moderate level of assessed risk, the social worker is torn by a duty to warn versus concern that the student may be imprisoned or deported if any threat of violence is revealed.

Assessment and Diagnosis

The code makes no provision for the ethical use of assessment and diagnostic procedures, let alone their application to diverse populations either domestically or internationally.

The *Code of Ethics* (National Association of Social Work, 1996) is forthright in acknowledging that moral values undergird ethical principles and standards of conduct. The preamble as well as values and principles focus on social justice, an agenda of great relevance for multicultural and international practice. The preamble, values, and principles use inclusive language, heighten awareness of contextual factors, encourage nontraditional professional roles, and advocate partnership and capacity building. Aside from occasional inconsistencies, the major drawback to the code is its failure to infuse values and principles into standards of conduct. While granting autonomy to resolve ethical dilemmas (e.g., multiple relationships), the standards lack the detail needed to guide social workers through key ethical issues encountered in multicultural and international practice. Though insisting on sensitivity to diversity and ending oppression, the standards are mostly silent on how to achieve these aims other than through advocacy (Freud & Krug, 2002). Moreover, the tentative individualistic, unilateral, and legalistic language of the standards sharply contrasts the collectivistic worldview embraced by the preamble, values, and principles, although several standards voice the need for international applications. The code, then, is "a necessary but insufficient guide to ethical practice" (Freud & Krug, 2002, p. 474).

Universal Declaration of Ethical Principles for Psychologists

The *Universal Declaration of Ethical Principles for Psychologists* (Gauthier, 2005) is an outgrowth of a motion approved by the General Assembly of the International Union of Psychological Science, and endorsed by the International Association of Applied Psychology and International Association of Cross-Cultural Psychology, to develop a framework for ethical practice that would have value for psychology associations and psychologists worldwide. The draft Declaration contains general principles common to ethics codes of the national psychology associations of several countries. These principles are not only universal, but also timeless in that their roots lie in Eastern and Western civilizations. The Declaration was presented for discussion during the 2006 International Congress of Applied Psychology. At present, the Declaration has a preamble followed by four sections, each tied to an ethical principle. Each section includes a statement outlining the moral values contained in the principle and a series of articles that derives from those values. Given the likelihood of further revision to the Declaration based on its relevance to indigenous values and local customs, I briefly review elements of the Declaration's principles that speak to multicultural and international practice (see Table 6.4).

General Statements and Principles

The preamble reiterates the moral grounding of professional ethics and ethical decisions, although it does not advocate that consumers participate in such decisions. It situates all practice within a social context, stressing the continuity of persons and communities with their past and future. It places the welfare of society (e.g., peace, justice, humanity) above that of the discipline in language that prioritizes collective over individual well-being. Its generic language shows regard for cultural variation in the expression of universal values.

The Declaration identifies respect for the dignity of all human beings as the most basic principle, implying that it should trump all others when resolving ethical dilemmas. Principle I recognizes the inherent worth of all human beings and the interdependence between individuals and their cultures. It balances respect for cultural differences in how values manifest themselves against a moral imperative to respect all people and groups. However, the Declaration does not articulate how to achieve this balance. Practitioners are hard-pressed to determine when respect for local beliefs and customs contravenes human dignity or causes harm. Do female virginity checks in conservative Muslim communities qualify as a violation of a young woman's dignity?

TABLE 6.4
Universal Declaration of Ethical Principles for Psychologists

Preamble
Principle 1: Respect for the Dignity of All Human Beings
Principle II: Competent Caring for the Well-Being of Others
Principle III: Integrity
Principle IV: Professional and Scientific Responsibilities to Society

Competent care for the well-being of others requires social and cultural sensitivity in order to apply knowledge and skills appropriately. Principle II also demands awareness of how values and culture mediate one's multicultural and international practice.

Integrity reflects an understanding of cultural definitions of professional boundaries, multiple relationships, and confidentiality and obliges practitioners to monitor these issues in order to avoid injurious conflicts of interest. Practitioners may assume that integrity includes open and direct communication, which, if expressed, would violate the more subtle norms of interaction found in many non-Western cultures.

Finally, professional and scientific responsibilities to society necessitate that knowledge be used to improve the conditions of individuals, groups, and society. Principle IV also encourages the development of social structures and policies for the benefit of all.

Before turning to ethical decision making, I should note that the ethics codes and Declaration tend to emphasize doing no harm rather than instruction on providing relevant services for diverse populations (Pedersen, 2002; Pettifor, 2001, 2005). The codes tend to be rule-governed and legalistic, mirroring the social-political-judicial process in the United States, which can lead to conformity by practitioners in order to avoid ethical sanctions. Alternatively, the codes are general and vague at places, which can contribute to self-interested outcomes that undervalue cultural realities and lead to substandard services for diverse persons and groups. Furthermore, the codes do not connect ethical principles, let alone values, to standards of conduct, and often present implicit Eurocentric assumptions at odds with such cultural values as interdependence and collective identity. Above all, with the exception of the ACA's code, the codes do not teach ethical multicultural and international practice as a morally grounded process that occurs within the context of a professional relationship (Kocet, 2006; Pedersen, 2002; Pettifor, 2001, 2005).

Ethical Decision Making

Promoting critical thinking in regard to ethical multicultural and international practice is long overdue (Cottone, & Claus, 2000; Hadjistavropoulos & Malloy, 2000; Herlihy & Watson, 2003; Pack-Brown & Williams, 2003). Rule-oriented ethics, which seek compliance with a "best" decision produced by logic, are slowly giving way to alternative approaches, having various names (e.g., contextual, moral dilemma, problem solving, process, relational), which seek an accommodation between the competing worldviews of different parties (Cottone & Claus, 2000; Pettifor, 2005). Few alternative approaches advocate overthrowing the mainstream intellectual and moral heritage that underlies current ethics codes; rather, they call for greater collaboration in identifying more culturally and internationally flexible applications of existing ethical principles and standards of conduct.

The decision-making approaches that follow are conceptually driven, rather than an atheoretical patchwork of disjointed ideas and techniques designed to guide practitioners sequentially toward an ethical choice (e.g., Frame & Williams, 2005). As others and I have stated, conceptual approaches articulate basic values and issues that are essential to ethical decisions, lend coherence to the decision-making process, improve the consistency of outcomes due to internalization of the decision-making process, and avoid the substitution of one set of formulaic rules with another that also risks being misapplied (e.g., presupposing ethnocentrism by practitioners aligned with the dominant culture; Cottone & Claus, 2000; Hadjistavropoulos & Malloy, 2000).

Rule-oriented approaches, including empirically tested models derived from theories of moral development (e.g., Rest, 1984), have been challenged by research showing that social service professionals do not employ odds-balancing strategies in making ethical decisions (see Downie, MacNaughton, & Randall, 2000). In fact, practitioners often depend on intuition rather than analytic reasoning because clinical data have limited validity, are presented en masse, lack organization, and must be processed quickly (Hammond, 1996). For example, expert practitioners typically arrive at a working diagnosis within 1 minute (Dumont, 1991), capturing whole the meaning of a symptom complex without calculating which is the best diagnosis among several alternatives. Although analytic reasoning is precise, it is prone to error; intuition, though imprecise, tends to be coherent, making it useful given the novelty, ambiguity, and complexity of multicultural and international practice. Is it not *intuitively* obvious that within a collectivistic framework privileged information may ethically be shared with selected members of a client's family and community? Thus, some have supported training in the application of intuition to ethical decision making in order to balance the current overemphasis on critical thinking (Cottone & Claus, 2000; Hill, Glaser, & Harden, 1995).

Existentialism represents an antidote to rational analysis and provides a conceptual foundation for authenticity in ethical decisions. It holds that practitioners, like all human beings, are free to forge meaningful choices and are responsible for the consequences of those choices, both to themselves and to the community of which they are a part. Existentialism, as applied to multicultural and international practice, entails openness to different ethical viewpoints and a commitment to identify values that are relevant to the particular context in which they are enacted. Through an authentic encounter, the practitioner and culturally diverse client struggle to find a mutual understanding of the boundaries of their professional relationship and then relate to one another based on this shared meaning (e.g., agreeing to meet once with the client's family for tea at their home before undertaking counseling).

The hermeneutic perspective situates knowledge within relationships and conceives of learning as a dialogic process that leads to meaning (Betan, 1997). From a hermeneutic standpoint, professional ethics are "a product of shared subjective experiences, which in turn are embedded in a context of cultural interpretation" (p. 356). Ethical decisions are co-constructed from the practitioner's worldview, the client's worldview, and the narrative that occurs in the professional relationship. Beyond acknowledging the culturally determined expression of universal values (e.g., altruism, justice, loyalty, responsibility), hermeneutics underscores the essential reciprocity between practitioners and culturally diverse clients along with their unfolding consensus on ethical decisions. For example, practitioners might come to understand corporal punishment as a local custom that makes a moral claim to prepare children to become upstanding adults. However, hermeneutics does not oblige practitioners to concur with such a claim; rather, the perspective encourages dialogue to resolve the ethical and legal dilemma of responding to corporal punishment as a reflection of a family's traditional culture versus the more permissive norms of society.

Like hermeneutics, feminist models (Hill et al., 1995) value collaboration in making ethical decisions, but focus more narrowly on institutional bases for potentially destructive differences in power between practitioners and clients. Feminist models stress awareness by practitioners of their socialized attitudes and feelings, and integrate analytical reasoning and intuition in fashioning mutually agreeable ethical solutions. Individual empowerment and ameliorating oppressive conditions are feminist values of great relevance to ethical multicultural and international practice. Feminist therapists engage their culturally diverse clients in dialogue about the parameters of ethically responsible intervention, such as ameliorating suffering and dysfunction by inspiring their clients to join grassroots organizations, whose goals might include liberating ethnic enclaves from predatory lending practices.

Social constructionism offers a more radical, but potentially more useful, approach to making ethical decisions in multicultural and international practice

(Cottone, 2001, 2004; D'Andrea, 2000; Gergen, 2001). Social constructionism speaks to the centrality of dialogue, in this case communication on a horizontal plane between practitioner and client, be it an individual, family, or community. Dialogue legitimizes the sharing of ethical worldviews and creation of ethical meaning, and empowers clients to assert their right to ethical service; it rejects the potentially injurious tradition of imposing an ethical decision unilaterally as if such decisions were unconditional (e.g., bartering *is* exploitive). Multiple ethical meanings are generated not merely through human interaction, but through interaction that takes place in cultural contexts. Cultural contexts evolve due to changing conditions and forces, such that ethical realities also change. It was not long ago that homosexuality was considered a psychiatric disorder, whereas today support is growing for the legal union of gays and lesbians. Thus, the ethical decisions that practitioners and clients make for themselves dismantle conventional interpretations that overlook divergent cultural traditions and, instead, actively seek and incorporate those traditions into alternative ethical actions (e.g., privacy as a communal construct). Finally, language functions to build or obliterate and sustain or modify cultural customs. Social constructionism sensitizes practitioners to terms that needlessly restrict effective multicultural and international practice (e.g., nontraditional professional roles lead to conflicts of interest). Thus, social constructionism is well suited to guide ethical decision making in multicultural and international practice. It views decision making as mutual and respectful, addressing both client and practitioner issues, rather than as private and possibly ethnocentric; it is "a process of negotiating (when necessary), consensualizing, and arbitrating (when necessary) . . . at critical moments" (Cottone, 2001, p. 79). It recognizes that, in order to serve the best interests of the client, ethical decisions should be value-driven rather than value-neutral; it adapts principles and standards to the contexts in which they are situated and encourages morally guided transformative action (e.g., the value of social justice) in addition to palliative cures (e.g., the value of caring and compassion; D'Andrea, 2000; Prilleltensky, 1997). Finally, social constructionism offers a parsimonious, nonsequential process of determining ethical responses that make it more likely to be used (Cottone, 2001, 2004).

Case Examples

I conclude with two ethical dilemmas that are likely to occur in multicultural and international practice, which I attempt to resolve through the precepts of social constructionism. Given the idiosyncrasies of most ethics codes on multicultural and international issues, I do not link specific principles or standards to each dilemma, although I invite interested readers to do so. I also refrain from settling on a particular course of action because social constructionism emphasizes the process of ethical decision making more than its outcomes. Instead, I identify a universal value(s) for each dilemma and illustrate how ethical decision making defined by social constructionism can yield options that reflect the universal value(s) in context.

Case 1: Multicultural Dilemma

Sadeghi and coworkers (2003) conducted a Delphi poll of 256 demographically representative members of the American Multicultural and Development Association with at least 5 years of professional practice and wide-ranging work experience with culturally diverse clients. Eighty percent of respondents encountered the following ethical dilemma at least once per year in their multicultural practice: struggling to foster the client's independence in solving his or her problem while honoring the client's culturally based expectation that the practitioner will offer solutions. The case below reflects this dilemma.

> Glafcos is a 21-year-old Greek-American education major at a medium-sized university in the Midwest. His family, immigrants from Greece where Glafcos was born, resides in a large city approximately 2 hours away by car or train. Glafcos's parents repeatedly encourage him to maintain close family ties and observe cultural traditions. Many of Glafcos's friends speak of moving away from home after they graduate. Glafcos enters counseling with a presenting concern of stress. He reports experiencing growing pressure from his family to return home after graduation, join his father's business, marry into his ethnic community, and start a family. Glafcos mentions that he has thought about relocating to either the east or west coast for a few years to begin his teaching career and meet different people. Of late, Glafcos has had difficulty concentrating on his studies and finding enjoyment in leisure activities; his grades have suffered. He seems stuck and asks you, a therapist at the university's counseling center, to give him advice and direction about his future life course.

The universal value most evident in this case is autonomy. The ethical dilemma reflects tension between the culture of mainstream clinical practice, which values self-determination, and the cultures of many diverse clients, which values interdependence. You may experience aversion to complying with Glafcos' request for advice because of internalized professional norms about taking personal responsibility for a client's life choices. Moreover, you may share the individualistic attitudes and lifestyle with the dominant U.S. culture, making it difficult to appreciate and remain unbiased toward Glafcos's ambivalence about individualistic mainstream culture and collectivistic family culture. Awareness of such personal reactions to Glafcos's request and impending life choices alerts you to the importance of culture as it impacts the professional relationship as well as the presenting concern.

Rather than complying with or rejecting Glafcos's request for advice based on a private consideration of relevant ethical principles and standards of conduct, you explore with Glafcos the meaning of his request, using language that conveys interest rather than judgment. Your exploration most likely will address personal motives, such as wanting to reduce confusion and relieve distress, as well as clarify cultural motives, such as respect for authority and your expertise as a professional. The ensuing dialogue will clarify for you and Glafcos how his struggle to balance the demands of competing cultures is recapitulated in the professional relationship, providing a therapeutic opportunity to demonstrate the power of conflicting cultural expectations and loyalties. Because social constructionism supports the incorporation of cultural traditions into professional practice, provided they do not pose obvious ethical violations, it is likely that you and Glafcos will co-create a cultural consensus about how autonomy is expressed within the professional relationship. Perhaps, you will find a midpoint between egalitarian and hierarchical relating, at which your professional advice is construed as one of several perspectives for consideration. Perhaps, you will redefine autonomy not as an imposed value of taking individual responsibility for life choices, but as a more communal construct whereby you and Glafcos can collaborate on life choices in a way that is culturally appropriate for both parties.

Case 2: International Dilemma

There are few published reports on ethical decision making in international settings. Yet, increasing numbers of psychologists and, to a lesser extent, counselors and social workers are practicing with international clients in nontraditional settings both domestically and abroad. This phenomenon will surely accelerate owing to the unstoppable force of economic and political globalization. In regard to the ethical dilemma in this example, practitioners who work with culturally diverse populations reported struggling often with the dilemma of recommending Western medically based interventions to avoid adverse health consequences versus honoring clients' nonmedically oriented beliefs about illness and health (Sadeghi et al., 2003).

> Several years ago, an earthquake inflicted more than 500,000 casualties in Pakistan. The dead, injured, and bereft included local villagers and a handful of European travelers. The Pakistani government has requested the assistance of social service professionals from around the world in the psychosocial reclamation of lives. You respond by registering with a newly formed NGO outreach program that is contracted to coordinate teams of practitioners to visit Pakistan and provide psychosocial aide to survivors in camps and shelters in particularly hard-hit areas. You are informed that your team will facilitate group therapy with children and adults using a biopsychosocial model of care. In addition to these sessions, your team will lead problem-solving groups in response to the massive physical and economic displacement of people. Having committed to a tour of service, you now experience misgivings because (a) your only training in disaster relief was a module on crisis intervention during practicum, a course that you completed years ago, and (b) you have only superficial familiarity with Pakistan, its peoples, and its cultures.

The universal value most evident in this case is nonmaleficence. The ethical dilemma reflects tension between fulfilling a moral responsibility to care for others in need, yet not inflict harm. You recognize that the validity of interventions based on a biopsychosocial model may not extend to Pakistani norms and could possibly further injure an already suffering populace. You also understand that, although problem solving is a universal socio-cognitive activity, its Pakistani form may depart radically from that in the United States. Given your minimal background in disaster relief and lack of familiarity with Pakistani culture, the overarching moral imperative is to do no harm. Should you withdraw from the project or go along with the intervention plan as prescribed by the NGO? Do you have recourse to a third option that allows facilitation of healing and restoration of village life in contextually appropriate and constructive ways?

Social constructionism gives you a collaborative alternative to private, dichotomous thinking about the ethical propriety of serving Pakistani earthquake survivors. In addition to the ethical mandate to remedy deficits in knowledge about disaster relief and Pakistani culture, you can advocate to ensure that planned interventions fit with local Pakistani health care traditions. By engaging the leaders of the NCO program in dialogue, perhaps with other team members, you initiate a collaborative process of negotiating ethical views of care that may yield a meaningful consensus on how to respond to the needs of survivors with both compassion and competence. Challenging language that presumes the general applicability of the biopsychosocial model and exploring different perspectives on the universal value of doing no harm reduces the likelihood of introducing conditions that could pose an additional health risk to Pakistanis. Respectful discourse also creates an opportunity for you and NGO leaders to identify health care customs that are situated in Pakistani culture, or at least heightens awareness of the need to include local Pakistani specialists to share their perspective of indigenous health care, and to incorporate these healing traditions wherever possible. For example, rather than forming artificial problem-solving groups, you and fellow team members can exploit "experience-near" arrangements, such as village meetings or religious assemblies, that constitute ready-made media for local problem solving. In other words, social constructionism affords providers and recipients of international humanitarian programs a method of co-creating approaches to care that meld sharply contrasting cultural perspectives, yet preserve the universal value of nonmaleficence, and even allow for beneficent intervention. Of course, you may withdraw from the Pakistani outreach program if negotiating and consensualizing with NGO leaders fails to resolve the fundamental ethical concern to do no harm.

Conclusion

Values are integral to ethical practice. Unfortunately, the ethics codes of many social service professions are not explicitly tied to values, even though values provide guidance in the application of principles and standards, especially in novel, ambiguous, and complex circumstances. Such guidance is sorely needed in contemporary multicultural and international practice. As I have shown, ethics codes have their distinctive strengths and weaknesses with respect to multicultural and, to a lesser extent, international practice. Most codes continue to improve by addressing such dilemmas as advocacy, bartering, confidentiality, and multiple relationships. However, the inconsistencies, vagaries, and general cautiousness of ethics codes mean that they are likely to fall further behind the accelerating demand for multicultural and international services. Because of their deficiencies and because prevailing models of ethical decision making tend to support private, hierarchical, and at times ethnocentric outcomes, I have supported an alternative approach to making ethical decisions that is grounded in social constructionism. This approach is highly relevant to multicultural and international practice due to its emphasis on values, collaboration, context, and language.

Considerable effort is needed to ready ethics codes for 21st-century professional practice. Perhaps, the most critical task involves the revision of ethics codes to ensure quality services that meet people's needs while avoiding the creation of barriers to such services. Each of us must join in constructing ethical principles, standards of conduct, and methods for their application that better serve diverse persons and communities, with diverse problems, in diverse ways and settings, both at home and across national borders.

References

American Counseling Association. (2005). *Code of ethics.* Alexandria, VA: Author.

American Psychological Association. (2002). *Ethical principles of psychologists and code of conduct.* Washington, DC: Author.

Bersoff, D. (2003). *Ethical conflict in psychology* (3rd ed.). Washington, DC: American Psychological Association.

Betan, E. J. (1997). Toward a hermeneutic model of ethical decision making in clinical practice. *Ethics and Behavior, 7,* 347–365.

Cottone, R. R. (2001). A social constructivism model of ethical decision making in counseling. *Journal of Counseling and Development, 79,* 39–45.

Cottone, R. R. (2004). Displacing the psychology of the individual in ethical decision-making: The social constructivism model. *Canadian Journal of Counselling, 38,* 5–13.

Cottone, R. R., & Claus, R. E. (2000). Ethical decision-making models: A review of the literature. *Journal of Counseling and Development, 78,* 275–283.

D'Andrea, M. (2000). Postmodernism, constructivism, and multiculturalism: Three forces reshaping and expanding our thoughts about counseling. *Journal of Mental Health Counseling, 22,* 1–16.

Downie, R. S., MacNaughton, J., & Randall, F. (2000). *Clinical judgement: Evidence in practice.* New York: Oxford University Press.

Dumont, F. (1991). Expertise in psychotherapy: Inherent liabilities in becoming experienced. *Psychotherapy, 28,* 422–428.

Frame, M. W., & Williams, C. B. (2005). A model of ethical decision making from a multicultural perspective. *Counseling and Values, 49,* 165–179.

Freud, S., & Krug, S. (2002). Beyond the code of ethics, Part 1: Complexities of ethical decision making in social work practice. *Family in Society: Journal of Contemporary Human Services, 83,* 474–482.

Gauthier, J. (2005, June). *Feasibility and relevance of a universal declaration of ethical principles for psychologists in today's world.* Invited address at the Interamerican Congress of Psychology, Buenos Aires, Argentina.

Gergen, K. J. (2001). Relational process for ethical outcomes. *Journal of Systemic Therapies, 20,* 7–10.

Hadjistavropoulos, T., & Malloy, D. C. (2000). Making ethical choices: A comprehensive decision-making model for Canadian psychologists. *Canadian Psychology, 41,* 104–115.

Hammond, K. R. (1996). *Human judgement and social policy: Irreducible uncertainty, inevitable error, unavoidable injustice.* New York: Oxford University Press.

Herlihy, B., & Watson, A. E. (2003). Ethical issues and multicultural competence in counseling. In F. D. Harper & J. McFadden (Eds.), *Culture and counseling: New approaches* (pp. 363–378). Boston: Allyn and Bacon.

Hill, M., Glaser, K., & Harden, J. (1995). A feminist model for ethical decision making. In E. J. Rave & C. C. Larsen (Eds.), *Ethical decision making in therapy: Feminist perspectives* (pp. 18–37). New York: Guilford.

Jennings, L., Sovereign, A., Bottorff, N., Mussell, M. P., & Vye, C. (2005). Nine ethical values of master therapists. *Journal of Mental Health Counseling, 27,* 32–47.

Jordan, S. (2006, February 24). Suggested guidelines for hosting division outreach programs in New Orleans. Message posted to DIVOFFICERS electronic mailing list, archived at http://www.apa.org/about/division/dialogue/ma06divnews.html#guidelines

Kocet, M. M. (2006). Ethical challenges in a complex world: Highlights of the 2005 *ACA Code of Ethics. Journal of Counseling and Development, 84,* 228–234.

McFall, R. M. (1991). Manifesto for a science for clinical psychology. *Clinical Psychologist, 44,* 75–88.

Meara, N. M., Schmidt, L. D., & Day, J. D. (1996). Principles and virtues: A foundation for ethical decisions, policies, and character. *Counseling Psychologist, 24,* 4–77.

National Association of Social Workers. (1996). *Code of Ethics of the National Association of Social Workers.* Washington, DC: Author.

New Zealand Psychological Society. (2002). *Code of ethics for psychologists working in Aotearoa / New Zealand.* Wellington: Author.

Pack-Brown, S. P., & Williams, C. B. (2003). *Ethics in a multicultural context.* Thousand Oaks, CA: Sage.

Pedersen, P. B. (2002). Ethics, competence, and other professional issues in culture-centered counseling. In P. B. Pedersen, J. G. Draguns, W. J. Lonner, & J. E. Trimble (Eds.), *Counseling across cultures* (5th ed., pp. 3–27). Thousand Oaks, CA: Sage.

Pettifor, J. L. (2001). Are professional codes of ethics relevant for multicultural counseling? *Canadian Journal of Counselling, 35,* 26–35.

Pettifor, J. (2005). Ethics and multicultural counseling. In N. Arthur & S. Collins (Eds.), *Culture infused counseling: Celebrating the Canadian mosaic* (pp. 213–238). Calgary: Counselling Concepts.

Pope, K., & Bajt, T. (1988). When laws and values conflict: A dilemma for psychologists. *American Psychologist, 43,* 828–829.

Prilleltensky, I. (1997). Values, assumptions, and practices: Assessing the moral implications of psychological discourse and action. *American Psychologist, 47,* 517–535.

Rest, J. R. (1984). Research on moral development: Implications for training counseling psychologists. *Counseling Psychologist, 12,* 12–29.

Sadeghi, M., Fischer, J. M., & House, S. G. (2003). Ethical dilemmas in multicultural counseling. *Journal of Multicultural Counseling and Development, 31,* 179–191.

Stevens, M. J., & Gielen, U. P. (Eds.). (2007). *Toward a global psychology: Theory, research, interventions, and pedagogy.* Mahwah, NJ: Erlbaum.

Sue, D. W., & Sue, D. (2003). *Counseling the culturally diverse: Theory and practice* (4th ed.). Hoboken, NJ: Wiley.

Tjeltveit, A. C. (2000). There is more to ethics than codes of professional ethics: Social ethics, theoretical ethics, and managed care. *Counseling Psychologist, 28,* 242–252.

Suggested Readings

Corey, G., Corey, M. S., & Callanan, P. (2007). *Issues and ethics in the helping professions* (7th ed.). Belmont, CA: Thomson Brooks Cole.

This book covers the ethics codes of the APA, ACA, American Psychiatric Association, Canadian Psychological Association, Canadian Counselling Association, and Canadian Association of Social Workers. The authors highlight the implications of ethics codes for community practice and for addressing the needs of underserved populations and service delivery in non-traditional settings. Chapter 4, "Multicultural Perspectives and Diversity Issues," presents guidelines on multicultural education and training, research, practice, and organizational change.

Freud, S., & Krug, S. (2002). Beyond the code of ethics, Part II: Dual relationships revisited. *Families in Society, 83,* 483–492.

This article highlights aspects of social work practice that are considered ethical, yet not easily accommodated by the 1996 ethics code. The authors question the prevailing concept of dual relationships, arguing that social workers in some settings, with particular populations, and in certain roles, face multiple relationships that are integral to their effectiveness.

Houser, R., Wilczenski, F. L., & Ham, M. (2006). *Culturally relevant ethical decision-making in counseling.* Thousand Oaks, CA: Sage.

This book presents a hermeneutic framework for addressing contextual issues in ethical decision making. The authors incorporate ethical perspectives that are grounded in various worldviews and are sensitive to cultural issues. Case studies are provided to illustrate how to negotiate between an ethical perspective based on diversity and codified professional standards.

Knapp, S., & VandeCreek, L. (2003). An overview of the major changes in the 2002 APA ethics code. *Professional Psychology: Research and Practice, 34,* 301–308.

This article summarizes the major changes to the 2002 APA ethics code, including its enhanced sensitivity to the needs of cultural and linguistic minorities. The authors discuss shortcomings of the code.

Kocet, M. M. (2006). Ethical challenges in a complex world: Highlights of the 2005 ACA code of ethics. *Journal of Counseling and Development, 84,* 228–234.

This article highlights changes in the 2005 ACA ethics code, including boundaries and relationships and multicultural and diversity considerations. The authors underscore the importance of cultural sensitivity in ethical decision making in counseling, teaching, and research.

Pedersen, P. B. (2002). Ethics, competence, and other professional issues in culture-centered counseling. In P. B. Pedersen, J. G. Draguns, W. J. Lonner, & J. E. Trimble (Eds.), *Counseling across cultures* (5th ed., pp. 3–27). Thousand Oaks, CA: Sage.

This chapter underscores the relevance of multiculturalism to effective counseling. The author describes pro-Western biases in counseling, competencies of multicultural awareness, ethical dilemmas faced by multicultural counselors, and how multiculturalism is becoming the "fourth force" in psychology. Criticisms of the former ethics codes of the APA and ACA are relevant to the revised codes.

Pettifor, J. (2005). Ethics and multicultural counseling. In N. Arthur & S. Collins (Eds.), *Culture infused counseling: Celebrating the Canadian mosaic* (pp. 213–238). Calgary: Counselling Concepts.

This chapter stipulates that ethical and competent professional practice cannot be separated from an examination of culture and cultural differences. The Canadian perspective on ethics is an alternative to the familiar U.S. view and emphasizes value-based decision making. The author also addresses the liabilities of ethics codes, social responsibility and justice, diversity-specific guidelines, and international developments, all accompanied by informative vignettes.

Web pages of professional associations on ethics and/or ethics-related issues in multicultural and international practice:

APA—http://www.apa.org/ethics
ACA—http://www.counseling.org/Resources/CodeOfEthics/TP/Home/CT2.aspx
NASW—http://www.socialworkers.org/practice/default.asp
IUPsyS—http://www.am.org/iupsys/ethicsdoc.html

Part II

Models of Multicultural Counseling

7

Functional Approaches to Evidence-Based Practice in Multicultural Counseling and Therapy

Junko Tanaka-Matsumi

Contents

Globalization, Diversification, and Multicultural Counseling and Therapy

The field of multicultural counseling and therapy has been steadily grow-ing in the last 25 years due to important and rapid societal changes around the world (e.g., Gielen, Fish, & Draguns, 2004; Hays & Iwamasa, 2006; Pedersen, Draguns, Lonner, & Trimble, 2002; Sue & Sue, 2003). The first source of societal change is globalization and the increase in frequency of direct and indirect cross-cultural interpersonal encounters that are facilitated by advanced technologies of transportation and telecommunications. The second source of change is the worldwide waves of migrations. Within the United States, large-scale immigrations from Latin America and Asia have contributed to ethnic diversity. According to the U.S. Census (U.S. Census Bureau, 2002), the minority population grew 11 times as rapidly as the non-Hispanic White population between 1980 and 2000. From 1980 to 2000, the percentage increases in the Asian and Pacific Islander population were 204% and for the Hispanic population, 142%. As a result, in the United States, the minority population increased from 20% in 1980 to 31% in 2000 with a corresponding decrease in the White non-Hispanic population. Today, the multicultural nature of society is a permanent feature and the cultures of the world have gained in complexity. Diversity has become an everyday word to characterize the world we live in today.

Marsella (1998) advocated the development of global community psychol-ogy whose goal is to recognize, acknowledge, and prize diversity by giving priority to the cultural analysis of human action. Global psychology advo-cates work on theory, research, intervention, and pedagogy from both uni-versal and indigenous perspectives (Stevens & Gielen, 2007). Along the same lines of reasoning, Leong and Leach (2007) promoted a global vision for counseling psychology with a goal of developing multiculturally sensitive models of counseling with flexible worldviews.

Turning attention to professional qualifications, Hall and Lunt (2005) investigated the global mobility of professional psychologists and assessed the feasibility of establishing global education and training standards in the United States, Canada, Europe, and other parts of the world. The authors described the European situation in detail, as a standard diploma in psychol-ogy (EuroPsy) was adopted for professional training within the European Union (EU). The European diploma system would provide impetus for professional mobility within the EU as it enables individuals to gain their qualifications in more than one country, including recognition in their own countries. At the same time, a mobile professional is faced with cultural and linguistic differences within EU. In this age of globalization, there is an increased need for training of culturally competent counselors and therapists to provide culturally informed and empirically supported counseling and therapy both within and outside of their home countries (Hall, 2006).

In the age of diversity and globalization, development of cultural competence has gained importance as a set of successful adaptive skills in one's environment (Sternberg & Grigorenko, 2004; Sue, 1998). Pedersen (2002) has long alerted the profession to the importance of training in multicultural awareness competencies. Multicultural competences should be generic to all forms of counseling and therapy (American Psychological Association, 2003; Hays, 2001; Sue & Sue, 2003) and encompass awareness, knowledge, and skills contributing to the development of "culture-centered counseling" (Pedersen, 1997).

Globalization and diversification facilitate dissemination of information to those who benefit from the knowledge. Relevant to the topic of this chapter, I note that cognitive-behavioral therapy has been practiced in various parts of Asia (Oei, 1998; Qian & Wang, 2005). The World Congress Committee (WCC) has the primary function of selecting organizations to host triennial congresses of the World Congress of Behavioural and Cognitive Therapy (WCBCT). The WCC includes the Association for Behavioral and Cognitive Therapies (ABCT) and other such organizations located in all continents of the world. The 2004 World Congress of Behavioural and Cognitive Therapies (WCBCT2004) was held in Kobe, Japan. The congress theme was "Toward a Global Standard." For the first time the WCBCT was held in Asia with approximately 1,400 participants. In her invited address, Qian analyzed the conceptual consistencies of behavior therapy, cognitive-behavioral therapy, and Chinese Taoism philosophy (Qian & Wang, 2005). Further, in 2006, the first Asian Cognitive Behaviour Therapy (CBT) Conference took place in Hong Kong. The conference theme was "Evidence-Based Assessment, Theory, and Treatment" with many participants from Asian countries (Japan, Korea, China, Thailand, Singapore, etc.) as well as Australia, among others. David Barlow delivered a keynote address titled "Psychological Treatments and Evidence-based Practices: The Future" with an emphasis on health care policy and the role of effective psychological treatments for various disorders (Barlow, 2004).

Both the 2004 WCBCT and the Asian CBT Conference advocated evidence-based therapy as the standard for clinical practice. The practice of cognitive-behavioral therapies has been extended well beyond the cultural boundaries of their developmental origins in North America and Europe. At the same time the programs of WCBCT and Asian Cognitive Behavior Therapy Conference included Eastern-oriented procedures such as meditation and mindfulness. The participants discussed the integration of Eastern practices as integral parts of cognitive-behavioral treatments in Asian countries. As cultural adaptations of cognitive behavior therapies develop in Asia, we can learn more specifically about universal and culture-specific aspects of their procedures. Muto's (2006) edited volume on acceptance and commitment therapy (ACT) is an example of Japanese adaptation of ACT originally developed by Hayes. Following the 2004 WCBCT in Kobe, publications of Japanese translations of Western books on cognitive behavior therapies have increased markedly. There has also been an increase in social skills training (SST) for children as part of regular classroom activities based on adapted or originally developed SST guidelines (e.g., Sato & Aikawa, 2005). The recent spread of cognitive-behavioral therapies to non-Western countries demonstrates their interest in evidence-based approaches in mental health service, school intervention, and consultation.

In assessment, cognitive-behavioral therapies use functional analysis as a means of gathering systematic data to analyze the interaction of target behavior and environmental events including responses from the social environment, and develop hypotheses on the cause and maintenance of the selected target behavior (Sturmey, 1996). Functional analysis emphasizes an ideographic approach to the assessment within the individual's immediate cultural milieu. To illustrate, symptoms of a panic attack (e.g., nausea, headache, dizziness, numbness) may be triggered by approaching a particular train station previously associated with a panic attack, and followed by running away from the station or avoiding the station in the future. The therapist assesses the interrelationships among the three elements of antecedents-behavior-consequences and develops hypotheses as to those environmental factors maintaining somatic symptoms of panic attacks and avoidance behavior. Although functional analysis would reveal systematic relationships between environmental cues associated with a train station and generation of somatic symptoms, the client may employ an alternative explanation of the same distressing experience based on cultural beliefs regarding health and illness behavior.

In this chapter, I address two growing domains in psychotherapy. They are multicultural psychotherapy and empirically supported psychotherapy (Chambless & Ollendick, 2001) with a focus on cognitive-behavioral therapy. Multicultural perspectives are eminently necessary to provide culturally responsive cognitive-behavioral therapy to people of diverse cultural backgrounds, both nationally and internationally (Hays & Iwamasa, 2006;

Tanaka-Matsumi, Higginbotham, & Chang, 2002). The purpose of this chapter is to integrate multicultural perspectives with functional approaches to cognitive-behavioral therapy.

Psychotherapy: Predicting Growth of Cognitive-Behavioral Therapies and Culture-Sensitive Therapies

Three decades ago, Draguns (1975) pioneered a culturally oriented definition of psychotherapy:

> Psychotherapy is a procedure that is sociocultural in its ends and interpersonal in its means, it occurs between two or more individuals and is embedded in a broader, less visible, but no less real cultural context of shared social learning, store of meanings, symbols, and implicit assumptions concerning the nature of social living. (p. 273)

Draguns (2004, 2007) recently confirmed these defining criteria for contextually oriented psychotherapy and reviewed the current status of psychotherapeutic interventions for a global psychology. Draguns' review clearly demonstrated the coexistence of diversity of therapeutic systems that ranged from culturally distinct, indigenous therapies (such as the Morita and Naikan therapies of Japan) to modern psychoanalysis, and to cognitive-behavioral therapies around the world. Different cultures practice psychotherapy in diverse forms that reflect indigenous views of health and illness together with ways to help the individual in distress (e.g., Gielen, Fish, & Draguns, 2004; Moodley & West, 2005).

Globalization has changed the way in which we conduct our profession. In the past decade, information has accumulated rapidly on empirically supported treatments for particular disorders such as anxiety and mood disorders, most notably in North America, Europe, and Australia (Chambless et al., 1996, 1998). The majority of empirically supported treatments are those broadly classified as cognitive-behavior therapy (Chambless & Ollendick, 2001; Roth & Fonagy, 2004). Worldwide, organizations such as the Agency for Health Care Research and Quality (AHRQ; http://www.ahqr.gov/) and the Cochrane Collaboration (http://www.cochrane.org/) regularly release, on the Internet, databases of effective treatments for all types of medical illnesses. Psychiatric disorders are included in both the AHQR and Cochrane

Collaboration resources. Outcome research is based on a scientific definition of therapeutic effectiveness. Accumulated data from controlled studies have been subject to meta-analysis in order to derive an effect size of a treatment for a particular disorder (Lambert & Archer, 2006; Lipsey & Wilson, 1993). Moreover, professionals and consumers have access to the same information on the Internet. Over time consumers will learn to expect the "best available treatment" that suits their cultures in the age of information technology.

Cognitive-behavioral therapy has made great strides in the past 30 years. In the United States, it is currently the leading theoretical preference among psychologists today (Hays, 2006a). In a survey conducted every 10 years using Delphi methodology, a panel of 62 psychotherapy experts in the United States predicted psychotherapy trends toward 2010 (Norcross, Hedges, & Prochaska, 2002). The experts had a mean of 30 postdoctoral years of clinical experience. The expert panel predicted that cognitive-behavior therapy, culture-sensitive/multicultural therapy, cognitive (Beckian) therapy, interpersonal therapy (IPT), and technical eclecticism would be the top five most influential theoretical orientations in psychotherapy. By contrast, classical psychoanalysis, implosive therapy, transactional analysis, and Adlerian therapy were predicted to decline. The panel predicted that 18 of 38 modes of interventions would increase by 2010. They were: homework assignments, relapse prevention, use of virtual reality, problem-solving techniques, computerized therapies, and cognitive restructuring, among others. The expert panel also predicated 23 future scenarios. The four top-ranking scenarios included: (a) mandatory licensure at the master's level; (b) required use of evidence-based psychotherapies by health care systems; (c) requirement to provide evidence-based treatment for certain disorders at health care facilities; and (d) the use of practice guidelines as part of standard clinical practice. These predictions are consistent with the current, increased demand for culturally sensitive and effective psychotherapy particularly for ethnic minority groups in the United States (Hall, 2001; Miranda et al., 2005).

Evidence-Based Practice, Acculturation, and Cultural Accommodation

Evidence-based practice in psychology (EBPP) is the integration of the best available research with clinical expertise in the context of patient characteristics, culture, and preferences. (APA Presidential Task Force on Evidence-Based Practice, 2006, p. 273)

Diversity considerations have gained momentum with the definition on the previous page, which includes an explicit reference to the individual's culture and preferences. The implications of adopting this definition of evidenced-based practice have been discussed in the literature (e.g., Goodheart, Kazdin, & Sternberg, 2006; Hunsley, 2007). One important question concerns the availability and access to the best available practice in a culturally diverse society.

Specifically, what are the competencies that are necessary to perform EBPP? The APA Presidential Task Force (2006, p. 10) identified eight competencies, each of which is highly relevant to the practice of culturally responsive assessment and psychotherapy. The eight competences are (a) assessment, diagnostic judgment, systematic case formulation, and treatment planning; (b) clinical decision making, treatment and monitoring of progress; (c) interpersonal expertise; (d) self-reflection and skills acquisition; (e) empirical evaluation and research; (f) understanding the influence of individual and cultural differences on treatment; (g) seeking available resources; and (h) having a cogent rationale for clinical strategies.

The eight competencies are linked by empiricism and multicultural perspectives. Demographic diversity due to the influx of immigrants and sojourners creates challenges for professional counselors and therapists. To witness the increasing diversification of the U.S. society, 31% of the population is now comprised of persons of non-European ancestry and they are expected to form the majority by 2050 (U.S. Census Bureau, 2002). Furthermore, more than 1.5 million Southeast Asian refugees have sought refuge in the United States since 1975 (Hinton & Otto, 2006), making the United States one of the largest refugee settlement countries in the world. It is widely recognized that refugees are a population with high risk for developing severe psychological problems because of the multiple and severe nature of traumas they have been experiencing. The premigration traumas include deprivation of basic needs, physical injury and torture, incarceration and reeducation camps, and witnessing torture and killing (Bemak & Chung, 2002). Refugees' postmigration may easily generate additional problems of resettlement and acculturation stress.

The journal *Cognitive and Behavioral Practice* devoted an entire issue to the cultural adaptation of cognitive-behavioral therapy for Southeast Asian refugees with post-traumatic stress disorder. In the foreword, Hoffmann (2006) stated:

> Culture actually seems to shape and determine our perception and reasoning in rather profound ways. Clearly, these are important directions for future research that go far beyond simply reporting the ethnic composition of our study samples. Acknowledging and incorporating

culture into our empirically supported treatments might enable us to translate the effective treatment components that we found in one culture into another culture. (p. 244)

This statement is a clear indication that cognitive behavior therapists are faced with treatment of diverse clients, and, unless culturally adapted, conventional cognitive behavior therapy practices may fail to meet their needs. Evidence-based clinical practice needs to be examined for suitability in a multicultural context.

Empirical assessment of acculturation should be an integral part of evidence-based assessment. In fact, there is an increased need for understanding the process of acculturation as evidenced in a recent comprehensive publication on acculturation psychology (Sam & Berry, 2006). Earlier, Redfield, Linton, and Herskovits (1936) defined acculturation as "those phenomena, which result when groups of individuals having different cultures come into continuous first-hand contact, with subsequent changes in the original cultural patterns of either or both groups" (p. 149). At the individual level, acculturation is defined as a psychological adaptation process affecting sojourners, immigrants, and refugees (Berry & Sam, 1997; Ward, Bochner, & Furnham, 2001). Acculturation outcomes refer to the degree of success of the acculturation process. Van de Vijver and Tanaka-Matsumi (in press) distinguished three kinds of acculturation outcomes. The first is called psychological adjustment and involves the psychological condition induced by acculturation and is usually associated with well-being and mental health. The second is called sociocultural competence in the host domain and involves knowledge of the language and culture of the host domain. The third outcome is sociocultural competence in the culture of origin (e.g., maintenance of the linguistic skills in the heritage culture) and changes in this competence as an outcome variable.

Acculturative stress refers to the stress induced by acculturation. The perceived cultural distance is probably the single best predictor of acculturative stress. It is also relevant to the therapist-client relationship in multicultural therapy and counseling (Comaz-Diaz, 2006; Muran, 2006). For example, Wong (2006) and Tanaka-Matsumi (2006) engaged in a dialogue on how differences in the cultural identities of therapist and client might affect therapeutic progress from the standpoints of psychoanalytic therapy and cognitive behavioral therapy, respectively. Acculturation orientations are also relevant for experienced stress of the client. A bicultural or multicultural integration strategy tends to be negatively associated with stress. In contrast, marginalization is often associated with high levels of stress (Arredondo, 2002). The knowledge of cultural and cross-cultural psychology is essential to formulate and conduct culturally sensitive assessment and intervention procedures with particularly acculturating individuals (Draguns & Tanaka-Matsumi, 2003; Tanaka-Matsumi & Draguns, 1997).

Access to Empirically Supported Therapies

By now, a large body of scientific evidence is available on the effectiveness of psychotherapy (Lambert & Archer, 2006; Wampold, 2001). Empirically supported psychological interventions have only recently begun incorporating assessment of diversity issues (Hall, 2001; Miranda et al., 2005; Okazaki & Tanaka-Matsumi, 2006). In a comprehensive review and evaluation of empirically supported psychotherapies, Roth and Fonagy (2004) reported the effectiveness of psychotherapy for at least 11 psychological disorders, including anxiety disorders. At the same time, they stated that the evidence was largely for Caucasian groups from North American or European cultural backgrounds. It is, therefore, important to develop evidence for the diverse populations of the world.

Cross-cultural researchers report large ethnic and cultural disparities in access to mental health care (Snowden & Yamada, 2005). In other words, mobility of potential clients is restricted. In the United States, the Surgeon General's Report indicated that African Americans, Latinos, Asian Americans, and Native Americans have less access to, and availability of, mental health services than Euro-Americans (U.S. DHHS, 2001). There are many possible reasons for the disparities in access to service. One of the basic reasons is cultural differences in expectations for therapeutic help. Cultural distance between the therapist and client works against establishing a collaborative relationship (Pfeiffer, 1996). Recent research continues to indicate that ethnic minority people do not receive the benefit of efficacious therapies, as many do not even reach professionals who provide such services. Two recent studies help clarify the sources of disparities within the Asian American group in help-seeking behavior.

Akutsu, Castillo, and Snowden (2007) assessed the differential referral patterns to ethnic-specific versus mainstream mental health programs of Chinese, Japanese, Filipino, and Korean American groups in Los Angeles County. Those who sought help at ethnic-specific centers were frequently (50–74%) referred by family/friends and preferred to speak an Asian language/dialect as their primary language of choice when compared to Asian Americans participating in mainstream programs. Japanese and Korean Americans had a greater tendency to seek help when their families and friends referred them to ethnic-specific centers than Chinese Americans. They could speak their own language and be seen by their own ethnic staff. For Filipino Americans, there was no significant association between family referrals and the use of ethnic-specific programs. Those who sought help at mainstream programs were self-referred (28–34%), or had been referred by criminal justice (17–23%) or medical services (12–21%). The authors attributed these significant differences to levels of acculturation and integration within social networks. Akutsu and Chu (2006) found that the English language proficiency, familiarity with cultural scripts about mental health issues, and baseline epidemiological rates may account for differential rates of help-seeking at ethnic-specific versus mainstream service centers for Asian American groups in California. These results demonstrate the importance of assessing acculturation status of immigrants and sojourners when they seek help. Culturally salient assessment of reasons for referrals can provide clues for differential dropout rates and reluctance to seek help among certain Asian Americans. Assessment of contextual factors would be helpful especially because contextual factors may interact with case formulation.

Cultural Adaptation of Empirically Supported Psychotherapy

In the context of the present chapter, I define cultural adaptation as incorporation of culture-relevant and culture-sensitive information into the practice of psychotherapy with diverse clients. The multicultural literature has generated a series of guiding questions in order to accomplish cultural adaptation of a particular therapy. Table 7.1 presents frequently collected information in multicultural assessment and therapy from client referral to follow-up.

Broadly speaking, culturally sensitive therapy integrates cultural context with therapy content (Tanaka-Matsumi et al., 2002). Multicultural therapists ask the following questions when working in a cross-cultural setting.

1. What is the culture-relevant definition of maladaptive behavior that is considered abnormal in the client culture?
2. What is the accepted standard of role behavior?
3. Who is sanctioned to provide help for the individual in distress?
4. What expectations does the client culture have for psychotherapy and counseling?

TABLE 7.1
Frequently Collected Information in Multicultural Assessment and Therapy

Assessment Steps	Individual Domain	Cultural Domain
Initiation referral	Presenting problems	Cultural beliefs Cultural idioms of distress
Background	History Developmental context ADDRESSING (Hays, 2001) (Age, developmental disabilities, religion and spiritual orientation, ethnicity, socioeconomic status, sexual orientation, indigenous heritage, national origin, gender)	
Cultural assessment	Cultural identity Acculturation Value conflict	Social support network Family Psychosocial environment
Explanatory model of illness	Perceived causes of problem Client's causal explanatory model General illness beliefs	Cultural explanation of the illness Cultural metaphors of health and well-being
Help-seeking	Help-seeking behavior and treatment	Community resource Culturally approved change agents
Motivation	Motivation for change	Significant other's motivation
Adaptation	Levels of adaptive functioning	
Relationship	Client–therapist relationship	Cultural preference of the relationship
Assessment	Functional Analysis Antecedent Behavior Consequence Systematic evaluation	Cultural context of ABC Cultural triggers for behavior Culturally accepted alternative behavior Cultural metacontingencies
Case formulation	Case formulation Hypothesis formulation	
Comparison	Negotiation Comparison of explanatory models	
Intervention	Treatment components Techniques Hypothesis testing	
Ongoing Assessment	Self-monitoring and data collection	
Evaluation	Evaluation Treatment efficacy Feedback	Social validity Clinical effectiveness

(Continued)

TABLE 7.1
Frequently Collected Information in Multicultural
Assessment and Therapy (Continued)

Assessment Steps	Individual Domain	Cultural Domain
Satisfaction	Client satisfaction	Community satisfaction
Follow-up	Follow-up assessment	Community function

Sources: Evans & Paewai (1999); Hays (2001); Kleinman (1980); Seiden (1999); Tanaka-Matsumi, Seiden, & Lam (1996); Weiss et al. (1992).

In addition to these, therapist guidelines are available to assist the development and training of culturally informed therapists. For example, Hwang (2006) developed the Psychotherapy Adaptation and Modification Framework (PAMF) to guide adaptation of empirically supported treatments. The PAMF consists of six therapeutic domains and 25 therapeutic techniques. The six domains are generic and would be helpful to increase cultural awareness of the therapist when assessing the client in cross-cultural context. Briefly, the domains are: (a) dynamic issues and cultural complexities; (b) orientation to psychotherapy; (c) cultural beliefs; (d) the client-therapist relationship; (e) cultural modes of communicating distress; and (f) culture-specific issues (Hwang, 2006). The PAMF provides a culturally supportive framework for the delivery of empirically supported treatments. Hwang and Wood (2006) developed a similar framework for conducting cognitive-behavioral therapy with Chinese Americans in three core areas: (a) understanding generic principles for adapting CBT to meet the needs of Chinese American clients; (b) strengthening the client-therapist relationship; and (c) understanding Chinese views of self and mental illness. Hwang and Wood then created a total of 18 principles to help implement the three core goals. The authors considered that these principles can be used across groups or generations.

Hays (2001) developed the ADDRESSING framework for multicultural counselors and therapists to develop awareness of their own ethnic and cultural views and biases. Regardless of the client they see, the ADDRESSING approach encourages therapist's self-awareness and self-monitoring of his or her own cultural identity. Therapists use the acronym to generate hypotheses about a client's beliefs, values, emotional expression, strengths, and symptom presentation. Specifically, the ADDRESSING acronym prompts the therapist to address each letter: Age, Developmental and Acquired Disabilities, Religion and Spirituality, Ethnicity, Socioeconomic status,

Sexual orientation, Indigenous heritage, National origin, and Gender. Hays (2006b) explained the formulation of cognitive-behavior therapy for Alaskan native people with emphases on positive coping skills and reinforcement of strengths and social supports. Hays also employed problem solving and cognitive restructuring. Hays explained cognitive restructuring as the changing of unrealistic, unhelpful, and distressing thoughts to more realistic and helpful ones, as it is consistent with the traditional substance worldview on surviving the harsh Alaskan environment. The implication of using the ADDRESSING framework is the convergence of multiple sources of information to assist formulation of culturally sensitive hypotheses about the client's distress.

Evans and Paewai (1999) developed a 15-item checklist called the Bicultural Evaluation in order to assist cognitive-behavioral therapists in developing case conceptualization that aims to build rapport, ensure cultural fairness, and utilize multiple sources of data. Similarly, Ridley, Li, and Hill (1998) developed the Multicultural Assessment Procedure. The authors emphasize a hypothesis building approach to case formulation in a step-by-step procedure of data gathering and clinical judgment. Counselors are trained to gain knowledge of indigenous views and explanatory models of illness. Further, Ridley and Udipi (2002) considered cultural empathy to be the basis for culturally sensitive communication with the client. Ridley and Udipi defined cultural empathy as a special case of empathy with five features: (a) Cultural empathy can be learned; (b) is multidimensional with particularly perceptual and communicative dimensions; (c) is clearly concerned with an interpersonal process; (d) facilitates gathering and interpretation of cultural data; and (e) conveys attitudes of concern to clients and helps them make therapeutic gains.

Another study focused exclusively on identifying popular Hispanic cultural constructs that would have important cognitive and behavioral implications for treatment (Andréas-Hyman, Ortiz, Añez, Paris, & Davidson, 2006). The research team used qualitative methods to identify culture-salient concepts helpful for the development of culturally competent behavioral health care for Hispanics in the United States. These concepts included *Dignidad y Respeto* (dignity and respect), *Familismo* (family values and the value of family), *Personalismo* (relating on a personal level), *Machismo* (controlling maleness, a stereotype), and *Marianismo* (traditional cultural prescriptions assigned to women), and religion and spirituality. The authors assert that an active accommodation of cultural scripts is likely to have an impact on treatment access, adherence, and outcomes. Culturally competent practices, therefore, aim to integrate cultural context with evidence-based practice.

We might question if culturally adapted therapies are really effective and, if so, to what extent. Griner and Smith (2006) conducted a comprehensive literature search on culturally adapted mental health treatments and then performed a series of meta-analyses to determine effectiveness. They found 76 studies, with a total of 25,225 participants. Typically, studies included the comparison of a culturally adapted psychological intervention to a "traditional" intervention. Across all 76 studies, the average effect size was $d = .45$, indicating a moderately strong effect. The results were especially promising when the intervention was targeted for a specific cultural group (e.g., Hispanics) rather than a mixed group. The authors reported that as high as 84% of the total studies explicitly included cultural values and contents into culturally adapted treatment such as the use of folk heroes for children. Cultural adaptations included: (a) reference to cultural values and stories; (b) racial/ethnic matching of client and therapist, (c) service in client's native language, (d) multicultural paradigm of agency, (e) consultation with a culturally familiar individual, (f) outreach efforts, (g) extra service to retain clients, (h) oral administration of materials for illiterate clients, (i) cultural sensitivity training for professional staff, and (j) referral to external agencies for additional services. Griner and Smith's (2006) careful metal-analysis review showed the benefit of cultural adaptation of psychotherapy regardless of the technical content of each therapy.

In sum, the literature converges on the process-oriented cultural accommodation in multicultural counseling and therapy (Okazaki & Tanaka-Matsumi, 2004). The culture-relevant variables are expected to interact with the client's presenting problems and the treatment process. Assessment is an ongoing process within the interactive cultural context of client and therapist.

Scientific Efficacy and Clinical Effectiveness: Dissemination of Empirically Supported Therapies

In the past decade, psychotherapy researchers have conducted active investigations of the interface between research evidence and clinical evidence. The issue concerns similarities and differences in the criteria used to evaluate the outcome in research and practice (Goodheart et al., 2006). An important distinction is drawn between treatment efficacy and treatment effectiveness. Psychotherapy outcome research has established outcome based on multiple types of research evidence. Currently, there are two criteria for evaluating effectiveness of empirically supported psychotherapy outcome. The treatment *efficacy* refers to outcome obtained in an experimental research study and treatment *effectiveness* refers to outcome in the naturalistic settings of clinical practice (Nathan, Stuart, & Dolan, 2000). Efficacy studies entail random assignments of participants to experimental and control groups. Participants are recruited for intervention studies. Client-participants receive standard treatments according to the therapist guidelines. The duration of treatment is typically the same for all participants in the study. The group average outcome data form the basis for evaluating significance of treatment effects. The treatment efficacy studies put priority on establishing internal validity, that is, demonstrating cause-effect relationships between treatment and outcome within the controlled experimental design. Empirically supported therapies are scientifically efficacious and internally valid for specific groups of clients treated. Empirically supported treatments are defined according to several criteria (Chambless & Ollendick, 2001). In addition to randomized controlled trials as criteria for evaluating scientifically efficacious treatment, the development of therapist manual, detailed descriptions of psychotherapy research participants, and at least two independent scientific studies with significant result are required to establish evidence for treatment efficacy. However, a further question concerns the extent to which these results generalize to the naturalistic practice environment with diverse clients and varied therapists in diverse clinical practice settings in the community. To what extent do counselors and therapists benefit from evidence-based treatments?

Treatment effectiveness studies, on the other hand, try to increase external validity of a therapy outcome study. The most common means of achieving this goal is conducting clinical research in the community where practice takes place routinely (e.g., Borkovec, Ragusea, & Ruiz, 2001; Schulz, Resick, Huber, & Griffin, 2006). The therapists are also regular clinicians in those settings, and the participating clients are those who routinely seek help in the community or are commonly referred to the clinical study setting.

Hunsley (2007) reported identifying at least three dozen effectiveness studies conducted in various practice-as-usual settings, including independent practice, community clinics, and hospital outpatient clinics. This line of investigation into psychotherapy effectiveness in the community settings is encouraging for multicultural therapy researchers, as more of cultural context will be reflected in the clinical procedure.

Specifically, if therapists use empirically supported therapies outside of the original boundaries of client culture, they need to incorporate relevant cultural accommodation features into standard treatment. The successful attempts to disseminate efficacious treatments into the community and for each individual client will depend on cultural accommodation and cultural adaptation with diverse client groups. Establishing a link between treatment efficacy and clinical effectiveness with culturally diverse client groups is an urgent research goal (Bernal, Bonilla, & Bellido, 1995; Hall, 2001).

Many of the empirically supported therapies use cognitive-behavior therapy techniques and are specific to disorders identified by the DSM system (Chambless & Ollendick, 2001; Roth & Fonagy, 2004). A total of 108 treatments for adults and 37 for children have been recognized as well-established treatments for various psychological disorders by the Division 12 Task Force of the American Psychological Association (Chambless & Ollendick, 2001). Examples of disorders for which efficacious psychological treatment exist include major depression, panic disorder, social phobia, bulimia, posttraumatic stress disorder, as well as psychophysical problems such as tension headaches and rheumatoid arthritis (Chambless et al., 1996, 1998). Children and adolescents also benefit from evidence-based psychotherapies (Kazdin & Weisz, 2003). Miranda et al. (2005) noted that some evidence demonstrates that culturally sensitive applications of cognitive behavior therapy can be successful with youths from diverse cultural backgrounds including Puerto Ricans, African Americans, and Latinos in the United States. These reviews suggest that the effectiveness of empirically supported therapies depends on specific assessment rather than on categories of client ethnicity or minority status per se.

Kazdin (2006) offered a more focused response to the "long-standing hiatus between research and clinical practice" (p. 153). Kazdin explained that the issue concerns the remarkably different ways of evaluating information in research and in clinical settings and the use of information to draw conclusions. He emphasized the importance of systematic evaluation in clinical practice of each individual case. Systematic evaluation entails five steps in clinical practice: (a) specification and assessment of explicit treatment goals; (b) specification and assessment of procedures and processes; (c) selection of measures; (d) ongoing assessment on multiple occasions to track course of treatment; and (e) evaluation of data. The complete assessment of the individual case has the advantage of systematic data collection without relying on group-average data, which do not really reflect the particular individual in therapy.

The present discourse on the pros and cons of efficacy and effective study designs informs us about the need for tracking the progress of the individual client to exercise best clinical judgment. Multicultural assessment can be conducted in a similar fashion generating data.

Multicultural Cognitive-Behavioral Therapy

To date, most of the empirically supported psychotherapies have earned their statuses on the basis of group comparison data derived from randomized control designs. Typically, clients are randomly assigned to either the experimental clinical treatment condition or to a control condition such as a placebo group or perhaps a waiting-list control group. The effects are measured by comparing average scores on various outcome measures. Eventually, all the qualified results are used to conduct meta-analysis to examine if the performance of the experimental treatment group was better than that of the control group. The literature reports exactly how large the effect size of each treatment was for specific disorders. Lambert and Archer (2006) reviewed the past meta-analytic studies and concluded that "the outcomes of psychotherapy are substantial" (p. 116). To summarize Lambert and Archer (2006), effects of psychotherapy are more substantial than those of informal support systems and placebo control. About 75% of clients who undergo a course of treatment show some positive benefit, with 40% to 60% returning to a normal state of functioning. The gains occur efficiently within 20 sessions in about 50% of the clients.

Functional Analytic Approaches

I turn attention to more individualized and functional data in cognitive-behavioral therapies. Behavioral assessment and therapy is founded upon the use of empirical single-subject designs and assessment of functional relationships between the client's behavior and the environment (Baer, Wolf, & Risley, 1987; Haynes & O'Brien, 2000). Figure 7.1 shows the ABC functional analysis framework, and Table 7.2 describes steps in conducting the Culturally Informed Functional Assessment (CIFA) Interview (Seiden, 1999; Tanaka-Matsumi, Seiden, & Lam, 1996), with additional steps included for the functional analysis part. Multicultural therapists can follow the interview steps as they overlap with those assessment variables listed in Table 7.1.

FIGURE 7.1
Functional analysis formulation.

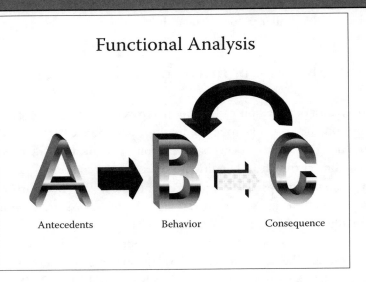

Functional Analysis

Antecedents   Behavior   Consequence

TABLE 7.2
Culturally Informed Functional Assessment (CIFA)
Interview

Client's cultural identity and level of acculturation

Client's presenting problems

Client's conceptualization of the problems and possible solutions

Functional assessment of the antecedent-target-consequence sequence

     Identification of problem behavior

     Assessment of antecedents and consequences

     Selection of target behavior(s) for change

     Selection of alternative behavior

     Selection of intervention techniques

     Selection of change agents

     Attention to motivational and developmental factors

     Evaluation of process and outcome

Negotiation of the functional analysis and the client's causal explanation of the problems

Development of a treatment plan acceptable to all parties involved

Data gathering

Discussion of treatment duration, course, and expected outcome

Sources: Nezu, Nezu, Friedman, & Haynes (1997); Seiden (1999); Tanaka-Matsumi, Seiden, & Lam (1996).

The goal of functional analysis is the "identification of important, controllable, causal functional relationships applicable to a specified set of target behaviors for an individual client" (Haynes & O'Brien, 1990, p. 654). Once the target behavior is selected, the task is to monitor the occurrence of the target behavior and its antecedent events and situations, and the target behavior's consequences, including response of others and one's own consequent behavior within the client's social network. For example, Toyokawa and Nedate (1996) reported a cognitive-behavior therapy case of a Japanese female client with a presenting problem of long-standing interpersonal problems including marital distress. The client was trained to use the Dysfunctional Thought Record to monitor thoughts and feelings she had whenever she had interpersonal difficulties. The purpose was to point out the irrational nature of her expectations and beliefs in social situations within the Japanese cultural context. The client was able to monitor her thoughts in social situations. Functional analysis provides information that is directly applicable to case formulation. That is, by recording the three-term contingency data of antecedents, target behavior, and consequences, in a repeated manner, the therapist begins to see consistently the predictable occurrence of the target behavior in specific situations. Careful monitoring of the consequent events also begins to predict whether or not the same behavior would occur more or less frequently in the future.

Functional analysis is an ongoing process by which the therapist monitors treatment variables and target behaviors throughout the duration of therapy, and provides an empirical approach to clinical case formulation, intervention, and evaluation (Haynes & O'Brien, 1990, 2000). Functional analysis involves the formulation and testing of hypotheses regarding variables that are determining the behavior of concern (Sturmey, 1996). The guiding principle underlying many of the evidence-based treatments for particular disorders is that of functional analysis of the individual client's behavior and his or her social environment. Culture is an integral part of the context, which should be evaluated carefully through functional analysis (Hayes & Toarmino, 1995; Tanaka-Matsumi, et al., 2002). The flexibility and empiricism underlying functional analysis should suit the assessment of cultural factors as they interact with the selected target problem of the client. This occurs in evidence-based practice with diverse clients in diverse settings (Tanaka-Matsumi, 2004).

Culturally Responsive Cognitive-Behavioral Therapy

The publication of the edited volume *Culturally Responsive Cognitive-Behavioral Therapy: Assessment, Practice, Supervision* (Hays & Iwamasa,

2006) marked a new beginning in cognitive-behavior therapy and multicultural counseling. The contributing authors to this volume placed priority on the assessment of diversity issues in the practice of cognitive-behavioral therapy. Culturally responsive, cognitive-behavioral therapists are trained to ask important questions with regard to the functional relationship between the expression of distress and cultural values, or the impact of client ethnicity and religiosity on coping with distress. Culturally sensitive, cognitive-behavioral analyses are available on such topics as somatic symptoms of PTSD (Hinton, Safren, Pollack, & Tran, 2006; Otto & Hinton, 2006; Schulz, Huber, & Resick, 2006) and panic attacks (Friedman, Braunstein, & Halpern, 2006; Zoellner, Feeny, Fitzgibbons, & Foa, 1999), among others. The functional analysis identifies antecedent events and consequences of problem behaviors within the client's social network. Cultural factors are viewed as embedded in the client's larger social environment and reinforcement history (Biglan, 1995; Skinner, 1971). Next, I review several studies that were published in the special issue of *Cognitive and Behavioral Practice* as the authors attempted to develop cultural adaptations of empirically supported cognitive-behavioral therapy of anxiety disorders. In each study, it was obvious that the therapist conducted functional assessment to identify fear-inducing triggers and the clients' consequent fear-reducing safety behaviors.

Hinton and Otto (2006) conducted a cultural analysis of somatic symptoms of a panic attack in traumatized Cambodian refugees who received cognitive-behavior therapy in Boston. The authors introduced the Cambodian cultural syndrome of "weak heart" based on the ethnographic account of "wind" as the causal agent of anxiety symptoms that produced somatization of trauma-related distress. They hypothesized that "weak heart" produces "syndrome-generated catastrophic cognitions and somatization" (Hinton & Otto, 2006, p. 251). Due to the cultural conceptualization of the "weak heart," Cambodian refugees experience multiple somatic symptoms during states of distress. Clients become hypervigilant of bodily symptoms as an indication of "weak heart." This self-focused attention activates the autonomic nervous system activities. Hinton and Otto (2006) observed that Cambodians usually construe a panic attack as a "wind attack" and consequently engage in self-statements to remove wind. These "coining" and "cupping" statements have the same function as the safety behaviors that maintain and perpetuate catastrophic cognitions about wind.

Somatic symptoms of panic attacks (such as dizziness, palpitations, and cold extremities) are triggered by certain antecedents. In this case, antecedents inducing somatic symptoms could be a loud noise, such as a sudden start of an automobile engine. This and similar noise generate considerable fear for Cambodians which, in turn, generated the target behaviors of dizziness, palpitations, and cold extremities. They may explain that the heart may be "weak," which starts the cycle of trauma associations. The individual may then engage in safety behaviors to escape from the wind. These safety behaviors are then reinforced due to fear reduction.

Hinton and Otto (2006) proposed that somatic-focused therapy for traumatized refugees would be most appropriate. Initially, they paid close attention to the traumatized refugees' somatic complaints and described how the sensations were induced as well as the nature of sensation-associated cognitions (e.g., trauma association, catastrophic cognitions). Assessment then focused on the assessment of somatic sensations and their antecedent and consequent events. The treatment followed the guidelines of CBT treatment of PTSD using the same components such as relaxation, exposure to somatic sensations, and relearning of the association of somatic symptoms with more positive events. Somatic-focused cognitive-behavior therapy is a culturally adapted cognitive-behavior therapy for panic attacks that suits Cambodian "explanatory model of the illness" (Kleinman, 1980).

In another article, Otto and Hinton (2006) elaborated on the core elements of exposure-based treatment. They worked with Cambodian refugee clients to negotiate the explanatory model, as they explored the significance of culture-specific beliefs about "wind" travelling through vessels in the body and creating a dangerous bodily condition. The therapists conducted sessions in a local Buddhist temple with interpreters. They also encouraged the use of cultural metaphors of somatic symptoms and Cambodian cultural concepts whenever possible. The authors stated: "Given evidence that interoceptive exposure, in combination with cognitive restructuring, is helpful in cases of panic disorder comorbid with PTSD, we felt confident in our application of these procedures, as long as we were sensitive to ways our treatment interacted with culturally specific beliefs" (Otto & Hinton, 2006, p. 265).

Another culturally appropriate treatment intervention for traumatized Vietnamese refugees used the Multiplex (TCMIE) Model of panic generation (Hinton, Safren, Pollack, & Tran, 2006; Iwamasa, Hsia, & Hinton, 2006). Based on the cognitive-behavioral model of trauma sensation, the authors explained the activation of various types of fear networks: "trauma sensations (T), catastrophic cognitions (C), metaphoric associations (M), and interoceptive conditions directly to psychological and somatic fear (I)" (Hinton et al., 2006, p. 271). Functional assessment can determine the causal mechanisms of fear-generating cues and subsequent associations with memories. Culturally adapted treatment included mindfulness, focusing on present state, and observing an observational attitude and controlling attentional focus (Hinton et al., 2006).

Friedman, Braunstein, and Halpern (2006) reported treatment outcomes of cognitive-behavior therapy of panic disorder and agoraphobia in a multiethnic, urban outpatient clinic. The study included a total of 24 African American and 16 Caucasian American clients with a primary diagnosis of panic disorder with or without agoraphobia, and it was based on a mean of 16.2 sessions.

Cognitive-behavior therapy of panic disorder consisted of a psycho-educational explanation of the biopsychosocial model of panic disorder; relaxation training; cognitive coping strategies; interoceptive exposure to somatic sensations; and in vivo exposure (Barlow, 2002).

Friedman and coworkers (2006) used multiple measures to assess the outcome. They reported that both African Americans and Caucasian Americans indicated significant reduction on measures of panic and agoraphobia symptoms. There was no significant effect of ethnicity, with the exception of the Beck Depression Inventory (BDI) scores. African Americans improved but had smaller declines in the BDI scores. The authors described African American cultural beliefs and therapeutic relationships. The results demonstrated that the culturally adapted cognitive-behavior therapy was effective for African American clients, and their treatment gains were similar to those of Caucasian American clients.

The examples reviewed here demonstrate the feasibility and effectiveness of culturally adapted cognitive-behavior therapy for anxiety disorders. At multiple clinical decision points, the clinician-researcher can develop hypotheses for individual clients and probe for the contribution of contextual variables. As part of the case formulation methods, the therapist gathers appropriate, idiographic data from the client and other informants (Bruch & Bond, 1998; Nezu, Nezu, Friedman, & Haynes, 1997; Persons & Tompkins, 1997). The step-by-step approach helps the therapist with clinical judgments in seven domains: (a) the problem list; (b) core beliefs; (c) precipitating and activating situations; (d) the working hypothesis; (e) origins or early history of the problem; (f) the treatment plan; and (g) predicted outcome of treatment (Persons & Tompkins, 1997). A major advantage of the case formulation approach is its process orientation and individualized approach. The multicultural guidelines (Tables 7.1 and 7.2) reviewed in this chapter should be of value when using the case formulation approach with diverse clients. The therapist's knowledge of the client's cultural definitions of problem behavior and cultural norms regarding behavior, change strategies, and the culturally approved change agents will enhance the degree of cultural accommodation (Tanaka-Matsumi, 2004). Assessment will then be both more accurate and more useful.

Conclusion

Multicultural counseling and therapy will continue to develop in response to the diversified needs of individuals and groups. Given that, as evidence-based practice is becoming a standard in some rapidly changing societies, the present chapter assessed the status of cognitive-behavioral therapy and ways to incorporate culture-relevant assessment. Functional analysis is well-suited to identify cultural contingencies of the presenting problem as it interacts with the client's social environment. The recent literature demonstrates the successful applications of empirically supported treatment to culturally diverse clients. Future research questions will include the definition of evidence within cultural context. From the perspective of narrative psychology, we may examine the nature of evidence as it links to values associated with modern science (McLeod, 2001). Finally, globalization will encourage training of multicultural mental health professionals who can apply universally applicable principles of behavior change and implement culturally specific treatment. Functional analysis is a flexible and individualized method that can identify culture-relevant content in cognitive-behavior therapy for diverse clients.

References

Akutsu, P. D., Castillo, E. D., & Snowden, L. R. (2007). Differential referral patterns to ethnic-specific and mainstream mental health programs for four Asian American groups. *American Journal of Orthopsychiatry, 77,* 95–103.

Akutsu, P. D., & Chu, J. O. (2006). Clinical problems that initiate professional help-seeking behaviors from Asian Americans. *Professional Psychology: Research and Practice, 37,* 407–415.

American Psychological Association. (2003). Guidelines on multicultural education, training, research, practice, and organizational change for psychologists. *American Psychologist, 58,* 377–402.

Andréas-Hyman, R.C., Ortiz, J., Añez, L. M., Paris, M., & Davidson, L. (2006). Culture and clinical practice: Recommendations for working with Puerto Ricans and other Latinas(os) in the United States. *Professional Psychology: Research and Practice, 37,* 694–701.

APA Presidential Task Force on Evidence-Based Practice (2006). Evidence-based practice in Psychology. *American Psychologists, 61,* 271–285.

Arredondo, P. (2002). Counseling individuals from marginalized and underserved groups. In P. B. Pedersen, J. G. Draguns, W. J. Lonner, & J. E. Trimble (Eds.), *Counseling across cultures* (5th ed., pp. 233–250). Thousand Oaks, CA: Sage.

Baer, D. M., Wolf, M. M., & Risley, T. R. (1987). Some still-current dimensions of applied behavior analysis. *Journal of Applied Behavior Analysis, 20*, 313–328.

Barlow, D. H. (2002). *Anxiety and its disorders: The nature and treatment of anxiety and panic* (2nd ed.). New York: Guilford Press.

Barlow, D. H. (2004). Psychological treatments. *American Psychologist, 59,* 869–879.

Bemak, F., & Chung, R. C. Y. (2002). Counseling and psychotherapy with refugees. In P. B. Pedersen, W. J. Lonner, J. G. Draguns, & J. E. Trimble (Eds.), *Counseling across cultures* (5th ed., pp. 209–232). Thousand Oaks, CA: Sage.

Bernal, G., Bonilla, J., & Bellido, C. (1995). Ecological validity and cultural sensitivity for outcomes research: Issues for cultural adaptation and development of psychosocial treatments with Hispanics. *Journal of Abnormal Child Psychology, 23,* 67–82.

Berry, J. W., & Sam, D. L. (1997). Acculturation and adaptation. In J. W. Berry, M. H. Segall, & Ç. Kağitçibaşi (Eds.), *Handbook of cross-cultural psychology: Social behavior and applications* (2nd ed., Vol. 3, pp. 291–326). Boston: Allyn & Bacon.

Biglan, A. (1995). *Changing cultural practices: A contextualist framework for intervention research.* Reno, NV: Context.

Borkovec, T. D., Ragusea, S. A., & Ruiz, M. (2001). The Pennsylvania Practice Research Network and future possibilities for clinically meaningful and scientifically rigorous psychotherapy effectiveness research. *Clinical Psychology: Science and Practice, 8,* 155–167.

Bruch, M., & Bond, F. (1998). *Beyond diagnosis: Case formulation approaches in CBT.* Chichester, UK: John Wiley & Sons.

Chambless, D. L., Baker, M. J., Beaucom, D. H., Beutler, L. E., Calhoun, K. S., Crits-Christoph, P., et al. (1998). Update on empirically validated therapies: II. *Clinical Psychologist, 51,* 3–16.

Chambless, D. L., & Ollendick, T. H. (2001). Empirically supported psychological interventions: Controversies and evidence. *Annual Review of Psychology, 52,* 685–716.

Chambless, D. L., Sanderson, W. C., Shoham, V., Johnson, S. B., Pope, K., Crits-Cristoph, P., et al. (1996). An update on empirically validated therapies. *Clinical Psychologist, 49,* 5–18.

Comaz-Diaz, L. (2006). Cultural variation in the therapeutic relationship. In C. D. Goodheart, A. E. Kazdin, & R. J. Sternberg (Eds.), *Evidence-based psychotherapy: Where practice and research meet* (pp. 81–106). Washington, DC: American Psychological Association.

Draguns, J. G. (1975). Resocialization into culture. The complexities of taking a worldwide view of psychotherapy. In R. W. Brislin, S. Bochner, & W. J. Lonner (Eds.), *Cross-cultural perspectives on learning* (pp. 273–289). Beverly Hills, CA: Sage.

Draguns, J. G. (2004). From speculation through description toward investigation: A prospective glimpse at cultural research in psychotherapy. In U. P. Gielen, J. M. Fish, & J. G. Draguns (Eds.). *Handbook of culture, therapy, and healing* (pp. 369–387). Mahwah, NJ: Lawrence Erlbaum Associates.

Draguns, J. G. (2007). Psychotherapeutic and related interventions for a global psychology. In M. J. Stevens & U. P. Gielen (Eds.), *Toward a global psychology: Theory, research, intervention, and pedagogy* (pp. 233–266). Mahwah, NJ: Lawrence Erlbaum Associates.

Draguns, J. G., & Tanaka-Matsumi, J. (2003). Assessment of psychopathology across and within cultures: Issues and findings. *Behaviour Research and Therapy, 41,* 755–794.

Evans, I. M., & Paewai, K. (1999). Functional analysis in a bicultural context. *Behaviour Change, 16,* 20–36.

Friedman, S., Braunstein, J. W., & Halpern, B. (2006). Cognitive behavioral treatment of panic disorder and agoraphobia in a multiethnic urban outpatient clinic: Initial presentation and treatment outcome. *Cognitive and Behavioral Practice, 13,* 282–292.

Gielen, U. P., Fish, J. M., & Draguns, J. G. (Eds.). (2004). *Handbook of culture, therapy, and healing.* Mahwah, NJ: Lawrence Erlbaum Associates.

Goodheart, C. D., Kazdin, A. E., & Sternberg, R. J. (Eds.). (2006). *Evidence-based psychotherapy: Where practice and research meet.* Washington, DC: American Psychological Association.

Griner, D., & Smith, T. B. (2006). Culturally adapted mental health interventions: A meta-analytic review. *Psychotherapy: Theory, Research, Practice, Training, 43,* 531–548.

Hall, G. C. N. (2001). Psychotherapy research with ethnic minorities: Empirical, ethical, and conceptual issues. *Journal of Consulting and Clinical Psychology, 69,* 502–510.

Hall, J. (2006). Working in cross-cultural and international settings. In J. Hall & S. Llewelyn (Eds.), *What is clinical psychology?* (4th ed., pp. 313–330). Oxford, UK: Oxford University Press.

Hall, J. E., & Lunt, I. (2005). Global mobility for psychologists: The role of psychology organizations in the United States, Canada, Europe, and other regions. *American Psychologists, 60,* 712–726.

Hayes, S. C., & Toarmino, D. (1995). If behavioral principles are generally applicable, why is it necessary to understand cultural diversity? *The Behavior Therapist, 18,* 21–23.

Haynes, S. H., & O'Brien, W. H. (1990). Functional analysis in behavior therapy. *Clinical Psychology Review, 10,* 649–668.

Haynes, S. H., & O'Brien, W. H. (2000). *Principles of behavioral assessment: A functional approach to psychological assessment.* New York: Plenum/Kluwer Press.

Hays, P. A. (2001). *Addressing cultural complexities in practice: A framework for clinicians & counselors.* Washington, DC: American Psychological Association.

Hays, P. A. (2006a). Introduction: Developing culturally responsive cognitive-behavioral therapies. In P. A. Hays & G. Y. Iwamasa (Eds.), *Culturally responsive cognitive-behavioral therapy: Assessment, practice, and supervision* (pp. 3–19). Washington, DC: American Psychological Association.

Hays, P. A. (2006b). Cognitive-behavioral therapy with Alaska native people. In P. A. Hays & G. Y. Iwamasa (Eds.), *Culturally responsive cognitive-behavioral therapy: Assessment, practice, and supervision* (pp. 47–72). Washington, DC: American Psychological Association.

Hays, P. A., & Iwamasa, G. Y. (Eds.). (2006). *Culturally responsive cognitive-behavioral therapy: Assessment, practice, and supervision*. Washington, DC: American Psychological Association.

Hinton, D. E. (2006). Culturally sensitive CBT. *Cognitive and Behavioral Practice* [Special issue], *13*, 246–248.

Hinton, D. E., & Otto, M. W. (2006). Symptom presentation and symptom meaning among traumatized Cambodian refugees: Relevance to a somatically focused cognitive-behavior therapy. *Cognitive and Behavioral Practice, 13*, 249–260.

Hinton, D., Safren, S. A., Pollack, M. H., & Tran, M. (2006). Cognitive-behavior therapy for Vietnamese refugees with PTSD and comorbid panic attacks. *Cognitive and Behavioral Practice, 13*, 271–281.

Hoffmann, S. G. (2006). The importance of culture in cognitive and behavioral practice. *Cognitive and Behavioral Practice, 13*, 243–245.

Hunsley, J. (2007). Addressing key challenges in evidence-based practice in psychology. *Professional Psychology: Research and Practice, 38*, 113–121.

Hwang, W. C. (2006). The psychotherapy adaptation and modification framework: Application to Asian Americans. *American Psychologist, 61*, 702–715.

Hwang, W. C., & Wood, J. J. (2006). Cognitive-behavioral therapy with Chinese Americans: Research, theory, and clinical practice. *Cognitive and Behavioral Practice, 13*, 293–303.

Iwamasa, G. Y., Hsia, C., & Hinton, D. (2006). Cognitive-behavioral therapy with Asian Americans. In P. A. Hays & G. Y. Iwamasa (Eds.), *Culturally responsive cognitive-behavioral Therapy: Assessment, practice, and supervision* (pp. 117–140). Washington, DC: American Psychological Association.

Kazdin, A. E. (2006). Assessment and evaluation in clinical practice. In C. D. Goodheart, A. E. Kazdin, & R. J. Sternberg (Eds.), *Evidence-based psychotherapy: Where practice and research meet* (pp. 153–178). Washington, DC: American Psychological Association.

Kazdin, A. E., & Weisz, J. R. (Eds.). (2003). *Evidence-based psychotherapies for children and adolescents*. New York: Guilford Press.

Kleinman, A. M. (1980). *Patients and healers in the context of culture*. Berkeley: University of California Press.

Lambert, M. J., & Archer, A. (2006). Research findings on the effects of psychotherapy and their implications for practice. In C. D. Goodheart, A. E. Kazdin, & R. J. Sternberg (Eds.), *Evidence-based psychotherapy: Where practice and research meet* (pp. 111–130). Washington, DC: American Psychological Association.

Leong, F. T. L., & Leach, M. M. (2007). Internationalising counseling psychology in the United States: A SWOT analysis. *Applied Psychology, 56*, 165–181.

Lipsey, M. W., & Wilson, D. B. (1993). The efficacy of psychological, educational, and behavioral treatment: Confirmation from meta-analysis. *American Psychologist, 48*, 1181–1209.

Marsella, A. J. (1998). Toward a "global-community psychology": Meeting the needs of a changing world. *American Psychologist, 53*, 1282–1291.

McLeod, J. (2001). *Qualitative research in counselling and psychotherapy*. London: Sage.

Miranda, J., Bernal, G., Lau, A., Kohn, L., Hwang, W. C., & LaFromboise, T. (2005). State of the science on psychosocial interventions for ethnic minorities. *Annual Review of Clinical Psychology, 1*, 113–142.

Moodley, R., & West, W. (Eds.). (2005). *Integrating traditional healing practices into counseling and psychotherapy*. Thousand Oaks, CA: Sage.

Muran, J. C. (Ed.). (2006). *Dialogues on difference: Studies of diversity in the therapeutic relationship.* Washington, DC: American Psychological Association.

Muto, T. (Ed.). (2006). *Akuseputansu & komittomento serapi no bunmyaku* [Context of acceptance and commitment therapy]. Tokyo: Brain Shuppan.

Nathan, P. E., Stuart, S. P., & Dolan, S. L. (2000). Research on psychotherapy efficacy and effectiveness: Between Scylla and Charybdis? *Psychological Bulletin, 126*, 964–981.

Nezu, A. M., Nezu, C. M., Friedman, S. H., & Haynes, S. N. (1997). Case formulation in behavior therapy: Problem solving and functional analytic strategies. In T. D. Eells (Eds.), *Handbook of psychotherapy case formulation* (pp. 368–401). New York: Guilford.

Norcross, J. C., Hedges, M., & Prochaska, J. O. (2002). The face of 2010: A Delphi poll on the future of psychotherapy. *Professional Psychology: Research and Practice, 33*, 316–322.

Oei, T. P. S. (Ed.). (1998). *Behaviour therapy and cognitive behaviour therapy in Asia.* Glebe, Australia: Edumedia Pty Ltd.

Okazaki, S., & Tanaka-Matsumi, J. (2006). Cultural considerations in cognitive-behavioral assessment. In P. Hays & G. Y. Iwamasa (Eds.), *Culturally responsive cognitive-behavioral therapy: Assessment, practice, and supervision* (pp. 247–266). Washington, DC: American Psychological Association.

Otto, M.W., & Hinton, D. E. (2006). Modifying exposure-based CBT for Cambodian refugees with posttraumatic stress disorder. *Cognitive and Behavioral Practice, 13*, 261–270.

Pedersen, P. B. (1997). *Culture-centered counseling interventions: Striving for accuracy.* Thousand Oaks, CA: Sage

Pedersen, P. B. (2002). Ethics, competence, and other professional issues in culture-centered counseling. In P. B. Pedersen, J. G. Draguns, W. J. Lonner, & J. E. Trimble (Eds.), *Counseling across cultures* (5th ed., pp. 3–28). Thousand Oaks, CA: Sage.

Pedersen, P. B., Draguns, J. G., Lonner, W. J., & Trimble, J. E. (Eds.). (2002). *Counseling across cultures* (5th ed.). Thousand Oaks, CA: Sage.

Persons, J. B., & Tompkins, M. A. (1997).Cognitive behavioural case formulation. In T. D. Eells (Ed.), *Handbook of psychotherapy case formulation* (pp. 314–339). New York: Guilford Press.

Pfeiffer, W. M. (1996). Kulturpsychiatrische aspekte der migration. In E. Koch, M. Özek, & W. M. Pfeiffer (Eds.), *Psychologie und Pathologie der Migration* [Cultural psychiatric aspects of migration] (pp. 17–30). Freiburg/Breisgau: Lambertus.

Qian, M., & Wang, A. (2005). The development of behavioral therapy and cognitive behavioral therapy in P. R. China. *Japanese Journal of Behavior Therapy, 31*, 111–126.

Redfield, R., Linton, R., & Herskovits, M. J. (1936). Memorandum on the study of acculturation. *American Anthropologist, 38,* 149–152.

Ridley, C. R., Li, L. C., & Hill, C. L. (1998). Multicultural assessment: Reexamination, reconceptualization, and practical application. *Counseling Psychologist, 26*, 827–910.

Ridley, C. R., & Udipi, S. (2002). Putting cultural empathy into practice. In P. B. Pedersen, J. G. Draguns, W. J. Lonner, & J. E. Trimble (Eds.), *Counseling across cultures* (5th ed., pp. 317–334). Thousand Oaks, CA: Sage.

Roth, A., & Fonagy, P. (2004). *What works for whom? A critical review of psychotherapy research* (2nd ed.). New York: Guilford.

Sam, D. L., & Berry, J. W. (Eds.). (2006). *The handbook of acculturation psychology.* Cambridge, UK: Cambridge University Press.

Sato, S., & Aikawa, M. (2005). *Jissen! Sosharu sukiru kyoiku* [Practice! Social skills education]. Tokyo: Tosho Bunka.

Schulz, P. M., Huber, L. C., & Resick, P. A. (2006). Practical adaptations of cognitive processing therapy with Bosnian refugees: Implications for adapting practice to a multicultural clientele. *Cognitive and Behavioral Practice, 13*, 343–344.

Schulz, P. M., Resick, P. A., Huber, L. C., & Griffin, M. G. (2006). The effectiveness of cognitive processing therapy for PTSD with refugees in a community setting. *Cognitive and Behavioral Practice, 13*, 322–331.

Seiden, D. Y. (1999). *Cross-cultural behavioral case formulation with Chinese neurasthenic patients.* Unpublished doctoral dissertation, Hofstra University, Hempstead, NY.

Skinner, B. F. (1971). *Beyond freedom and dignity.* New York: Bantam Vintage.

Snowden, L. R., & Yamada, A. M. (2005). Cultural differences in access to care. *Annual Review of Clinical Psychology, 1*, 143–166.

Sternberg, R. J., & Grigorenko, E. L. (2004). *Culture and competence: Contexts of life success.* Washington, DC: American Psychological Association.

Stevens, M. J., & Gielen, U. P. (Eds.). (2007). *Toward a global psychology: Theory, research, intervention, and pedagogy.* Mahwah, NJ: Lawrence Erlbaum Associates.

Sturmey, P. (1996). *Functional analysis in clinical psychology.* New York: John Wiley.

Sue, D. W., & Sue, S. (2003). *Counseling the culturally diverse: Theory and practice* (4th ed.). New York: John Wiley & Sons.

Sue, S. (1998). In search of cultural competence in psychotherapy and counseling. *American Psychologist, 53*, 440–448.

Tanaka-Matsumi, J. (2004). Behavioral assessment and individual differences. In M. Hersen, S. Haynes, & E. M. Heiby (Eds.), *The comprehensive handbook of assessment. Vol. 3: Behavioral assessment* (pp. 359–393). New York: John Wiley.

Tanaka-Matsumi. J. (2006). Cultural and acculturative inscrutability of Asian American clients. In C. J. Muran (Ed.), *Dialogue on difference: Studies of diversity in the therapeutic relationship* (pp. 208–213). Washington, DC: American Psychological Association.

Tanaka-Matsumi, J., & Draguns, J. G. (1997). Culture and psychopathology. In J. Berry, M. Segall, & Ç. Kağitçibaşi (Eds.), *Handbook of cross-cultural psychology* (2nd ed.), *Vol. 3: Social psychology, personality and psychopathology* (pp. 449–491). Boston: Allyn & Bacon.

Tanaka-Matsumi, J., Higginbotham, H. N., & Chang, R. (2002). Cognitive-behavioral approaches to counseling across cultures: A functional analytic approach for clinical applications. In P. B. Pedersen, J. G. Draguns, W. J. Lonner, & J. E. Trimble (Eds.), *Counseling across cultures* (5th ed., pp. 337–354). Thousand Oaks, CA: Sage.

Tanaka-Matsumi, J., Seiden, D., & Lam, K. (1996). The Culturally Informed Functional Assessment (CIFA) Interview: A strategy for cross-cultural behavioral practice. *Cognitive and Behavioral Practice, 3*, 215–233.

Toyokawa, T., & Nedate, K. (1996). Application of cognitive behavioral therapy to interpersonal problems: A case study of a Japanese female client. *Cognitive and Behavioral Practice, 3*, 289–308.

U.S. Census Bureau (2002, November). *Demographic trends in the 20th century: Census 2000 special reports.* Retrieved December 10, 2006, from http://www. census.gov/prod/ 2002pubs/ censr-4.pdf.

U.S. Department of Health and Human Services (2001). *Mental health: Culture, race, and ethnicity. A supplement to mental health: A report of the Surgeon General.* Rockville, MD: U.S. Department of Human Services.

Van de Vijver, F. J. R., & Tanaka-Matsumi, J. (in press). Cross-cultural research methods. In D. McKay (Ed.), *Handbook of research methods in abnormal and clinical psychology.* Thousand Oaks, CA: Sage.

Wampold, B. E. (2001). *The great psychotherapy debate: Models, methods, and findings.* Mahwah, NJ: Lawrence Erlbaum Associates.

Ward, C., Bochner, S., & Furnham, A. (2001). *The psychology of culture shock.* London: Routledge.

Weiss, M. G., Doongaji, D. R., Siddhartha, S., Wypij, D., Pathare, S., Bhatawdekar, M., et al. (1992). The Explanatory Model Interview Catalogue (EMIC) contribution to cross-cultural research methods from a study of leprosy and mental health. *British Journal of Psychiatry, 160,* 819–830.

Wong, P. S. (2006). The inscrutable Doctor Wu. In C. J. Muran (Ed.), *Dialogue on difference: Studies of diversity in the therapeutic relationship* (pp. 187–202). Washington, DC: American Psychological Association.

Zoellner, L. A., Feeny, N.C., Fitzgibbons, L. A., & Foa, E. B. (1999). Responses of African American and Caucasian women to cognitive behavioral therapy for PTSD. *Behavior Therapy, 30,* 581–595.

Suggested Readings

Draguns, J. G. (2007). Psychotherapeutic and related interventions for a global psychology. In M. J. Stevens & U. P. Gielen (Eds.), *Toward a global psychology: Theory, research intervention, and pedagogy* (pp. 233–266). Mahwah, NJ: Lawrence Erlbaum Associates.

This gives a broad overview of the practice of psychotherapy around the world. Readers will appreciate the diverse psychotherapies and research outcome on their effectiveness.

Hays, P. A., & Iwamasa, G. Y. (Eds.). (2006). *Culturally responsive cognitive-behavioral therapy: Assessment, practice, and supervision.* Washington, DC: American Psychological Association.

This is a first volume with a title indicating culturally responsive cognitive-behavioral therapy with an emphasis on the practice of CBT. Chapters are organized according to ethnicity, age, gender, and disabilities.

Miranda, J., Bernal, G., Lau, A., Kohn, L., Hwang, W. C., & LaFromboise, T. (2005). State of the science on psychosocial interventions for ethnic minorities. *Annual Review of Clinical Psychology, 1,* 113–142.

This is a review article on the psychological interventions for ethnic minority groups in the United States. It covers minority children, youth, and adults. Authors call for more research and increased access to effective mental health services for minority clients.

On-line Readings in Psychology and Culture (2002–2006), Center for Cross-Cultural Research, Western Washington University. Retrieved from http://www.ac.wwu.edu/~culture/readings.htm

This is a unique Internet text with free access to close to 100 articles by cross-cultural authors. Unit 10 is about counseling across cultures.

Otto, M.W., & Hinton, D. E. (2006). Modifying exposure-based CBT for Cambodian refugees with posttraumatic stress disorder. *Cognitive and Behavioral Practice, 13*, 261–270.

This article describes specific aspects of cultural adaptation of cognitive-behavioral therapy (CBT) with specifically PTSD problems. CBT is embedded in cultural analyses of the meanings of illness and culture-specific interpretations of somatization.

Tanaka-Matsumi, J., Seiden, D., & Lam, K. (1996). The Culturally Informed Functional Assessment (CIFA) Interview: A strategy for cross-cultural behavioral practice. *Cognitive and Behavioral Practice, 3*, 215–233.

This article describes eight steps in conducting the CIFA Interview with culturally different clients using functional analysis as a main tool. It also includes a case example to illustrate each CIFA step.

8

Multiculturalism and School Counseling

Creating Culturally Relevant Comprehensive Guidance and Counseling Programs

Hardin L. K. Coleman and Jennifer J. Lindwall

Contents

The profession of school counseling is working to respond to two external pressures that highlight the need to systematically create and implement culturally responsive comprehensive guidance and counseling programs (CR-CGCPs). The first is globalization. Preparing students to compete within a global economy has many dimensions about which professional school counselors need to be aware and to which they need to respond as they develop effective school counseling programs. The second is the achievement gap that is a function of race and class in American society. As Thernstrom and Thernstrom (2003) have noted, targeted ethnic minorities in the United States underperform their European American peers, whereas many immigrant populations, particularly from Asia and India, outperform their European American peers. These achievement gaps create a challenge to American schools in their efforts to provide an equitable educational experience. Although there is a growing literature on the multicultural competence of school counselors, the focus of these investigations is more on the awareness, knowledge, and counseling skills than on the ability of counseling and guidance programs to prepare students to be effective citizens in a pluralistic society or to close the achievement gap. The purpose of this chapter is to present emerging ideas concerning multiculturalism within school counseling programs that can be used to address globalization, the achievement gap, and the social-emotional needs of diverse youth. It is our intent to provide guidance for how school counselors can become more effective instruments of educational equity.

In this chapter we will first summarize the literature on multicultural competence in school counselors. Then we will outline the central components for culturally responsive comprehensive guidance and counseling programs, illustrating how these components are put into practice. We will use the American School Counseling Association's (ASCA) framework for school counseling to organize this discussion. The third focus of the chapter will be on ways in which school counselors can address salient factors in minority student achievement, followed by a summary of the literature on the role of school counseling for preparing students to become citizens in a global economy. The next section of the chapter will describe programmatic suggestions, including implications for the training and ongoing professional development of school counselors.

Multicultural Counseling Competence

Sue (2001) has set the current standard in the field for understanding multicultural counseling competence. Although there have been challenges to this construct (e.g., Weinrach & Thomas, 2004), the research and policy development in this area has been dominated by Sue's supposition that multicultural competence involves the following three dimensions: a) *awareness,* which is the understanding that cultural factors such as race, gender, or class have a substantial impact on human development and the counseling process; b) *knowledge* concerning the ways in which cultural processes have this impact across different groups; and c) *skills,* which includes the ability to effectively integrate the impact of cultural factors into the provision of professional services. In the field of professional counseling, these three dimensions have been discussed in a variety of ways. In this section, we will summarize how the literature has described the types of awareness, knowledge, and skills that a professional school counselor needs to develop in order to be considered multiculturally competent.

Awareness

As with all counseling professionals, it is a consistent request that a multiculturally competent school counselor become aware of his or her own cultural being. This includes being aware of how cultural factors have influenced his or her personal development and how they affect an individual's personal worldview. It is a standard within the field that the more aware one is of how cultural factors affect one's own values and behaviors, the better able one is to understand how these factors influence the behaviors of others. Within the literature, there are some specific suggestions about which school counselors must become aware, including one's own cultural background and characteristics (Baruth & Manning, 2000), one's assumptions and beliefs about working with culturally diverse families (Bryan, 2005), the interplay between the cultures of the child, school, larger community, and the school counselor him- or herself (Coleman & Baskin, 2003), and the differences in power among individuals within the context of the school (Constantine & Yeh, 2001). Furthermore, school counselors should engage in a continuous "cultural self analysis" (Harris, 1999) that includes reflecting on the ways in which the school counselor's culture impacts his or her life, considering how aware he or she is of racism and how it impacts the experiences of diverse individuals. This also involves thinking about the expectations that he or she has for culturally diverse youth. This type of self-awareness is critical in understanding how a school counselor approaches his or her work with youth and families.

Knowledge

One of the challenges to becoming an effective school counselor is the wide range of factors one needs to come to master—from issues in vocational development and career guidance, through behavior management, to effective developmental guidance. To be multiculturally competent, a school counselor must also understand how cultural background interacts with these processes. For example, one must understand how a student's cultural background and personal experiences affect his or her perception of vocational possibility or choice. This might include having an understanding of the multiple factors (e.g., poverty, racism, violence) that impact the career development of youth and the opportunities that are available for them. This knowledge will come into play when a school counselor facilitates discussions about career development with students. The school counselor can be sure to integrate topics including poverty, racism, and violence into these dialogues and introduce ways in which youth can cope with these and other challenges they might encounter on their career development journey (Constantine, 1998). Creating and implementing programs without integrating this knowledge will lead to programs that do not serve all students within a pluralistic society.

Some of the general cultural factors about which a school counselor needs to be knowledgeable are (a) the effects of social stratification, (b) racial, gender, and class bias, (c) acculturation processes, (d) immigration, (e) cultural learning styles, and (f) culturally responsive pedagogy. In addition to these general factors, a school counselor also needs to understand how racial and ethnic background as well as current geographic context interact with these factors to affect a particular student. One example is being knowledgeable about how these factors impact youths' career expectations and the opportunities that are available for them. In turn, the school counselor can have an understanding of various career interventions that allow students to explore their career interests and improve their understanding about the education and training that is needed for different career paths (Constantine, 1998).

As Green, Conley, and Barnett (2005) have advocated, it is important for school counselors to be knowledgeable about and able to use an ecological perspective to conceptualize their practice. We believe that an ecological perspective represents a significant departure from the understanding of cultural processes that have dominated the conversation concerning multicultural competence for the past three decades. As Coleman, Norton, Miranda, and McCubbin (2003) have described, the primary theory of culture that has been used to understand cultural processes in counseling has been structural. Structural theories of culture emphasize the influence of historical institutions and groupings on current behavior. In these theories, the impact of group membership, most often determined by race, class, and gender, takes on a dominant role in a person's understanding of self and his or her place in the world. The influence of structural theories can be noted in the focus that is placed on developing theories of ethnic psychologies and the normative role of racial or group membership on the counseling process.

The understanding of cultural processes proposed by Bronfenbrenner (1979) is more inclusive and dynamic. His ecological perspective suggests that an individual's behavior is the result of a dynamic interaction between historical factors, institutional structures, social context, and the individual's meaning-making processes. This dynamism requires the school counselor to move beyond constructions of individuals as a function of their race or gender, and asks them to conceptualize the individual within both an historical and contextual perspective. This perspective asks the school counselor to understand how historical and contextual factors have influenced the individual's development, how the current context is serving to re-create historical processes (e.g., poor academic performance for lower income individuals), and to use this understanding to create change in both the context and the individual to facilitate positive outcomes.

Skills

This is the most challenging dimension within the Sue construct of multicultural competence. It is the dimension that generates the most suggestions and has the least empirical support. Reading the literature on multicultural skills for school counselors highlights the lack of support for substantive research on effective or efficacious interventions within schools. There are many calls for this type of work, but a relative paucity of examples. What exists tends not to directly address the skills of the counselors, but the effectiveness of particular interventions. It is assumed that running an effective intervention is equivalent to demonstrating effective skills. Despite the lack of empirical support for these skills, it is important to review those skills that have been suggested within the literature as being relevant to multicultural school counseling. For example, Green and Keys (2001) describe that it is critical for school counselors to possess strong collaboration skills in order to better meet the needs of youth in today's society through their comprehensive guidance and counseling program. These authors suggest that, through collaboration with school staff members and families, the school counselor is better able to address the multiple needs of youth by offering comprehensive services. Furthermore, the school counselor should utilize his or her collaboration skills to form relationships with community members to whom they can refer youth and families for additional supportive services. The school counselor is also utilizing leadership skills through the establishment of these collaborative relationships within and beyond the school context.

Due to the lack of literature on the specific skills of culturally responsive school counseling, we will now attempt to illustrate some of those skills that are fundamental to the work of a school counselor who is operating within a culturally responsive comprehensive guidance and counseling program (CR-CGCP). In particular, this discussion will be applied to the ASCA model for comprehensive guidance and counseling programs (CGCPs). By doing so, we hope to illustrate how culturally responsive school counseling can be applied to the national model to make it a more appropriate one for school counseling in a global society.

Culturally Responsive Comprehensive Guidance and Counseling Programs (CR-CGCPs)

With the growing acknowledgement of the school counselor as an integral component of the school environment (e.g., ASCA, 2003, 2005; Beale & McCay, 2001; Borders & Drury, 1992; Dahir, 2001; D'Andrea, 1996; Gysbers & Henderson, 2001) along with our country's increasing cultural diversity, school counselors have been called upon to develop comprehensive guidance and counseling programs (CGCPs) that appropriately address multicultural issues (e.g., Baruth & Manning, 2000; Bemak, 2005; Bradley, & Jarchow, 1998; Bryan, 2005; Butler, 2003; Butler-Byrd, Nieto, & Nieto Senour, 2006; Coleman & Baskin, 2003; Constantine, 1998; Green et al., 2005; Green & Keys, 2001; Harris, 1999; Holcomb-McCoy, 2004; Johnson, 1995; Lee, 2001, 2005; Sink, 2002; Smith-Adcock, Daniels, Lee,

Villalba, & Indelicato, 2006). There are several themes within the literature that advocate for the incorporation of multicultural practices into CGCPs. We will now summarize how these themes relate to the ASCA's general framework for CGCPs. First, we will suggest that an ecological framework needs to be incorporated into the definition of a CGCP in an effort to create a CR-CGCP. Next, the four primary systems that encompass a CGCP (Foundation, Delivery System, Management Systems, and Accountability; ASCA, 2005) will each be discussed from a culturally responsive school counseling perspective. This discussion will assist school counselors in understanding how to conceptualize, structure, and implement a CGCP that is attentive to the cultural needs of youth in today's society and allows the school counselor to continually be cognizant of how his or her work impacts the development of youth.

Utilizing an Ecological Framework

Comprehensive school counseling programs (CSCP) are defined as "comprehensive in scope, preventative in design and developmental in nature" (ASCA, 2005, p. 13). Comprehensive guidance and counseling programs are "comprehensive" in the sense that they provide services to *all* students, equipping them with the knowledge and skills that are necessary for a healthy development in academic, personal-social, and career domains. These programs are also "preventative" because they offer services to youth in a "proactive and preventative manner" that assists in their development across the various domains. Finally, CGCPs are "developmental" in that they facilitate student development by allowing youth to acquire specific competencies at various stages of development (ASCA, 2005).

In reviewing the definition of CGCPs, we suggest that there is a missing critical dimension directly related to addressing issues of equity in education and the preparation of students to become citizens in a global economy. We are suggesting that the fourth component of a CGCP is the application of an ecological perspective. Therefore, to complete the definition, we believe that the phrase "utilizes an ecological perspective" should be added. As a result, the definition of a CGCP will better capture the way in which school counselors consider the contextual factors that impact a student's well-being (e.g., individual, family, school, and community factors) and choose interventions based on this consideration.

As mentioned earlier in this discussion, operating from an ecological perspective is an important aspect of the knowledge base of multiculturally competent school counselors. A number of authors support the utilization of an ecological perspective in CGCPs and have written about this issue in different ways. Reviewing these various writings assists in grasping how using an ecological perspective enhances the CSCP. For example, Green and Keys (2001) suggest that the current model of school counseling is incomplete, and that it often results in the use of individual approaches that fail to consider the larger systems and cultural factors that impact a child's well-being. In order to address this problem, they suggest employing a "development-in-context" framework as an important way to more appropriately address the needs of diverse youth. This allows for factors within a youth's context and culture to be considered to ensure that a more complete picture of his or her concerns are understood, and the framework further assists in choosing appropriate interventions. Similarly, Coleman and Baskin (2003) state that "the ability to serve the needs of students within their ecological context is the essence of multiculturally competent school counseling" (p. 104). They suggest that the school counselor must utilize this perspective when he or she engages in activities such as assessment and intervention, developmental guidance, individual and group counseling, consultation, and program planning and management. Both sets of authors suggest that using an ecological approach, such as that proposed by Bronfenbrenner (1979), allows the school counselor to consider the ways in which interventions might be implemented that target both the individual as well as his or her context.

As a result, integrating an ecological perspective into the framework of a CGCP will help prevent the school counselor from using a deficit model targeting solely the individual and/or the family as the sole source of concerns. Rather, an ecological approach considers how the context might also be contributing to the issues of concern. In this way, the school counselor acts as a culturally responsive "student advocate" who identifies obstacles within the school and larger societal systems that may be preventing youth from having a positive educational experience (Lee, 2001). This ecological perspective also calls for the collaboration with the various systems such as school, family, and community (Bemak, 2000). Furthermore, the school counselor must demonstrate cultural awareness by continually examining how his or her professional and personal identity influences the way in which he or she engages in these activities and the impact that they have on his or her work within the school (Coleman & Baskin, 2003; Green & Keys, 2001).

Green and coworkers (2005) also advocate utilizing an ecological perspective in their discussion of urban school counseling. These authors propose that utilizing an urban school counseling approach allows for the consideration of cultural and contextual factors, including those that are salient in the larger urban setting (e.g., violence, low achievement, and poverty). Holcomb-McCoy (1998) speaks specifically of six factors that impact the work of school counselors in urban settings: diversity of students, lack of resources, poverty, family issues, violence, and high dropout rates. She describes the necessity for school counselors working in urban settings to address these factors that create unique issues for the school community. Furthermore, today's school counselor needs to consider the interplay between his or her cultural self, the cultures of the students with whom he or she works, and the culture of the school within the larger urban context (Green et al., 2005).

Collectively, the literature that promotes the utilization of an ecological perspective in school counseling addresses a gap that is missing from the current national model. It is imperative that a school counselor consider contextual factors that impact the well-being of individual youth, their families, the school as a whole, and the greater community in order to provide the most comprehensive and beneficial services. In practice, an example of how the school counselor employs an ecological perspective can be seen in the way in which he or she conceptualizes a student performing poorly in school. The school counselor will consider the multiple individuals and contexts in the student's life in order to understand what factors contribute to this issue and where interventions can best be implemented. For example, the school counselor will consider the student's family, such as the degree to which parents can be available to provide academic support at home; the classroom and school context, including the degree to which the student feels that he or she belongs and feels valued by teachers and peers; the student's neighborhood, including the levels of safety and violence that the student experiences on a regular basis and how it may impact his or her ability to become fully engaged in the learning that takes place at school. After engaging in this process, the school counselor can then determine the types of interventions that are best for the student, such as those that promote parent support and involvement in school, increase the degree to which the student feels cared for by the school community, and allow the youth to become involved with positive activities within the neighborhood.

Adding the ecological perspective as a fourth characteristic that defines a CGCP, in an attempt toward creating a CR-CGCP, is a step in the right direction for school counseling in the 21st century. Furthermore, as suggested by Sink (2002), the student competencies that are fostered through CGCPs must be reconsidered to include multicultural outcomes. We will attempt to emphasize and expand upon this idea by discussing how school counselors can consider the way in which culturally responsive school counseling can be integrated into the four components of CGCPs: Foundation, Delivery System, Management Systems, and Accountability (ASCA, 2005).

Integrating Culturally Responsive School Counseling Into the ASCA Model

Foundation

The ASCA (2005) describes the "Foundation" component of the CGCP as the "what" of the program, encompassing the knowledge and the skills that are fostered within each student in the school. It includes a philosophy or shared set of ideas that are at the core of the school's CGCP program; a mission that describes the CGCP's purpose that is in line with the school and the district; the developmental domains of academic, career, and personal/social in which the CGCP promotes student growth; and the ASCA national standards and competencies that describe the specific knowledge and skills that students should acquire as a result of receiving the services of the CGCP.

When applying a multicultural school counseling framework to the Foundation component, the literature on culturally responsive schooling becomes quite relevant. In writing about culturally responsive classrooms, Shade, Kelly, and Oberg (1997) indicate that an important aspect of culturally responsive education is understanding the following: "Students bring certain characteristics that have been shaped by their socializing group to the classroom, and teachers must be able to recognize these traits and build upon them. The cultural, social, and historical backgrounds of children have a major impact on how they perceive school and the educational process" (p. 11). In a similar manner, Bradley and Jarchow (1998) discuss how school counselors can help to "globalize" the school context in an effort to address and celebrate cultural diversity. Through efforts to promote diversity, school counselors can serve as key individuals in creating a positive learning environment that respects all cultural backgrounds (Harris, 1999). These efforts must be embraced by the school counselor as core to his or her philosophy of working with youth and must also be shared among other educators working in the school. Together, those in the school district can form goals and objectives that will guide the initiative, an important first step in the process of forming a "comprehensive multicultural relations initiative" (Johnson, 1995).

It should be part of the mission of both the CR-CGCP and the larger school and district, reflecting the fact that addressing multicultural issues is at the forefront of not only the school counselor's work but also that of the teachers, administrators, school psychologists, school social workers, and other K–12 educators. Staying committed to this shared philosophy of providing a culturally responsive educational experience and maintaining a CR-CGCP that reflects this goal is critical. For example, Johnson (1995) suggests that "the most significant contribution that the school counselor can make toward fostering a school environment supportive of cultural diversity is to be culturally responsive in working with all students" (p. 106).

In addition to the literature on culturally responsive education, the school counselor and the greater school community can draw from the literature that advocates for creating schools to function as cohesive communities (e.g., Battistich, Solomon, Watson, & Schaps, 1997; Noddings, 1992; Sergiovanni, 1994). Lindwall and Coleman (2008) argue that creating caring school communities is essential for helping youth feel as if they belong and are valued within the school context. It is also one way to conceptualize how the educational context can specifically be addressed to promote the positive development of youth and facilitate learning. Lindwall and Coleman (2008) suggest that the school counselor is a key individual who can be involved in the process of creating and maintaining schools that actively attempt to promote belongingness of students and families. We suggest that this may be particularly critical for diverse youth, who may feel disconnected from their school environment if mainstream Eurocentric values are dominant in the school. Therefore, part of the mission of the school counselor, as well as the larger school, can include not only being culturally responsive but striving to ensure that students and their families feel connected to school. The school counselor can implement efforts in individual, small group, classroom, and school-wide levels that build a caring community. For example, the school counselor can work individually with a student who feels isolated from peers and would benefit from the development of appropriate social skills; offer small groups for youth who are experiencing a common difficult experience, such as divorce or death of a loved one, and are looking for support from others within the school; teach developmental guidance lessons that emphasize themes of respect, friendship, and trust; and help assist in the development of mentoring relationships for youth who would benefit from a supportive older peer or adult within the school.

Maintaining a shared philosophy of providing a culturally responsive educational experience that involves creating a sense of a caring school community requires the school counselor to engage in collaborative efforts with his or her colleagues within the school as well as with families and the greater community to promote an environment that addresses the cultural issues of its diverse school community (Green & Keys, 2001; Johnson, 1995). Through this collaboration, the school counselor will be operating from the ecological perspective that calls for addressing the multiple individuals and contexts that impact the well-being of a child (Green & Keys, 2001; Johnson, 1995). One important type of collaboration that should be done in order to better formulate the goals and objectives of the school or district is conducting a needs assessment (Green & Keys, 2001; Johnson, 1995). Johnson (1995) explains that this process allows the school community to understand the unique culture of the school/district, creating a "blueprint for action." Johnson goes on to describe that this needs assessment might include activities such as reviewing enrollment patterns, curriculum, instructional techniques, staff recruitment practices, and scheduling to better understand the culture of the school and the most important areas that can be addressed by the school counseling program.

Lee (2001) articulates many of the changes in the school context that are necessary to help facilitate the acquisition of these competencies. He suggests that there are several elements that should be present in a culturally responsive school. The first is a focus on true integration, what he calls the "salad bowl," rather than to expect non-European members to assimilate into the mainstream culture, what Lee calls the "melting pot." The second is a sense of community that is fostered within the school that centers on the value of cultural diversity for the school rather than a more passive recognition of diversity. Furthermore, Lee argues that the values of the school would not be centered on one cultural background to which all other groups need to aspire, but that the values of all the represented cultures in the school would have a valued voice and place. The fourth is shared expectations for academic accomplishment for all students regardless of class or ethnic background and, we would add, that instructional strategies are suitably differentiated so that all students are provided the structures and opportunities that facilitate their academic accomplishment. The fifth element that Lee espouses is to ensure that multicultural (and global) issues are integrated across the school curriculum rather than segmented into one celebration or class. The sixth is the existence of opportunities for students to share ideas and perspectives about cultural diversity with their peers outside of the classroom. The seventh is the establishment of well-defined policies within the school that are followed when dealing with cultural tension. The eighth is staff commitment to seeking continuing professional development in relation to multicultural-ism. The ninth is an active effort to recruit a culturally diverse school staff to provide multiculturally competent role models for all students. The tenth is family involvement from all backgrounds in the school, and staff working effectively with all families regardless of linguistic or cultural differences. Finally, the last element is that the school uses a broad and inclusive definition of multiculturalism that goes beyond race/ethnicity to include factors such as religion, sexual orientation, and ability. Those schools that illustrate a sub-stantial number of these factors are more likely to be successfully addressing cultural issues within the educational process. These characteristics provide a helpful understanding of the shared philosophy that the school counselor and the larger school can uphold in striving to provide a culturally responsive educational experience for youth.

The Foundation also includes the school counselor's conceptualization of the three domains of youth developmental: academic, career, and personal/social. Addressing student development by providing a CR-CGCP includes two important tenets. First, the school counselor needs to believe that all youth are capable of learning and have a desire to learn, and cultural dif-ferences exist and must be addressed (Lee, 2001). Second, school counsel-ors need to conceptualize that there are skills in these domains that today's youth need to acquire in order to develop into citizens who can successfully live in a culturally diverse society (Bradley & Jarchow, 1998; Green & Keys, 2001; Lee, 2001; Shade et al., 1997; Sink, 2002). For example, Lee (2001) describes five ways in which a culturally competent school counselor facili-tates student development to prepare them for a global society. These five areas of development fall into one of the three domains of the ASCA model: fostering academic achievement and fostering the attitudes and the skills that are important for youth to experience success in school (academic domain); assisting in career goal-setting and exploration (career domain); and facilitat-ing healthy, positive identities in youth and effective relationships with cul-turally different peers (personal/social domain). These areas can serve as the foundation upon which the school counselor creates his or her interventions that promote the development of diverse youth in a culturally responsive manner.

Delivery System

The "Delivery System" is described by the ASCA (2005) as "how" the CGCP will be put into practice. This component is comprised of the Guidance

Curriculum that is provided to all students; Individual Student Planning, or programmatic activities that facilitate individual and small group development in youth; Responsive Services to address the immediate concerns of youth through consultation, individual and group counseling, referrals, crisis consultation, and peer facilitation; and Systems Support, which includes the activities that allow for the successful continuation of the CGCP services such as professional development, consultation and collaboration, working with families and community members, community outreach, advisory councils, and district committees (ASCA, 2005).

The Foundation, as described previously, provides the guiding philosophy from which the school counselor can create the programs, initiatives, and interventions that will put the philosophy into practice to serve all students in a culturally responsive manner. When integrating cultural diversity into the various school counseling services, this can take multiple forms in the academic, career, and personal-social domains. First, in the academic domain, the school counselor can help students acquire the skills and the attitudes that are helpful for academic accomplishment. This may take the form of teaching study skills, organizational skills, and test-taking skills in guidance lessons or in small groups (Lee, 2001). On an individual level, school counselors can take an active role in pupil service and individual education plan (IEP) meetings in developing goals and interventions that will better support a student's academic experience. School counselors might also consider providing more intensive services for those students who need more support, which could take the form of individual counseling to work through identity issues or personal and societal challenges that may be impacting their academic accomplishment. School counselors can also involve the family in trying to identify and work through these challenges and develop ways in which the family can support the student's academic success at home. For example, it might be the case that the student is responsible for caring for younger children while a parent is at work, which may make it difficult for the student to complete schoolwork at home. In this case, the school counselor might work with the student and his or her teachers to create some time during the school day to complete homework and get extra support from an adult tutor or mentor during this time.

When considering interventions in the career domain, Constantine (1998) provides several important ideas. For example, she describes that some students may have experienced adults having lower expectations for their future careers because of certain cultural characteristics such as gender, race/ethnicity, or socioeconomic status. The school counselor can be attentive to students' career goals and ascertain whether or not youth have indeed experienced lowered expectations from adults. Then, the school counselor can provide career development activities that allow youth to explore and increase their career expectations, such as connecting youth with community members who hold various jobs that are of interest to youth. These connections could include job shadowing and other mentoring activities that allow youth to learn and experience different jobs and careers. Constantine (1998) also suggests providing activities that enable youth to brainstorm career options in order to better understand the career development process. This can be incorporated into developmental guidance lessons and in individual and small groups for students who express greater interest in receiving this type of guidance. Throughout these different activities at the individual, small group, and classroom levels, the school counselor can integrate discussions about cultural factors, such as acculturation and racial/ethnic identity development, and other challenges (e.g., financial hardships, stereotypes, discrimination) that impact the career development process. These activities can also include teaching youth problem-solving and coping skills that are helpful in dealing with challenges that arise. Furthermore, school counselors can engage classrooms or small groups in role-plays about job interviews or career exploration. These and other activities that promote collaboration can be used to increase youth's skills working cooperatively with others (Constantine, 1998; Sink, 2002). Through this process, the school counselor can explicitly teach youth how to work as a team, including the skills that teamwork requires, and emphasize how these skills will be important in being successful in future jobs.

Finally, in the personal-social domain, school counselors can provide a number of activities and interventions that are important for positive youth development. For example, they can help to foster an environment that celebrates diversity. This can be accomplished by facilitating discussions and teaching lessons about diversity within the classroom or in small groups, helping youth to appreciate and respect diverse worldviews related to their own and others' cultures (Bradley & Jarchow, 1998; Green & Keys, 2001; Sink, 2002), and developing multicultural awareness (Johnson, 1995). This can also be done on a school-wide level in the form of assemblies, or in the classroom through lessons and discussions that embrace the unique aspects of multiple cultures. Second, the school counselor can help to raise awareness and educate students about prejudice and stereotyping (Bradley & Jarchow, 1998) and sociocultural and political issues (Sink, 2002) through developmental guidance lessons in the classroom or in small group and one-on-one contexts. Third, the school counselor can facilitate youth's development of identity, which includes the consideration of various cultural issues including gender, race, and socioeconomic status (Green & Keys, 2001). This can be done by providing opportunities for students to talk with diverse peers in a small group context where the school counselor leads these discussions. Through these activities, school counselors assist youth in developing a positive self-awareness and cultural identity. This includes helping youth to become aware of the various factors that have an impact on their lives, which will help them to adjust to different contexts in their future interactions and development (Green & Keys, 2001). Fourth, school counselors can engage classrooms in a process of creating rules or a code of conduct so students can collectively and respectfully share in the establishment of these expectations (Sink, 2002). Finally, school counselors can think about ways in which they can help students feel a sense of belongingness or connectedness to their school community to ensure that youth of all cultural backgrounds feel as if they are valued in the school context (Coleman & Baskin, 2003). For the school counselor, this may take the form of providing individual support through counseling or providing opportunities for youth to form relationships with peers through small group counseling or mentoring relationships with peers (Sink, 2002) or adults in the school or community. Johnson (1995) describes several multicultural initiatives that can also be considered part of facilitating belongingness, such as orientations and clubs for new and transitional students, peer helper programs, and parent education groups.

In the Delivery component, it is also important to consider the Systems Support aspect which includes collaboration, working with families and the community, and the school counselor's continued professional development. Several authors in the literature (e.g., Bemak, 2000; Bryan 2005; Carpenter, King-Sears, & Keys, 1998; Harris, 1999; Keys & Bemak, 1997; Lee, 2001; Sink, 2002) emphasize the need for school counselors to collaborate with school staff (e.g., teachers, administrators, support services), families, and the larger community (e.g., mental health agencies, local businesses) in order to best meet the needs of students. In doing so, the school counselor can be instrumental in setting up prevention and intervention programs such as community service opportunities, mentoring relationships, and consultation relationships with mental health providers. School counselors can provide parent groups that serve as a forum for discussion and support related to cultural issues that impact their family's experience within the educational context (Bradley & Jarchow, 1998). Finally, school counselors need to take initiative in participating in ongoing professional development activities such as workshops, courses, and reflection with peers. This is especially critical because it has been reported that school counselors often have not been adequately trained in multicultural issues and/or report feeling the need for more training in this area (e.g., Butler, 2003; Carey, Reinat, & Fontes, 1990; Constantine & Yeh, 2001; Hobson & Kanitz, 1996). With ongoing professional development, school counselors can also collaborate with their colleagues within the school by serving as consultants regarding multicultural issues. Harris (1999) describes how school counselors can collaborate with administrators in promoting cultural diversity within the school. For example, he suggests that school counselors can lead staff members in activities that raise their multicultural awareness, knowledge, and skills, and also can serve as a consultant for integrating multicultural issues into the curriculum. This may take place one-on-one, in "teacher support groups," or in the context of school-wide in-services. In sum, "The multiculturally sensitive counselor presents a viable partner, collaborator, mentor, and resource for teachers who seek to become multiculturally aware; for those who are multiculturally unaware, the counselor can act as a role model" (Herring & White, 1995, p. 55).

Management Systems

The third component, "Management Systems," pertains to the "when," "why," and "on what authority" aspects of the CGCP. Management Agreements include the agreed-upon responsibilities of the school counselor; an Advisory Council reviews the CGCP; the Use of Data reflects the data-driven nature of the CGCP; Action Plans address the guidance curriculum and closing the achievement gap; Use of Time includes an outline of the amount of time school counselors should spend on various responsibilities; and Calendars refer to master schedules of the school counselor's activities (ASCA, 2005).

When considering the responsibilities of the school counselor within a CR-CGCP, several roles emerge from a review of the relevant literature. First, the school counselor can act as a "team facilitator" (Bryan, 2005) or "group process facilitator" (Keys & Lockhart, 1999) by utilizing his or her training in group dynamics and communication, problem-solving, and conflict resolution. For instance, this role would be helpful when the school counselor consults with a grade-level team of teachers who are seeking consultation regarding the integration of multicultural issues into their curriculum (Bryan, 2005). Second, the school counselor plays the role of an "advocate" (Bryan,

2005; Keys & Lockhart, 1999; Lee, 2001) for youth and families by helping staff members conceptualize the concerns of their students. They can do this by pointing out the multiple cultural factors that impact a child's performance in school rather than solely focusing on individual characteristics. Part of this process includes helping the staff to reflect upon their own cultural selves and how this impacts their perceptions and interactions with a student. Third, school counselors play the role of "collaborator" (Bemak, 2000; Bryan, 2005) when they establish themselves as safe individuals with whom staff, families, and community members can engage in honest dialogue about cultural issues and increase their own cultural awareness. Providing opportunities for these dialogues to take place at in-services or parent nights is one example of how the collaborator role might play out within the school context (Bryan, 2005). Another example is the school counselor providing staff development trainings or workshops that increase the knowledge of culturally responsive educational practices. Fourth, the school counselor serves as "student development facilitator" when he or she promotes the development of multicultural competencies in the academic, career, and personal-social domains (Lee, 2001), examples of which were provided earlier in this discussion.

Depending on the specific needs of the school and its unique environment, the school counselor may choose to take on some roles more than others. A needs assessment (Green & Keys, 2001; Johnson, 1995) will be particularly helpful in deciding how the school counselor can best structure his or her time within the school in an effort to address its salient issues. The school counselor can work together with his or her school administrators and staff to establish a general daily schedule of his or her day that clearly articulates the ways in which the CR-CGCP offers services to the school's youth and families. As advocated by ASCA, a team of individuals at the school can serve as an "Advisory Council" to periodically review the structure of the CR-CGCP to ascertain whether it is meeting the needs of the school.

The Management Systems component also includes the use of data. The importance of using data in a CR-CGCP is supported by a number of individuals within the literature. For example, Johnson (1995) advocates for ongoing assessment of efforts to facilitate a climate that embraces diversity to determine what components are working well and what aspects need to be adjusted. Eschenauer and Chen-Hayes (2005) suggest using functional behavioral assessment and single-case designs to determine the most appropriate intervention for a particular student and to understand how he or she responds to that intervention. Evaluation on a larger scale, which includes collecting, analyzing, and interpreting data, is described by Green and Keys (2001) as a critical piece of school counseling in the 21st century. In particular, these authors advocate for the use of evidence-based practices in establishing the efficacy of their CR-CGCP and the consideration of alternative frameworks to design and implement CR-CGCP, such as logic models (see http://www.uwex.edu/ces/pdande/evaluation/evallogicmodel.html for a logic model proposed by the University of Wisconsin-Extension). Helpful resources for reviewing and choosing evidence-based practices that support the efforts of a CR-CGCP include the Substance Abuse and Mental Health Services Administration (http://modelprograms.samhsa.gov) and the Center for Substance Abuse Prevention's Center for the Application of Prevention Technologies (http://captus.samhsa.gov/western/western.cfm).

Accountability

The final component of the CGCP, "Accountability," addresses the impact that the CGCP has on the students that it serves. It is comprised of Results Reports that are shared with stakeholders; School Counselor Performance Standards that act as a foundation for school counselor evaluation; and Program Audit, which evaluates how well the CGCP is structured in accordance with the ASCA model (ASCA, 2005).

This component of the ASCA model is the area most in need of future research and scholarship in order to fully implement CR-CGCPs. This is the aspect of the model that ensures that the program is appropriately designed, provides positive benefits for students in the critical areas of development, and makes certain that the school counselor is carrying out his or her role effectively. The literature that has been reviewed thus far in this discussion provides a starting point. For example, the outcomes and characteristics of CR-CGCPs and schools that are offered by Sink (2002) and Lee (2001) provide a foundation for providing standards by which CR-CGCPs can be evaluated for youth outcomes and school counselor performance in acting in a culturally responsive manner. School counselors, along with their colleagues within the school, need to utilize outcome measures that appropriately capture the impact of the CR-CGCP on the youth in the school.

Much of our conversation to this point has addressed the general ways in which an ecological perspective can be integrated into school counseling and guidance programs, and how a CR-CGCP is mapped out onto the various components of the ASCA model. In the next sections, we want to discuss the manner in which this integration can have an impact on two of the challenges to creating effective CR-CGCPs, minority student achievement and producing students prepared to become effective citizens in a global economy.

Minority Student Achievement

Coleman (2007) has presented a model suggesting that ethnic minority students who are successful in schools are actually demonstrating resilience. This is a particularly useful construction for school counselors, whose primary role in schools is to help students develop the social and emotional skills and attitudes that facilitate learning. Resilience is certainly a set of attitudes and skills (Coleman, Karcher, & Biscoe, 2001) that facilitate learning. In this model, Coleman suggests that minority student achievement is a resilient outcome because social stratification factors (e.g., class, race, ethnicity, and gender) are more predictive of academic outcomes than quality of schooling or intellectual competence. In the United States, if one is poor and a member of a targeted ethnic minority group, one is more likely to fail in school than if one is wealthy and a member of the ethnic majority. This puts ethnic minorities at risk for academic failure. Those who succeed, therefore, are overcoming the expected probabilities and are resilient.

Coleman goes on to discuss the factors which help ethnic minorities to succeed. In addition to contextual factors (e.g., parental involvement, quality teachers in each classroom, and a caring school community), there are personal factors that help minority students overcome their risk status. In this review of the literature on minority student achievement, the factors which contribute to resilient outcomes that are of particular interest for school counseling programs include a well-developed cultural identity, social skills, and bicultural competence. Coleman (2007) argues that these constructs are important foci of a developmental guidance program that is designed to help close the achievement gap between minority and majority students.

Coleman, Yang, and Kim (2008) discuss the important role that cultural identity plays in helping ethnic minorities take full advantage of opportunities in schools. They build on the literature which suggests that many ethnic minorities find schools to be a culturally challenging experience. For many of these students, success in schools demands letting go of their cultural sense of self. For children and adolescents who are in the process of acquiring a sense of cultural and personal self, this challenge can be overwhelming. Depending on the student's family, the climate in the school, and other contextual variables, many students withdraw from this challenge and choose to remain within their own cultural framework. This may not serve to facilitate learning in school or assimilate to school-based expectations of their cultural group, which also may not serve to facilitate learning in schools. Coleman and coworkers (2008) cite a growing body of evidence which suggests that minority students who develop a strong and positive sense of cultural self are better able to manage the challenge of working with the Eurocentric value system of most American schools. Those students who have this strong cultural identity are better able to engage in the process of learning with a positive impact on their academic performance. It is important for CR-CGCPs to integrate curriculum and groups that help students develop a positive sense of cultural self (see Coleman et al., for examples of such programs).

The second personal factor that Coleman (2007) suggests is a central part of resilience among ethnic minority students involves the development of the social skills that facilitate learning among students. These skills are a central focus of all CR-CGCPs. There are many ways in which these skills have been described, from the ASCA model with its focus on being able to manage conflict, to other paradigms such as those which focus on social competence (Webb, Brigman, & Campbell, 2005). In general, these characteristics involve what Goleman (1995) calls emotional intelligence, the Search Institute (2005) calls individual protective factors, and Wolin and Wolin (1993) call resilience. The core idea is that students need high levels of social skills to effectively negotiate the school environment. The importance of these skills is supported by the effectiveness of the Knowledge is Power Program (KIPP) Schools (2006), which make the learning of these skills a central part of their curriculum. These skills should be part of the universal curriculum that all students receive in schools, with a focus on mastery. School counseling programs need to focus on demonstrating the manner in which these skills have an impact on academic performance and advocate for more time to develop these skills among those students who have not mastered them.

An example of the importance of these skills is represented in most programs that are designed to reduce school violence or alcohol and other drug abuse (AODA) issues among children and adolescents. Each of these programs has different outcomes and shares different information. They do, however, focus on a common set of personal and social skills that are core to emotional intelligence such as the ability to self-regulate, awareness of one's emotions, ability to communicate needs in an assertive manner, ability to take the perspective of others, decision-making skills, and the self-efficacy to act in congruence with one's values. These are the skills that should be the focus of CR-CGCPs as well as the information to apply them in particular situations.

A CR-CGCP that is focused on being culturally responsive needs to understand that these skills have a cultural context. Specifically, what may be an effective approach in one's culture of origin may not be effective within the school context, and vice versa. An important part of the instructional role of the school counselor is not only to understand this process but to help his or her students learn to apply their social skills in a contextually appropriate manner. Bass and Coleman (1997), in a program designed to enhance cultural identity among African American adolescent males, found that real change in school performance did not occur until the participants were explicitly taught how to apply their identity within the context of school. LaFromboise, Coleman, and Gerton (1993) found that this type of bicultural competence is an important aspect of psychological well-being of ethnic minorities as they manage the challenges of working within the majority culture.

LaFromboise and coworkers (1993) have identified a set of skills and attitudes that makes up bicultural competence. These are knowledge both about one's culture and the culture into which one is seeking a place, a positive attitude toward both cultures, communication competency in both, a substantive role in both, the self-efficacy to negotiate the demands of both cultures, and a sense of belonging in both cultures. It is clear that a CR-CGCP can help students develop these skills and attitudes and provide them opportunities to practice these skills. We also suggest that a CR-CGCP will evaluate its effectiveness by the degree to which it can stimulate bicultural competence in all the students within the school. It is important not to isolate these skills as only useful for minority students to acquire as a way to overcome the achievement gap, but as a useful set of skills for all students to acquire as our society becomes increasingly pluralistic and our economy becomes more global.

Preparing Students for a Global Society

Friedman (2005) has laid out a compelling rationale for the importance of thinking in global terms about educational, social, and economic planning and change. His central hypothesis is that the technological revolution has rendered the world flat in real terms. Describing the effects of this revolution on economic practices, Friedman challenges us to think through the types of attitudes, knowledge, and skills American workers must develop in order to be productive participants in an increasingly global society. From our perspective, it is very easy to describe the need to produce students who are better prepared to perform at high levels of proficiency in the areas of science, technology, engineering, and mathematics (increasingly referred to as the STEM fields). However, it is more difficult to think about the values and social skills these students will need to fully participate in the global economy while preserving a well-functioning democratic and pluralistic society within the United States. Without creating citizens who are simultaneously able to compete in a global economy and function as effective citizens, we will be at risk for maintaining the types of economic and social disparities with which we are already struggling and which are significant threats to the future prosperity and stability of the other major economic powers, such as China, India, and Russia. Our position is that educational equity and preparation for participation in a global economy are not separate issues, but are deeply intertwined. As such, we believe that a CR-CGCP needs to focus on the development of citizens who are committed to responsible globalization and educational equity.

Sink (2002) does an excellent job of summarizing the current thinking concerning the types of competencies such students should acquire by the time they reach 12th grade in American schools (see Table 8.1). Essential to this perspective is the understanding that academic skills are important, but so are the skills and values that an individual uses to apply those academic skills within a social context. It is core to the assumptions about multiculturalism within school counseling that the focus of a CR-CGCP is to help all students to develop the values, attitudes, and skills that will enable them to work toward a democratic and equitable social system. The competencies outlined by Sink are central to this process.

TABLE 8.1

Summary Competencies of a Multicultural Student-Citizen Within the Framework of a Comprehensive Guidance and Counseling Program (Sink, 2002)

By Grade 12, students will demonstrate:

An understanding and appreciation for their own culture and the cultures of others

Critical thinking in the exploration of sociocultural and political ideas

An ability to reason about issues from local, national, and global perspectives

An understanding of important American values (e.g., justice, tolerance, responsibility)

An understanding of the basic rights of all human beings as embodied in the Bill of Rights

The ability to express appropriately an opinion on important social and political issues while listening and respecting the views of others

The ability to cooperate/collaborate with others in school and community settings

The ability to resolve interpersonal conflicts peacefully

As we discussed earlier, Lee (2001) articulates many of the changes in the school context needed to help facilitate the acquisition of these competencies. Many authors (e.g., Bradley & Jarchow, 1998; Lee, 2001; Sink, 2003) argue that the school counselor has a vital role in this process. As we outlined earlier in this chapter, the baseline for multicultural competence within a school counselor is an awareness of how social stratification factors influence academic performance in school and how the counselor's personal worldview (Yeh & Pituc, 2008) will affect how he or she responds to this issue. A school counselor who integrates the ecological perspective into his or her practice, as described earlier, will seek to find ways to help his or her students develop a multicultural and global worldview together with the competencies that Sink has suggested are needed in our modern society.

To be effective, a culturally responsive school counselor must have knowledge about a variety of issues. Yeh and Pituc (2008) suggest that they must know about issues related to worldview, cultural values, racial identity, White privilege, and acculturation processes. Lee (2001) argues that a school counselor who runs a CR-CGCP should be able to facilitate the process of developing positive identities of youth, assist in the development of positive relationships among students of various cultural backgrounds, assist with academic accomplishment by focusing on "inherent cultural potential" and creating activities that integrate individuals from diverse cultural backgrounds, emphasize and teach skills that foster a positive attitude about school (e.g., academic planning, study skills), and deliver career development activities that include examining nonstereotyped jobs and careers. Bradley and Jarchow (1998) go on to suggest that the multiculturally competent school counselor should be able to teach both staff and students about diversity, engage in efforts to educate about and reduce prejudice and stereotyping, help individuals understand and appreciate diverse worldviews, and facilitate dialogue about diversity within the school and the community.

We argue that the school counselor is the person in the building who should be trained to understand how developmental, cognitive, emotional, and cultural processes contribute to the growth of a child and who is in a position to influence these processes through a CR-CGCP, through interactions with teachers and other school personnel, and through interactions with parents in a systematic and comprehensive manner. We believe that school counselor training programs lay the groundwork for these competencies, but that the school counselor needs ongoing and systematic professional development to become highly qualified in these areas. With the changes in certification requirements which allow individuals who have not been classroom teachers to become certified school counselors, it is important that professional school counselors be very conscious of the need to develop proficiency in the pedagogy needed to create culturally responsive classrooms.

Because the achievement gap has become persistent, despite efforts to eliminate structural desegregation and to highlight educational inequities, the need to understand and implement into practice educational techniques that respond to cultural diversity (e.g., Shade et al., 1997) is pressing. Because creating an effective workforce to address the demands of globalization is essential to our economic and social well-being, the ability to educate all of our students is becoming an increasingly practical as well as moral imperative. School counselors need to expand their knowledge of culturally responsive pedagogy to be able to be effective consultants with the teachers with whom they work to serve the needs of all students within schools. Because school counselors receive social science training, they are well positioned to select evidence-based practices that can effectively stimulate the academic and social competence of all students (Green & Keys, 2001).

Implications

In this chapter, we have made the argument that multiculturalism in school counseling is a multidimensional phenomenon, but that the outcome of an effective integration of a multicultural perspective into the field will allow us to address the major issues of educational equity and create global citizens. We argue that the acquisition of multicultural counseling competence for school counselors serves as the foundation for this integration. We believe this process begins in preservice training, but needs to be an ongoing focus of a school counselor's professional development activity. From an ecological perspective, because culture is constantly evolving, it is vital for the professional who is providing leadership in a CR-CGCP to constantly be in training. This means that those who train school counselors must be actively engaged in the process of in-service training. Counselor educators have a responsibility not only to understand the changes in the field, but to be engaged in the ongoing professional development of the graduates from their programs and the supervisors of the preservice students in their programs.

Once a school counselor has acquired a foundation of multicultural competence, he or she needs to develop the awareness, knowledge, and skills to design and implement a CR-CGCP. We have suggested that such a program needs to incorporate an ecological perspective as an addition to the ASCA expectation that such a program be comprehensive, preventative, and developmental in nature. We suggest that a professional school counselor not only needs to understand the effects of social stratification factors on student achievement, but he or she also needs to know how to systematically intervene to ameliorate the negative effects. In addition to being able to provide high-quality individual, group, classroom, and school-wide interventions, a multiculturally competent school counselor needs to know how to apply an ecological perspective when engaging in system change as well as collaborating and consulting with teachers in the creation of a an educational context that promotes a sense of belongingness and value within students. One way in which to foster this type of context is the creation of culturally responsive classrooms and fostering a school community that focuses on the success of all students (Lindwall & Coleman, 2008). Finally, we are suggesting that addressing the social, emotional, and behavioral issues that are associated with educational equity will have a direct and positive impact on preparing students to become effective citizens in a global economy. The social and academic competence of all students needs to be addressed in order to create the types of students who are able to find a productive and meaningful role in society, the desired long-term outcome of any school counseling program.

We believe that there are several changes that need to occur to institutionalize CR-CGCPs. The first is that more resources are made available to support the science of school counseling. We need support to develop, implement, and evaluate culturally responsive and effective school-based interventions that are designed to address educational equity and globalization (see Gysbers, 2008; Kim & Alamilla, 2008, for a more in-depth discussion of evaluation and research in school counseling). We call on the Department of Education to provide more calls for research on school counseling, and on the National Institute for Mental Health and the National Science Foundation as well as nongovernmental foundations to recognize that schools constitute the appropriate places to develop, implement, and evaluate programs to prevent violence and substance abuse and facilitate the development of youth into effective citizens.

The other change is an ongoing relationship between school counselors and counselor education programs that extends beyond preparation for a degree. School counselor training programs need to be involved in an ongoing consultation and training relationship with their graduates and local schools. Counselor educators need to engage in research that provides models for how to address issues of educational equity and globalization within schools and be active in disseminating this information.

School counselors need to become vocal and active advocates for educational equity and preparing students to become effective citizens in a global society. Much has been written about the need for school counselors to move beyond a practice that is focused on individual counseling or being overburdened with clerical tasks. A multiculturally competent school counselor needs to build on his or her counseling skills to take on an active consultation and leadership role in all aspects of the school (e.g., Beale, 2003; Bemak, 2000; Butler-Byrd et al., 2006).

Finally, we believe that school counselors need to demonstrate how their activities affect educational equity and student preparation for a modern economy. We believe that demonstrating multicultural competence goes beyond awareness, knowledge, and skills and includes being effective.

References

American School Counseling Association. (2003). The ASCA national model: A framework for school counseling programs. *Professional School Counseling, 6*(3), 165–168.

American School Counseling Association (2005). *ASCA national model: A framework for school counseling programs* (2nd ed.). Alexandria, VA: Author.

Baruth, L. G., & Manning, M. L. (2000). A call for multicultural counseling in middle schools. *The Clearing House, 4*, 243–246.

Bass, C., & Coleman, H. L. K. (1997). Enhancing the cultural identity of early adolescent male African Americans. *Professional School Counselor, 1*, 48–51.

Battistich, V., Solomon, D., Watson, M., & Schaps, E. (1997). Caring school communities. *Educational Psychologist, 32*(3), 137–151.

Beale, A. (2003). The indispensable school counselor. *Principal Leadership, 4*(1), 68–71.

Beale, A., & McCay, E. (2001). Selecting school counselors: What administrators should look for in prospective counselors. *The Clearing House, 74*(5), 257–260.

Bemak, F. (2000). Transforming the role of the counselor to provide leadership in educational reform through collaboration. *Professional School Counseling, 3*(5), 323–331.

Bemak, F. (2005). Reflections on multiculturalism, social justice, and empowerment groups for academic success: A critical discourse for contemporary schools. *Professional School Counseling, 8*(5), 401–406.

Borders, L. D., & Drury, S. M. (1992). Comprehensive school counseling programs: A review for policy makers and practitioners. *Journal of Counseling and Development, 70*(4), 487–498.

Bradley, L.J., & Jarchow, E. (1998). The school counsellor's role in globalizing the classroom. *International Journal for the Advancement of Counseling, 20*, 243–251.

Bronfenbrenner, U. (1979). *The ecology of human development.* Cambridge, MA: Harvard University Press.

Bryan, J. (2005). Fostering educational resilience and achievement in urban schools through school-family-community partnerships. *Professional School Counseling, 8*(3), 219–227.

Butler, S. K. (2003). Multicultural sensitivity and competence in the clinical supervision of school counselors and school psychologists: A context for providing competent services in a multicultural society. *The Clinical Supervisor, 22*(1), 125–141.

Butler-Byrd, N., Nieto, J., & Nieto Senour, M. (2006). Working successfully with diverse students and communities: The community-based block counselor preparation program. *Urban Education, 41*(4), 376–401.

Carey, J. C., Reinat, M., & Fontes, L. (1990). School counselors' perceptions of training needs in multicultural counseling. *Counselor Education and Supervision, 29*(3), 155–169.

Carpenter, S. L., King-Sears, M. E., & Keys, S. G. (1998). Counselors + educators + families as a transdisciplinary team = more effective inclusion for students with disabilities. *Professional School Counseling, 2*(1), 1–9.

Center for Substance Abuse Prevention's Center for the Application of Prevention Technologies (2007). Retrieved January 15, 2007, from http://captus.samhsa.gov/western/western.cfm

Coleman, H. L. K. (2007). Minority student achievement: A resilient outcome? In D. Zinga (Ed.), *Navigating multiculturalism: Negotiating change.* Cambridge Scholars Press.

Coleman, H. L. K. (2008). School counseling and student accomplishment. In H. L. K. Coleman & C. Yeh (Eds.), *Handbook for school counseling.* Mahwah, NJ: Lawrence Erlbaum Associates.

Coleman, H. L. K., & Baskin, T. (2003). Multiculturally competent school counseling. In D. B. Pope-Davis, H. L. K. Coleman, W. M. Liu, & R. L. Toporek (Eds.), *Handbook of multicultural competencies* (pp. 103–113). Thousand Oaks, CA: Sage.

Coleman, H. L. K., Karcher, S., & Biscoe, B. (2001). *Adolescent resiliency attitudes scale: A content and factor analysis study.* Paper presented at the annual meeting of the American Psychological Association, San Francisco, CA.

Coleman, H. L. K., Norton, R. A., Miranda, G. E., & McCubbin, L. D. (2003). Toward an ecological theory of cultural identity development. In D. B. Pope-Davis, H. L. K. Coleman, W. Liu, & R. Toporek (Eds.), *Handbook of multicultural competencies* (pp. 38–58). Thousand Oaks, CA: Sage.

Coleman, H. L. K., Yang, A., & Kim, S. C. (2008). Cultural identity development: An applied focus. In H. L. K. Coleman & C. Yeh (Eds.), *Handbook for school counseling.* Mahwah, NJ: Lawrence Erlbaum Associates.

Constantine, M. G. (1998). Challenges to the career development of urban racial and ethnic minority youth: Implications for vocational intervention. *Journal of Multicultural Counseling and Development, 26*(2), 83–95.

Constantine, M. G., & Yeh, C. J. (2001). Multicultural training, self-construals, and multicultural competence of school counselors. *Professional School Counseling, 4*(3), 202–207.

Dahir, C. A. (2001). The National Standards for School Counseling Programs: Development and implementation. *School Counseling, 4*(5), 320–327.

D'Andrea, M. (1996). Promoting peace in our schools: Developmental, preventive, and multicultural considerations. *School Counselors, 44*(1), 55–64.

Eschenauer, R., & Chen-Hayes, S. F. (2005). The transformative individual school counseling model: An accountability model for urban school counselors. *Professional School Counseling, 8*(3), 244–248.

Friedman, T. L. (2005). *The world is flat: A brief history of the 21st century.* New York: Farrar, Strauss, & Giroux.

Goleman, D. (1995). *Emotional intelligence.* New York: Bantam Books.

Green, A. G., Conley, J. A., & Barnett, K. (2005). Urban school counseling: Implications for practice and training. *Professional School Counseling, 8*(3), 189–195.

Green, A. J., & Keys, S. (2001). Expanding the developmental school counseling paradigm: Meeting the needs of the 21st century student. *Professional School Counseling, 5*(2), 84–95.

Gysbers, N. C. (2008). Evaluation of school guidance and counseling programs: Past, present, and future. In H. L. K. Coleman & C. Yeh (Eds.), *Handbook for school counseling.* Mawah, NJ: Lawrence Erlbaum Associates.

Gysbers, N. C., & Henderson, P. (2001). Comprehensive guidance and counseling programs: A rich history and a bright future. *Professional School Counseling, 4*(4), 246–256.

Harris, H. L. (1999). School counselors and administrators: Collaboratively promoting cultural diversity. *NASSP Bulletin, 83*(603), 54–61.

Herring, R. D., & White, L. M. (1995). School counselors, teachers, and the culturally compatible classroom: Partnerships in multicultural education. *Journal of Humanistic Education & Development, 34*(2), 52–64.

Hobson, S. M., & Kanitz, H. M. (1996). Multicultural counseling: An ethical issue for school counselors. *School Counselor, 43*(4), 245–255.

Holcomb-McCoy, C. (2004). Assessing multicultural competence of school counselors: A checklist. *Professional School Counseling, 7*(3), 178–183.

Holcomb-McCoy, C. C. (1998). *School counselor preparation in urban settings. ERIC Clearinghouse on urban education.* (ERIC Document Reproduction Service No. ED418343).

Johnson, L. S. (1995). Enhancing multicultural relations: Intervention strategies for the school counselor. *School Counselor, 43*(2), 103–113.

Keys, S. G., & Bemak, F. (1997). School-family-community linked services: A school counseling role for changing times. *School Counselor, 44*(4), 255–263.

Keys, S. G., & Lockhart, E. J. (1999). The school counselor's role in facilitating multisystemic change. *Professional School Counseling, 3*(2), 101–107.

Kim, B. S. K., & Alamilla, S. G. (2008). Research in and on school counseling. In H.L.K. Coleman & C. Yeh (Eds.), *Handbook for school counseling.* Mahwah, NJ: Lawrence Erlbaum Associates.

KIPP (2006). *Knowledge is power program.* Retrieved January 10, 2007, from, http://www.kipp.org/

LaFromboise, T. M., Coleman, H. L. K., & Gerton, J. (1993). Psychological impact of biculturalism: Evidence and theory. *Psychological Bulletin, 114,* 395–412.

Lee, C. (2001). Culturally responsive school counselors and programs: Addressing the needs of all students. *Professional School Counseling, 4*(4), 257–261.

Lee, C. C. (2005). Urban school counseling: Context, characteristics, and competencies. *Professional School Counseling, 8*(3), 184–188.

Lindwall, J. J., & Coleman, H. L. K. (2008). Creating caring school communities. In H. L. K. Coleman & C. Yeh (Eds.), *Handbook for school counseling*. Mahwah, NJ: Lawrence Erlbaum Associates.

Noddings, N. (1992). *The challenge to care in schools: An alternative approach to education*. New York: Teachers College Press.

Search Institute (2005). *40 developmental assets*. Retrieved July 13, 2005, from http://www.search-institute.org/assets/forty.html

Sergiovanni, T. J. (1994). *Building community in schools*. San Francisco, CA: Jossey-Bass.

Shade, B. J., Kelly, C., & Oberg, M. (1997). *Creating culturally responsive classrooms*. Washington, DC: American Psychological Association.

Sink, C. (2002). Comprehensive guidance and counseling programs and the development of multicultural student-citizens. *Professional School Counseling, 6*(2), 130–137.

Smith-Adcock, S., Daniels, M. H., Lee, S. M., Villalba, J. A., & Indelicato, N. A. (2006). Culturally responsive school counseling for Hispanic/Latino students and families: The need for bilingual school counselors. *Professional School Counseling, 10*(1), 92–101.

Substance Abuse and Mental Health Services Administration (2007). Retrieved January 15, 2007, from http://modelprograms.samhsa.gov

Sue, D. W. (2001). Multidimensional facets of cultural competence. *Counseling Psychologist, 29*(6), 790–821.

Thernstrom, A., & Thernstrom, S. (2003). *No excuses: Closing the racial gap in learning*. New York: Simon & Schuster.

University of Wisconsin-Extension (2007). *Logic model*. Retrieved January 15, 2007, from http://www.uwex.edu/ces/pdande/evaluation/evallogicmodel.html

Webb, L. D., Brigman, G. A. & Campbell, C. (2005). Linking school counselors and student success: A replication of the student success skills approach targeting the academic and social competence of students. *Professional School Counseling, 8*(5), 407–413.

Weinrach, S. G., & Thomas, K. R. (2004). The AMCD multicultural counseling competencies: A critically flawed initiative. *Journal of Mental Health Counseling, 26,* 20–35.

Wolin, S., & Wolin, S. (1993). *The resilient self: How survivors of troubled families rise above adversity*. New York: Villard Books.

Yeh, C. J., & Pituc, S. T. (2008). Understanding yourself as a school counselor. In H. L. K. Coleman & C. Yeh (Eds.), *Handbook for school counseling*. Mahwah, NJ: Lawrence Erlbaum Associates.

Suggested Readings

Coleman, H. L. K., & Yeh, C. (Eds.). (2007). *Handbook of school counseling*. Philadelphia: Taylor and Francis.

This handbook provides a comprehensive perspective on the practice and science of professional counseling. The purpose of the handbook is to give information to entry level school counselors as they develop a school counseling program and for scholars who are looking for a current summary of issues in the field of school counseling.

Green, A. J., & Keys, S. (2001). Expanding the developmental school counseling paradigm: Meeting the needs of the 21st century student. *Professional School Counseling, 5*(2), 84–95.

Green examines the current comprehensive developmental guidance framework and addresses how it fails to meet the needs of diverse student populations. In order to address this issue, the authors present a "Development-in-Context" perspective that is more effective for working with urban students by looking at the ecological factors that must be considered in an urban environment.

Lee, C. (2001). Culturally responsive school counselors and programs: Addressing the needs of all students. *Professional School Counseling, 4*(4), 257–261.

Lee advocates that school counseling programs must address the needs of culturally diverse youth. In this discussion, Lee describes the important elements of culturally responsive schools and school counseling programs, and describes the roles and responsibilities of school counselors who take an active role to promote the development of culturally diverse youth.

Miller, W. R., & Rollnick, S. (1991). *Motivational interviewing: Preparing people to change addictive behavior.* New York: Guilford Press.

Professional school counselors are consistently faced with students, teachers, administrators, and families who are committed to a sometimes difficult status quo. The principles of motivation outlined in this book are extremely helpful in understanding how to motivate individual, group, and institutional change.

Sink, C. (2002). Comprehensive guidance and counseling programs and the development of multicultural student-citizens. *Professional School Counseling, 6*(2), 130–137.

Sink argues that comprehensive guidance programs should help youth to develop into "multicultural student-citizens" in order to prepare them to successfully live and work in our increasingly global society. Sink provides examples of competencies that students should acquire, and asserts that these can be fostered through comprehensive guidance and counseling programs that effectively promote the development of culturally diverse youth.

9

Group Therapy With Mexican American and Mexican Adolescents
Focus on Culture

Joan D. Koss-Chioino, Louise Baca, Luis A. Vargas

Contents

Introduction

With the increasing emphasis on using evidence-based therapies, a debate is
taking place between proponents who favor the development of therapies for
specific cultural groups and those who favor making cultural adaptations to
existing evidence-based therapies. Shirk (2005) notes that it is highly likely
that empirically supported treatments (ESTs) will be optimized by developing culturally specific treatment variations, and by ensuring that therapists
are sensitive to cultural factors. However, he asserts that it does not mean
that the core components of ESTs need to be abandoned because of cultural
differences. In other words, he believes that ESTs can be optimized by being
culturally adapted but they must still maintain treatment fidelity.

Nagayama Hall (2001) contrasts culturally sensitive therapies (CST) with
empirically supported treatments that are considered by many research psychologists to be the gold standard for all persons. He asserts that the inclusion of culture in psychotherapeutic interventions is a significant ethical issue
because psychological processes are invariably related to the "social, cultural
and political contexts of ethnic minority persons" (p. 505). Nagayama Hall
suggests that the cross-cultural and cross-ethnic factors that should be considered are interdependence, spirituality, and discrimination. Yet, most EST
studies have done little more than label their ethnically diverse subject/clients
as a particular group and include their culture only as some discrete variable,
such as language, rather than integrate culture into treatment as content or
context.

Hwang (2006) has noted that the term *adaptation of treatments* has been
used loosely, with few studies clearly describing how they actually adapted
the treatments. A direction of integration, at least for adults, is detailed in
a recent book edited by Hays and Iwamasa (2006), which focuses on making cognitive-behavioral therapy culturally responsive for a variety of ethnic

groups. Cognitive-behavioral therapy is widely considered to be effective for all persons yet these authors describe cultural adaptations they consider necessary. The study described in this chapter describes how a group therapy model was culturally adapted while adhering, in part, to methods and processes that are evidence-based.

Group Therapy in the Southwest Study of Treatment Outcomes

In this chapter we discuss how our Southwest study of treatment outcomes in Mexican-descent and Mexican American youths intended to be culturally responsive, focused on an innovative group therapy, in order to explore the general question: What is the role of culture in the treatment of adolescents? It is to be noted that the movement for "cultural competence" in treatment has taken a firm stand on this question, advocating that treatments must employ cultural factors (American Psychological Association, 2003; Sue, 1998). However, questions remain: What are the cultural factors that make a difference in treating adolescents? Are there specific factors integral to the content of the treatment, the clients' culture, their level of acculturation, the treatment modality, the quality of the treatment alliance, or ethnic matching (the latter two suggested by Sue, 1988, and Sue & Sundberg, 1996)? We will suggest answers to these questions, based on the treatment study of Mexican and Mexican American youths and families which compared Strategic-Structural Family Therapy to an innovative, culturally adapted group therapy developed specifically for the project (Baca & Koss-Chioino, 1997). Our focus is on a description of the group treatment we carried out, some culturally relevant responses to that treatment, and a few outcomes. Statistical results are reported when they are relevant as adjuncts to description.

The Southwest Treatment Study for Mexican and Mexican American Adolescents

Our clinic sample was composed of 369 families, and 371 adolescents, 12 to 18 years of age (mean: 14.6 years), self-identified as Mexican or Mexican American and referred for substance use and other behavior problems by school counselors, juvenile justice intake workers, social service agencies, parents or other relatives, or (in three cases) by the adolescent. Adolescents and their families were assigned to a treatment group if they were eligible under the following criteria: Subject was (a) between 12 and 18 years old; (b) identified himself/herself as Mexican or Mexican American; (c) fluent in English; (d) living locally with at least 2 family members, one of whom was an adult; (e) lived with his/her family in the United States for at least 2 years; and (f) identified as having substance use and/or behavior problems. Exclusion criteria were as follows. The potential participant was not (a) receiving treatment for or exhibiting suicidal ideation; (b) receiving treatment for or exhibiting delusional behavior; (c) receiving treatment for or exhibiting hallucinatory behavior; (d) needing detoxification; (e) moderately or severely retarded; (f) having a member of the household currently receiving treatment for or exhibiting psychosis, suicidal behavior, or homicidal behavior; or (g) currently receiving treatment for or having been diagnosed with any of the following DSM-III-R disorders: anorexia nervosa, bulimia nervosa, bipolar disorder, major depression, schizophrenia, or other functional psychosis (psychotic disorders not elsewhere classified). Fifty-two subjects were found to be ineligible during the intake visit due to the severity of psychiatric or addiction problems and were referred to other mental health care services. Of the remaining 319 families and youths, 197 were males and 122 females. In 64% of the families, parents were born in the United States; in 36% of the families, parents were born in Mexico and most preferred to speak Spanish. Of the youths, 270 were born in the United States and 49 were born in Mexico. Families had a narrow range of socioeconomic backgrounds with most heads of household holding blue-collar jobs, many temporary in nature.

Clinic Setting

In order to replicate community mental health services in the greater metropolitan area, but to do so in a culturally responsive way, we set up a "parallel center" in the Hispanic community focused on serving Mexican American and Mexican clients and families (see Yeh, Takeuchi, & Sue, 1994). All of the support staff, and all but 3 of 10 therapists, were bilingual Latinos. The clinic was located on the edge of a Mexican barrio close to public transportation. Clinic hours were held from 3 p.m. to 9 p.m. during the week and on Saturdays from 9 a.m. to 4 p.m. The furnishings and site of the center were informal; the decor was oriented to Mexican and Mexican American tastes and preferences. All of the staff, from receptionists to research assistants and therapists, were carefully and repeatedly instructed on the need to put client youths and families at ease, in order to establish a family-like ambience and *confianza* (trust).

Interventions

Three treatment conditions were tested: (a) Brief Structural/Strategic Family Therapy (BSFT; see Santisteban et al., 1996); (b) the BSFT modality enhanced by an engagement intervention (Santisteban et al., 1996) referred to as the "Structural Strategic Systems Engagement" (SSSE); and (c) an innovative, culturally responsive group therapy, model developed specifically as a comparison treatment. A manual was created for the group therapy, and the model was pilot tested before it was utilized as a comparison treatment condition. The family therapy interventions (with and without engagement) have been extensively described by Szapocznik, Santisteban, and colleagues in numerous publications and will not be included in the discussion in this chapter.

The three treatment groups did not significantly vary by gender composition, age, or number of immigrant versus native born subjects. There were no significant differences in typical patterns of drug use or in scores on the drug use consequences scale at baseline, making the treatment groups basically similar.

Culturally Adapted Group Therapy

The only intervention model specifically adapted for Latino children that is described in the literature is that of Cuento Therapy, developed by a group at Fordham University. Cuento Therapy uses folktales as triggers for the discussion of cultural values and problem solving with children, 9 to 13 years of age, and heroic biographies for older adolescents (Costantino, Malgady, & Rogler, 1986; Malgady, Rogler, & Costantino, 1990). A storytelling therapy along the same lines was also developed, in which TEMAS pictures (a culturally adapted projective test) are used to elicit designated themes or stories. Therapists facilitate discussion of the resolution of problems represented in the stories (Costantino, Malgady, & Rogler, 1994). The authors report significant effectiveness of this therapy in treating conduct problems in school, and anxious and fearful symptoms in both Latino males and females. However, they note lack of effectiveness with symptoms of depression.

Although the Fordham group systematically measured outcomes of their interventions and found significant results, they raise the important question of whether "cultural sensitivity operates like a catalyst, enabling the effectiveness of a standard therapeutic technique . . . or whether cultural sensitivity is itself therapeutic?" (Costantino et al., 1994, p. 19). The two major elements of storytelling therapy, the narrative format and cultural content, may synergistically account for positive outcomes. Because culture is pervasive in our thinking about life and about ourselves, perhaps these elements cannot be split apart. In any case, Cuento Therapy and its successor, storytelling therapy, provide excellent models of how therapeutic interventions might be designed differently to respond to cultural content and context.

The group therapy model proposed in this chapter is based in part on the assumption that an established personal/ethnic identity provides psychological protection against a range of symptoms associated with problem behavior (Harter, 1990). An example of the role of ethnic identity is given by Vigil (1988), who views the attraction of the gang as related to problems around ethnic identity. Ethnic identity was an often verbalized issue among the youths in our clinic cohort. Even though immigrant youths seem to accommodate within 1 to 2 years to the larger, multicultural society (e.g., learning English and teenage mores regarding dress and attitudes), this process is different than retaining a Mexican ethnic identity within the social milieu of the United States, where discrimination by members of the dominant society may provide the impetus to either attempt to assimilate or to identify with one's ethnic group (such as identifying oneself as Chicano, Latino, and so on) experiencing the discrimination. Mexican identity may be the only choice for many immigrant youth given darker skin color and negative attitudes in the dominant society that block assimilation to mainstream culture. This process may parallel that of many youths of Mexican descent born in the United States. One could even hypothesize that embracing a "traditional" (albeit somewhat modified) identity model serves a stabilizing function in troubled youths' chaotic lives.

It is of interest that data on a summary acculturation measure with the first 80 youths in our clinic cohort showed that 36% reported an overall lower (i.e., more traditional) level of acculturation than did their parents, the reverse of the direction described in the work of Szapocznik (1981).

Key Components of Our Group Therapy Model for Mexican American Adolescents

Developing a culturally responsive group therapy model included integrating aspects of various theoretical models with those considered most relevant to Mexican and Mexican American adolescents. Various approaches were reviewed in order to find those with the best potential for being effective for Mexican and Mexican American youths. Work on the theoretical underpinnings of group therapy suggests that considerable overlap exists among at least 10 common models (Dies, 1992). The model described here does not fall into one theoretical niche but borrows from several of the most widely used models in the field, given hypotheses about what is culturally responsive for Mexican and Mexican American youths. For example, the here-and-now orientation of the group comes from Yalom's model (1985) but is congenial to conceptions of adolescent development that specify that youths lack a focus on the future, a characteristic of over 95% of our clinic cohort. Present time orientation is also culturally responsive in terms of the values that typify the worldview of most Mexican and Mexican Americans (Sue & Sue, 2008).

Social Skills Training (SST) aims to teach effective interpersonal skills, and assumes that social behavior is learned via structured teaching, role playing, and modeling. Tiffen and Spence (1986) found SST to be an effective modality for Anglo adolescents but their findings were not replicated with Cuban youth (Szapocznik, personal communication). The foci of our group model for Mexican and Mexican American youth are on affective expression, personal/ethnic identity, and life choices, especially in relation to drug use and delinquent behavior. A major focal point for each session in the group model is attention to affect as the primary factor related to symptom reduction (Hardy-Fanta & Montana, 1982). A conceptual viewpoint underlying this technique is that a focus on affect presents the challenge of attending to pain and conflict without moving into either a pure problem-solving mode or one of denial. By facilitating adolescents' ability to tolerate anxiety and verbalize feelings, rather than withdrawing or acting out, a foundation for other therapeutic work is established. This is accomplished through sensitivity to the cultural nuances of the expression of affect, especially by working with silences.

From a behavioral perspective, emphasis on communication skills has been shown to be an effective component of intervention. For example, "I" messages (labeled in the model as "talking from the heart") are taught in order to underscore the importance of communicating feelings and as a means of taking responsibility for what is said (in contrast to the blaming that can occur with "you" messages). A focus on interpersonal relating and on the affective components of relationships, especially nonverbal ones, is, according to our studies, culturally responsive for Latinos in general (Koss-Chioino & Cañive, 1996).

Another focus of the model is attention to anger, which surfaces as youths attempt to deal with family distress and racial/ethnic prejudice and discrimination encountered at school and in the larger metropolitan community. Expressing anger with words without injuring others emotionally or physically or blaming and accusing others, accessing and communicating the emotional or physical injury that gives rise to anger, and learning how to use physical exercise or sports as a means to cope with stress and tension emerge as productive ways of coping with these negative feelings in group. Once the anger is expressed productively, the way is open to discuss group members' ideas about societal oppression in their local worlds. This is one means by which these youths can learn to cope with feelings of helplessness and hopelessness, which research has shown to arise through the process of acculturation (Vega, Gil, Warheit, & Apospori, 1993).

Gang activity was often discussed by the youth, described as a way of attempting to replace the lack of support from families and of trying to overcome their sense of powerlessness and vulnerability in a dominant society that is often perceived as oppressive, callous, and inaccessible. Although our group therapists allowed discussion of gang involvement, glorification of gang activities or acting out (such as the "throwing of signs") was not permitted. The focus was on the needs the gang fulfills, the replacement of needs unfulfilled at home or school, and the sense of belonging and self-efficacy that is so important in adolescence. In this context, the topic of alternative ways of belonging was addressed, as well as the themes of "loyalty," "honor," and "protection," which are highly charged concepts integral to idealized familial relationships among Mexicans and Mexican Americans.

We observed that most Mexican and Mexican American adolescents do not respond well to the therapist taking a passive stance, nor to the blank-screen approach, nor to the uncovering techniques derived from psychoanalysis (Khantzian, 1986). Instead, an active, empathic, and supportive stance from the group leaders is appreciated. Strategic expressions of vulnerability by therapists as well as clients have been noted to be particularly important with those who abuse substances (Khantzian, Halliday, & McAulifee, 1990). In line with sensitivity to cultural patterning, the expression of vulnerability by therapists was encouraged only in areas where adolescents had parallel concerns. Trust in the therapist was established during initial group sessions by the juxtaposition of strength/firmness and vulnerability.

Group as a "Fourth Life Space"

Overall, the suggested group process was aimed at creating a "fourth life space" (neither home nor school nor the streets) in which some basic social and psychological needs could be met. In group, as a created life space, the formation of new types of peer and adult relationships and the construction of new narratives that reflect a culturally compatible balance between affiliation and self-efficacy was designed to be a primary vehicle for change by doing the following:

1. Promoting more direct, affectively oriented communication in the interpersonal sphere
2. Suggesting new patterns of self-care, self-efficacy, and caring for others
3. Facilitating a positive, more integrated sense of personal and ethnic identity focused on nondestructive methods of developing a sense of self-worth and self-efficacy within a culture that values family and community affiliation
4. Confronting issues around drug use, negative peer pressure, loss/death, family conflict or disintegration, economic disadvantage, school experiences, sexuality, sexism, discrimination, and oppression
5. Empowering participants with increased self-awareness and increased perceptions of self-efficacy in dealing with the primary life spaces of family, school, and street/neighborhood

A New Group Therapy Model: Within the Fourth Life Space

Following the model suggested by Vargas and Koss-Chioino (1992), the group therapy we developed can be described as consisting of two interrelated dimensions: *structure* and *culture*. The *structural* dimension is further subdivided into *form* and *process*. *Form* is the style by which therapy is carried out according to its underlying theory, manual, and/or characteristic methods and procedures, including the physical environment in which the therapy is carried out. *Process* refers to the course or changes that produce a particular result in therapy. The *cultural* dimension is subdivided into *content* and *context*. *Content* refers to specific and patterned meanings through which social phenomena are constructed, deconstructed, and reconstructed, including self- and worldviews, perceptions of developmental landmarks, and roles and relationships. *Context* refers to intra- and extra-clinical situational and environmental spheres that a therapist and client occupy. These include the physical setting in which the therapy is conducted; social ecology, such as family, school, work, and community, of the client and therapist; and the aspects of these institutions that influence a client's and therapist's attitudes and behavior.

The Structural Dimension: Form

In the clinic setting, there are furnishings and decoration focused on creating a homelike environment and facilitating a feeling of acceptance and ease. Both rules and environmental arrangements relate to the overall goal of developing a culturally responsive approach to not only the therapy but also its context. For example, in our study the group therapy space and its accoutrements were oriented toward a feeling of *confianza* (familiarity in the sense of family feeling and trust).

The clinic's reception area is geared toward passive family activity and equipped with a television, toys, and bilingual reading materials for all ages. Coffee for the adults and cookies for everyone are set out. Both the adult reading material and the decor include items of local Latino interest, and the staff is trained to provide referrals to other agencies or community services according to the family's needs. Mexican holidays are celebrated through decoration. In the group therapy room, as in the reception area, there is a purposeful informality (chairs and beanbags are provided for seating, for example) in contrast to the ordered formality of some institutions that deliver mental health services. These various arrangements, together with the limitation of services to one ethnic group, classify the Southwest Study of Treatment Outcomes as a parallel center (see Yeh et al., 1994).

Confianza was encouraged in our clinic from the time of initial contact by a client's parent. A bilingual receptionist recorded any information the parents offered and assured the parents that they would be called by their child's therapist within a 24-hour period. Therapists were mostly Latino; a few were of another ethnic minority group with explicit training in Hispanic cultural awareness. All intake information was collected by the therapist during the initial intake. The client and the entire family were invited to come in for the initial assessments. Parents and youths were free to select the language of their preference. Both Spanish and English were spoken interchangeably throughout the clinic.

Therapists

The efficacy of group therapy is due in great part to the particular strengths and characteristics of the group leader(s). Therapists should ideally be young (under 35 years of age) and trained at the master's level or beyond. Preferably, all of the therapists and the clinical supervisor should be Latino or of ethnic minority descent in order to spontaneously identify with the struggles, needs, and strengths of the adolescent participants (Sue and Sue, 1991). This does not exclude therapists who have been trained to identify with the life experiences of ethnic minority youths. In our experience, those therapists who have had similar life experiences are more likely to be successful through a covert process of identification with the youths. Youths seem to recognize this similarity in life experience, even if it is not verbalized.

The particular attributes of therapists that were important to carrying out this group therapy in our clinic were as follows:

1. Culturally appropriate displays of firmness and clear boundaries
2. Culturally appropriate expression of nurturing, warmth, caring, accepting, genuineness, and openness
3. Actively able to engage participants in either English or Spanish, including the use of culturally relevant humor
4. Enthusiasm for cultural heritage expressed in language, clothing, and knowledge of cultural events
5. Sincere appreciation of youth
6. Capable of facilitating a sense of commonality and sharing

Format

Sixteen 90-minute sessions formed the modal therapeutic period. Four-session blocks focused on one of the following four goals:

1. Increase ability to express feelings and emotions in the service of increasing the effectiveness of communication among peers and between youths and adults.
2. Increase the effectiveness of interpersonal skills and the belief or awareness that one can become an important, contributing member of society.
3. Improve self-concept through the enhancement of positive and integrative aspects of ethnic identity.
4. Increase awareness of what it means to have a positive self-concept and strategies in order to displace drug use, delinquent behavior, and other self-destructive behavior.

In our clinic, whenever a member joined the therapy group, a pregroup orientation was conducted by one of the group therapists. Preparation for group therapy has been shown to be an effective deterrent of high attrition rates (Sklare, Keener, & Mas, 1990). Client and therapist previewed together the expectations of the group leaders for group members. The therapist demystified the group experience by describing the group and allowing questions about group therapy. Moreover, fears or concerns about being in group therapy were addressed. Each client was then asked to consider some personal goals that might be achieved during the course of group therapy. We observed that most youths found it very difficult to describe any goals.

The Structural Dimension: Process

The main focus in developing this group therapy was to create an alternative life space as a counterpoint to other social arenas in which problems have occurred. As discussed by Morales (1992) and reflected in our clinical experience, it is the rejection that youths experience in other groups (family, schools, churches) that seems to lead to many potentially self-destructive behaviors. These include gang affiliation and drug and alcohol abuse. Our group model attempts to provide a group experience that embraces and welcomes its members, and is culturally familiar. Throughout the course of the group, group members were permitted a wide range for expression, as long as there was respect and safety for all group members. For example, discussion of gang affiliation was allowed but the group itself was designated as "neutral territory."

Four main principles guided therapeutic process in our group therapy.

Flexibility   The therapy group sessions were structured by a specific topic for each session, a goal addressed in the session, and suggested questions for initiation of discussion within the group. However, the group process itself cannot be prestructured. It is assumed to be a vital and healing component of the intervention (Millan & Chan, 1991). As suggested by Delgado (1983), the adolescents were allowed to use whatever language each felt most comfortable with, be it Spanish, street slang, or a combination, which allowed for spontaneous emotional expression. During the group session, an initial topic was introduced but all topics for discussion were welcomed and woven into the theme of the particular session.

Expansion Into Life Spaces   Due to the high value placed on family in Latino culture, which intersects with developmental needs, both the nuclear and the extended *familia* (family) were introduced for discussion. This included close family friends, godparents (referred to as *compadres*), and especially grand-parents. Self-work was promoted through developing awareness of an inter-nal life space facilitated by discussion of autobiographical narratives framed by an ethnic and cultural context. This sharing of personal space built group cohesion and provided a basis for discussion of ethnic identity. Typically, feelings about ethnicity were charged with confusion, a search for meaning, and need for affirmation and acceptance.

Empowerment Group leaders (therapists) empowered group members to lead the group toward concerns that felt pressing at the moment. This weaving of self-determination and responsibility by group members with the structural consistency provided by group leaders constitutes a novel and complex model of group therapy for Mexican American adolescents.

Therapeutic process includes working with the acknowledged and previ-ously unacknowledged individual strengths of group members, highlighting them in group as means to achieving desired positive changes, and utiliz-ing them to suggest more personally and socially satisfying alternatives to self-destructive or delinquent behavior. These then can be tied into skills to develop and maintain a positive self-concept. By processing emotional responses to death, divorce, and other interpersonal losses, normalization and reinforcement of appropriate coping is encouraged, along with the devel-opment of a positive sense of self.

The underlying principle of empowerment plays a large part in the healing process. Every opportunity was taken to emphasize personal choice in rela-tion to the ways group members interacted with each other, as well as with the outside world. The peer group in this fourth life space is encouraged to be honest rather than "hip" or "cool" when confronted by group members and therapists. Confrontation is a carried out through an invitation to hear feed-back rather than as an opportunity to instigate conflict or punish an indi-vidual. Expressions of vulnerability, low self-esteem, anger, and confusion are embraced with warmth, active listening, and empathic understanding. It might be noted that these are very new responses for most youths in these groups. Such factors have been shown to be related to positive therapeutic outcomes for substance-abusing adults (Khantzian et al., 1990).

Integration of Skills Training With Process Group process was stressed dur-ing the social skills training portions of the treatment protocol. As teens learned about improving communication skills, they were encouraged to practice the use of these skills in every group session. Therapists were active in directing peer interaction and clarifying feelings and statements which occurred between group members. The processing of nonverbal behavior and long silences (making the covert overt) by the therapists facilitated the expression of anger and the management of conflict within the group. These skills could then be generalized to other settings by suggesting that they try out their new skills in social arenas outside the group therapy setting.

Culturally Responsive Techniques

A number of projective devices in the form of stories were used to cue discussion around sensitive subjects, such as sexuality and drug use. This facilitates the telling of personal stories which many of the youths are reluctant to do (McAdams, 1993). Poetry written by Mexican American authors, excerpts of documentaries of famous Mexican artists, and film clips with contemporary Chicano themes and actors were used to elicit responses and suggest ideas for discussion. These narrative devices often highlighted discrepancies in perceptions between family and peers in assessing the accuracy of information and the ability to use communication skills. For example, a film clip might describe differences in parental interactions with sons and with daughters. This is one aid to facilitate discussion of perceptions of what it takes to be a respected and honorable man or a woman in the Mexican American community—in the family, at school, or in the streets. The discussion might then lead to comparisons that arise spontaneously, regarding conflicts or complementarities with the Anglo world, as suggested by group members' experiences.

Cultural responsiveness was enhanced by targeting certain topics for exploration in each session, such as the following:

1. Issues around ethnic identity and acculturation
2. Identifying special communication styles and patterns
3. Identification of gender-role definitions and expectations
4. Family relationships and struggles around dependency
5. Coping with major losses such as deaths, divorce, and relocation
6. Interfacing with the dominant society (school, churches, community)
7. Dealing with discrimination, prejudice, and more subtle forms of oppression

These topics were explored at least once during the 16 sessions and continued according to the judgment of the therapists leading the group.

Termination

The process of termination for each individual was systematic and addressed with enough time to allow for preparation of what may have constituted the first positive "good-bye" a youth had ever experienced. Each group member received feedback from other group members and was encouraged to respond to the feedback. A certificate of accomplishment was given, along with a key ring depicting the Mexican flag. Sharing of food and applause at the end of the session captured a sense of graduation. These rituals were tailored to each group.

Some Outcomes of the Culturally Adapted Group Therapy

We examined the outcomes of group therapy for the first 35 youths, 14 females and 21 males, ages 12 to 18 years. Assessments were made prior to the first session and immediately subsequent to completion of eight or more sessions. We report here on some positive changes on selected measures, as well as lack of change on other measures.

Paired t tests evaluating pretreatment–posttreatment changes were performed for all therapy groups. The Comprehensive Addiction Severity Index for Adolescents (CASI-A; Meyers, 1991) assessed several domains: educational problems, legal problems, sexual problem behavior, and drug use. A modified version of the Kiddie Schedule of Affective Disorders and Schizophrenia (K-SADS; Puig-Antich & Chambers, 1987) was used to measure symptoms of oppositional defiant disorder; major depression, minor depression, and dysthymia; conduct disorder; anxiety disorders; and attention deficit/hyperactivity disorder. A cutoff score of 3 or above (at least moderate severity or frequency of symptoms) classified adolescents according to diagnostic category. Scores were summed responses of youths and a parent. The Family Assessment Measure (FAM III; Skinner, Steinhauer, & Santa-Barbara, 1983) measured family dysfunction, using the General Scale and the Self-Rating Scale. The Parent-Adolescent Communication Scale (PAC; Barnes & Olson, 1982) assessed communication relative to three factors: open family communication, problems in family communication, and selective family communication.

Two scales on the Comprehensive Addiction Severity Index (CASI-A) showed significant, positive differences in means: Educational problems decreased ($t[34] = 4.173$, $p < .001$), and the quality of family interactions improved ($t[34] = 2.588$, $p < .05$). Other scales (drug use and severity, peer problems, high-risk sexual behavior and legal problems) were not significantly improved, although legal problems showed a positive trend.

The K-SADS showed highly significant improvements in symptom expression for the following categories: attention deficit/hyperactivity disorder ($t[33]$ = 3.852, p = .001); oppositional defiant disorder ($t[33]$ = 7.191, p < .001); depression ($t[33]$ = 6.917, p < .001); conduct disorder ($t[33]$ = 6.826, p <.001); and anxiety disorder ($t[33]$ =3.914, p <.001). There was no significant change in symptoms of obsessive-compulsive disorder.

There were no significant changes in family functioning or parent–adolescent communication, as reported by the youths themselves or by their parents. However, analysis of outcome data showed significant improvement in the areas of educational problems, quality of family interactions, as reported by the youths, and significant decreases in symptoms of psychopathology, especially depression, conduct problems, and oppositionality/defiance.

The rate of retention (defined as 8 or more sessions within 20 weeks) was 48%. This exceeded our hypothesized rate of 24% based on a study of Hispanic youths in a clinic in New Mexico. Although this is only one aspect of outcomes, it raises the question posed by Yeh and coworkers (1994) of whether this retention rate, along with other positive outcomes, is due to the culturally tailored group model, to our arrangement of the clinic as a culturally familiar setting, and/or to some other factors. Replication and refinement of the model would help answer these questions, as well as a search for the essential ingredients of positive outcomes. We also need to know if the model will be effective for Latino youths other than Mexican and Mexican Americans, if it is tailored to other Latino groups as it was for Mexican and Mexican American youths. We are planning to assess group process along culturally responsive dimensions in order to rate the extent to which culture plays a significant role in this modality. Outcomes should also be assessed from this perspective (Vargas & Koss-Chioino, 1992).

Conclusions and Summary: Group Therapy for Mexican and Mexican American Youths

A review of the literature reveals that group therapy is widely used for mainstream adolescents who exhibit behavior problems (McCord, 1990; O'Brien & Kelly, 1990). Foci of group treatments are poor school performance (Campbell & Myrick, 1990); peer relationship difficulties (O'Brien & Kelly, 1990); nonsevere psychiatric disorders (Loftus, 1988); and substance abuse

(Weis, Zarski, & Perkins, 1988). However, there is little written that specifically addresses group therapy for Latino adolescents, although several articles describe group interventions with Hispanic adults (Delgado, 1983; McKinley, 1987; Olarte & Masnik, 1985; Organista, 2006). Treatment studies of Hispanic adolescents deal mainly either with Puerto Ricans (Costantino, Malgady, & Rogler, 1994; Hardy-Fanta & Montana, 1982; Malgady, Rogler, & Costantino, 1990; Millan & Chan, 1991) or Cubans (Szapocznik & Kurtines, 1989). There are only a few treatment outcome studies of group therapy with Mexican American adolescents, and it appears that there are as yet no published manuals of a group intervention with this population. A recent search found only four articles and book chapters on some form of group therapy for ethnic minority adolescents apart from those for Latino youth cited in this chapter (DeCarlo & Hockman 2003; Franklin, 1989; Kahn, Lewis, & Galvez, 1974; Salloum, Avery, & McClain, 2001).

Behavioral group therapy, based on social learning principles, is considered effective for adolescents in general. Improvement in social and communication skills has been shown to improve a youth's management of life situations (O'Brien & Kelly, 1990). Groups allow for a large variety of techniques such as behavior contracting, peer feedback, behavior rehearsal, problem-solving skills, social reinforcement, and generalization to situations outside the group, all enhanced by the social influences the group generates. Some programs have been successful when focused on restructuring social reinforcers for nondelinquent behavior (Fawzy, Coombs, Santana, & Wolcott, 1984).

However, when culture and socio-psychological development simultaneously are taken into account, other requirements are suggested that augment an exclusive focus on behavior. Millan and Chan (1991) review themes such as: ethnocultural perspectives on the nature of adolescent development; the organization and quality of Hispanic family life; and the articulation of gender roles as essential baseline characteristics of group therapy with Hispanic adolescents. Of primary importance for interventions is the need to focus on issues around ethnic identity during adolescence, a highly vulnerable period of the youth's life. Research into adolescent development examines self-definition within the context of identity formation. During adolescence, the self is described as differentiating according to social role and context (Harter, 1990). One of the domains for differentiation of the self is ethnic identity.

Our definition of problems, issues, and contexts among Mexican American adolescents is broader and more varied than usually included in existing group therapy models. A goal of this chapter has been to examine an innovative approach to the development of a culturally responsive group therapy model. Toward this end, the assumptions and components of a newly developed manual for group therapy with Mexican American and Mexican adolescents have been described in some detail.

References

American Psychological Association (2003). Guidelines on multicultural education, training, research, practice and organizational change for psychologists. *American Psychologist, 58*(5), 377–402.

Baca, L. M., & Koss-Chioino, J. (1997). Development of a culturally responsive group therapy model. *Journal of Multicultural Counseling and Development, 25,* 130–141.

Barnes, H. L., & Olson, D. H. (1982). Parent adolescent communication scales. In D. H. Olson, H. I. McCubbin, H. Barnes, A. Larsen, M. Muxen, & M. Wilson (Eds.), *Family inventories: Inventories used in a national survey of families across the family life cycle* (pp. 33–48). St Paul: Family Social Science, University of Minnesota.

Campbell, C. A., & Myrick, R. D. (1990). Motivational group counseling for low performing students. *The Journal for Specialists in Group Work, 15,* 43–50.

Costantino, G., Malgady, R. G., & Rogler, L. H. (1986). Cuento Therapy: A culturally sensitive modality for Puerto Rican children. *Journal of Clinical and Consulting Psychology, 54*(5), 639–645.

Costantino, G., Malgady, R. G., & Rogler, L. H. (1994). Storytelling through pictures: Culturally sensitive psychotherapy for Hispanic children and adolescents. *Journal of Clinical Child Psychology, 23,* 13–20

DeCarlo, A., & Hockman, E. (2003). RAP therapy: A group work intervention method for urban adolescents. *Social Work With Groups, 26*(3), 45–59.

Delgado, M. (1983). Hispanics and psychotherapeutic groups. *International Journal of Group Psychotherapy, 33,* 507–520.

Dies, R. R. (1992). Models of group psychotherapy: Sifting through confusion. *International Journal of Group Psychotherapy, 42*(1), 1–17.

Fawzy, F. I., Coombs, R. H., Santana, F. O., & Wolcott, D. L. (1984). Activity workshops to reduce clinical attrition among adolescents. *Journal of Drug Issues, 14*(2), 419–426.

Franklin, A. J. (1989). *Therapeutic interventions with urban Black adolescents.* Berkeley, CA: Cobb & Henry.

Hardy-Fanta, C., & Montana, P. (1982). The Hispanic female adolescent: A group therapy model. *International Journal of Group Psychotherapy, 32,* 351–366.

Harter, S. (1990). Developmental differences in the nature of self-representations: Implications for the understanding, assessment, and treatment of maladaptive behavior. *Cognitive Therapy and Research, 14*(2), 113–142.

Hays, P. A., & Iwamasa, G. Y. (Eds.). (2006). *Culturally responsive cognitive-behavioral therapy: Assessment, practice, and supervision.* Washington, DC: American Psychological Association.

Hwang, W. (2006). The psychotherapy adaptation and modification framework: Application to Asian Americans. *American Psychologist, 61*(7), 702–715.

Kahn, M. W., Lewis, J., & Galvez, E. (1974). An evaluation study of a group therapy procedure with reservation adolescent Indians. *Psychotherapy: Theory, Research & Practice, 11*(3), 239–242.

Keefe, S., & Padilla, A. (1987). *Chicano ethnicity*. Albuquerque: University of New Mexico Press.

Khantzian, E. J. (1986). A contemporary psychodynamic approach in drug treatment. *American Journal of Drug and Alcohol Abuse, 12,* 213–222.

Khantzian, E. J., Halliday, K. S., & McAulifee, W. E., (1990). *Addiction and the vulnerable self: Modified dynamic group therapy for substance abusers*. New York: Guilford Press.

Koss-Chioino, J. D., & Cañive, J. M. (1996). Cultural issues in relational diagnosis: Hispanics in the United States. In F. W. Kaslow (Ed.), *Handbook of relational diagnosis* (pp. 137–151). John Wiley and Sons.

Loftus, M. (1988). Moving to change: Action groups in an out-patient setting. *Journal of Adolescence, 11*(3), 217–229.

Malgady, R. G., Rogler, L. H., & Costantino, G. (1990). Culturally sensitive psychotherapy for Puerto Rican children and adolescents: A program of treatment outcome research. *Journal of Consulting and Clinical Psychology, 58*(6), 704–712.

McAdams, D. P. (1993). *The stories we live by*. New York: Morrow.

McCord, J. (1990). Problem behaviors. In S. S. Feldman & G. R. Elliot (Eds.), *At the threshold: The developing adolescent* (pp. 414–431). Cambridge, MA: Harvard University Press.

McKinley, V. (1987). Group therapy as a treatment modality of special values for Hispanics. *International Journal of Group Psychotherapy, 37,* 255–268.

Meyers, K. (1991). *Comprehensive addiction severity index for adolescents*. Center for Studies of Addiction, University of Pennsylvania/VA Medical Center.

Millan, F., & Chan, J. (1991, Summer). Group therapy with inner city Hispanic acting out adolescent males: Some theoretical observations. *Group, 15,* 109–115.

Morales, A. (1992). Therapy with Latino gang members. In L. A. Vargas & J. D. Koss-Chioino (Eds.), *Working with culture: Psychotherapeutic interventions with ethnic minority children and adolescents* (pp. 129–154). San Francisco: Jossey-Bass.

Nagayama Hall, G. C. (2001). Psychotherapy research with ethnic minorities: Empirical, ethical and conceptual issues. *Journal of Clinical and Consulting Psychology, 69,* 502–510.

O'Brien, C. G., & Kelly, J. A. (1990). Behavioral group therapy with adolescents. In E. L. Feindler & G. R. Kalfus (Eds.), *Adolescent behavior therapy handbook* (pp. 421–448). New York: Springer.

Olarte, S. W., & Masnik, R. (1985). Benefits of long-term group therapy for disadvantaged Hispanic outpatients. *Hospital and Community Psychiatry, 36,* 1093–1097.

Organista, K. C. (2006). Cognitive-behavioral therapy with Latinos and Latinas. In P. A. Hays & G. Y. Iwamasa, *Culturally responsive cognitive-behavioral therapy: Assessment, practice, and supervision* (pp. 73–96). Washington, DC: American Psychological Association.

Peña, J., Koss-Chioino, J. D., & Bay, C. (2003). Searching for universals: Evidence for the validity of substance abuse subtypes in a sample of Mexican American youth, *American Journal of Substance Abuse and Addictions, 2,* 145–169.

Puig-Antich, J., & Chambers, W. (1987). *The Schedule of Affective Disorders and Schizophrenia for school-age children (Kiddie-SADS)*. New York: New York Psychiatric Institute.

Rogler, L. H., Malgady, R. G., & Rodriguez, O. (1989). *Hispanics and mental health: A framework for research.* Malabar, FL: Krieger.

Salloum, A., Avery, L., & McClain, R. P. (2001). Group psychotherapy for adolescent survivors of homicide victims: A pilot study. *Journal of the American Academy of Child & Adolescent Psychiatry, 40*(11), 1261–1267.

Santisteban, D. A., Szapocznik, J., Perez-Vidal, A., Kurtines, W. M., Murray, E. J., & LaPerriere, A. (1996). Efficacy of intervention of engaging youth and families into treatment and some variables that may contribute to differential effectiveness. *Journal of Family Psychology, 10*(1), 35–44.

Shirk, S. R. (2005). President's message: Dialogue and persistent polarities between research and practice. *In Balance: Society of Child and Adolescent Psychology Newsletter, 20*(3), 1–2.

Skinner, H. A., Steinhauer, P. D., & Santa-Barbara, J. (1983). The Family Assessment Measure. *Canadian Journal of Community Mental Health, 2*(2), 91–105.

Sklare, G., Keener, R., & Mas, C. (1990). Preparing members for here-and-now group counseling. *Journal for Specialists in Group Work, 15*(3), 141–148.

Sue, D. W., & Sue, D. (1991). *Counseling the culturally different: Theory and practice.* New York: Wiley.

Sue, D. W., & Sue, D. (2008). *Counseling the culturally diverse: Theory and practice* (5th ed.) Hoboken, NJ: John Wiley and Sons.

Sue, S. (1988). Psychotherapeutic services for ethnic minorities. *American Psychologist, 43*, 301–308.

Sue, S. (1998). In search of cultural competence in psychotherapy and counseling. *American Psychologist, 53*(4), 440–448.

Sue, S., & Sundberg, N. D. (1996). Research and research hypotheses about effectiveness in intercultural counseling. In P. B. Pedersen, J. G. Draguns, W. J. Lonner, & J. E. Trimble (Eds.), *Counseling across cultures* (pp. 323–352). Thousand Oaks, CA: Sage.

Szapocnik, J. (1981). Treatment of depression among Cuban American elders: Some validational evidence for a life enhancement counseling approach. *Journal of Consulting and Clinical Psychology, 49*(5), 752–754.

Szapocznik, J., & Kurtines, W. (1989). *Breakthroughs in family therapy with drug abusing problem youth.* New York: Springer.

Tiffen, K., & Spence, S. H. (1986). Responsiveness of isolated versus rejected children to social skills training. *Journal of Child Psychology and Psychiatry, 27*(3), 343–355.

Vargas, L. A., & Koss-Chioino, J. D. (Eds.). (1992). *Working with culture: Psychotherapeutic interventions with ethnic minority children and adolescents.* San Francisco: Jossey-Bass.

Vega, W. A., Gil, A. G., Warheit, G. J., & Apospori, E. (1993). Acculturation and delinquent behavior among Cuban American adolescents: Toward an empirical model. *American Journal of Community Psychology, 21*(1), 113–125.

Vigil, J. D. (1988). *Barrio gangs: Street life and identity in Southern California.* Austin: University of Texas Press.

Weis, D. M., Zarski, J. J., & Perkins, S. E. (1988). Family therapy and group counseling: Therapeutic factors and the chemically dependent adolescent. *The Journal for Specialists in Group Work, 13*, 218–223.

Yalom, I. D. (1985). *The theory and practice of group psychotherapy* (3rd ed.). New York: Basic Books.

Yeh, M., Takeuchi, D. T., & Sue, S. (1994). Asian-American children treated in the mental health system: A comparison of parallel and mainstream service centers. *Journal of Clinical Child Psychology, 23*(1), 5–12.

Suggested Readings

Vargas, L. A., & Koss-Chioino, J. D. (Eds.). (1992). *Working with culture: Psychotherapeutic interventions with ethnic minority children and adolescents.* San Francisco: Jossey-Bass.

In four chapters each, this book explores cultural adaptations used by therapists of similar ethnicity with their child and adolescent clients in the four major ethnic minority populations: Latino, Asian Americans, African Americans, and Native Americans. An introduction and concluding chapter by the editors provide theoretical perspectives and procedures by which to construct culturally responsive interventions.

Koss-Chioino, J. D., & Vargas Luis, A. (1999). *Working with Latino youth: Culture, context and development.* San Francisco: Jossey-Bass.

This book presents a synthesis of cultural-ecological, developmental, and contextual theories as grounding for an innovative approach to interventions with Latino youth. Cultural variations within the group of Latino youth seen in the United States are integrated with the approaches outlined.

McCabe, K. M., Yeh, M., Garland, A. F., Lau, A. S., & Garcia, G. (2005). The GANA program: A tailoring approach to adapting parent–child interaction therapy for Mexican Americans. *Education and Treatment of Children, 28*(20), 111–129.

The authors develop a culturally modified version of the Parent Child Interaction Therapy (PCIT), called *Guiando a Niños Activos* (GANA), for use with Mexican American families. Modifications were made based on information gleaned from the clinical literature, and based on qualitative data (focus groups). The modifications were reviewed by an expert panel of Mexican American therapists, a group of consultants with expertise in cross-cultural and mental health services research, and by Sheila Eyberg. The final version was revised according to their recommendations to arrive at a version that was both culturally acceptable and faithful to the original intervention.

Hwang, W. (2006). The psychotherapy adaptation and modification framework: Application to Asian Americans. *American Psychologist, 61*(7), 702–715.

The author notes that "adaptation of treatments" has been used loosely, with few studies clearly describing how they adapted the treatments. He cites the lack of methodological vigor (e.g., nonrandom assignment to groups, small sample sizes, use of simplistic structural or single point adaptation strategies) that weakens the conclusions that can be drawn from current studies. He presents a very thoughtful psychotherapy adaptation and modification framework model for use with Asian American immigrants.

Bernal, G., & Scharrón-del-Río, M. R. (2003). Are empirically supported treatments valid for ethnic minorities? Toward an alternative approach for treatment research. *Cultural Diversity and Ethnic Minority Psychology, 7*(4), 328–342.

The authors argue that insistence on generalization in the absence of data to support a particular position is an illusion. They propose an integration of hypothesis-testing (contemporary) and discovery-oriented (alternate) research. Discovery-oriented research aims to provide a closer, exploratory look at the psychotherapeutic process. It might provide tools and methods to move researchers beyond traditional methodologies and toward a consideration of research questions that are more exploratory. They see these two methodologies as complementary to each other.

Part III

The Practice of
Multicultural Counseling

10

A Clash of Cultures
A Case Study

Pittu Laungani

Contents

Preamble

This case study deals with several problems—marital, cultural, religious, familial, and psychological—between a married couple: a Muslim architect, Asif Mohammad from Kuala Lumpur in Malaysia, and his Chinese wife, a linguist who originally came from Taipei in Taiwan. They were both students in Hong Kong. They met at their university, and after completing their postgraduate studies, decided to get married—despite strong opposition from their respective families, which manifested itself in their refusal to attend the wedding. Asif Mohammad and his wife Mary Chung lived in a rented apartment in Kuala Lumpur and avoided meeting their families. But upon the sudden death of Asif's mother 2 years later, the estranged couple returned to Asif's parental home in Kuala Lumpur. It was soon after moving into their family home that their disagreements and conflicts began to surface.

My own meeting, initially with Mary and subsequently with her husband, Mohammad, was a matter of chance. I had gone to Taipei about a decade or so ago to attend an international conference (organized by the International Council of Psychologists), where I had been invited to present a couple of papers. One of my Indian relatives who lived with her husband and their daughter in Taipei knew Mary well—they were close friends—and she was aware of the serious rift between the couple and was justifiably worried that, unless their conflicts were resolved, their marriage was unlikely to survive for long.

By sheer coincidence Mary had come to Taipei to visit her ailing mother. My cousin, who really ought not to have done so, persuaded Mary to meet me in the hope that I might be in a position to help her. I hesitated. I could not see the purpose of one brief meeting because I knew I would not be staying long in Taiwan. My cousin insisted. I gave in and met Mary at my cousin's home, getting to know her briefly. Nothing of any importance or significance was discussed or disclosed. But because I had already planned to go to Kuala Lumpur to spend a couple of weeks with my nephew who lives there and whom I had not seen for several years, I promised to meet Mary and her husband in Kuala Lumpur—if of course they wanted to.

The essay discusses my 10 two-hour meetings with them. I could not ask them to come to my nephew's home without disclosing the purpose of the meeting. I felt it was morally and professionally incumbent upon me to protect their privacy and anonymity. To ensure privacy we met in Mohammad's office after office hours. I should also like to make it clear that both Mohammad and his wife Mary gave me leave to tape all our sessions. What follows is an edited account of their marital, cultural, religious, social, and familial conflicts and our mutual attempts to find a satisfactory solution.

I have no idea how Mary managed to persuade Asif to meet me. Both the husband and the wife were in their late 20s, perhaps a bit older. Asif was smartly dressed in a light grey suit with an open collar. Mary wore a knee-length silk dress, and around her neck a matching scarf asserted by a diamond brooch. They seemed a bit uneasy and even rather nervous as they offered me a seat. The reception room in which we sat was elegantly furnished: comfortable armchairs, a large leather sofa, architectural prints and drawings on the walls, a large desk in one corner of the room covered with a few architectural drawings. Mary offered me Chinese tea, which I accepted.

Mr. Mohammad asked me a few questions related to my professional and personal life, which I was happy to answer. To get them to relax I gave them a few snippets of my life, exaggerating my follies to elicit a smile. From past experience I have found that there is a tendency among people from several Eastern and Middle Eastern countries and regions, including Kuwait, Saudi Arabia, Oman, Egypt, Syria, parts of Africa, India, Pakistan, Bangladesh, Sri Lanka, Malaysia, Indonesia, China, and even Japan, to look upon healers as gurus—in some instances even as messiahs—with religious, supernatural, and magical powers, which they can use to tame ruffled tempers, calm winds of distress, recite magical incantations, placate malevolent demons, and perform soothing rituals to alleviate the sufferers from their afflictions (Al Issa, 1995; Kakar, 1982; Laungani, 1999; Roland, 1996). Not surprisingly, several healers and therapists, not just in the East but also in the West, seldom shy away from playing the role of omniscient gurus. It would seem that it has never been too difficult for humans to learn to play god! But in presenting a "chink in my armor," an exaggerated projection of one or two my own genuine inadequacies—forgetfulness, the tendency to swear, "calling their bluff," and careless movements of my hands, which has occasionally resulted in dropping glasses, or spilling tea—often brings me down as an equal, without their imbuing me with a halo, or looking upon me as a kindly, benevolent, all-knowing guru. I also make no promises. I seldom or hardly ever offer any guarantees.

After a while I got them talking about themselves, and gradually over the days, our conversations began to flow more smoothly. Mr. Mohammad eventually got around to telling me about where he and his wife had met, when they had got married, that much to their sorrow they did not have any children, and other such details. They were both very keen to have children, but it had not occurred to either of them to consider having gynecological examinations, or if it had, they did not to talk about it with me. Mohammad, however, had placed all his faith in God; he was convinced that they would have children when Allah willed it; Mary was more circumspect. She would not be drawn into offering an opinion. I made a mental note to pursue this point later, when I got to know them better.

Mohammad and Mary's Account

Mohammad explained that his was an old, well-known Sunni family that had lived in Indonesia for several generations. They came from a priestly family. It appears that his father, who was an Imam in Jakarta, decided to leave Indonesia and move to Kuala Lumpur, where he was offered the position of Chief Imam in a mosque. For a moment my own fantasies soared and I wondered if he was indeed the Chief Imam of the world renowned *Sultan Salahuddin Abdul Aziz Shah Mosque: Masjid Negara* in Kuala Lumpur. That, as it turned out, was not the case. He was the Chief Imam of a less well-known mosque.

Mohammad had no sisters, just two older brothers who, after graduating, had migrated to California, one of them working in Silicon Valley as a computer programmer, the other in the food industry. He had not seen either of them for over 4 years. It appears they were content to live in America and did not feel the need to come to Malaysia to visit their aged parents. Neither of them was married. "Playing the field, I guess," Mohammad said with a conspiratorial wink.

A God almighty row broke out at home when his parents learned that their son had decided to get married to a Chinese girl—a non-Muslim. They were not opposed to her being Chinese, but to being a non-Muslim. Upon reflection I realized that the distinction made no difference.

"Would your parents have been equally angry," I asked instead, "if you had decided to get married to a Shia Muslim instead of to a Sunni Muslim?"

"Difficult to say. But I think they would have been more distressed than angry. I suppose it is like a Protestant wanting to marry a Catholic, or vice versa. Same God. Different rites. Different rituals. Different customs. Irreconcilable animosities. You must understand, my father is an Imam—still is. For an Imam to have his *only son* wanting to marry outside his religion came as a shock."

"Why *only* son? What about your two brothers?"

He explained that they didn't count, partly because they didn't live in Kuala Lumpur, and from what he knew of their lives in California one would hardly refer to them as devout Muslims. He doubted that they had ever been to a mosque in all their years of stay in California.

"Assuming there are mosques in Silicon Valley," said Mary.

"Quite. So, you see, they don't count. They don't live here. It doesn't matter a damn what they get up to, what they do with their own lives. Out of sight … out of mind, so to speak. What the eye does not see, the ear does not hear, the mouth does not condemn."

"So the pressure was upon you to do the honorable thing?"

"He was worried that I would bring shame and disgrace upon the family. Don't forget, he is an Imam. A man highly respected, highly venerated. All the pressure was on me. I had to be the model son and marry according to my parental wishes. We are an extended-family orientated society, he explained.

"We tend to live within the orbit of our family members, and it has always been important for us to live that way. Also it is our duty to obey and respect our parents, and as far as possible act in accordance with their wishes."

"But not your two brothers," I said.

"It was their departure that created the vacuum, which ..."

"... was filled by Asif!" Mary completed. "He really was pushed around by his parents—but of course in the gentlest possible way. After all, his father is a well-known Imam—a man of God! But as you can see, my hero, my Superman, handled the pressure well. He defied the dictates of the man of God and we married."

"Do you regret the decision?" I asked gently, turning once again to Asif.

"You cannot make an omelet without breaking an egg."

That was not the answer I was looking for. I wasn't quite sure what he meant by it. Did he mean he regretted the hurt he had caused his parents, or did he regret having married an outsider? I made a mental note of the point and decided to pursue it later when the opportunity presented itself.

"Come the Day of Judgment Asif will certainly not go to paradise. No *houries* for him, I'm afraid. To make matters worse, he's married an infidel— what's that other wonderful word in Arabic, Asif?" asked Mary.

"Kaffir!" he replied automatically.

"Right. My dear husband has married a Kaffir, an infidel, a heathen—a bloody philistine! Aren't I right, dear?" Her veneer of sarcasm did not quite conceal the deep hurt, which simmered within her.

Mohammad looked at his wife. "I don't see it that way."

"I'm sure *you* don't! But *I* do! How can I not be a *Kaffir*? My family and all my ancestors subscribe to Confucianism. Confucianism isn't exactly what one would refer to as a religion in its literal sense of the word—as other religions, such as Islam, Hinduism, and Christianity are. Confucianism is more a spiritual philosophy—in some ways like Taoism, almost a way of life. Islam accepts established religions and does not look upon their believers as Kaffirs, but I am not at all sure it accepts Confucianism as an established religion."

I made a mental note to think over these distinctions, which Mary had just articulated. But by now she was in full spate.

"They obviously could not prevent us from getting married but they made their disapproval clear by not attending our wedding."

"I understand *your* parents too did not come to your wedding."

"True. They too would have preferred me to have married a Chinese, but, if I'd had some time on my side, I am sure I would have got them round to my way of thinking."

Whether that was a face-saving bluff or an oblique attempt to needle her husband, I could not tell.

"At any rate," she continued, "I was in Kuala Lumpur, and had no desire to go to Taipei and spend time with my parents. We had taken the decision to get married—and we married. And because there was no place for a *Kaffir* in an Imam's home, we found a flat to rent and moved our stuff into it a few days prior to our wedding. A few of our friends came to the wedding—and that was all. Neither of our parents attended the wedding—although we *did* invite them. Our wedding was not what one would call a joyous family gathering. It was a simple affair in the Registry, with a few of our mutual friends in attendance, followed by a party in a smart restaurant with no alcohol. Strangely enough our simple wedding did not go unnoticed. A few days after our marriage, one or two of the local newspapers reported our marriage. I cannot even to this day imagine what my father must have gone through. In my case the sins of the son, namely mine, were visited upon my parents, instead of the other way round."

I asked him if any of his relatives in Indonesia were informed of their marriage.

He shook his head. "Bad news always seems to travel unbidden, faster than lightning. They knew. But no one wrote. No one phoned. Ghostly silence."

Two years later Mohammad's mother, who had had a coronary bypass, died of a heart attack, or rather, as Mohammad put it, of a broken heart. He was also aware of his aged father's failing health and knew that he would not be able to live on his own, despite a couple of faithful man-servants that had been in his employ for over 20 years. "I finally persuaded Mary to move into our family home. What reinforced my decision to return to the family home was the fact that neither of my two brothers who lived in California came to mother's funeral."

"Why not?" I asked.

"You know what Muslim funerals are like. They are performed swiftly—within 24 hours of death. They wouldn't have been able to make it on time, even if they wanted to. They phoned, offered their condolences, and asked me if we needed any money. I said no. They have got so used to an American way of life that they have virtually severed all their cultural roots. They now stand on arid, rootless ground. Money to them is all. Money buys everything. Money solves all problems. That's the grand illusion that my brothers along with 250 million other Americans cling to. Poverty of imagination in the land of plenty! That is America."

On moving into the family home, the relationship between father and son underwent a gradual change. His father lavished all his attention and affection on Mohammad, keen to instill in him (and in his Chinese wife too) an Islamic way of life, which consisted of regular visits to the mosque, particularly on Fridays, daily prayers, sermons from the Koran, avoidance of certain foods, acts of charity, fasts during the month of Ramadan, and suggestions of annual pilgrimages (*hajj*) to Mecca.

In his own subtle way, he tried to woo his daughter-in-law into the Islamic fold, but she too resisted in a manner that was too subtle to be seen as a direct confrontation with her father-in-law.

Mohammad's father, not content with his son's gradual involvement in Islam, engaged a teacher who would teach Mohammad to read Arabic so that he might read the Koran and profit from its teachings. Because he was already conversant with the Arabic script, because of his knowledge of Urdu, it did not take him long to acquire some understanding of the language. In less than a year he was able to read the Koran, and to decipher and interpret some of the *suras*. The more he read, the more absorbed he became in Islam. When speaking to me, he occasionally broke into Urdu, which he spoke fluently. This suited me fine, for it now gave me the opportunity to speak in two languages, English and Urdu, both of which I had learned to speak since childhood in India. The fact that we could now converse in English and in Urdu in a sense brought us closer to each other. I did, however, feel guilty in leaving Mary out when we both spoke in Urdu.

Let me interject for a moment with an important point. The process of intercultural counseling, guidance, or therapy is likely to progress more smoothly when both the counselor and client are able to converse fluently in each other's languages, understand each other's nuances and subtleties of expression, and share the use of metaphors, colloquialisms, proverbs, similes, and aphorisms (Gombrich, 1979). Each culture produces its own range and repertoire of such phrases, which carry specific meanings, not easily discernable to outsiders.

For instance, words such as *imam, bey-imam, raham, bey-raham, haram, halal, shaitaan, zaalim, izzat, bey-izzat, baksh, barkhurdar, mast qalandar, qauamat, houri, adab,* and so forth, carry culturally loaded meanings in Urdu. The use of such metaphors allows us to articulate, interpret, and reinterpret our own world of experience to ourselves and hopefully share it with others. It is this understanding and the mutual sharing of those culture-specific meanings mediated through the use of metaphors that facilitate meaningful interactions. It is therefore necessary for the counselor and/or the therapist to acquire a fairly sophisticated insight into the client's cultural and linguistic background. Such knowledge enables the therapist to "go beneath" the surface, and arrive at a meaningful understanding of the ongoing encounter.

The same argument would also apply to non-Western therapists dealing with English-speaking Western clients. How many counselors and therapists from Eastern cultures for instance, although familiar with the English language, would make sense of some of the following metaphors commonly used among the educated middle classes in Britain—*Trojan horse, Draconian laws, stoic endurance, quixotic, Dionysian, Apollonian, platonic, Promethean, Faustian, Kafkaesque, Confucian, Elysian, the Playing Fields of Eton, meeting one's Waterloo, being in limbo, the patience of Job, Jacob's ladder, the burning bush,* and so on?

The use of such metaphors does not necessarily reflect classical education. It is through repeated usage of such metaphors within the home that their underlying meanings become clear. Another point to be noted here is this: The types of metaphors one employs in conversation to a large measure are also class related. The above metaphors reflect a certain kind of learning and upbringing and are less likely to be understood by all and sundry. On the other hand, metaphors such as *it's not cricket, he had a good inning, a sticky wicket, pull your finger out, between the devil and the deep blue sea, sour grapes, up the creek without a paddle, thick as two short planks, a lemon, driving a wedge, in for a penny, in for a pound,* and so on are more commonly employed metaphors. Thus, metaphors range from the very simple to the very complex—even elitist. But whether the metaphors used are complex or simple, *knowledge of their meanings serves as a solid basis for meaningful communication.* Unfamiliarity with the meanings of metaphors is likely to restrict, if not impede, effective cross-cultural communication between client and counselor. This obvious fact is not always recognized nor is it given the serious consideration it deserves by Western counselors when dealing with clients from non-Western cultures.

I turned to Mary and asked her if she'd ever considered learning Urdu.

Before she could respond, Mohammad intervened. "Not Urdu. It's Arabic that I'd like her to learn. In fact, my teacher who comes every day would be happy to teach her as well. We could practice it together. I have been trying to persuade her but she doesn't wish to."

"I have never objected to learning Arabic. You know, I am a linguist and can pick up languages relatively easily. I am quite sure it is an extremely rich, poetic, and romantic language. It sounds melodious too. I am sure I would enjoy learning it. I've read translated works of a few Arab, Persian, and Urdu poets such as Rumi, Omar Khayyam, Mahmoud Durwish, Hafiz, Khalil Gibran, and Ghalib; I find them fascinating."

At this Mohammad seemed very puzzled, even quite troubled and upset. He looked at me and then at his wife. "I wasn't aware you were fond of Sufi poetry."

"Why shouldn't I be?"

"I just find it strange. That's all." He paused for a while and continued. "Translations of poems never quite work out right. I'm sure you'd enjoy them more if you read them in their original languages."

I could not tell why her reference to Sufi poetry had upset him so. I was sure he was keeping something back. But now was not the time to question him on it. My own knowledge and understanding of Sufism was limited, but I couldn't help feeling that I was witnessing a scenario that had been played out in different forms several times before. I waited. They went round, and round, and round over this issue, without reaching any agreement on the problem.

"I'd rather you learned Arabic instead of reading Sufi poetry."

"I'd like to. But for the moment I am tied up with learning Mandarin, which is far closer to my heart than Arabic."

"Isn't it a dead language?"

Mary laughed. "Who's told you that? Do you know how many people speak it? Over 800 million people! And not just in China. It is spoken in Singapore, Indonesia, Philippines, Taiwan, *and even* in Malaysia. What language do you think the Chinese living in Kuala Lumpur speak? Mandarin!"

It was clear that Mohammad, influenced partly by his father, wanted her to learn Arabic, and she showed not the slightest inclination to abide by their wishes. She explained that she felt far greater cultural affinity to Chinese languages than to Arabic or Persian, or Urdu. Evidently, they had reached a deadlock over this issue. I felt that it was up to me to initiate a strategy, a more amicable dialogue between them, which would break the deadlock—well before it broke their hearts. I brooded over the words that were exchanged and those that were left unsaid. From past experience I have found that quite often what has *not* been said turns out upon reflection to be of far greater importance than what has been articulated. I decided to throw out some feelers when I met them again the following evening.

From the discussions we had had thus far, it seemed to me that, Mary's present conflict with her husband (and his with her) sprang from the following sources:

1. Their not having any children was a bone of contention between them. Mohammad's response to my question on this issue was vague; he said he left it to the Will of Allah! If Allah wanted them to have children, they would have them by the dozen. I restrained myself from making

the prurient remark that God also helped those who helped themselves. The fact that neither of them independently nor jointly had considered a medical examination seemed strange. It was of course possible that they had sought medical guidance but were unwilling to confide such intimate details to me. And because I could not bring myself to inquire into their sex life, I failed to arrive at a rational explanation. At the same time I wondered if I were reading more into this than was actually there.

2. Their religious differences, which, although they had not boiled over, kept simmering under the façade of equanimity, which they both did their best to display.

3. I also had the distinct but uneasy feeling that some subtle pressure was being brought to bear upon Mary to convert her to Islam. Although the pressure came largely from Mohammad's father (perhaps with Mohammad's connivance), it was extremely subtle and seemingly innocuous. But the strain, I felt, was beginning to tell on her. The fact that Mohammad was keen to have Mary learn Arabic indicated an unvoiced "conspiracy" between father and son. But Mary, I felt, was wise to the pressures and in her own equally subtle and skillful way had thus far been able to resist it. Conversion would have meant a surrender of her cultural and religious identity, which one could see she was unwilling to do.

There could be other reasons too, of which for the moment I was unaware. I decided to probe with extreme caution into her own religious beliefs, her relations with her parents, and with her siblings, if any. In so doing, I was hoping that I might acquire a deeper insight into some of her conflicts.

Mary's Account

The following day I was surprised to see that Mohammad was not in his office. Mary sat by herself, on the same sofa, drinking a cup of Chinese tea, a bubbling, steaming samovar beside her. Before I could inquire as to where her husband was, she explained that he had to attend an important business meeting with a large multinational group of clients who were sending out feelers to architectural companies such as the ones Mohammad worked for, which would design the plans for the construction of yet another large skyscraper of the size of the Petronas Twin Towers.

"He asked me to apologize to you for not being here, but he had to attend that meeting. Besides he was keen to meet the great Mr. Cesar Pelli, the chief architect of the Petronas Twin Towers, who was also coming to the meeting."

"Would you rather we met tomorrow?"

"No, no, not at all. In fact, it might be better that from time to time I saw you on my own and Mohammad, too on his own. That way..."

I welcomed the God-sent opportunity. For so far, I had heard and pondered over her husband's side of the story, if it can be called such. During the last six meetings, Mohammad had been the centerpiece, and all the accounts had revolved around him and his family members. But now that she was on her own, it gave me the opportunity to hear her side of the story without any constraints, which her husband's presence might otherwise have imposed. I was keen to learn more about her life, her own relations with her parents and siblings, if there were any, and why, despite her disclaimers, her parents had refused to attend their daughter's wedding.

At this point the reader—particularly the Western reader—might wish to know why I was so interested in learning about the families of Mohammad and Mary. What had their respective families to do with the problems of the couple? As several cross-cultural psychologists have pointed out elsewhere (e.g., Kim, 1997; Laungani, 2003, 2004), unlike Western cultures, which operate on an individualistic model, Eastern cultures tend to operate on a communalistic (or collectivist) model, where family dynamics and religious beliefs play an influential role in interactions. Quite often the needs and the wishes of an individual (in this case, the needs and wishes of the couple) may be subordinated to the wishes and desires of the elders within the family. Thus, if one is to understand behaviors of individuals within family structures, one cannot afford to ignore the important role of family dynamics and the power exercised by the elder family members over each individual. In the West, because individualism is the ruling ideology, it would be less likely for parents to succeed in imposing their will upon their children.

"Mary," I said, "for the last 5 or 6 days we have been talking mainly about your husband, his father, and such other matters. I am aware that there are some serious differences between the two of you and of course between you and his father."

"Please don't get me wrong. Asif's father is a real gentleman, a man of— how shall I put it—impeccable integrity and honor, a man of great love and tenderness. You should see the number of people that come to our house to meet him every day, seeking his advice and his blessings. I hold him in very high esteem and have the greatest respect for him, but …"

"But what?"

"How shall I explain it to you? I think it is his very gentleness, his kindness, his integrity, his humility, and his decency that I find harder to put up with. I am sure in his heart of hearts he loves me. How can one have a row, a fight with such a noble person! If only he would show some anger, some resentment! Then I'd know what to do, how to respond. I would even fight back."

"Would you really?"

She thought for a while. "No, perhaps not. Right from childhood we are brought up to respect, obey, and revere our parents. Filial piety is an enshrined ethic in Confucianism. Unquestioning loyalty to one's parents is taken for granted. We are also expected to care for our parents in their old age, and to produce descendents who would continue the family line, and to perform all the ancestral rites and rituals. Like Islam, ours too is a hierarchical society. Women are considered to be the embodiments of *yin energy*, which means they are expected to be passive and nurturing. And men, on the other hand, are seen as being dynamic, possessing *yang energy*."

She said that such ethical caveats had been so strongly ingrained in her that she would have found it impossible to challenge or quarrel in any way with Mohammad's father. Although he was not her father, but her father-in-law, he was nonetheless seen as a symbolic father—*in loco parentis*. It would be her duty to respect, obey, and revere him.

I was rather relieved that she had chosen to remain silent over the matter. To have gone on the offensive would have done no one any good; least of all her. It might even have led to a serious rift between Mary and her husband.

I asked her if she could tell me a bit more about herself. "I have learned a lot about Mohammad, but little about you and your life. All that my cousin in Taiwan told me about you was that you were very unhappy and—"

"Which she had no business to!"

"I'm sure she meant well. We would not be sitting here otherwise."

"Yes, I suppose so," she replied after a while. "I'm sorry."

Mary, I learned, came from a reasonably affluent, middle-class, cohesive, united family. As is common in most extended families, they had their share of differences, dissensions, and disagreements, but none so intractable as to be irreconcilable. Her father was a biochemist who worked as a research scientist in a multinational pharmaceutical organization. Mary had no brothers; she had two sisters, one older, and one younger than her. Her mother was a schoolteacher in Taipei. Her older sister worked for a travel agency, and her younger sister was a postgraduate student at the university, reading Chinese history. Neither of her two sisters was married. For over three to four generations the family, including several cousins and other relatives, had lived in Taiwan. They were all ardent followers of Confucianism, abiding by the tenets of Confucian philosophy, which emphasized ancestor worship, a faithful and sincere performance of rituals, and learning to live in peace and harmony with others. They attempted to lead a life that emphasized the practice of virtue, morality, and the five *jen,* which were respectfulness, tolerance, worthiness, diligence, and generosity, and which were all extremely important considerations in their daily lives.

Her father, an extremely well-read person, had over the years acquired a huge library of books on world religions; from time to time, he read out the famous sayings of Confucian writings and also from Taoism, Buddhism, Christianity, Hinduism, and Shinto. Over the years the three girls had acquired a fairly sophisticated understanding of the six religions, but not of Islam, which for some unknown reason had not featured in their teachings.

From what I could gather it seemed an idyllic family unit. Given their closeness, I failed to understand why none of the family members had attended Mary's wedding in Kuala Lumpur. Were her parents upset at the idea of her wanting to marry a Muslim? Were there unconscious prejudices against Islam that had led to their boycotting her marriage? Or were there other considerations? Would they have displayed a similar intransigence had she decided to marry a Hindu, a Buddhist, or a Christian? I was not even sure if any of the family members had met Mohammad and his parents, or whether Mohammad had visited them in Taipei.

It was time to probe. I questioned her on this issue.

"Tell me, Mary, did a family reconciliation or a family reunion ever take place?"

"Asif and I have been to Taipei quite a few times. My father and he get on like a house on fire. You won't believe it—but they hit it off within the first few minutes of their meeting one another. My two sisters envy me for marrying such a good-looking, handsome, hardworking architect, who they believe will one day achieve fame."

"Why didn't they come to the wedding?"

"They were afraid that I might have made a dreadful mistake."

"And have you?" I asked bluntly.

Suddenly she started to cry. I sat silently and waited.

"I don't know. I honestly don't know. I am sick with worry. I just don't know what will happen. When I first met Mohammad, he seemed so cheerful and carefree. He was fun to be with, a real joy and full of good humor. We had good friends we met regularly. Although gambling and alcohol are disallowed in Islamic religion we occasionally went with some of our friends to Genting's Hill Top Casino, which is about 50 kilometers away from Kuala Lumpur. But since we moved into his parental home, he's changed. He has become more serious, more distracted—even a bit grumpy. I really don't know what to do." She thought for a while and said, "The funny thing is that I love them both, for in their heart of hearts both father and son are very decent and in their own way very caring persons."

Although I had my own views as to where their problem lay, I took a gamble and asked a blunt question.

"Mary," I said gently. "I have been seeing you and Mohammad for the last so many days, during which period I think I have got to know you and your husband quite well, and in a tangential way, also your father-in-law and your parents in Taipei. I have some inkling as to where your tensions and conflicts lie. But I could be wrong and barking up the wrong tree. Why don't you—if you can bring yourself to—tell me where you feel your own problems lie, and how you personally feel they might be resolved."

"I'm being pushed into a corner by Mohammad and his father. I feel they would like me to convert to Islam. ... I was born into a Chinese family that has for generations subscribed to Confucianism; I am happy and content in leading my life in accordance with Confucian and Taoist teachings; I don't see why I should adopt another religion just because my husband and my father-in-law want me to do so."

"Has your husband or your father-in-law actually asked you to convert to Islam?"

"Not in so many words. But the writing is clear. Why else would Mohammad want me to learn Arabic?"

I could not find an appropriate answer to her question. It was of course possible that her fears had more than a ring of truth about them, and their wanting her to learn Arabic was part of an elaborate strategy. "Let me think about what you have told me. We shall return to this theme tomorrow."

"I shan't be able to see you tomorrow."

"Oh, why not?"

"I thought it would give you a chance to talk alone with Mohammad."

I wondered who was handling the counseling sessions, she or I? On the one hand, I was pleased that I would get to see Mohammad and talk to him as freely as I had been able to with Mary. But I was also rather cross with her for deciding on my behalf what was good for me without consulting me.

In doing that, she had trapped me into a conspiracy of silence. I did not relish the idea of being led by her.

Mohammad's Account

Mohammad was delighted to see me the following evening. I looked longingly at the samovar, which I noticed was cold. He apologized for not being able to see me the previous day. He apologized for his wife's absence; she was feeling poorly, he explained, and had decided to stay in bed. For a while, he went around in circles, going over and over again what we had discussed and talked about during all our meetings, and after a while he fell silent. I felt he either did not wish to bring up whatever was in his heart or that he was gathering the courage to put into words what was on his mind. Because I was used to playing such waiting games, I said nothing. The silence lingered, stretching to the breaking point. I sorely missed the jasmine tea.

"What do you think I should do?" he asked abruptly.

"About what?"

"You *know* what!"

"No, I don't know what." He could not bring himself to put his feelings into words.

"Aren't you supposed to be the expert in these matters?"

"What matters are you referring to?" I replied, pushing him a bit further.

"You know perfectly well what I am referring to."

"I want to hear it from you in your own words."

He brooded. "I'm confused. I don't know what to do. Mary is a wonderful girl. And I love her dearly. But there is a stubborn streak in her. She won't listen to anything. She decides what's right and what's wrong and once she's decided nothing will make her change her mind. She believes that Abajan [father] and I are anxious to convert her to Islam."

"And are you?"

"Of course not!"

"Why then has she formed this impression?"

Mohammad found it difficult to offer a clear explanation. He denied that he and his father had conspired to brainwash her; her fantasies, he said, were running away with her. Having married into a Muslim family, all that he wanted her to achieve was a closer and more mature understanding of Islam and Islamic culture. There was nothing wrong with that suggestion, was there? I asked him if he would agree to learn Cantonese if she asked him to so that he could acquire a closer understanding of her language and culture. He wasn't interested in learning Cantonese, nor was he particularly interested in Confucianism.

"Can you not accept her lack of interest in Arabic and leave it at that?"

It wasn't that easy, he explained. She had married into a Muslim family, a conservative and orthodox family with an even more orthodox extended family in Kuala Lumpur, Indonesia, India, and Pakistan. He, Mohammad, was the first person within his own community to have strayed, so to speak, by marrying a Muslim girl—his brothers didn't count; they lived in America, and what they got up to there was their business. They had, in a sense, been written off by the family and by their extended community. But if he was to live within his community and among his own people, it was essential that his wife fit into their lifestyle and culture.

To me, it didn't seem a compelling reason. "Come on, Asif," I said, pushing him a bit, "that doesn't sound a particularly convincing reason. Does it?"

For a long, long while, he sat in silence, immobile, as though carved out of stone. And then suddenly, the dam burst, the floodgates opened, and it all came hurtling down.

Since childhood, Mohammad had been deeply attached to his mother, almost as an embryo that had miraculously never left its mother's womb. Her death had come as a mortal blow. He had been totally devastated. As custom dictated he participated in all the rituals, visited his father regularly, and spent many a solitary hour by his mother's grave.

It was of course possible that somewhere within the nether regions of his unconscious he was tormented by a sense of guilt, which like cancer in one's entrails tore into his febrile psyche, but he could not bring himself to accept his involvement in her death. All he could bring himself to admit was that, by forces unknown, forces unseen, he *had been led astray* from the path of Islam. Had he but abided by his parental wishes and married a Sunni Muslim girl, his mother, he believed, would still be alive. He had lost his mother, and his poor father was staying on his own, while he, a strong, healthy young man, was living comfortably with his Chinese wife. *If only* he had married a Muslim girl!

His revelation did not come as a surprise. His insistence that his wife learn Arabic, that she read the Koran, and that she learn to understand and even imbibe Islamic teachings were all part and parcel of his attempts to *undo* what had already been done. It is a common enough experience; unfortunately none of us can ever turn back the inexorable march of time. Freud, I knew, had written a lot on the concept of "undoing." I now felt that it was upon me to convince Mohammad that he was asking for the impossible and that any further attempts to pursue such a course would lead to greater misery for all parties concerned but, far more importantly, for his wife, who, it was evident, was an innocent party. In the kindest possible way I tried to make him understand that he was using his wife as a whipping boy, a scapegoat, instead of accepting his own involvement in this tragedy.

"Asif, please don't mind my saying so but I do believe that you should *not* implicate your wife in your mother's death. Remember, your mother had had a coronary bypass; she was frail, she had a weak heart. The fact that she died of a heart attack may have been because of her critical condition rather than due to her sorrow at being parted from her son."

"But she was genuinely distressed at the idea," he pleaded.

"I'll grant you," I continued, "that that may have been a contributory factor, Asif. That's all. But if you *have to* apportion blame then you need to hold *yourself* culpable—not Mary. You were aware of your mother's critical condition. Not your wife. If you felt that your proposed marriage to a non-Muslim would have far-reaching consequences upon your mother's health, then naturally it was up to you to decide on a course of priorities—and you chose to get married."

I begged him to think about this with a true, open heart, and hopefully he would then learn to accept his own involvement in the matter. Acceptance, I explained, was the first step in expiation. And genuine acceptance of one's responsibility would gradually lead to his coming to terms with himself. This would then enable him to be less harsh both upon himself and on his dear wife.

We wrestled with each other for a while, unable to arrive at any agreement.

I decided to raise the problem once again the following day when I saw them together. I had only two more meetings left with them. But he surprised me. He made it clear that the last session was to be theirs, which sounded strange to say the least. He and Mary had planned to take me out to dinner, along with a few of their close friends.

"Over dinner we shall put *you* on the rack and have the sadistic pleasure of grilling you for a change."

"You *shaitaan* (devil)!"

"A benevolent devil," Asif retorted, smiling.

I spent a sleepless night worrying about how I would handle the last session when I met Mary and Asif in the evening at the usual after-office hours. I desperately wanted to help them to solve their interrelated marital, religious, cultural, and familial differences so that they henceforth learn to accept and respect their differences, even transcend them. Intuitively I felt that, over the last eight sessions, to a certain extent I had succeeded in persuading them to consider not only their own intractable positions but also each other's. There was, I was convinced, no right or wrong, no true or false in the positions they held—and entrenched though they were, they merely reflected the individual values they had imbibed since childhood. But in so doing, they had failed to consider the vast areas of similarities and synchronicities that united their respective religious and ethical beliefs. They had instead chosen to focus on the differences and divergences in their respective value systems, even believing that they were worlds apart and therefore irreconcilable.

But over the last two or three sessions I had started to notice subtle positive changes within each of them: They smiled at each other more often; they seemed less tense, more relaxed than they had been before. I also noticed that Asif, who for the past five sessions had sat behind his desk, now sat next to her on the sofa, and from time to time even placed his arm around her shoulders. I felt that they might have reached a stage where they were each genuinely prepared to find mutually acceptable ways of resolving their differences and learning to live together in peace and harmony. I sincerely hoped that the final session would bring them closer to the reconciliation I prayed for and they both sought.

Prior to going to bed I made some notes, which I intended to use at our meeting. I looked forward to the final session. I also dreaded it intensely.

The Final Session

There was an atmosphere of expectancy when I entered their smart office at the appointed hour. Soon after the preliminaries of jasmine tea were over, I cleared my throat, thus bringing our last meeting to order.

"I have given a great deal of thought to the meetings we have had so far. During those meetings both of you have been honest and open and unafraid to express your own views on your disagreements and differences. The fact that you have both been able to express your differences so openly suggests that underneath those disagreements there lies, within each of you, a core of mutual trust, respect, and love. And that is what I have been endeavoring to establish and bring out into the open."

They smiled. Asif put his hands round his wife's shoulders.

"Trust," I continued, "is the main foundation on which one can attempt to build an edifice of peace and harmony, love and affection, care and being cared for. This applies not just to individuals but also to societies, countries, and nations all over the world. Nations that expect to go to war do in fact go to war, as a famous American psychologist had pointed out several years ago. People that expect to fail, do in fact fail, and vice versa. Paranoia breeds paranoia, mistrust breeds mistrust. There is thus a self-fulfilling prophecy, referred to as an Oedipus Effect by Sir Karl Popper in his book *Objective Knowledge,* which he wrote in 1972."

I then went on to explain to them that they had become so entrenched in their religious and cultural *differences* that they had ignored the vast areas of congruence and unity within their seemingly incompatible religious beliefs.

I tried to argue them out of it. "If you consider some of the main tenets of Islam and of Confucianism and even of Taoism for that matter, you will not fail to notice the vast number of similarities that enjoin them: love, respect, obedience toward one's parents, living in peace and harmony, ancestor worship, diligent performance of all the required rites and rituals, being charitable, filial piety, so on and so forth. Although one might argue—as many have done—that Confucianism is not, strictly speaking, a religion in the traditional sense of the word, it is nonetheless concerned like all religions are with moral and ethical actions. Well, what do you think?"

"I'm sure you are right." Mohammad paused, thought for a while, and continued. "I don't disagree with you on this point. But there are, you will admit, fundamental differences between religions."

"Sure. And this precisely is where most of the problems arise."

There are, I explained, proselytizing religions and nonproselytizing religions: Christianity, Islam, and, perhaps, one or two others that would also fall into that category. But if one considered Confucianism and Taoism, Shinto and Buddhism, and to a certain extent Hinduism, they could all be classified as nonproselytizing religions. Most, if not all, proselytizing religions, I elaborated, assert the superiority of their own religion over all others. If they didn't, there would be no need for them to proselytize. ("There is no god but God and Muhammad is His Messenger.") Their believers consider it their moral duty to proselytize, spread the word, and convert the nonbelievers to their religion.

"But, here's the rub. The superiority of one religion over others can neither be established by rational argument, nor can it be established on any empirical evidence. It rests fundamentally on the premise of faith. And who is to say that one form of faith, one set of beliefs, one set of practices, one set of rituals is superior to that of others? This is the dilemma, which no proselytizing religions have been unable to successfully rebut—except by the use of the sword—as the Crusaders did in centuries past."

The protracted silence once again raised some fears in me: Without waiting for a response, I turned to Mohammad. "As a devout Muslim, would you not agree that your life is a gift from Allah, that your stay on earth is determined—and even predetermined, as many astute commentators on Islam have pointed out—by the Creator, and that nothing happens without the Will of Allah? You can call it *kismet, taqdeer, naseeb,* or whatever."

At this he bucked up and said, "Yes, yes, yes. That is absolutely right."

"If you agree with this, then you must also agree that your marriage to Mary was also determined, even predetermined by the Will of Allah."

Once again, he lapsed into silence. Mary sat on the sofa, hardly daring to breathe. To press the point home, I said, "You might recall the lovely line from *Hamlet*, '... providence in the fall of a sparrow.'" Mary went a step further. "Better still," she said, "are the lines from Omar Khayyam [as translated by Edward Fitzgerald], the Persian Sufi poet, which reflect the theme of determinism, or predeterminism":

> The Moving Finger writes; and having writ,
> Moves on: nor all thy Piety nor Wit,
> Shall lure it back to cancel half a Line
> Nor all thy Tears wash out a Word of it.

I felt I had reached the end of my efforts to persuade them to accept, if not reconcile, their differences and focus more on their commonalities and similarities. And the more commonalities—social interests, hobbies, reading, being together, culinary preferences, travel, art, painting, music, and so on—the less they would concern themselves with their differences. Over time they would cease to matter.

I had tired myself out and did not feel the need to continue anymore. Besides, it was time for me to leave. I rose.

Both wife and husband rose with me. They thanked me profusely for all the help that they said I had offered them. It had been a Herculean task. They switched off the tape recorder, retrieved the cassette, and handed it to me as they had done after each session. They said they would take into very serious consideration all that I had said and would even phone me in London within the next few weeks to let me how it was all going. As I was getting ready to leave, they reminded me not to forget the party they were giving in my honor the following evening at their club. As I stepped into the taxi, they said they had already compiled a list of questions, which they would fire at me, and, laughing fiendishly, they reentered their office.

About 5 months later, I received a letter from Mohammad, which said that they were expecting their first child and all apparently was going well.

References

Al Issa, I. (Ed.). (1995). *Culture and mental illness: An international perspective.* Madison, CT: International University Press.

Berry, J. W., Poortinga, Y. H., Segall, M. H., & Dasen, P. R. (1997). *Cross-cultural psychology: Research and applications.* New York: Cambridge University Press.

Fitzgerald, E. (2002). *Rubaiyat of Omar Khayyam.* Calcutta, India: Rupa.

Gombrich, E. H. (1979). *Ideals and idols: Essays on values in history and in art.* Oxford, UK: Phaidon Press.

Kakar, S. (1982). *Shamans, mystics and doctors: A psychological inquiry into India and its healing traditions.* London: Mandala Books.

Kim, U. (1997). Asian collectivism: An indigenous perspective. In H. S. R. Rao & S. Sinha (Eds.), *Asian perspectives on psychology.* New Delhi: Sage.

Laungani, P. (1999). Client centred or culture centred counselling? In S. Palmer & P. Laungani (Eds.), *Counselling in a multicultural society.* London: Sage.

Laungani, P. (2002). The counselling interview: First impressions. *Counselling Psychology Quarterly, 15*(1), 107–113.

Laungani, P. (2003). Changing patterns of family life in India. In J. Roopnarine & U. P. Gielen (Eds.), *Families in global perspective* (pp. 85–103). Boston: Allyn & Bacon.

Laungani, P. (2004). *Asian perspectives in counselling and psychotherapy.* London: Brunner-Routledge.

Laungani, P. (2005). Caste, class and culture: A case study. *Counselling Psychology Quarterly, 18*(1), 61–71.

Popper, K. R. (1972). *Objective knowledge: An evolutionary approach.* New York: Oxford University Press.

Roland, A. (1996). *Cultural pluralism and psychoanalysis. The Asian and North American experience.* New York: Routledge.

Triandis, H. (1994). *Culture and social behavior.* New York: McGraw-Hill.

Suggested Readings

Kakar, S. (1982). *Shamans, mystics, and doctors: A psychological inquiry into India and its healing traditions.* New York: Alfred A. Knopf.

India's leading psychoanalyst vividly describes the unique approaches of indigenous healers such as Muslim *Pir*, Ayurvedic doctors, shamans, and Buddhist monks.

Laungani, P. (2004). *Asian perspectives in counseling and psychotherapy.* London: Brunner-Routledge.

This volume uses philosophical discussion, theoretical perspectives, practical advice, and vivid case studies to elucidate differences between Eastern and Western perspectives on counseling.

Roland, A. (1988). *In search of self in India and Japan: Toward a cross-cultural psychology*. Princeton, NJ: Princeton University Press.

Roland, a practicing psychologist in New York City, reflects upon his experiences in India and Japan with therapists and patients. Of special interest are his comparisons between the familial self found in Asian cultures and the individualized self-concepts more typical of the United States.

11

The Practice of Counseling in Kuwait
An Interview With Jasem M. A. Al-Khawajah

Uwe P. Gielen and Jasem M. A. Al-Khawajah

Contents

In 2002 and 2006, I (U. P. G.) had the opportunity to visit the Psychology Department of Kuwait University in the context of site visits. The visits were designed to evaluate the strengths and limitations of the graduate (2002) and undergraduate (2006) programs in psychology. During these visits, and again in late 2006, I had the pleasure of meeting the chairman of the Psychology Department, Professor Jasem M. Al-Khawajah, on various formal and informal occasions. Professor Al-Khawajah is a very engaged counseling psychologist who has been trained in psychology in three countries: Kuwait, the United States, and the United Kingdom.

In the following, Professor Al-Khawajah discusses his experiences as a Kuwaiti counseling psychologist and professor of the university. It is important to keep in mind that his experiences differ in various ways from those described in many American textbooks of multicultural counseling. Whereas such textbooks frequently describe counseling situations involving a counselor from a mainstream cultural and ethnic background and a client from a minority group, Professor Al-Khawajah's clients typically are members of the same Muslim-Arab majority culture as he himself. However, this culture is now in rapid flux and includes both traditional and modern value systems that sometimes clash with each other. Because counseling psychology is a newcomer with Western roots, traditional Kuwaitis may look at it with skepticism and distrust. At the same time, counseling did gain some legitimacy in the public eye following Kuwait's liberation from the Iraqi occupation in 1990–91, a time when counselors proved their usefulness by helping Kuwaitis to adjust to the aftereffects of their memories and traumatic experiences during the occupation period.

When counseling clients in Kuwait, it is important to keep the prevailing patrilineal kinship and patrilocal residence systems in mind. This holds true especially for marriage and family counselors. Patrilineal systems emphasize that descent is traced through men. Furthermore, when a Kuwaiti woman gets married she is frequently expected to move into the house of her husband and his family, a custom that places the young wife under considerable pressure to adapt to the norms, expectations, power structure, and varied personalities of her husband's family. In divorce cases, she will frequently return to her extended family of origin whose members, however, may feel ambivalent or unhappy about such developments. For Kuwaiti family counselors such as Professor Al-Khawajah, it is crucial to align one's counseling activities with the local expectations without, however, losing sight of the fact that these expectations may lead to conflicts both within and between family members. Special problems may also arise in the case of polygamous marriages which are, however, on the decline. Polygamy is most frequently found among the older generations of conservative Bedouin families who, at any rate, are unlikely to avail themselves of psychological counseling services.

One of the central tensions described in the cross-cultural psychology literature is that between universalists and cultural relativists. Universalists emphasize that certain psychological processes can be found across most or all cultures whereas relativists stress the extensive cultural variability of social norms and belief systems. Professor Al-Khawajah, it seems to me, is somewhat closer to the universalist position. He argues that basic counseling skills and even some diagnoses derived from the *DSM-IV-R* have proven to be of value in the Arab-Islamic culture of Kuwait, although the counselor must at the same time be prepared to adjust the counseling process to different family norms, gender roles, legal requirements, religious conceptions, and cultural expectations. His Western training in cognitive-behavioral counseling techniques and skills, he believes, has generally proved useful in this dynamic sociocultural environment.

Let me add a word about psychology training in Kuwait. The Psychology Department at Kuwait University offers both an undergraduate and a master's degree program in psychology. The predominantly female students are instructed in Arabic by Kuwaiti, Egyptian, and other professors, yet are to various degrees exposed to psychology literature in both Arabic and English. The contents of most of their psychology courses and assigned readings tend to resemble those found at most American universities.

There exists, however, one important difference between the Kuwaiti educational system and that to be found in the United States and Europe. After receiving their BS in psychology, most Kuwaiti graduates will then proceed directly to positions in schools, hospitals, social welfare institutions, businesses, and so on. As holds true also in many Latin American countries, a bachelor's degree in psychology is (at present) deemed sufficient preparation for practicing psychology in various applied settings. A small group of students, however, will subsequently enter the psychology master's degree program at Kuwait University. Only a very few are likely to apply later on to doctoral programs in the United States and the United Kingdom.

Here now is the interview that was conducted via e-mail from December 2006 to April 2007.

Interview

UPG: I wonder, Professor Jasem, whether you could tell our readers something about yourself. Where and how did you grow up? What are your present life circumstances?

J. Al-K.:   My name is Jasem Mohammad Al-Khawajah. I was born in Kuwait in 1954, and I lived with my family and my eight brothers and sisters in our home in the capital city of Kuwait. The family house was divided into two sections, one for my father and the other for my uncle. I entered kindergarten at age 4. After 2 years at kindergarten I went to elementary school for 4 years, to intermediate school for 4 years, and then to high school for an additional 4 years.

During intermediate school I became ill twice. The first time I suffered from rheumatism and stayed in bed for almost 2 months.

After 1 year I got ill again but this time from sickle-cell disease and with alpha thalassemia disorder. This illness forced me to stay in bed for many months instead of interacting with other children my own age. At that time I began to read many books, mainly about psychology and education, but also about religion, poetry, literature, and even some books in the English language. When attending high school I had another attack of sickle cell disease which confined me to bed for many months. Again, I used this time to read many books.

After I finished high school I initially studied psychology at Kuwait University, even though I had been given the opportunity to study medicine abroad. Furthermore, I worked at Kuwait University as a scientific research assistant after I had finished my BS in psychology there. With the help of a scholarship from Kuwait University, I attained my master's degree at the University of Wisconsin–Milwaukee, USA, and then my PhD at the University of Surrey in the United Kingdom. I have taught at Kuwait University for quite a few years. In addition, I have also worked as a counselor at the Mental Hospital in Kuwait, Social Development Office, and with the family courts to help families overcome their problems before seeking divorce. In addition, I have served part-time as a supervisory counselor for a crisis hotline.

UPG: How did you become involved in psychology, and later on in counseling psychology?

J. Al-K.: I was already interested in psychology in high school where I studied scientific subjects and read some translated books about many different subjects within psychology. Those books were translations by Egyptian psychologists and aimed to improve parents' understanding of their children. After I finished high school I had the option to study medicine but felt that psychology, for me, was a more exciting and interesting way to help people. During my 4 years at Kuwait University I studied many subjects in psychology, for example: counseling and clinical psychology, psychopathology, abnormal psychology, physiological psychology, experimental psychology, intelligence and abilities assessment, personality assessment, industrial psychology, cross-cultural psychology, environmental psychology, research methodologies in psychology, social psychology, organizational psychology, and cognitive psychology. After receiving a BS in psychology, I applied for a scholarship at the Department of Psychology to study counseling because it was the best way I could see myself helping other people. I used the scholarship to go to the United States to study counseling psychology, and, later, I completed my PhD in the United Kingdom in psychology.

When I returned to Kuwait, the Department of Psychology refused to let me teach counseling psychology but asked me instead to teach social psychology and introductory psychology. However, after the liberation of Kuwait from the Iraqi occupation in 1991, the opportunity was given to me to work as a teacher and a counselor in my original field of interest, namely counseling psychology.

UPG: What did your graduate training in counseling psychology emphasize? Were you satisfied with it?

J. Al-K.: I took many courses dealing with community counseling and with counseling techniques. For example, our trainer asked us to do audio tape for the session and then to transcribe it for him. Naturally, I found it difficult at first to understand the American speakers and their accents, but in time my ability to understand them improved. Another training exercise focused on helping clients develop problem-solving strategies for finding a job, coping with stress, and so on. We also used a room equipped with video cameras to record sessions with clients. The supervisor and about five students would watch the video and then comment on it. This type of training helped me to understand many issues in counseling psychology.

I used many techniques which I had learned in previous courses such as the importance of observing and deciphering clients' body language and how to collect information from clients through open-ended questions. Such training, in my experience, is very helpful in becoming a counselor. In addition, I received a variety of trainings after I finished my PhD, as well as later on when working in a Kuwaiti mental hospital under a supervising psychotherapist and psychiatrist. Much of my training focused on stress management, treatment of PTSD, and the use of cognitive therapy. For instance, I took courses dealing with general counseling skills, treatment of PTSD, cognitive therapy with clients suffering from personality disorder, cognitive restructuring, Ericksonian hypnosis psychotherapy, crisis intervention, treatment of depression and grief, and quite a few others.

UPG: It seems to me that you have had extensive training in cognitive-behavioral approaches and techniques that fall squarely within the mainstream of Anglo-Saxon counseling psychology. What are your present professional positions and duties with regard to counseling?

J. Al-K.:   My present professional duties can be divided into four kinds. The first one consists of teaching counseling at Kuwait University, both at the BS and MS levels. Second, I work at the Social Development Office providing counseling for individuals to help them in coping with psychological problems due to trauma or any other personal and/or social problems. Third, I work with the courts to help families cope with their problems and avoid divorce by helping them to resolve their difficulties and cope with stressful situations. Fourth, I am a supervisor for two counseling groups: the first group runs a hotline office and the second is in Kuwait's Social Development Office.

UPG: Who are your clients? What brings them to your counseling offices?

J. Al-K.:   There are two types of clients whom I see. The clients who come to see me at the Social Development Office mostly suffer from PTSD, depression, anxiety, and sexual difficulties. The clients are usually adults, both male and female, plus a small number of adolescents 16 years old and older. A few of them come to my office because their parents bring them there.

The clients I see as part of the court system usually come for three reasons: (a) both male and female clients seek our help in finding suitable spouses, (b) they wish to resolve difficulties in their marriages, and (c) they are seeking help to successfully marry or divorce.

UPG: What kinds of sexual difficulties are the most common? How do you try to deal with them?

J. Al-K.:   There are many types of sexual difficulties that married couples encounter. Males complain about premature ejaculation, inhibited male orgasm, and erectile disorder. Among newly married females, we find sexual problems such as vaginismus, sexual arousal disorder, inhibited orgasm, and dyspareunia.

I use cognitive-behavioral therapy to help married couples overcome these difficulties that affect their relationships as well as themselves. I have also used successfully many of the techniques discussed by Virginia E. Johnson and Robert C. Kolodny, who have written extensively on sexual dysfunctions and gender-related disorders.

UPG: Could you present a typical divorce case? What are some common problems that lead to divorce (or the possibility of divorce), and how do you deal with them?

J. Al-K.: A 34-year-old female had been married for 15 years. She had four children, one boy and three girls. Having received a BA in teaching, she was working as a high school teacher while her 38-year-old husband had a high school degree and served in the army. They were living at the husband's family house. The husband's family gave them two rooms with only one bedroom for the couple and the children, and only one bathroom for them. The wife complained about the husband's behavior which included his lack of care toward her and a lack of communication both between them as husband and wife and also between the husband and the children. She stated that her husband did not spend any money on her or on their children. Not only did they eat from what his family provided for them, but she also had to spend all her salary on clothing for herself and the children, including buying everything the children needed for school. The husband spent most of his time at the *dewaniyah* (a place where men gather especially during the evening to talk and at times to play games). The husband and his family always blamed her for the problems of the family. When she asked her own family to help her they blamed her for the aforementioned problems as well and ordered her to remain in her husband's family house. After many years of fighting and much evidence that her husband did not take care of her either emotionally or economically, her family began to give her some support yet they would not support her in court so that she could get a divorce.

UPG: How was the case resolved?

J. Al-K.: I saw the wife and later the husband at a court family consultation office. In Kuwait, any person who wants to divorce their spouse has to go to a special court office where couples are helped in overcoming their problems and in reaching an agreement so that, if possible, they may avoid a court case. In most of the cases the husband and the wife blame each other. Should this happen, I will try to counsel them at the Center of Marriage Counseling, a court office nearby, by using various cognitive-behavioral techniques. About 30% of the couples resolve their problems even though they had originally intended to obtain a divorce.

In this specific case, an agreement was reached so that the couple would move to a separate home. Furthermore, the husband promised that he would give more money to his wife and spend less time at the *dewaniyah*. In other words, the husband agreed that he would behave more in accordance with Kuwaiti norms regarding how a husband should ideally behave.

UPG: What are some of the most common problems leading to family tensions and divorce?

J. Al-K.: The Family Consultation Office at the Ministry of Justice has reported the following problems as frequently leading to divorce: lack of communication; various forms of abuse; lack of expressing love; carelessness; not taking responsibility; interference by either the husband's or the wife's family; lack of economical spending on the family; anger; making decisions without taking into consideration the opinion of the partner; complaining about everything; excessive moodiness; spending too much time in *dewaniyah*; differences between couples in educational or cultural level; authoritarian attitudes; low economic status; and the husband not providing good housing for the family.

UPG: Many of these problems sound familiar to my Western ears. Could you please tell us something about the nature of family life in Kuwait and how this influences both your clients and your counseling activities?

J. Al-K.: Kuwaiti families, even when they consider themselves to be nuclear families, are nevertheless largely extended families. The members may endorse many kinds of family values and attitudes, some of which present us counselors with considerable challenges in our work. Some family members refuse to seek help from counseling psychologists because they consider it to be humiliating for the whole family. Some clients tell us never to contact their family because they came to counseling without their family's permission. Indeed, most Kuwaiti families will not avail themselves of counseling nor allow any member of the family to use it. They think each member should rely solely on the social support which the family provides for its members. If they go to a counselor, they believe it will bring shame upon not only the family member who sought it, but the whole family. They fear that someone in their community will learn about their problems and believe that they failed to resolve them on their own. Some of these families are conservative

Bedouins coming from a tribal and originally nomadic system, and they will reject totally any family member who uses counseling. In their view, family members should approach the tribal chief for advice, or else they should go seek the opinion of an elderly person and be guided by it.

UPG: Can you describe the methods that Kuwaiti elderly heads of household have traditionally employed to resolve disputes and counsel members of their families? Have you incorporated any of these methods into your own counseling approach?

J. Al-K.: Usually the senior male member of a family or, on rare occasions, an elderly female will be asked to resolve family disputes. Household heads will be asked to intervene on behalf of those family members who experience problems because the heads are believed to have more knowledge and better abilities to solve family and other disputes. In some situations, the elderly may intervene in family disputes even when nobody asked them for help. In both situations the senior members will ask to have a general meeting including the family members that are involved in the quarrel as well as elderly from both sides. The household senior will ask each member to speak and explain what the problem is. The family members usually expect the senior member to suggest a solution to the problem. If any of the members involved in the dispute reject the proposed solution, the family leader will be furious. Sometimes he will ask everyone to punish the family members who refuse to accept his solution. However, in many situations the "interference" from the elderly will actually increase the dispute between family members. That is why many families are asking for counseling services. They believe that the elderly lack many of the skills required to help resolve disputes between family members.

Because elders may not have the skills needed to resolve family problems I never ask them to attend counseling sessions unless they are part of the family problem under discussion. They will not be asked to attend the counseling unless the family member approves of it. However, I do ask fathers or mothers of family members to attend counseling so that they can provide more information which will improve counseling.

UPG: What type of approaches to counseling do you adopt, and why?

J. Al-K.: I have adopted cognitive-behavioral psychotherapy as my main approach to counseling. Many specific techniques, especially those of Aaron Beck and his followers, have proven useful for both husbands and wives.

I believe that our perceptions and beliefs are the main factors influencing our lives. Our perceptions of ourselves, our parents and siblings, and our relationships with other people and the environment constitute the main determining factors in our psychological well-being. An individual who has negative, unrealistic, or illogical perceptions of himself/herself, other people, or his/her environment will develop many forms of psychological disorder. At the same time, conditioning also exerts a strong influence on our psychological well-being. Individuals with psychological disorders need to change their perceptions and then they can work together with the counselor on changing their behavior in order to achieve psychological well-being.

Our Kuwaiti culture is strongly influenced by our adherence to Islam, which teaches about the influence of ideas, perceptions, and learned responses on all kinds of behavior, and it considers how these affect the individual and his or her world. If an individual has a misperception of himself and his world, he will suffer from many types of problems that will affect his life and also his world.

UPG: Do you tell your clients that your approach agrees well with Islamic ideas about the influence of ideas, perceptions, and learned responses?

J. Al-K.:   Usually I do not mention that there is agreement between my therapeutic approach and certain Islamic ideas but rather let the clients themselves reach that conclusion. I believe that this will improve both their self-esteem and the therapeutic relationship. However, many clients had unsuccessfully consulted religion advisers prior to asking for marriage counseling and that's why they might not want to hear that marriage counseling overlaps with religious advice.

UPG: Are there any traditions in Islam that you have found it either useful or necessary to implement in your counseling approach?

J. Al-K.:   Islam strongly emphasizes individual responsibility for one's actions. God will reject any excuse for wrongdoing or blaming others or the situation for one's wrongdoing. I use this fundamental idea in my counseling approach. According to Islam, if any individual wants to change his/her behavior and tries hard to change it, God will help him or her in this endeavor. This idea I use as well with my clients. Clients need to work hard to change their behavior by using all those skills they learn in their counseling sessions. I teach them to assume responsibility for changing their behavior. In addition, Islam emphasizes the use of other ideas that can be used in counseling such as planning, social support, rewards, the importance of free choice, respecting clients' needs, the counseling relationship, respecting clients' privacy, and various errors of thinking. Sometimes when it is necessary to make my clients understand or prove to them what the real counseling goals are, I use some *Surah* (chapter) from the Holy Quran. The Holy Quran includes many *Surah* that have names, and each *Surah* includes many *Ayah*. It is very difficult to translate the Holy Quran, but the following are some of the *Surah* and *Ayah* that can be used to present the Islamic point of view on responsibility.

Whatever benefit comes to (O man!), it is from Allah, and whatever misfortune befalls you, it is from yourself; and we have sent you (O Prophet!), to mankind as an apostle; and Allah is sufficient as a witness.
Woman *Surah* (4), *Ayah* (79)

Allah will say: This is the day when their truth shall benefit the truthful ones; they shall have gardens beneath which rivers flow to abide in them forever: Allah is well pleased with them and they are well pleased with Allah; this is the mighty achievement.
The Food *Surah* (5), *Ayah* (119)

And if they call you a liar, say: My work is for me and your work for you; you are clear of what I do and I'm clear of what you do.
Yunus *Surah* (10), *Ayah* (41)

Surely you cannot guide whom you love, but Allah guides whom He pleases, and He knows best the followers of the right way.
The Narrative *Surah* (28), *Ayah* (56)

And the soul and Him Who made it perfect,
Then He inspired it to understand what is right and wrong for it;
He will indeed be successful who purifies;
And he will indeed fail who corrupts it.
The Sun *Surah* (91), *Ayah* (7, 8, 9, 10)

These and many other *Surah* from the Holy Quran make it clear that the individual alone is responsible for his or her behavior.

The *Ayah* prepare my clients to understand more easily how counseling can solve some of their problems. They emphasize that they must accept full responsibility for their behavior. However, counselors must be very careful when they use any part of the Holy Quran or touch upon religious issues. Any misuse or misinterpretation of the Holy Quran or of any religious issue will damage the counselor-client relationship. In addition, counselors should be careful when they are using religious ideas and issues because some clients will conceive them differently.

UPG: Could you please describe for us a typical case or two that can shed light on your counseling activities?

J. Al-K.: Case one: A 36-year-old female who was married for 20 years and had four girls and one boy came to the office asking for help. As a first step, she provided us with some information about her life including her marriage, her relationship with her mother and father, and her education, working conditions, and health. As a second step she was interviewed by me. She said that she was feeling sad and unhappy about her life with her husband and children. She stated, "I have sat alone for many hours crying until even if I had wanted to, I couldn't cry anymore. I find it difficult to sleep, I sit awake for many hours, and when I fall asleep I find myself waking up many times. I feel hopeless thinking I can't do anything to change my life. I planned many times to kill myself but what stopped me was thinking about my children, how they will suffer after I die. In addition, my belief in God stopped me from killing myself... I used many types of medication and drugs to control my sadness and unhappiness, I visited many doctors to treat me for many physical problems, but they told me that I didn't have any physical problems and commented that I should see a psychotherapist... I hesitated many time to see a psychotherapist because I feared that my husband and my society would consider me crazy but 2 weeks ago I felt that I couldn't take it any more and that I needed help." She told me further that her main goals were controlling her sadness and stopping her husband and children from abusing her.

After a diagnosis was made according to the *DSM-IV-R*, I used a cognitive-behavioral approach including a number of different techniques to help her resolve her problems and achieve her goals. The number of sessions for her was 23. (The usual number of sessions for my clients ranges from 10 to a maximum of 25.) After we helped her resolve her difficulties, a follow-up session was arranged for the next month and then in 3 months. As the progress seemed to continue, the case was closed. This is the type of work that is carried out by members of the Social Development Office.

Case two: A 40-year-old male with four children was divorced after 17 years of marriage, and this occurred 6 months prior to counseling. His wife had gone to court in an attempt to gain custody of the children and be awarded alimony for them. There were many problems that led to the divorce. First, the husband accused his wife that she didn't respect him and did many thing against his will. The wife, in turn, accused the husband that he didn't discuss many issues about their joint life and their children's needs, and she also complained that her husband didn't give her any money to cover her expenses and those of their children. She asked that either her husband change his behavior and give her all she needs or else give her a divorce. They challenged each other and refused to respect each other's demands, and that is why they divorced.

One of the major things I did with them was to find out whether there were psychological elements that caused the divorce. Next I tried to find out how they handled their family affairs and how they communicated with each other. If in such cases there are psychological problems, I would deal with those first and later on discuss the legal aspects. He discussed with me what happened during the process of divorce and what type of legal arrangements had been agreed to by the couple. I next met with his ex-wife to discuss the issue from her point of view. Then the three of us sat down together to reach a new arrangement without going to the court. I also encouraged them to use all of the techniques that had been employed in our sessions for any future issues that they might face instead of seeking legal solutions.

UPG: How do cultural factors including religion and Kuwaiti belief systems and customs enter into the lives of your clients? How does this influence the type of counseling you are involved in?

J. Al-K.: Traditional Kuwaitis see counseling in a negative light because they believe that it interferes with one's private life. Kuwaitis dislike talking about their private lives, something they tend to see as a violation of their personal integrity and as a source of humiliation for themselves and their families. If people talk about their private lives, they will lose respect in the eyes of others. This consideration keeps many people from using counseling and psychotherapy.

Traditionally, many Kuwaitis considered such people as being more or less the same as an "insane" person and thus unfit to take care of themselves or to hold any responsibilities. That is why almost everyone who needs psychotherapy or counseling will hide the fact that they are receiving psychological help.

This type of cultural value changed dramatically after the Iraqi invasion of Kuwait as many Kuwaitis began to develop psychological disorders resulting from their traumatic experiences. We saw an increase in the number of offices which opened to provide help or counsel after the invasion, and a large number of Kuwaitis did seek out counseling and psychotherapy after the invasion.

The influence of religion on the client's life, especially in cases of marriage and divorce, is quite important. There are many Islamic traditions that define how husband and wife should communicate with and take responsibility for their families. The husband should respect the needs of his wife and children. He should work and take care of all family expenses. In the same way, Islam assigns the responsibilities conducive to the family's well-being to the wife. A wife should take care of the needs of the husband and the children at home. However, cultural norms and practices sometimes contradict religious traditions. For example, the Islamic tradition maintains that a husband should not cheat on his wife, and if he does he will be banished. But the cultural reality in Kuwait is that he will be excused in such a case and he is not banished. In contrast, if the wife commits adultery she will be banished. This double standard is approved culturally as well as religiously, although strictly speaking, it contradicts traditional Islamic teachings.

UPG: Aside from the anticounseling bias present in traditional Kuwaiti culture, have you encountered any other cultural conflict while using Western counseling methods, such as cognitive-behavioral therapy, with your clients—for example, concepts that do not easily translate into Kuwaiti language and culture?

J. Al-K.:   The cognitive-behavioral therapy focuses most of all on perception and learning, an idea that is accepted by Kuwaiti culture. Indeed, the Arabic language includes many words and meanings equivalent to those in Western counseling theories. Therefore, I did not encounter any cultural conflicts while using Western counseling methods.

UPG: How important are gender roles in all of this? Are they now changing?

J. Al-K.: In Kuwait, as in other societies, some clients prefer to have a counselor of the same gender whereas others do not specify a gender preference in choosing a counselor. Other clients agree to have a counselor of the opposite sex, but then find it difficult to discuss their sexual experience with him or her. They feel ashamed to disclose such information in front of a member of the opposite sex. Other clients in marriage counseling say that they would like to have a counselor of the opposite sex so that they could understand better what their partner thinks and feels. They think that all men (or all women) think alike and that an opposite sex therapist will think in a way similar to their spouse.

UPG: Could you please describe a case or situation that sheds some special light on the cultural dimensions of counseling in Kuwait?

J. Al-K.: A female client who had married 6 months earlier felt depressed because of continuous arguments with her suspicious husband about where she was going and whom she was meeting. Her session ended after 1 hour at 8 p.m. As I was leaving the building a man called and said that he was her husband. He told me that according to religious law I should tell him everything his wife had told me during the session and that it was his right to know what his wife had said about him. I told him that although it is true that our religion and culture gave him this right, I was working with her as a counselor. Therefore, I could not give any information to anyone except after the client had given me written consent to do so. I invited him to come with his wife to the next session and participate in couple counseling. He became very upset and angry. He told me that he would force me to release all information on file. I tried to explain to him that as my client, his wife had a right to privacy. To this he responded that our culture gave him the right to have access to all information about his wife and that she had no private life. Moreover, he claimed, her mother would support him in this. He also told me that our social values allowed him to either give or withhold permission for her to participate in the next session.

UPG: How was this situation resolved?

J. Al-K.: I told him that I was looking forward to seeing him with his wife in the next counseling session. In response, his attorney sent an official letter to the Office of Conciliation claiming that I had to go to his office to answer some question about the wife's claim that her husband had misused the power of attorney that she had given him. I called the attorney to explain to him that I couldn't be a witness in this case, but he insisted. And so I became the first Kuwaiti therapist to be ordered by an attorney to serve as a witness in a husband-wife court case. However, the judge did not require me to go to court because the Office of Family Consultation interfered and explained my role as a family and marriage counselor. I am glad to report that the judge accepted our role as counselor in helping the family and that we should not be asked to break confidence by testifying what had happened in the counseling sessions.

UPG: Some people say that Western counseling approaches are not applicable—or only with major modifications—in Arab cultures. Do you agree with this statement? Why or why not?

J. Al-K.: There are many ways to organize counseling interviews, just like there are many other steps involved in counseling. There are also many ways to define the role of a counselor. Some of these approaches will generally be agreed on in both Arabic and Western cultures as they are based on general counseling skills which can be used in any culture. Other approaches will have to be modified or abandoned because they may merely reflect Western cultural preferences such as, for instance, traditional Freudian forms of counseling, with their strong emphasis on sexual needs and how they purportedly affect human behavior.

UPG: Could you tell us something about the general situation of counseling and counseling psychology in Kuwait?

J. Al-K.: Several government offices and some private offices provide various types of counseling. However, both are facing the same problem, namely the absence of a code of ethics and a control system by a professional association to protect clients. The counselors who follow a code of ethics usually adopt either the APA (American Psychological Association) or the BPS (British Psychological Society) code of ethics. Furthermore, there exists a lack of supervision for counselors in Kuwait except at the Social Development Office where they insist that their counselors should meet weekly with their supervisor both as a group and as individuals in order to discuss their cases and learn new techniques.

I should add that the situation of counseling psychology in Kuwait resembles that to be found in other Gulf countries such as United

Arab Emirates, Saudi Arabia, and Bahrain. These countries share many cultural components and similarities in educational development. However, the situation in other Arab countries such as Egypt and Jordan is rather different because of different economic, cultural, and educational conditions.

UPG: You are the Chairman of the Kuwait University Psychology Department, and therefore you must have a pretty clear idea of where your students end up after they graduate from your department. How are they trained and what happens to them afterward? How many of them become involved in counseling activities? How many join the school system?

J. Al-K.: The Psychology Department includes in its curriculum many courses which aim to train students to become involved in counseling activities. They have to finish the following psychology courses: counseling psychology, clinical psychology, psychopathology, abnormal psychology, physiological psychology, experimental psychology, intelligence and abilities assessment, personality assessment, industrial psychology, cross-cultural psychology, environmental psychology, research methods in psychology, social psychology, organizational psychology, cognitive psychology, and many other courses.

When the students graduate with either a BS or MS degree, they will apply for jobs at a government employment office. Usually, they will be sent to work in the school system, a mental hospital, a social welfare office, the family courts, or the prison system for adults and minors. A few of them will work in factories or banks. There exists no precise information about how many of them end up working as counselors, but most of them will work for the Ministry of Education as school psychologists. As school psychologists they conduct interviews with students that have psychological problems and difficulties in learning and they encourage them to build good relationships with other students and their teachers. They may also help drug-addicted students either by providing face-to-face counseling or by giving them detailed information about various forms of addiction through lectures and handouts.

UPG: Professor Jasem, thank you so much for taking time out of your busy schedule to answer all these questions. It is indeed instructive to hear from you about the opportunities and challenges that you as a counseling psychologist are facing in Kuwait.

Suggested Readings

Al-Issa, I., & Al-Subaie, A. (2004). Native healing in Arab-Islamic societies. In U. P. Gielen, J. M. Fish, & J. G. Draguns (Eds.), *Handbook of culture, therapy, and healing* (pp. 343–365). Mahwah, NJ: Lawrence Erlbaum Associates.

A useful overview of traditional healing practices that remain influential among many Arabs in North Africa and the Middle East.

Al-Khawaja, J. M. A. (1998). Counseling psychology. In R. A. Ahmed & U. P. Gielen (Eds.), *Psychology in the Arab countries* (pp. 447–461). Menoufia, Egypt: Menoufia University Press.

This chapter constitutes a brief overview by the interviewee of counseling psychology as an emerging profession in the Arab World.

Dwairy, M. (2006). *Counseling and psychotherapy with Arabs and Muslims: A culturally sensitive approach.* New York: Teachers College Press.

A Palestinian psychologist summarizes his experiences with Arab clients gained mostly in a minority group context.

McGoldrick, M., Giordanao, J., & Garcia-Preto, N. (Eds.). (2005). *Ethnicity and family therapy* (3rd ed.). New York: Guilford Press.

Section VI (Middle Eastern Families) contains three brief chapters respectively by Nuha Abudabbeh, Karen L. Haboush, and Nuha Abudabbeh that describe, in turn, Arab families, Lebanese and Syrian families, and Palestinian families.

Soueif, M. I. (1998). Clinical psychology. In R. A. Ahmed & U. P. Gielen (Eds.), *Psychology in the Arab countries* (pp. 425–446). Menoufia, Egypt: Menoufia University Press.

The father of clinical psychology in the Arab world provides a brief overview of the field, with some emphasis on the situation in Egypt.

The Holy Quran. Translated by M. H. Shakir (1984). Tahrike Tarsile Qur'an, Inc. (Elmhurst, NY).

12

A Clinical Toolbox
for Cross-Cultural
Counseling and Training

Judy Kuriansky

Contents

This chapter presents techniques, which constitute a "toolbox," for clinical intervention in varied cross-cultural settings. The toolbox contains a collection of exercises that practitioners and healers can select to apply within an intervention design chosen for a particular situation and population. The exercises are meant to facilitate personal growth, interpersonal relations, healing from trauma, as well as peace between people from cultures in conflict.

The tools presented here are the result of the author's decades of experience in many cultures and contexts, doing trainings and counseling for individuals, couples and groups, within traditional and modern theoretical disciplines (cognitive-behavioral, analytic, humanistic, shamanistic), in varied societies (American, western European, Eastern, and indigenous), and using diverse modalities (face-to-face, large audiences, on-the-ground disaster relief, and advice-giving on media). The techniques were applied in diverse settings, including disaster relief (after the World Trade Center terrorist attacks, the Asian tsunami, and suicide bombings in the Middle East); psycho-education workshops for HIV/AIDS prevention (with youth in China and high-risk teens in America); classes of elementary school-age children of multiracial and multiethnic background; weekend workshops to enrich couples' relationships; and varied seminars and trainings throughout China and India, and cities of diverse cultures from Tokyo and Prague to Teheran, Vienna, Kathmandu, Belgrade, and Dubai (Kuriansky, 2000a, 2001a, 2001b, 2001c, 2002a, 2003a, 2003b, 2003c, 2003d, 2004a, 2004b, 2004c, 2005a, 2005b, 2006a).

Many of the techniques involve nonverbal activities, to accommodate cultural limitations in language and relative comfort level with verbal communication. Most are group interventions, requiring experiential interactions and postactivity sharing. Although grounded in psychological theory, many of the techniques evolved from unexpected conditions (which typically occur in remote areas or disaster sites) which presented opportunities as well as challenges, and required flexibility and creativity for effective intervention. Several exercises accomplish multiple goals, in which case specific instructions and postprocess discussion was focused on one or the other dynamic (e.g., balance of power or general dynamics of communication). Many exercises reflect an integration of approaches (Eastern and Western, traditional and modern) consistent with best practices in cross-cultural counseling as described by experts in the field (Gielen, Fish, & Draguns, 2004; Pedersen, Draguns, Lonner, & Trimble, 2002; Sue & Sue, 1999; Tseng, 2001).

The techniques presented here are intended for personal growth and "psychological first aid" and are not meant to be "therapy" in the formal sense of providing either long-term or reconstructive work. They are also intentionally simple enough to be implemented by early-career counselors or taught to local individuals. This is intended in order to achieve sustainability and continuity of care which is particularly important in developing countries with a dearth of trained mental health providers—as was the case in a remote area of Sri Lanka after the tsunami, where translators and community members could be trained to provide ongoing emotional support (Kalayjian, Kuriansky, Moore, & Aberson, 2007).

Most of the individual exercises take about 10 to 20 minutes, but as modules within a longer intervention process, they can be abbreviated or extended according to the needs of the population and circumstances (e.g., time allowed, number of participants, handing out materials, amount of explanation or processing desired or required). The modules should be combined to form an experience lasting an hour; but can also be mixed and matched for workshops that can be 1 or 2 days, with individual exercises selected for follow-up sessions of varying length.

Concept of a "Toolbox"

The concept of a clinical toolbox has been described in various contexts regarding health and mental health, including weight management, drug abuse, career counseling and even providing smoke-free homes for children (Foreyt, 2005; National Institutes of Drug Abuse, 2005; Smoke Free Homes, 2005). For example, government manuals about treating cocaine addiction include cognitive-behavioral techniques, community reinforcement and vouchers, and individual drug counseling. Strategies in a toolbox for obesity include behavioral management and education about self-monitoring.

Psychological techniques in a toolbox format are also being made available to the general public through internet sites. One of these—promising "fun" and self-improvement—describes various techniques including reframing, guided imagery and visualization, journalizing, eye movement desensitization and reprocessing, and Reiki energy work, and even invites diversity with the note, "I honor your race, religion, culture, and way of life" (Ruth, 2006).

The related concept of a "tool kit" is used by the American Psychological Association in the Practice Directorate's materials for professionals to use to educate the public about psychological issues. Various topics of such toolkits include "resilience" and "the mind-body connection" (http://www.apa.org.)

The present toolbox offers "mix and match" modules which can be combined with each other or with techniques presented elsewhere. These modules represent a wide variety of specific exercises, using various media, and are meant to be matched together given specific purposes (Kuriansky, 2006b).

Guiding Theoretical Principles

Selection of individual techniques in a toolbox should be guided by a theoretical model. One useful multimodal model of coping addresses six facets of experiencing the world: the physical mode (achieving relaxation, establishing boundaries); cognitive mode (restructuring thoughts); imaginative mode (being creative); social mode (establishing interpersonal trust and support); affective mode (facilitating expression); and belief mode (Ayalon, 2006). The toolbox techniques presented here reflect my "4M" model of intervention: multidisciplinary, multidimensional, multimodal, and multicultural. Individual techniques draw on various orientations (psychoanalytic, humanistic, cognitive-behavioral, spiritual, indigenous); address various modes of functioning (cognitive, emotional, spiritual, behavioral, social, imaginative, and ritualistic) and relationships (personal, interpersonal, social, and global); and draw on diverse clinical skills (intellectual, creative, responsive, empathic).

Design: The 3 Ps

Selective use of toolbox techniques depends on several factors, including the intention and goals of an intervention, available assistance, logistics (time, setting, space and even costs of supplies. travel, etc.) and design. A design consists of what I call the "3 Ps": (a) presence, meaning establishing awareness within oneself and the environment; (b) process, referring to selection of techniques to accomplish intended goals; and (c) parting, to accomplish closure of the experience and session.

Techniques

Presence

Becoming present means being fully conscious and aware in the moment, to fully experience the self, others, and the environment. Such a state is fundamental to Buddhism; as a result, people with this orientation are responsive to related exercises. Exercises to establish presence which I use in groups are meant to facilitate awareness of one or more of three levels: self, others, and the environment.

Grounding   Grounding means feeling rooted in one's body, in stark contrast to engaging in mental processes and cognitions. A lack of grounding can lead to simply being "lost in thought" or feeling separated from others, or to more serious derealization or depersonalization. To achieve levels of groundedness, I ask participants to close their eyes and inhale deeply, put a hand on the place on the body where the breath seems to go, and concentrate on feelings in the body. I invite them to lower the hand and inhale into this deeper place. In the next stage, they open their eyes, and concentrate on their feet feeling rooted to the ground/floor like a firmly planted tree, twisting the feet to feel them more definitively. Then, they walk around the room, stomping to feel their feet increasingly firmly rooted while in motion. The next stage involves feeling grounded while connecting to another person (i.e., relating without losing the self"). To accomplish this, they continue walking and feeling rooted while moving toward others in the room, making eye contact as much as possible. This exercise takes about 5 minutes.

Space Comfort   Becoming comfortable with the environment requires being aware of the surrounding space. Treatment of public speaking anxiety, for example, includes becoming comfortable in the room before speaking (Woy & Efran, 1972). In one exercise to accomplish this, I ask participants to draw their dream (for their future) on a piece of paper and place (or post) it anywhere in the room they choose. They then give a short description (2 to 3 sentences) about it to the group. Give participants about 10 to 15 minutes to do this. To accommodate culture sensitivity and multiculturalism of groups, they are instructed that this rendering can be in any words or images they choose. In variations of the exercise, they can be asked to draw other themes (e.g., their happiest moment).

In another technique, I ask participants in mixed-culture groups to find a space in the room where they feel most comfortable. Besides grounding, a related goal of this experience is self-awareness—by describing how qualities of the space evoke similarities to qualities of the self. For example, one Japanese participant gravitated to curtains in the room, describing their texture as enfolding her like a child in a blanket. This description helped her realize that she often hides from people because she is shy and afraid to reveal herself. Another participant sidled next to the refrigerator in the room, making an association to her use of food as a way to escape pain from past relationships. Allow the group at least 20 minutes for this process, longer if more extended processing is desired.

Relaxation   Being relaxed is key to feeling self-confident, calm, anxiety-free, and present and, as such, is fundamental to help those in crisis or post-disaster. Most practitioners use some variation of breathing exercise to help clients achieve relaxation. My favorite is simply breathing in through the nose to the count of three and breathing out through the mouth to the count of five or more. This takes only 2 to 3 minutes, with explanation. An increased length of time spent on the inhale compared to the exhale is activating, whereas a decreased amount of time exhaling compared to inhaling achieves relaxation. This technique works well when it precedes the emotional release process described later in this chapter.

Greeting   In introductions commonly used in group process, participants announce their name and say a few sentences about who they are, why they came, or what they expect from the experience. When working with multiple culture groups, I invite participants to use culture-specific words and gestures—for example, Hindu *Namaste* (meaning "the divine in me salutes the divine in you") accompanied by pressing the hands together in front of the chest with a slight bow; Hebrew *Shalom*; Islamic *Salamu Alaikum* (meaning "peace be upon you"); Chinese *Ni Hao*; Tamil *Vanakkum* or Sinhalese *Ayubowan* (meaning "may you live long") in north and south Sri Lanka respectively; or the "soul brother handshake" for African American teens, (a gesture of brotherhood which began in the 1960s as a three-move procedure: clasping palms, touching thumbs, and clasping fingers), or modern palm slaps ("Gimme five"), fist bumping, knuckle knocking, or even chest bumping.

Each individual greeting is short, but the time required depends on the size of the group, as each person needs a turn.

Synchronized Breathing   Breathing at the same pace with another person achieves the experience of being more connected (Kuriansky, 2004d). Pairs face one another and inhale and exhale at the same time and pace. On the exhale, they make a noise to signal the exhale more obviously to the partner. The sequence is repeated three times. The individual interaction takes about 1 minute. Participants repeat the exercise, pairing with other group members—creating more group cohesion.

Soul Gaze   This exercise involves pairing with a partner and looking into each other's eyes; with a key instruction: look beyond noticing a person's eye shape or color, to "look behind the eyes, into the other person's soul." This can be done with one partner (at random) or with several different partners, with each interaction lasting only about a minute. People in Asian cultures stereotypically hesitate to make eye contact, lowering the eyes out of respect or embarrassment. However, I have observed that Asian participants are more willing than would be expected to participate in this exercise, and make even more sustained eye contact than some Western participants. In one mixed cultural group in India, an Iranian male doing this eye gazing with a Western female noted that although such contact is traditionally unacceptable in his culture, he found the experience extremely freeing. Years later, he emailed the woman to thank her again for the experience he still thinks about.

Process

This stage consists of various exercises that reflect varied constructs intended to manifest the desired outcome.

Safety   Fundamental to any growth or healing experience is feeling safe intrapersonally, interpersonally, and within the environment. Safety has been pointed out as a necessary condition in a clinical intervention, especially for people who are in crisis. As a result, I always use exercises to create a sense of safety when I am working with people, especially those who have suffered a disaster.

Safety Mantra   This exercise, which I devised, is based on an Eastern approach to healing by directing energy. It establishes three dimensions of safety: personal, interpersonal, and within a broader social context, through motions and affirmations (mantras) in a group's native language. In one application with child and adult survivors in Sri Lanka after the 2004 tsunami, participants gathered in a circle and (a) held their hand to their own heart, saying, "I am safe"; (b) turned to the person next to them and said, "You are safe"; and (c) turned to face the circle and said, "We are safe." The actions allow for somatic imprints of the experience of safety by putting one's hand on one's own heart when saying "I am safe," putting one's hand either on or directed at the other person's heart area (allowing for distance depending on participants' comfort level) while saying "You are safe," and then turning to the group and extending one's hand while saying "We are safe." With a small group this can take about 10 minutes. This exercise can be combined with in-vivo desensitization, as I did in Sri Lanka, whereby participants repeated the exercise at various stages closer to the anxiety-provoking situation (being at the water in this case or "sea"), which was the source of destruction.

In some cases (judging by the appropriateness and by receptivity of the participants), I adapt this exercise by adding an Eastern energetic aspect that can amplify the power of the experience. Participants are invited to imagine accumulating energy from the earth (symbolic of grounding, strength, love) and bringing it into their body—by actually bending down and making a scooping motion and bringing the hands up to the heart as if drawing the energy upward. Then, they symbolically draw energy down from the sky (symbolic of intellectual clarity, enlightenment) by lifting their hands above their head and scooping imaginary energy down into their heart. This is a variation of a tantric exercise called in Sanskrit the *shiva-shakti mudra*, which symbolizes the union of the masculine and feminine divine energy.

Trust   Trust is essential in any relationship. Significantly, people of varied cultures respond positively to the trust exercise in which I hand out blindfolds and ask people to pair up, with one person putting on the blindfold, to be led by the partner around the room, without talking. Although this exercise has another lesson about being a leader or follower, instructions can focus participants on the experience of trust by emphasizing, "Put yourself fully into your partner's hands when you are being led around," and "If you are the leader, feel what it feels like to be trustworthy by being in charge of someone else's safety and experience." Give each person about 2 minutes to be in each role. Instructions should point out that (a) the partner who is leading should guide the blindfolded person with the deliberate intention of showing him or her an interesting experience, and that (b) each person should fully experience what it feels like to trust whoever is leading or to be trusted when leading.

Both partners then share with each other and the group, about the level of comfort they experienced in each role. Adolescents can become rowdy during this exercise, but this can lead to growth as happened in one group where an African American teen female became exceptionally angry with her male partner for allowing her to bump into chairs and walls, accusing him of being abusive. This triggered memories of many abusive experiences and males in her past which she was able to express—and process—for the first time.

Individualization   Exercises of this nature attune participants to the expression and realization of the self, consistent with Maslow's (1970) hierarchy.

"Dream Affirmation"   This exercise involves presenting a dream for the future. Hand out drawing paper and instruments (preferably of different colors). People in Asian cultures are considered traditionally family- and group-oriented as opposed to the individualized orientation of Westerners. Yet, groups in Asia with whom I have worked appear to increasingly value individualization (likely due to increased exposure to Western cultures, globalization, and economic and social development). In a class at Aoyama Gakuin University in Tokyo, for example, I asked the students to write down their dream for their future and blocks to this pursuit. Allow about 4 to 5 minutes to do this, and invite participants to share with the group. In a large class, it is best for only a select number to share, taking another 6 to 8 minutes total. Many students expressed deep appreciation for permission to announce their previously held secret desires, particularly those who felt that they had unorthodox career goals which would incur parental disapproval. One dramatic example of this is a female student who said she wanted to be a photographer—considered an unusual and unacceptable profession for Asian females.

"Walk This Way"   Another exercise that confronts conformity and facilitates individual expression, which I have used widely at universities and public groups, is derived from a scene in the film *Dead Poet's Society* where actor Robin Williams plays a prep school professor. For example, I asked hundreds of Japanese women in a large auditorium to stand up, move into the aisles, and make a long line. One woman was arbitrarily picked as the leader, to walk in whatever style, whereas the others were instructed to copy her movements exactly. Then, another woman was picked to walk in her way, with everyone imitating. The instructions were, "Become fully aware of what it feels like to copy someone else's actions exactly…to submerge your own impulse into following someone else's way." Then, I said, "Now, walk in your

own way, paying attention to what it feels like to break the pattern of copying someone else, and instead to express yourself." This can take at least 10 minutes. The instructions stress the importance of walking in a fully conscious way, similar to exercises of mindfulness (Germer, Siegel, & Fulton, 2005), and to be aware of such walking as a self-expression. At first, most of the women were hesitant, glancing around to see what others were doing; then, while some walked self-consciously, others became very demonstrative, walking in a distinctly idiosyncratic manner, clearly enjoying themselves.

Given enough time and a small enough number of participants, every person can have a turn to lead with the group mimicking their walk. To help participants become fully aware of the experience of leading, I ask them to look back at the group following in their footsteps. I also ask them to notice any fear or embarrassment, and to switch their concentration at times to enjoy the experience of leading. To amplify the experience of self-expression and self-control over behavior, I invite the group to exaggerate their way of walking (e.g., swing arms higher or take broader steps).

Power   Because trauma can render one feeling helpless, exercises that build a sense of personal power are helpful. Two somatic exercises that I like to use help activate the body through motions and breathing, in an adaptation of Eastern techniques used by lamas in Tibet. In what I call the "arm pull," participants breathe in as they make a fist and raise one arm high in the air; then they exhale with a loud *whoosh* noise as they bring their arm forcefully straight downward. Do this three times with each arm. Hesitate after each motion to feel sensations in the body. In what I call the "train ride," participants inhale as they raise their arms straight out at their sides, and then exhale, making an explosive *choo* sound each time they lower their arms toward their side, stopping four times along the way. This is repeated three times, and takes no more than a minute.

Power Balance: Giving and Receiving   Power imbalances are at the root of distress in relationships within various cultures (particularly where women are considered inferior) and between cultures. The acts of giving and receiving can be considered as a metaphor for power relations, such that repeated giving can reflect codependence or subservience on one hand, or dominance over the receiver on the other hand. Many personal relationships are defined by one or the other partner being a giver or a taker, creating problems, for example, when takers feel guilty or resentful of codependency and become withdrawn or aggressive, or when givers feel depleted and exploited and become withdrawn or passive aggressive. A balance of giving and receiving is essential for healthy relations.

Such dynamics also manifest on cultural levels. For example, many Palestinians express feeling humiliation as a result of living in conditions inferior to Jewish Israelis, or being treated without respect (Lindner, Walsh, & Kuriansky, 2006). In order to resolve such power imbalances, peace building requires negotiating the best helping arrangement where receiving help does not stimulate degrading dependency but rather a transient dependency leading to personal dignity and pride (Nadler, 2006). In these exercises, I give each party a chance to lead and follow for an equal amount of time (about 3 minutes each), to serve as a metaphor for balance of power, equality, and being in control or being controlled. These activities also constitute lessons in nonverbal communication skills.

The Thumb–Palm Exercise   This short exercise helps participants first identify their proclivity to giving or receiving. Participants put their thumb in the palm of their opposite hand and determine what they "feel" more: their thumb rubbing their palm (giving), or their palm being rubbed (receiving). Whichever they feel more, they are asked to purposefully focus on the opposite experience. The exercise can be expanded to touch other body parts on one's own—or a partner's—body (making sure to be culture-sensitive about comfort levels with physical contact).

Hand Mirror Dance   The group forms pairs, and puts their hands up to chest level, (as if about to play paddy-cake). They can touch hands or maintain whatever is a comfortable distance. Similar to the "walk this way" exercise, the person identified to go first moves his/her hands and the partner mirrors those actions exactly, without talking. Then, the other person has a turn moving his/her hands idiosyncratically, with the partner following the motions exactly. In the third stage, each person moves his/her hands in whatever way he or she chooses. The point is to pay particular attention to who moves independently, or leads or follows the partner, and also to notice what it feels like in each condition. Then, they share their experience, including which role feels more comfortable. For example, someone may say, "I feel out of touch (separate, lonely, angry, etc.) when you move differently from me" or "I worry about whether you will not like what I am doing." This exercise can be expanded to move the entire body, as opposed to just the hands.

Communication

Backtalk   Some cultures stereotypically restrain from expressing emotions directly or verbally (especially anger or affection). In this exercise, pairs stand back-to-back and "communicate" through movements of their backs instead of through words. They are instructed in three stages: (a) "Say hello to your partner with your back"; (b) "Have an argument or disagreement with your partner through your back"; and (c) "Make up (resolve the argument) and show how much you care about the person by movements of your back." Allow about a minute for each stage. Some participants hesitate at first, but invariably get into the exercise. Some people who would culturally be expected to be very reticent become very active, because moving with their back is less threatening than direct confrontation. Participants often giggle, as a form of not only anxiety release but also enjoyment.

Animal Encounters   Children are especially amenable to this exercise, inviting them to think of themselves as an animal and to walk around the room like that animal, making motions and noises, and "greeting" other children as that animal. This need only take about 5 minutes.

Make a Toy   To explore cooperation with others of another orientation, background, or culture, I ask participants to pair with someone they consider "different" from themselves. I hand out one sheet of paper and two differently colored pencils to each pair, and ask them to draw a toy together, without talking and with each person taking a turn making a mark on the paper. Allow about 5 minutes for the drawing. This exercise is part of extensive brain style workshops that help people get in touch with different communicating styles (Herrmann, 1996; Kuriansky, 2001d). Then the pairs share with each other and the group about what it felt like to work with that person, how they experienced "differences," and how this reveals their way of relating to people in real life. For example, a European male drew the outline of a truck, and an Asian woman found herself reacting traditionally, continuing his marks at each of her turns, and then sharing how compliance is characteristic of her behavior. In another example, a participant from Belgrade consistently made more abstract lines in response to his partner making circles (meant to be wheels on a realistic toy), realizing how this interaction triggered memories and residual anger about the NATO bombing of his city and aggression over the ethnic cleansing conflict in his region.

Boundary Setting

Boundary-setting is fundamental in child development, to establish independence, especially in the process of separation-individualization (Mahler,

1975). Yet, many people from some cultures passively follow or fulfill others' desires, even if internally resenting such compliance.

Yes–No   In this exercise, participants are asked to identify three things that they normally say yes to and to imagine themselves saying no to these things instead, as well as to note three things that they normally say no to and imagine saying yes to these things. Allow participants about 2 minutes to write these down and 2 minutes each to share with a partner; however, it is possible to ask them to think of, and share, only one thing—taking a shorter amount of time. This exercise has been used to help women develop assertiveness, especially when they are brought up in cultures which inhibit women's self-expression, or where they are excessive "people pleasers." Such behavior inhibits responsiveness in all aspects of relationships, including sex (Barbach, 2000; Braiker, 2002).

"Yes–No Tug-of-War"   This exercise is a variation of the traditional tug-of-war used in many groups. It facilitates boundary setting and highlights control issues. With participants in pairs, I hand out a handkerchief (or strong rope) to each pair to hold at the ends. They are instructed to tug at their end of the rope, while saying yes or no, and given turns with each word. Participants might be tentative while others tug strongly, pulling the other person off balance. Some say yes loudly and no in a weak, small voice. One or two minutes is adequate for each turn. Afterward, they share feelings evoked by each word (which felt more powerful, energetic, or comfortable); describe personal meaning attached to yes and no (e.g., yes feels more agreeable, so others will like you); experience being on the other end of someone else's yes or no (e.g., angry or resistant); and connections to real-life relationships (e.g., one woman shared, "I realized that I always give in to my boyfriend and do whatever he likes even when I really want to say no").

Emotional Release   Because pent-up emotions can erupt into psychological or physical symptoms, emotional release defuses psychological stress and prevents somaticizing symptoms. The latter is common in various cultures, especially in response to disaster, where people develop headaches, stomach-aches, and nightmares. A simple process taking only a few minutes is to combine deep breathing with a symbolic releasing action. Participants inhale deeply to a count of three, holding up one, two, or three fingers consistent with counting and visible to the group, in order to emphasize the breathing pace. On the exhale, they blow out the anxiety symbolically, making a loud whooshing sound to emphasize the release. They are asked to imagine the upset emanating from a body part (e.g., the head in case of headaches or nightmares, or the stomach in case of stomachaches), put their hands on that part as if collecting the energy, and then to dump the upset into an imaginary hole in the ground in the center of the group, to symbolically be rid of the anxiety. With tsunami survivors, I incorporated this exercise into an in-vivo desensitization and into drawing exercises.

Acknowledgment   People in some cultures stereotypically reject self-praise, considering the activity as a sin of pride or a bad omen. For example, Jewish parents warn against praising a child lest the opposite characteristic manifests. Similarly, a Chinese mother may say that her child is ugly, even if objectively beautiful. Yet, positive descriptions about the self and others build self-esteem and rapport essential for healthy development and relationships. A Japanese therapy tradition, Naikan therapy, fundamentally consists of expressing appreciation for people, objects in one's life and the self (Murase, 1976).

My Good Qualities   In this exercise, participants note or write down a quality—preferably three—about the self that they most like. Then, noticing any resistance or embarrassment, they turn to the person next to them and take turns stating these qualities, saying, "What I like about myself is that I am …" In an important second step, the listener repeats back to the speaker what he or she said, which allows the person to feel accepted and appreciated for his or her good qualities. This takes about 5 minutes.

In extensions of this exercise, participants pair with others in the group to repeat the exercise. Or, they announce their qualities to the larger group ("I am Raoul and I am real" or "I am Lakshmi and I am kind"), and the group repeats back to them ("Raoul, you are real" "Lakshmi, you are kind"). The repetition of the quality paired with the person's name deepens the experience of being acknowledged by others. To further reinforce acknowledgment and also facilitate group cohesion, participants randomly announce another group member's name and quality ("Raoul, you are real") until everyone takes a turn and everyone is announced. Although some Asians are hesitant at first, many express considerable appreciation for the experience of being acknowledged by a large group.

In a variation of this exercise, which I developed for use with orphans after the tsunami, I asked children in the group to answer the question, "What quality did your (lost parent) most appreciate about you?" Several children said, "My mother said I was a good student." The group then repeats the quality to the child, using their name (e.g., "Ardu, you are a good student"). Many children responded very positively to this exercise.

Self-Awareness

Cherished Item Projection   Because people from particular cultures stereotypically have difficulty talking about themselves directly to others and to a group, exercises founded in object relations theory facilitate such sharing. In one such exercise, I ask participants to pick something that they like or value that they are wearing or that is in the immediate environment and to describe the importance of that item and how it reflects something about themselves. Each turn should be about 2 minutes, but takes longer when deep emotions are aroused and need to be processed. With preparation time, I ask participants to bring that item to the session. One man in a postdisaster group brought an item reminding him of his deceased wife's love for family, leading to his unprecedented sharing of suicidal feelings as a result of losing her and his family. In using this exercise with a group of inner-city African American teens (where revealing personal information is traditionally considered "unmanly"), one male brought a pair of dice to the group, and described how life is a like a "crap shoot." Another male showed a baseball which was gift from his father, and was close to tears when describing how he loved his father but rarely saw him because he was in jail.

Love Qigong

Qigong is a unique system of Chinese exercises to build health and prevent illness by preserving the body's *Qi*, or "vital force," using breath, gentle movements, and mental concentration to circulate spiritual power through energy channels in the body (Garripoli, 1999). I developed "love qigong" exercises for use in China, deliberately using the word *qigong* to evoke the concept of energy flow, because many Chinese understand that concept and its related practices. The movements are derived from ancient Indian and Chinese tantric tradition meant to develop relationship skills and remove blocks between people (Kuriansky, 2005c; Saraswati & Avinasha, 1996). As such, the exercises apply not only to intimate partners but also to strangers extending love to a broader community. Partners can stand as close or far away from each other, reaching out with as much space, as comfortable.

Heart Tap   In this exercise, partners face each other and place their right hand on the partner's heart area and cover their partner's hand on their heart with their left hand. On the exhale, they imagine sending love energy down their arm and through their hand into the partner's heart. On the inhale, they imagine love energy being transmitted from their partner out his or her arm into their own heart, creating a cycle of caring, support, and loving energy. This exercise can be expanded to send that energy to the group: To do this, they turn back into the circle and extend their right hands into the circle and place their left hands on their own hearts, while imagining sending and receiving love energy in the circle. This energy can be transmitted further if participants lift their right hands outward, toward the sky, or in a sweeping motion, imagining sending love energy to the broader universe, loved ones, strangers, disaster survivors, or people in war zones. This can take at least 10 minutes.

The Five-Step Energy Process

The five-step energy process is based on Eastern tantric techniques of energy movement (Avinasha, 2002), which I adapt according to specific circumstances in innumerable workshops and trainings on relationships in different countries (Kuriansky, 2000b, 2001f, 2002b, 2003c). I have further adapted this process to suit varied growth and healing experiences in mixed cultural groups, particularly in conflict situations and postdisaster recovery (Kuriansky, 2003b, 2005b). The process facilitates inner peacefulness, re-establishes trust in others, and encourages reconnection with the broader community. For example, I used this exercise with a group of Jewish American, Canadian, and Arab students attending a university in Jerusalem after a suicide bombing took place on campus (Kuriansky, 2007).

The steps I use are (a) activation, by shaking body parts at an increasing rate, starting with the feet and hands and then including the entire body, and moving around the room at an increasingly fast pace (which causes physiological arousal through stimulation of the autonomic nervous system and chemicals like adrenalin) accompanied by culturally appropriate music; (b) quieting the mind, by stopping abruptly to become fully still and quiet (invoking the parasympathetic nervous system similar to mediation) and concentrating on feelings within the body (tingling, pulsing, quivering, electrical sensations, indicating energy flow empowerment and aliveness, serving as an antidote to "deadened" or desensitized feelings that often accompany trauma); (c) reactivation, emerging from the quiet state, opening the eyes and moving around the room, feeling grounded and connected to the earth (facilitating personal strength and security essential in trauma recovery); (d) transmuting the energy into connection, openness, and compassion toward others, using eye gazing and the heart tap described earlier or a simple version by holding out hands on top of one another at a safe distance and sensing the energy between them; and (e) play, around a theme easily acceptable to most cultures, like free-form dance, or imagining oneself as animal. This can take 20 minutes to a half hour (or longer) or be abbreviated into a shorter time if necessary.

Participants are asked to be mindful of the intention of the exercises: to feel secure within oneself, to appreciate the other person's being (neutralizing preju-dices), and to experience commonality (of hurts, anger, and need for human connection). Synchronized breathing (as described) achieves harmony on a deep level that counteracts separation and judgment that contributes to intolerance.

Changing Thoughts and Behavior

Reframing This technique—widely used in Western cognitive therapies—involves restating upsetting cognitions, issues, or problems in a more positive way. When I used this technique with orphans after the tsunami, one young girl who suffered from recurrent nightmares (being in a coconut tree watch-ing her mother being washed out to sea crying for help) was able to reframe the dream so that her mother was smiling at her saying, "Even if I die, know that I am okay and you must live and be happy" (Kuriansky, 2005d).

In Vivo Desensitization Exposure to the anxiety-provoking situation with systematic desensitization is a behavior modification technique proven effec-tive in various cases, as with survivors of abuse and trauma (Foa & Meadows, 1997). In working with Sri Lankan adults and children who lost loved ones in the tsunami, I brought group members closer and closer to the "sea" start-ing from the refugee camp and stopping at progressively closer stations on the journey to the seaside. At these stages, participants collected in a circle, indicating their level of anxiety by a show of fingers (from 0 to 10, indicat-ing increasing intensity), and performing the safety mantra and emotional release exercises described earlier. The final process involved play, tossing a ball. This process can take several hours.

Anchoring Actions or items can serve as ways to ensure that a more constructive or desired behavior or thought process is "set" in a new pattern and repeated.

Transitional Objects Toys are useful in various cultural groups, espe-cially with children, as a reward (for doing the exercise), contact comfort, a transitional object, or to anchor a relaxed experience. For example, for play with a group of tsunami survivors at the seaside, I used a ball-like object with fur-like covering (for softness), and bold colors (for cheerfulness). Also, tsunami orphans who completed a drawing exercise were given a small stuffed animal (in male or female versions) to take to bed with them to facilitate peaceful sleep free of nightmares, and which they were encouraged to share when playing with other children. To ensure culture sensitivity, the toy should be consistent with those available in local stores.

The REASSURE Model

The REASSURE model of advice-giving was developed over several decades of my doing crisis counseling and radio call-in advice in America and Japan, which I have also used in trainings throughout China (Kuriansky, 2006c). I have also used it in internet advice (Kuriansky, Larsen, Zappa, Mora and Carty, 2007b). The model is useful for various cultures, by health professionals in a variety of settings, because it can easily be easily learned and applied by the practitioner.

The word *reassurance* specifically refers to the overall intention of offering the person/client confidence that (a) he or she is "normal"; (b) he or she is not the only one with his or her problem; and (c) there is help and hope for his or her problem. The word is an acronym which describes the various elements of the advice, applied individually or collectively and in whatever order seems appropriate. For example, *R* refers to reassurance of normality and hope; *E* stands for explanation of the problem; *A* refers to asking questions to elicit more information; *S* stands for identifying the person's social support network; the second *S* stands for offering specific suggestions; *U* stands for understanding deeper dynamics, including the impact of childhood experiences; *R* stands for offering referrals; and *E* stands for encouragement. Reports have described this model (Portis, Tettey, and Gadsden, 2003; Kujac, Golia, Sottile, Nenova and Kurinasky, 2006); described its applications (Kuriansky, 1996); and provided preliminary validation (Golia, 2005). Although these words are spelled differently in different languages, which would lead to a different anagram, many cultures can relate to the English words and translations are always made into words in the local language, even though they do not start with the same letters.

Using this model with a young Chinese husband who was distraught over infertility (having a child is highly prized in China) produced dramatic results. His anxiety was reduced and hope increased when I helped him trace his anxiety to traditional cultural shame over not starting a family, and deeper shame and fear that his manliness was being challenged. I also encouraged him to continue sexual relations, because the couple's withdrawal was preventing any possibility of pregnancy, and reassured him that reducing anxiety alone can lead to success in some cases.

Art Therapies   The value of art therapy has been well established, particularly with regard to the use of drawing as a tool for self-expression as well as healing (Malchiodi, 2002). I devise many creative arts experiences with groups and classes, often consulting the participants to determine culture appropriateness, value, and metaphoric significance of the experience. For example, orthodox Jewish males painted a "happy experience" on the traditional kippot head coverings in a class about psychology and trauma recovery. One student, who drew a bright sunshine, explained that the skullcap is a symbol of being close to God; therefore, in the face of terrorism prevalent in the world today, his sun was meant to be a symbol from God of shining hope.

Drawings   In different settings, I ask participants to make multiple drawings in order to move through a traumatic experience toward a more positive state. For example, child survivors of the tsunami did four sets of drawings: (a) their family; (b) the stressful situation; (c) a happy moment; and (d) drawing a bridge (Kuriansky, 2005e; Yedida & Itzhaky, 2004). The latter two drawings assisted participants to process the traumatic experience by balancing it with happy moments, and helped the children make a transition from focusing on the trauma to a more positive view of life. Allow about 10 minutes for drawing.

Media-Based Techniques

Using films and videos as an educational tool and aid in therapy has been established, including showing videos to clients about a topic or videotaping patients in sessions and watching these tapes as feedback of their behavior. Such video-assisted therapy has been applied in varied clinical settings, including treatment of eating disorders (Matsumoto et al., 2006) and as an adjunct to sex therapy (Sommers, 1999). The use of visual aids has been shown to be helpful in multicultural settings where limited language skills hamper therapeutic progress (Sommers, 1999). A project in Israel gives Israeli and Palestinian youth cameras to document and share their experience (Givat Haviva News, 2006).

Trigger Films   When playback equipment is available, I often show trigger films—short films related to topics that stimulate discussion relevant to a selected topic. These may be professionally produced films, clips of television news stories from my own reporting, news stories I have collected over the years, or even commercials. The usefulness of video material has been established (Ber & Alroy,

2002). One short video I use with many Chinese groups shows Chinese men and women, particularly couples I interviewed at a wedding festival in Hainan, China, answering my favorite question: "What can you do to please your partner?" (Kuriansky, 2001e). In remote areas where equipment is not available, I show these films on the screen of my handheld SONY video camera.

Videos Home   Because the use of video can greatly enhance not only communication but also healing, I have developed variations of what I call "media-assisted healing" (Kuriansky, 2006d). In an example of this, I invited international students attending a university in Jerusalem where a suicide bombing killed several people on campus to videotape personal messages to their parents, who were understandably anxious about their children after such an event. The students spoke into the camera directly addressing their parents ("Hi Mom, hi Dad, I am safe and I love you and wanted you to know I am going to stay here and you should not worry."). I also filmed the students in some activity of their daily lives (dancing in the street, walking arm in arm with friends) to give their parents a sense of their lives. After the parents received the tapes, I followed up with phone calls to offer help processing feelings after viewing the tape.

Healing Homework   Another example of media-assisted healing is homework assignments given to students in my graduate class in psychology to help students process the tragic events of the attacks on the World Trade Center on September 11, 2001. One student who was also a professional musician wrote a song with lyrics about honoring the heroes and acknowledging ongoing emotions and the need for closure (http://www.towersoflightsong.com). Encouraged to show his work and spread his message more publicly, he performed the song in class, as well as at meetings at the United Nations and at a peace summit in Hiroshima honoring Nobel Peace Prize laureates (the Dalai Lama, Reverend Desmond Tutu, and Betty Williams).

In a similar example of using performing arts for healing, students at the Shevat Moffet high school in Israel—a school that lost the most number of students as a result of a 2001 terrorist attack in a disco—produced a video titled "We Will Never Stop Dancing." The video showed memorials to the seven classmates who died, as well as scenes of students dancing and singing and getting on with life, as a message of resolve to survive.

"Guerrilla Encounters"

This term describes encounters intended for growth and recovery after disaster or in war zones, which take place impromptu in the field. For example,

I have conducted such encounters with couples near the site of the World Trade Center, and on campus after a terrorist bombing in Jerusalem. In the latter, I and another psychologist (of Middle East origin) encountered students informally, on benches near dorms, in cafeterias and at bus stops, using processes similar to "compassionate listening" where peace activists listen to people's stories in public sites (Green, 2002, 2007; Kuriansky, 2003a). Students of various backgrounds in pairs or groups expressed disparate views, with the psychologists facilitating dialogue to foster understanding and acceptance. For example, a British student criticized the settlements and Israeli occupation as inciting Palestinian rage, whereas an American student defended actions as necessary security measures in reaction to suicide bombings. In several encounters, students of various nationalities (including French and Jewish American) challenged Arab students to explain terrorism. Students were assisted to explore belief systems and emotions and to listen compassionately and nonjudgmentally to each other. As a result of these encounters, some students expressed more positive feelings toward the "other," especially when Arab students expressed similar nonacceptance of suicide bombing and similar post-event trauma (e.g., inability to study; or increased pressure to graduate).

Rituals

Rituals common to many cultures play an important role in healing. In some postdisaster situations where circumstances or destruction of religious centers prevent people from worshipping or performing normal cultural rituals, I have facilitated improvisations. For example, after the tsunami, when many survivors could not perform burial rites for lost loved ones because temples were destroyed and bodies were missing, I created an experience whereby orphans painted candles for widowers (depressed over loss of their spouse and children) and then both the children and fathers gathered in newly constituted group "family" units to light the candles and recite indigenous prayers. Children displayed enjoyment and fathers expressed deep appreciation for this exercise.

Parting

The third stage of the 3 Ps of group process involves closure. Group closings, in my view, should be an uplifting and moving emotional experience with a celebratory quality. I also intend that such exercises extend the value of the energy created in the group to the broader universe.

The Web   My favorite closing exercise to accomplish the above goals is creating a web. For this process—versions of which are used by other practitioners (http://www.womanwithin.org)—I buy yarn of different colors (to metaphorically evoke differences between people) and wrap them around a ball (e.g., crunched-up newspaper or Styrofoam balls from arts and crafts stores) to create a mass and weight so the ball can be thrown. The group forms a circle, and I toss out the balls of yarn arbitrarily to different members who hold one end of the string and throw the ball to someone else across the circle, until a web is formed of the different colored yarns. Then I ask the group, "What does the creation seem to connote?" Invariably someone notes, "We are all different, and yet we are connected." Others are invited to share anything about their feelings, thoughts, or prayers. This process can take about 15 minutes.

The web works well for adults as well as children, and particularly well for groups of diverse backgrounds. Adults at one workshop with participants from various cities and countries (e.g., Sudan, Singapore, and Malaysia) were so moved by this exercise that it created bonds leading to lasting connections.

Occasionally I use the web at the beginning or in the middle of a group to facilitate bonding and fun. I also adapt the exercise and integrate it into the "play" part of the five-step process described above; for example, I gave children in one group strips of colorful material to swirl over their heads while they danced around in a circle, and then I asked them to form a circle and grab opposite ends of the strips of material to create the web.

Pairing, Extended Partnering, and Puja Techniques

In exercises that require dyads, I ask participants to turn to the person nearest them, or to roam around the room and stop in front of whoever is nearest to them when I say "stop," or to stop in front of anyone to whom they feel "drawn." Even in cultures which are typically gender-separate, I often find people willing to work with the opposite gender. To extend the exercise, I ask them to move on to another partner, allowing an opportunity to experience a variety of partners, and therefore an expanded awareness of differences and similarities. Sometimes I orchestrate a *puja*—asking the group to form an inner and outer circle, facing a partner with whom to do a particular process, and then stepping to the left to face another partner for the next process. When dyads share, I usually suggest that the person with the longest hair goes first; this is an easy method and also makes people laugh, which encourages joy but also anxiety relief.

Discussion

An Eclectic Approach

The field of cross-cultural counseling is rich with increasing possibilities for new ideas and interventions, especially given opportunities for cross-pollination among professionals afforded by the Internet, travel, and international conferences. As a result, innumerable exercises can be added to any toolbox. These will inevitably increasingly represent hybrids of approaches which are traditional and modern, East and West, and right- and left-brain.

The techniques in this toolbox individually and collectively represent a blend of Western and Eastern approaches, whereby an Eastern theoretical orientation is based on energy, compared to a focus on cognitions and behavior, which is typical of a Western orientation. An energy system can be considered similar to the formulations of physics—an association called "ontological strangification" by Austrian philosopher Fritz Wallner (2001) to refer to overlaying lessons and principles of one micro/cultural/religious world on another. Such an Eastern view has its source in Buddhist and ancient tantric practices and beliefs whereby energy moves through the body (driven by the breath) and can be channeled inward toward the self or outward to others or to the broader universe. This process creates states of enlightenment and bliss, or can act as a healing force to combat addictions and illness, and to facilitate racial and ethnic tolerance and peace (Avinasha, 2002; Kuriansky, 2001f, 2004d). Such Eastern views are increasingly being revived and adapted by Western professionals, including myself, and taught in Eastern countries, returning them to their roots (Kuriansky, 2001g, 2002b, 2003b, 2006e).

In becoming more familiar with Middle Eastern counseling, I note with interest that although Arab cultures are still unfamiliar with Western examinations of childhood as the source of psychological problems, some Arab psychologists trained in Western culture who return to their roots find this context useful in their treatments (Srour, 2006). Western cognitive therapy techniques are also being applied; for example, a Palestinian social worker has found the use of the flooding technique from behavior modification particularly helpful in desensitizing young children's fear of soldiers (AlArja, 2006).

Techniques in a toolbox can also mix traditional and modern approaches. Practices such as astrology, energy practices, and bodywork may not be evidence-based by Western standards, but can be well received and practiced by local cultures. For example, auspicious timing and feng shui (flow of energy dependent on location or harmonious placement) are held in high regard in countries like China and Nepal. Counselors must take this into account, as was necessary for me regarding a Chinese couple suffering from infertility who faulted the direction of their home.

Equally important is being aware of instructions, descriptions, and even specific words used during the implementation of various techniques, adjusting them to be culture-specific. For example, in China, rather than using the term "healthy" to describe a relationship—which is common in America—I use the word "harmony" when describing relationships, which is easily translatable and better understood.

An increasing number of Western practitioners, including myself, are seeking training in indigenous therapies. At one such training in Tamang Buddhist shamanism in Nepal, we made daily observations of a local shaman who received villagers in her home where she performed various divinations to free them from bad spirits considered to cause infidelity, headaches, and even infertility. Such techniques involve chanting, divinations using a knife, water, and salt, and transmissions from animal spirits (Dietrich, 1998; Muller-Eberling, Ratsch & Shahi, 2000; Peters, 2002; Kuriansky, 2001g). In one session, the shaman hit me over the head with a live chicken, for bad spirits to exit my body into the chicken, which was then slaughtered. To further excise bad spirits, she led the student group in a ritual of wrapping colored string around a large tree while chanting.

The toolbox techniques presented here further reflect dominance by either right-brain processes (which are creative, emotional, and imaginative) or by left-brain processes (which are logical and cognitive). Whereas Western cognitive therapy relies on left-brain techniques like reframing and thought-stopping, an Eastern worldview's guiding techniques (like those of American Indians as well as Asian cultures) is more right-brain in its emphasis on harmonious aspects of the world, intuitive functioning, and a holistic approach. In many workshops, I select techniques from my toolbox which use both orientations. For example, to help participants identify difference in their style of functioning (thinking and relating) which leads to either compatibility or conflict in their relationships, I administer a shortened version of an extensive computer test of brain dominance (Herrmann, 1996) which constitutes a left-brain exercise. Once they have identified their own and their partner's styles, and potential areas of cooperation or friction, I may ask them to do the toy drawing exercise, which is a more right-brained activity. To give participants an experience of increased intimacy, I may also follow this with the five-step process previously described.

Many of my toolbox techniques evolved from trusting my intuition, thinking "outside the box," and allowing myself to freely create new applications that fit the situation and people. For example, the safety mantra described earlier was created "in the field" in reaction to the situation and people's needs for safety after a traumatic event. In another example, I developed some of the love qigong exercises at a book fair in China when I was asked to make a presentation on a large stage in front of thousands of people who spoke only Chinese. Realizing the need to be demonstrative as well as informative, I abandoned my prepared formal lecture and improvised useful activities. That experience also convinced me to expand my definition of "counseling" to include occasions where a trained counselor addresses an audience, affording an opportunity to present what counseling is, to demonstrate growth-producing techniques, and to evoke growth-producing experiences.

Consequently, I approach counseling and training, especially in another country than my own, by being prepared, but without a rigid or preconceived notion of what to do or what will happen. Being responsive to situations means that implementing methods from this toolbox requires "inner knowing," intuition, and clinical skill to know when, where, and with whom these techniques would be helpful. Such an approach is often discussed on the Listserv of the Humanistic Division of the American Psychological Association and is supported in the three-pronged mantra of "Open Space Technology": Trust the people; trust the process; trust yourself (Heft, 2006).

Because of these aforementioned trends, I am convinced of the value—which I first learned in graduate school decades ago—of being "eclectic" in one's approach. As a result, early-career counselors can benefit from diversity in their training and learning about all disciplines. Although the contemporary focus of the counseling field is on cognitive-behavior approaches—which more easily lend themselves to scientific measurement—other approaches which cannot be as easily tested should also be studied and tried.

The importance of developing methods to effectively work with diverse cultures is especially important in regions mired in seemingly intractable conflicts (e.g., the Middle East). Grassroots efforts in these regions are increasingly employing a binational as opposed to uninational approach—bringing together members from opposing sides (Albeck, Adwan, & Bar-on, 2002; Kuriansky, 2007c). Many people-to-people programs aimed at reconciliation and also trauma recovery use dialoguing—a technique which requires verbal skills but is effective in facilitating mutual understanding (http://traubman.igc.org). In these contexts, I also find the five-step nonverbal method described earlier to be useful.

Cultural and Counseling Competence

This toolbox approach, as in all cross-cultural counseling, assumes that practitioners are culture-sensitive, skilled in the theories and practices of dealing with different cultures, and aware of personal values, biases, and cultural background which influence behavior and attitudes. Because general counseling competence underlies cultural competence, using these techniques and integrating them into a meaningful intervention requires clinical skills essential for positive client outcome (rapport, compassion, and empathic listening) consistent with person-centered counseling (Rogers, 2003); a "loving presence" as described in Buddhist tradition (Martin, 2003); and integrity, meaning respect for the individual and for his/her culture, as well as for the training required to implement responsible interventions.

Challenging Cultural Preconceptions

My experience in developing and implementing these toolbox techniques has challenged certain preconceptions or generalizations about working with varied cultural groups. One of these is the widely held view that Eastern cultures do not respond to verbal therapy, or do not value insight. To the contrary, I have encountered many Chinese individuals intrigued with analytic understanding of family dynamics. For example, one young Chinese woman, upset over her boyfriend's selfishness, came to a new appreciation for why she chose him in the first place, once she made the connection that her mother was exceptionally narcissistic and self-centered.

Another commonly held generalization is that men and women in various cultures would never participate in groups together. Of course, one must always be gender sensitive; yet, I have found certain situations where both men and women—even from Muslim communities—were receptive to mixed-gender groups. Some mixed-gender groups were even the result of self-selection.

Furthermore, although experts (reasonably) point out difficulties with international cross-cultural mental health responses and trauma relief (Shah, 2006), I have found that people in certain cultures can not only be receptive to intervention by a practitioner from another culture but can be even more responsive to a foreigner than to a local. This was evident to me when I expressed surprise that many men and women at my public lectures, and many Chinese doctors in my trainings, participated so readily in the exercises I proposed. In response to my surprise, I was told that participants would not cooperate as fully with a local Chinese, but were also not only gracious, curious, and stereotypically deferent to an authority figure, but were appreciative of my "fresh" active approach in comparison to very formal didactic lectures typical of the local teaching and lecturing style. Research has confirmed that the aspects of my trainings to health professionals about American counseling which were rated highest were the active techniques, like the trust exercise (Hu, Kuriansky, & Shen, 2003). Occasionally, three-quarters of a group from mixed or Eastern cultures participates, whereas one-quarter retreats to the sides of the room to observe. Besides being due to culturally specific reticence, power positioning may contribute to objection to participation, as was revealed by one male participant in a training of medical professionals who said, "I am a doctor, not a patient."

To respect individuals' rights to voluntary participation, I always introduce exercises as an invitation (i.e., "I invite you to …") rather than as a command. Individuals in certain cultures, particularly in the East, may appear reluctant to participate when in fact they are waiting for permission, and therefore respond well to being called upon (Fisher-Yoshida, 2006). I have noted this in many groups with Asian participants. When using attuned intuition about who is likely to respond, the invitation to speak up is received exceptionally well. Individuals who do not participate can benefit from observing or just from being offered the opportunity to confront their shyness.

I have further found striking similarities among cultures with regard to psychological concerns. Questions from people in all cultures—including Chinese, Singaporeans, and even Persians in Iran—cover the same topics as I have been asked by Americans over many decades of giving advice to thousands of men and women of all ages (Zhu, Kuriansky, Tong, Xu, Chen, & Cheng, 2001; Gwee, 2002; Kuriansky, 2000c, 2004e, 2006f). For example, one Persian man approached me in the hall at a conference in Tehran and asked, "Is it okay for a younger man to be attracted sexually to an older woman?"—a common question in Western cultures.

The Issue of Evidence-Based Therapy

Scientific validation of these toolbox techniques has been limited due to lack of opportunity, time, or funding, but preliminary findings of some research projects using selected techniques suggest their effectiveness. For example, process analysis of the Reassure model is proving its validation (Golia, 2005).

Also, an evaluation of my workshops with mixed-culture adults (in India and Singapore) is suggesting that participants report less shyness, more openness, and increased self-awareness. And self-reports before and after my workshops for youth at risk for sexually transmitted diseases show an increased self-esteem necessary for making wise decisions about relationships and behavior. Other research with groups—using related techniques like breathing, drawing, movement, and meditation with participants in Israel and Gaza—showed a substantial decrease in post-traumatic symptoms from 88% to 38% (Gordon, 2006).

Much anecdotal evidence supports the value of various exercises in this toolbox. For example, one participant in the workshop for Jewish and Arab students after a campus bombing said, "You normally keep relationships shallow but this brings you closer together and to see where your boundaries are … I know now that for there to be any peace between people in the world, we have to examine the walls we put up between people … I am grateful that I now know I can connect with another human being on a deeper level that you cannot do with words, that has changed me forever."

Logistics

In many cross-cultural situations, especially after disasters, it is necessary to be flexible not only in selecting techniques, but also regarding logistics. For example, although the optimum size for a group may be 6 to 20 participants, many more individuals may wander in or attach to a group when the session is being held in an open area or a unique setting like a refugee camp. Additionally, even though private enclosed spaces are optimal to ensure maximum safety, confidentiality, and comfort for participants, groups may have to be held in improvised spaces. For example, groups for Sri Lankan tsunami survivors had to be held in classrooms at converted schools serving as the survivors' residence. Because one wall was exposed and onlookers wandered by, a local had to be enlisted to stand "sentry." Rooms were also often devoid of furniture, making it necessary to do drawing exercises on the floor. Such flexibility is consistent with principles utilized in open space technology (Heft, 2006).

A Good "Fit" for the Practitioner and the Participants

Choosing among these toolbox techniques requires clinical judgment as well as determining whether the technique suits the practitioner's personality style.

Because my personality, training, and clinical style are "eclectic," I am well suited for the multidisciplinary, multimodal, and multidimensional and multicultural nature of the techniques described in this chapter. Any practitioner, especially a student, must examine his or her own attitudes, experience, comfort, and orientation to determine whether he or she is a good match.

Choosing the mixture of modules also requires clinical judgment taking into account many factors, including the appropriateness for the participants based on their needs, situation, comfort, and receptivity. Furthermore, the order of the modules depends on many factors including the needs and sophistication level of the group. An important guiding principle requires being sensitive to the energy of the group, alternating activities which are activating with those that are calming; with the goal to facilitate an experience—and create a flow—which moves the energy of the participants in a way that is empowering and healing.

Conclusion

A toolbox of techniques such as those presented in this chapter, which have been developed and implemented in diverse cultures, can be a valuable resource for clinicians doing cross-cultural work, especially in unpredictable circumstance such as after a disaster. To maximize benefits of an intervention, such a toolbox should be multidisciplinary, multimodal, and multidimensional. Practitioners well trained in general counseling can choose techniques to formulate into a useful intervention design.

Ultimately, it is not the individual technique which determines a positive outcome, but rather the intention of the practitioner to be helpful, the client's experience of empathy and care, and the resulting rapport that goes beyond language skills and exists on a more energetic plane. No matter what a counselor "does," the most important "tool" is to "be present" with attention, care, emotional support, nonjudgment, empathy, listening, and love. Consequently, a most valuable "tool" is the practitioner's open heart.

References

AlArja, N. (2006). Cries for help: A Palestinian social worker's story. In J. Kuriansky (Ed.), *Terror in the Holy Land: Inside the anguish of the Israeli-Palestinian conflict* (pp. 123–131). Westport, CT: Praeger.

Albeck, J., Adwan, S., & Bar-on, D. (2002). Dialogue groups: TRT's guidelines for working through intractable conflicts by personal storytelling. *Peace and Conflict: Journal of Peace Psychology, 8*(4), 301–322.

American Psychological Association. (n.d.). *Public education campaigns.* Retrieved November 16, 2006, from http://www.apa.org/practice/publicedu.html

Avinasha, B. (2002). *The Ipsalu Formula: A method for Tantra bliss.* Valley Village, CA: Ipsalu Publishing.

Ayalon, O. (2006). Dealing with demonization of the "other" in the Middle East by metaphoric tools to transform foe into friend. In J. Kuriansky (Ed.), *Terror in the Holy Land: Inside the anguish of the Israeli-Palestinian conflict* (pp. 183–189). Westport, CT: Praeger.

Barbach, L. (2000). *For yourself: The fulfillment of female sexuality* (rev. ed.). Garden City, NY: Anchor Press.

Ber, R., & Alroy, G. (2002). Teaching professionalism with the aid of trigger films. *Medical Teaching, 24*(5), 528–531.

Boraine, A. (2000). *A country unmasked: South Africa's Truth and Reconciliation Commission.* New York: Oxford University Press.

Braiker, H. (2002). *The Type E* woman: How to overcome the stress of being everything to everybody.* Lincoln, NE: iUniverse Publishing.

Dietrich, A. (1998). *Tantric healing in the Kathmandu valley.* Delhi: Book Faith.

Fisher-Yoshida, B. (2006, December 15). Reframing conflict: Intercultural conflict as potential transformation. Presented at the 8th Annual HumanDHS Meeting: *2006 Workshop on Humiliation & Violent Conflict,* Columbia University Teachers College, New York.

Foa, E. B., & Meadows, E. A. (1997). Psychosocial treatments for posttraumatic stress disorder: A critical review. *Annual Review of Psychology, 48,* 449–480.

Foreyt, J. P. (2004). *Weight loss: Counseling and long-term management.* Retrieved November 13, 2006, from http://www.medscape.com/viewarticle/493028

Garripoli, G. (1999). *Qigong: Essence of the healing dance.* Deerfield Beach, IL: Health Communications.

Germer, C. K., Siegel, R., & Fulton, P. (Eds.). (2005). *Mindfulness and psychotherapy.* New York: Guilford Press.

Gielen, U. P., Fish, J. M., & Draguns, J. G. (Eds.). (2004). *Handbook of culture, therapy, and healing.* Mahwah, NJ: Lawrence Erlbaum Associates.

Givat Haviva News (2006, Spring). New York: *Newsletter of the Givat Haviva Educational Foundation,* p. 7.

Golia, L. (2005, April 15). *The Reassure Model: Principles and process analysis of a unique and brief advice-giving approach.* Presentation at the Graduate Society for the Advancement of Psychological Sciences, Columbia University Teachers College, New York.

Gordon, J. (2006, Winter). Healing the wounds of war in Gaza and Israel: A mind-body approach. In J. Kuriansky (Ed.), *Terror in the Holy Land: Inside the anguish of the Israeli-Palestinian conflict* (pp. 203–216). Westport, CT: Praeger.

Green, L. (2002). Just listen. *Yes! A Journal of Positive Futures,* 20–25.

Green, L. (2007). Compassionate listeneng with Israelis and Palestinians. In J. Kuriansky (Ed.), *Beyond bullets and bombs: Grassroots peacebuilding between Israelis and Palestinians* (pp. 105–109). Westport, CT: Praeger.

Gwee, E. (2002, November 19). Thrill me, love me. *Singapore Straits Times,* Weekend Today Life section, p. 3.

Heft, L. (2006). *The open space technology idea book*. Workshop materials based on H. Owens, *Open space technology: A user's guide* (2nd ed.). San Francisco, CA: Berrett-Koehler Publishers.

Herrmann, N. (1996). *The whole brain business book*. New York: McGraw-Hill.

Hu, P., Kuriansky, J., & Shen, Z. (2003). The analysis of American sex therapy training. *The Chinese Journal of Human Sexuality*, *12*(3), 42–44.

Kalayjian, A., Kuriansky, J., Moore, N., & Aberson, C. L. (2007). *A psychosocial outreach program for tsunami survivors in Sri Lanka: Psycho-educational and training approaches* (submitted for press).

Kujac, H., Golia, L., Sottile, G., Nenova, M. and Kuriansky, J. (2006, November 10). The Reassure Model: Description and preliminary process evaluation of an advice-giving short-term intervention applied in America and China. Paper presented at the 18th Greater New York Conference on Behavioral Research. St. Francis College, Brooklyn, New York.

Kurinasky, J. (1996). *Generation sex*. New York: Happer.

Kuriansky, J. (2000a, October 21). *Talking to teens about sex: Emotional, relationship and sexual problems of adolescents, giving advice in the mass media and lessons of America that can be helpful to China*. Presented at the International Symposium on Reproductive Health Research and Policy Issue of Adolescent and Unmarried Young Adults, Shanghai Institute for Planned Parenthood Research, Shanghai, China.

Kuriansky, J. (2000b, October 27). *Tantric healing and sacred sex*. Workshop at the 3rd Annual Conference on Spirituality, Psychotherapy and Healing: Merging Old/New Paradigms, organized by the National Institute for the Psychotherapies, Mt. Sinai Hospital, New York.

Kuriansky, J. (2000c, October 31). *Common problems of couples in China, America and around the world: Steps to increase sexual and marital satisfaction to improve family planning and reproductive health practices*. Seminar at the 20th anniversary of the Shanghai Center for Reproductive Health Instruction, Shanghai, China.

Kuriansky, J. (2001a, March 25). *Common relationship problems and American counseling techniques that help: Lessons for Nepal*. Public lecture. Kathmandu, Nepal.

Kuriansky, J. (2001b, September 12–17). *American counseling techniques for Chinese health professionals*. The 5-day training course for the China Sexology Association, Chengdu, China.

Kuriansky, J. (2001c, September 19). *Techniques of couples counseling for family planners*. Training for the Shanghai Center for Family Planning Technical Instruction, Shanghai, China.

Kuriansky, J. (2001c, December 5). *Brain style empowerment in professional and personal life*. Presented at the Women in Business Conference, Hong Kong.

Kuriansky, J. (2001d, December 23). Two by two: The annual international wedding festival. *South China Morning Post*, p. 9.

Kuriansky, J. (2001e, October 23). *Systems and strangification of couples therapy in the U.S. and China*. Presented at the Second International Meeting of Science of Culture, Chinese Academy of Sciences, Beijing, China.

Kuriansky, J. (2001f, August 23). *Applying American counseling to Chinese couples: Techniques for immediate use*. Workshop at conference on "Dialogues between East and West," International Conference on East–West Psychotherapy, Kunming, China.

Kuriansky, J. (2001g, Spring issue). Trekking the other Nepal: the Katmandu Valley. *Spiritually and Health Magazine*.

Kuriansky, J. (2002a, July 15). *Dealing with the aftereffects of terrorism: The 9/11 experience.* Presented at the conference of the World Council of Psychotherapy, Vienna, Austria.

Kuriansky, J. (2002b, July 13–14). *A new model of East/West therapy for peace in an age of terrorism.* Workshop at the World Congress of Psychotherapy, Vienna, Austria.

Kuriansky, J. (2003a). The 9/11 terrorist attack on the World Trade Center: A New York psychologist's personal experiences and professional perspective. *Psychotherapie-Forum.* [Special edition on terrorism and psychology], *11*(1), 37–47.

Kuriansky, J. (2003b, September 15). *Counseling skills: Crisis intervention trends, theories, techniques and models.* Presented at the meeting of the China Mental Health Association, Huangzhou, China.

Kuriansky, J. (2003c, November 13–14). *An experiential workshop for clinical application of East/West techniques: Reviving ancient Indian practices for intra-psychic and interpersonal growth.* Workshop at the 1st International Conference of the Asian Federation for Psychotherapy. Psychotherapy, Yoga and Traditional Therapies: Dialogue between East and West, Sagar, India.

Kuriansky, J. (2003d, December 13). *Peace and healing in troubled regions: Impact on relationships. What East & West can learn from each other about treating trauma and a new integrated therapy model.* Presented at the Middle East/North Africa Regional Conference of Psychology, Dubai, United Arab Emirates.

Kuriansky, J. (2004a, May 24). *Therapy in times of terrorism: International models and clinical skills.* Keynote address at the International Conference on Counseling, Psychotherapy and Mental Health Education, Nanjing, China.

Kuriansky, J. (2004b, September 29). *New methods of psychotherapy in modern times: Combining Eastern mystical techniques with Western practices.* Presented at the 2nd Asian Conference on Psychotherapy, Tehran, Iran.

Kuriansky, J. (2004c, June 26). *Unique clinical interventions for peace and healing in troubled regions.* Presented at the 12th European Congress of Psychotherapy, Belgrade, Serbia.

Kuriansky, J. (2004d). *The complete idiot's guide to tantric sex* (2nd ed.). New York: Alpha Books.

Kuriansky, J. (2004e, October 1). *Common relationship and intimate problems in America and other countries.* Public seminar, Tehran, Iran.

Kuriansky, J. (2005a, July 20). *Unique programs for teens and safer sex.* Presented at International AIDS Day: Trauma, Families, and HIV/AIDS. National Institute for Mental Health Scientific Conference on the Role of Families in Preventing and Adapting to HIV/AIDS, Marriott Hotel, Brooklyn, New York.

Kuriansky, J. (2005b, August 28). *Children in conflict zones: Psychotherapeutic techniques to aid Palestinian and Israeli children.* Presented at the 4th World Congress for Psychotherapy, Buenos Aires, Argentina.

Kuriansky, J. (2005c, October 22). *Achieving harmony in relationships: Love qigong and other Western and Eastern techniques.* Public seminar, Chongqing, China.

Kuriansky, J. (2005d). *Finding life in a living hell.* Posted February 21. Retrieved November 20, 2006, from http://www.nydailynews.com/front/story/283039p-242333c.html

Kuriansky, J. (2005e, November 15). *Innovative cross-cultural techniques for psychosocial relief: Efforts for children affected by the tsunami.* Plenary presentation at the Asian Applied Psychology International-Regional Conference, Bangkok, Thailand.

Kuriansky, J. (2006a, July 20). *Unique psychosocial recovery efforts for children survivors of the tsunami.* Presented at symposium on "Post Tsunami Mental Health" at the 26th International Congress of Applied Psychology, Athens, Greece.

Kuriansky, J. (2006b, July 20). *Achieving peace and AIDS prevention with unique intervention models: A toolbox from radio to rituals.* Presented at the 26th International Congress of Applied Psychology, Athens, Greece.

Kuriansky, J. (2006c, November 10). *The REASSURE model: Principles and application of a short-term intervention in various cultures.* Presented at the 18th Greater New York Conference on Behavioral Research, St. Francis College, Brooklyn, New York.

Kuriansky, J. (2006d, June 22). *Unique clinical techniques for psychosocial healing after trauma: Group rituals with students, media assisted therapy, and skills building.* Presented at the 4th International Congress of Psychic Trauma and Traumatic Stress, the Argentine Society for Psychotrauma, Buenos Aires, Argentina.

Kuriansky, J. (2006e, July 17). *A new model of counseling: Application of integrated Western and Eastern techniques.* Workshop at the International Congress of Applied Psychology, Athens, Greece.

Kuriansky, J. (2006f). Eros in the dragon empire: The open door to sex in China. In M. S. Tepper & A. F. Owens (Eds.), *Sexual health* (Vol. 3, pp. 243–278). Westport, CT: Praeger.

Kuriansky, J. (2007a). Healing after a terror event on campus in Israel: Unique workshops and other techniques for International, Jewish and Arab students, staff and extended community. In J. Kuriansky (Ed.), *Beyond bullets and bombs: Grassroots peacebuilding between Palestinians and Israelis.* Westport, CT: Praeger.

Kuriansky, J., Larsen, E., Zappa, K., Mora, L., and Carty, G. (2007b). E-advice: Approaches and techniques for online advice-giving, application of the Reassure Model and evaluation of emails to a psychological-topic driven newspaper column (manuscript in preparation for publication).

Kuriansky, J. (2007c). (Ed.) *Beyond bullets and bombs: Grassroots peacebuilding between Israelis and Palestinians.* Westport, CT: Praeger.

Lindner, E. tG, Walsh, N. R., & Kuriansky, J. (2006). Humiliation or dignity in the Israeli-Palestinian conflict. In J. Kuriansky (Ed.), *Terror in the Holy Land: Inside the anguish of the Israeli-Palestinian conflict* (pp. 99–105). Westport, CT: Praeger.

Mahler, M. S., Pine, F., & Bergman, A. (1975). *The psychological birth of the human infant.* New York: Basic Books.

Malchiodi, C. (Ed.). (2002). *Handbook of art therapy.* New York: Guilford Press.

Martin, D. (2003). *The heart of hakomi: The practice of loving presence.* Retrieved November 21, 2006, from http://www.hakomi.ca/lovingpresence/appliedbuddhism.html#Anchor-THE-47857

Maslow, A. H. (1970). *Motivation and personality* (2nd ed.). New York: Harper & Row.

Matsumoto, R., Tsuchida, H., Wada, Y., Yoshida, T., Okamoto, A., Yamashita, T., et al. (2006). Video-assisted cognitive behavioral therapy for anorexia nervosa. *Psychiatry and Clinical Neurosciences, 60*(6), 780.

Morita, M (1998). *Morita Therapy and the true nature of anxiety-based disorders (Shinkeishitsu).* New York: SUNY Press.

Muller-Eberling, C., Ratsch, C., & Shahi, S. B. (2000). *Shamanism and tantra in the Himalayas.* Rochester, VT: Inner Traditions.

Murase, T. Y. (1976). Naikan therapy. In W. P. Lebra (Ed.), *Culture-bound syndromes, ethnopsychiatry and alternate therapies* (pp. 259–269). Honolulu: University Press of Hawaii.

Nadler, A. (2006, December 15). *Intergroup helping as status relations: Effects of status stability, identification, and type of help on receptivity to high status group's help.* Presented at the 8th Annual Human DHS Meeting: 2006 Workshop on Humiliation & Violent Conflict, New York, Columbia University Teachers College.

National Clearinghouse for Alcohol and Drug Information (2005). *NIDA clinical toolbox: Science-based materials for drug abuse treatment providers.* Retrieved November 20, 2006, from http://www.nida.nih.gov/TB/Clinical/Clinical Toolbox.html

Pedersen, P. B., Draguns, J. G., Lonner, W. J., & Trimble, J. E. (Eds.). (2002). *Counseling across cultures.* Thousand Oaks, CA: Sage.

Peters, L . G . (2002). *Cultural psychology and shamanism in Nepal.* New Delhi: Pratik.

Portis, C., Tettey, N., and Gadsden, O. (2003) The process of brief psychotheraphy and the development of the Reassure Model. Unpublished manuscript.

Rogers, C. R. (2003). *Client centered therapy: Its current practice, implications and theory.* London: Constable & Robinson.

Ruth, D. (2006). *Coaching/counseling toolbox.* Retrieved November 16, 2006, from http://www.dynamicresources.net/Coaching-Counseling_Toolbox.htm

Saraswati, S., & Avinasha, B. (1996). *Jewel in the lotus* (rev. ed.). Valley Village, CA: Sunstar Publishing.

Shah, S. A. (2006). Resistance to cross-cultural psychosocial efforts in disaster and trauma: Recommendations for ethnomedical competence. Retrieved on November 20, 2006, from http://www.massey.ac.nz/~trauma/issues/20 06-2/shah. htm

Smoke Free Homes (2005). *"Professional Toolbox." Pediatric clinicians making children's homes smoke free.* Retrieved November 16, 2006, from http://www.kidslives mokefree.org/toolbox/index.php?mode=c

Sommers, F. G. (1999, August 13–17). Multicultural sex therapy. *Proceedings of the 14th World Congress of Sexology.* Hong Kong.

Sommers, F. G. (2003). Visually enhanced psychosexual therapy (VEST) in a multicultural community. *Canadian Journal of Psychiatry, 48*(11), 773–774.

Srour, R. (2006). Challenges becoming a young Palestinian clinician during the intifada. In J. Kuriansky (Ed.), *Terror in the Holy Land: Inside the anguish of the Israeli-Palestinian conflict,* (pp. 197–202). Westport, CT: Praeger.

Sue, D. W., & Sue, D. (1999). *Counseling the culturally different: Theory and practice* (3rd ed.). New York: Wiley.

Tseng, W. S. II. (2001). *Handbook of culture and society.* San Diego, CA: Academic Press.

Wallner, F. (2001, October 23). *Ontological strangification.* Presented at the Second International Conference on Culture and Science, Chinese Academy of Sciences, Beijing, China.

Woy, J. R., & Efran, J. S. (1972). Systematic desensitization and expectancy in the treatment of speaking anxiety. *Behavior, Research and Therapy, 10*(1), 43–49.

Yedida, T., & Itzhaky, H. (2004). A drawing technique for diagnosis and therapy of adolescents suffering traumatic stress and loss related to terrorism. In N. Webb (Ed.), *Mass trauma and violence: Helping families and children cope* (pp. 283–303). New York: Guilford Press.

Zhu, H., Kuriansky, J., Tong, C., Xu, X., Chen, J., & Cheng, L. (2001). *China repro-ductive health hotline: Professionals solve problems on sex and emotion*. Shanghai: Sanlian Press.

Suggested Readings

Gielen, U. P., Fish, J. M., & Draguns, J. G. (Eds.). (2004). *Handbook of culture, therapy, and healing*. Mahwah, NJ: Lawrence Erlbaum Associates.
Useful resource which includes chapters by experts from varied disciplines (psychology, anthropology, psychiatry) presenting a multidimensional view (psychosocial, biological, cultural) of cross-cultural interventions. Details healing traditions from various cultures, including with Arabs, African Americans, and Asians, as well as Western and non-Western therapies applied both in their own and in different cultural contexts.

Kuriansky, J. (Ed.). (2006). *Terror in the Holy Land: Inside the anguish of the Israeli-Palestinian conflict*. Westport, CT: Praeger.
Includes chapters about the psychological dynamics and approaches to counseling in a Middle Eastern context contributed by Palestinians and Israelis. Of particular interest are chapters about Palestinian counselors integrating Western therapy approaches with children, as well as a very readable and detailed description of a medical doctor's mind–body workshops, which include Eastern- and Western-style techniques that have been applied with cultures in conflict, specifically Israelis and Palestinians.

Kuriansky, J. (2004). *The complete idiot's guide to tantric sex* (2nd ed.). New York: Alpha Books.
An easy-to-read and comprehensive guide to Eastern techniques and exercises which derive from ancient practices but have been adapted for modern use with both Western and Eastern populations. The techniques can be applied without the sexual component to enhance intimacy, overcome addictions, heal illness, promote tolerance, and create peaceful relations in conflict situations.

Tseng, W., & Streltzer, J. (Eds.). (2001). *Culture and psychotherapy: A guide to clinical practice*. Washington, DC: American Psychiatric Association.
An overview of culture and psychotherapy with contributed chapters about clinical interventions for early-career as well as experienced professionals to learn about cross-cultural interventions. Includes approaches for individuals as well as group with various backgrounds, e.g., Hispanic, African Americans, and Southeast Asians.

Uno, M. (Ed.). (2006). *Buddhism and psychotherapy across cultures: Essays on theories and practices*. Somerville, MA: Wisdom Publishing.
Contributions present the synergy and intersection between Buddhism, psychology and psychotherapy, with some chapters specifically addressing cross-cultural work. Experts explain ways to bridge Western talking cures with Eastern energetic sensing and somatic practices, as well as Japanese Naikan therapy.

Webb, N. B. (Ed.). (2004). *Mass trauma and violence: Helping families and children cope*. New York: Guilford Press.
Chapters cover theory as well as specific psychological interventions to address psychological trauma in children and families. Includes group support, music and play therapy, and a bridge-drawing technique used as a diagnostic tool to assess youth trauma.

13

Rethinking Counseling in Refugee Work
Post-Traumatic What?

Geoff Denham

Contents

Survivors of all systematic torture/trauma face a daunting task in their attempts to restore shattered lives. Their lives are irrevocably altered by the death of loved ones, or by injuries, or through surviving experiences of chronic subjection to routine harassment, persecution, and threats of death. I will argue that multicultural counseling with the survivors of torture/trauma is a professional activity that must draw on a number of disciplinary knowledge bases to find a substantial theory-of-practice base. A bare knowledge of post-traumatic stress disorder will not adequately equip the counselor for work in this area, nor will knowledge provided by texts on multicultural counseling, which lack the required specificity. In this chapter, 12 major points gleaned from multicultural counseling with survivors of torture/trauma will be put forward to assist in comprehending the task facing multicultural counselors working with this client population.

My aims here are twofold: first, to make a contribution toward a more integrated theory of multicultural counseling with torture/trauma survivors; and second, to prepare counselors for the huge demands the work places on their capacity to acknowledge and address social suffering. As the adage goes, forewarned is forearmed. Burnout is a common occurrence in this particular work. In my view, it can be avoided or minimized through the passing on of knowledge gained in these circumstances of professional work, and in providing counselors with an opportunity to reflect on the issues raised.

Responding to Social Suffering

Kleinman, Das, and Lock (1997) use the phrase *social suffering* and introduce it as follows:

> Social suffering are conditions that are usually divided among separate fields, conditions that simultaneously involve health, welfare, legal, moral, and religious issues. They destabilize established categories ... the trauma, pain, and disorders to which atrocity gives rise are health conditions; yet they are also political and cultural matters. (p. ix)

Torture/trauma survivors typically face assaults on their way of life, on their person, and on their cultural practices—in short, genocide. I have worked with the survivors of torture/trauma accepted as refugees or humanitarian entrants to Australia under successive Australian governments' commitment to refugees worldwide.[1] In addition to this counseling and resettlement work, I was involved in a special government-initiated humanitarian response to Albanian Kosovars from former Yugoslavia who were brought to Australia under the aegis of Operation Safehaven in mid-1999. The Australian government responded to the United Nations Human Commission on Refugees' (UNHCR, 1999) call for help in providing emergency accommodation for people displaced from Kosovo, following Slobodan Milosevic's ethnic cleansing campaign, and almost 4,000 refugees were brought to Australia in June 1999.

The work with the torture/trauma survivors from Kosovo[2] and surrounding districts in former Yugoslavia presented counseling staff at Bandiana Safehaven with many challenges. A more detailed account of the work can be found in Denham (2002).

The counseling staff of our agency wore identifying badges that said in literal Albanian: "Caring, sharing, and listening to your bad experiences." This was the translation of a pithy motto—caring, listening, sharing—we thought would help identify our professional role. In the first month of the Safehaven, counseling staff walked around the dormitories making contact with at least one member of every family living on-site. This was relationship building. In a highly visible way, the central and formative aspect of all counseling engagements was highlighted in this very painstaking work of knocking on doors, making introductions, meeting members of these displaced households, and getting to know each person by name—*Avni, Ramadan, Makfire, Shpresa, Fatos, Emin, Fetije, Bexhet, Shyrete, Xhelal.* (I quickly learned to write my first name as *Xhef* so that Albanian native speakers could pronounce it perfectly!)

First point: All counseling and psychotherapeutic endeavor is premised on communication and relationship. Communication fails when generosity is extinguished.

Border Crossings and Ambiguity

We met people in the canteen and other communal spaces, and later in their dormitories. The articulated identity on our badge was a starting point. We took interpreters with us when they were available. We made contact and did our best to build relationships with these people. Rosaldo (1989) has called these transcultural encounters "border crossings." Border crossings describe meetings between people where different cultural practices, assumptions about meaning, and codes of behavior come into play. It was much harder to do "being ordinary" in these contexts because we didn't know what ordinary practices were for Kosovars. We quickly learned. Most travelers have experienced the discomfort arising from ambiguity in unfamiliar social situations (e.g., Do these people really drink coffee this strong with six spoonfuls of sugar? Did I say something embarrassing or inappropriate to the lady I just met?). Counselors at Bandiana Safehaven[3] could never be quite sure that they were conducting themselves in a socially and culturally appropriate manner, despite prior briefings on customs and manners. As we encountered these people, our interpreters helped us to understand subtle matters of social exchanges.

Some counselors were drawn to these ambiguous social encounters, and some were worn down by them. A male psychiatric nurse on the counseling team asked me whether we had to go out and introduce ourselves "all over again" to the new influx of residents following camp consolidations. Of course we did, but his decision to resign was an indication of the energy-sapping nature of the work and the unusual circumstances of that work. Border crossings can be exhausting encounters, whereas routine cultural practices provide continuity and knowledge in the familiar. Many people do not leave the comfort of their homeland.

Second point: In border-crossing settings, relationship building should be a highly visible activity. The onus is on the counseling staff to clearly identify themselves and to openly acknowledge difference.

We welcomed new residents; we said farewell to those who returned to their homeland during the life of the camp; we attempted to address their social suffering; we helped arrange specialist medical consultations, massage from trained practitioners, and professional counseling; we encouraged and supported productive activity; we took our place alongside other service providers at the camp including medical practitioners, dentists, teachers, Red Cross workers, army personnel, interpreters, catering staff, and the management team from the Department of Immigration.

This was a fragile and changing community in several ways.

A temporary camp that brings together a group of 400 survivors of torture/trauma is a fragile community from the outset because of the nature of the experiences the survivors have endured. A defining characteristic of refugee experience is the act of fleeing, or escaping, or being forced to evacuate one's homeland.[4] A refugee community finds itself in a temporary location chosen by others. During 1999 many of the Kosovars had first been evacuated to Skopje in Macedonia, and then had been flown to East Hills holding camp in Sydney, subsequently bussed to Singleton Safehaven in NSW, and then bussed to Bandiana Safehaven[5] in Victoria. This was a typical relocation pattern.

Bandiana also witnessed changes to the service staff. Few of the nongovernmental agencies (including our own) were guaranteed funding for the work beyond a 1-month time frame. We were routinely on the verge of closure. Counselors made decisions about their working future in response to these uncertainties.

And most importantly, there was a changing political landscape in relation to survivors of torture/trauma driven by domestic and international events.[6] Counselors were increasingly called upon by the residents to interpret this changing landscape and offer advice to them concerning the decisions they faced. For example, survivors had to decide how to respond to financial inducements to return to their homeland by October 31, 1999 (the Winter Reconstruction Allowance),[7] and whether to seek refugee status and apply for permanent residency in Australia.

Third point: Counselors working with refugees will be called upon to address the issue of the refugee family's uncertain future, and will be cast into a role of interpreter/adviser of government policy. They need to be ready to take on this role with particular regard to government policy changes.

A Medical/Educational Model of Service Delivery

If social suffering raises health, welfare, legal, moral, and religious issues, as Kleinman, Das, and Lock (1997) contend, those involved in the planning of Operation Safehaven focused on the provision of suitable housing, health, counseling, and educational services to alleviate the social suffering of the Kosovars. Representation at the planning meetings in June 1999 (prior to the Kosovars' arrival at Bandiana) was primarily from government health, armed services, and immigration sectors, with the Adult Migrant Education Service, our own counseling service for torture/trauma survivors, the Red Cross, local police, the local Albanian community, and the Salvation Army also represented. The need for interpreters was quickly identified, and hasty preparations were made to augment the supply of Albanian interpreters by running 40-hour "courses" for competent local native speakers of Albanian. At the peak of Operation Safehaven almost 4,000 residents were housed in 8 army camps around Australia.

A very high standard of medical and dental care was offered. This is now a well-established first professional response to refugee and humanitarian entrants to Australia, whether they come into temporary Safehavens, or whether they come as permanent settlers to Australia. It was clear that the Kosovars had not experienced as sophisticated a level of medical and dental care in the Drenica or Pristina areas of their homeland (where most of them came from). For example, the poor quality of dental care was confirmed by a glance at most residents' teeth.

The role of counseling was largely unknown to them, although some knew of the role of psychologist in a hospital setting. For them, engaging with a counseling service was a new experience.

A very high-standard education program was provided by both local teachers and specialist teachers from the Adult Migrant Education Service (AMES). The establishment of regular classrooms on the camp site did much to reestablish the routines of everyday life for the Kosovars, though the government response to the request for work permits was ambivalent and restrictive (see footnote 6).

The dormitory-style accommodation was clean, well maintained, and solidly built, and the residents were able to manage their own laundry and reestablish the domestic routines of everyday life with one exception—preparation of food. Army barracks function in Australia on the assumption that recruits are young, mainly male, and require a canteen and linen service. There were few opportunities for residents to prepare their own foods (because of contractual arrangements between the army and the private catering firm), and this inhibition on the expression of a people's eating practices became a more salient irritation as time went on.[8] The importance of the rituals of the birthday cake in family life, and fasting arrangements during Ramadan were two instances of the issue which were partially addressed.

Fourth point: The reassertion of a people's familiar cultural practices is quite important in establishing safety and everyday routines in a small translocated community. The routines of everyday life are important in reaffirming a sense of well-being in members of the community. These are seldom noticed mental health issues, because communities are rarely deprived of their everyday life routines, but become evident when routines are disrupted or no longer available, as frequently occurs in refugee camps or safehavens.

Slowly at first, we began to realize that what we took to be "natural" in providing health and counseling services was indeed "cultural." In our planning meetings, we constituted the social suffering of these people in a manner informed by our cultural interpretations, preoccupations, and emphases. This was not an active choosing on our part, simply something that we "naturally" did. Of course it is important not to assume that such delivery of service is unequivocally good and to begin to recognize the substantial differences in interpretations of illness among such populations.

Fifth point: Healing practices vary from culture to culture. Psychological counseling (as a healing practice) is not universal in its application and may undergo changes in its attempt to be a relevant resource for people of different cultural backgrounds.

Looking at the Survivors of Torture/Trauma Through the Lens of Post-traumatic Stress

Counseling services for the Kosovars were part of a suite of services including medical assessment, diagnosis, and treatment. Survivors were presented with a seamless integration of medicine and counseling, and it is hard to conceive of the delivery of services to survivors of torture/trauma without taking into account the success of the medicalization of human suffering and distress through psychiatric diagnoses and explanation (Kleinman, Das, & Lock, 1997).

The medicalization of human suffering can be illustrated as follows: Certain universal features of life—aging is probably the best example—become medicalized to the extent that medical solutions are offered and taken up, and proceed to become a normal expectation of those who experience problems associated with the aging process (of course with the proviso that a medical response to the problem is available and affordable). For example, the prescription of antidepressants is in part a medical response to the problems of depression, loneliness, isolation, and despair in old age. But loneliness and isolation can also be addressed by companionship, and frequently this is an antidote for depression and despair. Thus the problem of aging can be addressed in both medical and social ways.

The suffering of torture/trauma survivors can similarly be addressed in medical and social ways. It is here that a key distinction helps to clarify our professional response to the suffering of torture/trauma survivors (and indeed to suffering of the aged and infirm). On the one hand, we can distinguish between suffering as somatic pain and an awareness of such suffering, whereas on the other, suffering is understood as an existential, psychological, or spiritual state that is made meaningful by local understandings deriving from ideas about "redemption, merit, responsibility, justice, innocence, expiation" (Young, in Kleinman, Das, & Lock, 1997, p. 245). Although these two understandings of suffering overlap, it is important to distinguish them.

Professionals working with survivors of torture/trauma medicalize the experience of torture/trauma survivors in their application of the psychiatric syndrome: post-traumatic stress disorder (see Wilson & Drozdek, 2004, for a recent collection of articles by workers in the field). Post-traumatic stress disorder focuses attention on both suffering as somatic pain and an awareness of such suffering as indicated in the following diagnostic statement.

> The person has been exposed to a traumatic event in which he/she experienced, witnessed, or was confronted with an event … that involved actual or threatened death or serious injury, or a threat to the physical integrity of oneself or others … [and] the person's response to the traumatic event involved intense fear, helplessness, or horror.[9] (Zimmerman, 1994, p. 50)

In short, it emphasizes the first meaning of suffering as previously articulated.

This attempt at a pan-cultural formulation of a set of symptoms for diagnostic purposes has been applied to a number of groups (e.g., Vietnam veterans, victims of chronic abuse, torture/trauma survivors). This formulation of the diagnosis post-traumatic stress disorder removes the cultural contextual features of suffering described in the second meaning presented here—those existential, psychological, and spiritual aspects. Such an approach is *pathognomonic*—it identifies sets of characteristic symptoms but indicates no causal mechanisms (Young, in Kleinman, Das, & Lock, 1997, p. 248). Put slightly differently, relevant cultural contextual features are excluded from the diagnostic criteria in its ambition to become a universal system of classification (Mezzich et al., 1999). These authors offer a summary of a substantial critique of the transcultural limitations of the *DSM-IV* in the following:

> Some of the major biases of DSM-IV concern ontological notions of what constitutes real disease or disorder, epistemological ideas about what counts as scientific evidence, methodological commitments to how research should be conducted, and pragmatic considerations about the appropriate uses of the DSM. Contrary to its frequent portrayal as an atheoretical, purely descriptive nosology based on scientific evidence, the DSM is a historical document with a complicated pedigree and many theoretical notions expressed in its structure and content. Most of the disorders of the DSM are syndromes in search of underlying pathological mechanisms. (Mezzich et al., 1999, p. 461)

Sixth point: Psychiatric nosologies vary from culture to culture. A diagnostic category developed in one culture can be applied in another cultural setting, but it may not make sense to apply it.

When we spoke to one Kosovar man about children being kidnapped, and whole families going missing without a trace, he said, in effect with a shrug of his shoulders, "This is what I have always known; this is the kind of community I was born into; I am used to it." Post-traumatic stress disorder would appear to have a greater capacity for marking out the singular event in a society where ethnically motivated abductions, violence, and forced home evacuations are not a daily occurrence, and where systematic and institutional neglect is not pandemic. On the other hand, my vague sense of "trouble in the Balkans following World War II" was quite an insufficient knowledge base for continued helpful "therapeutic" dialogue, and so this set me on a course of finding out more about happenings in the Balkans, both recent and past.

Mertus (1999) provides a comprehensive account of recent events in former Yugoslavia from the point of view of its victims. The following quote is indicative of the comprehensive picture she assembles of life in the region of Kosovo in her book.

> In one of the walled gardens in Pristina, the provincial capital of Kosovo, Flora sits patiently on a stone bench fiddling with a picture book. The five-year-old's left leg is propped up with a large pillow; two wooden bars prevent her from moving her knee. A piece of grenade has been in her knee for over a month ... the local hospital would not treat her. [She goes on to analyze the social and political causes of the conflict] ... The root cause of the conflict in Kosovo is two-pronged. On one level, conflict has been prompted by power struggles among elites, that is, states or quasi-states. On another level, conflict has been propelled by historically conflicting national identities, human development needs, misunderstandings among the general populace, and a culture of failing to accept responsibility for social problems. Structural violence, including institutionalized poverty and institutionalized discrimination against Kosovo Albanians, only perpetuates and widens divisions. (Mertus, 1999, pp. 231–232, 276)

Seventh point: It is the very features of post-trauma omitted from the *DSM* criteria that are the salient features of the torture-trauma survivors' accounts of their suffering, flight, and upheaval. To engage with these accounts meaningfully the counselor must draw on an expanded knowledge of significant local and historical events in the lives of the speakers.

Hacking's Ecological Niche

Hacking (1991) has provocatively suggested that post-traumatic stress disorder will turn out to be a transient mental illness, and will disperse and become a nonusable classification along with the dissociative disorders (p. 100). He proposed the notion of an "ecological niche" to describe the social circumstances in which it is possible for a particular mental illness to appear. An ecological niche is made up of social vectors or forces.

> I mean nothing technical by the word vector, whose origins are in mechanics, and which is also used in epidemiology. Here I use it as a

metaphor. In mechanics, a force vector is a force acting in a direction. When there are several forces acting in different directions, the resultant force is the product of the different forces and their directions... the metaphor has the virtue of suggesting different kinds of phenomena, acting in different ways, but whose resultant may be a possible niche in which a mental illness may thrive. (Hacking, 1991, p. 81)

For Hacking, the relevant vectors are a medical taxonomy, cultural polarity, observability, and release. Respectively, a new diagnosis must be capable of fitting into a medical taxonomy or promote controversy regarding its place in such a system (e.g., post-traumatic stress disorder, acute stress disorder, or major depression or comorbidity); the mental illness is located at the juncture of contemporary and controversial social phenomena (the legitimacy of retrieved memories of abuse; the question of whether painful memories are to be remembered or forgotten; the question concerning the effect on audiences of horrific images on film and television; the alleged potency of publicly represented memory as compared to privately accessed memories); the mental illness must be capable of detection (this requires detectors in the case of post-traumatic stress but also requires sufferers to be able to self-recognize and self-identify their forms of illness); the mental illness needs to provide an escape, a kind of career trajectory (to know that one suffers from post-traumatic stress brings relief to some torture/trauma survivors—their suffering now has a name and they have [medical] status as a sufferer).

If there are no secondary benefits in being diagnosed with post-traumatic stress disorder; if there is no intention on the part of the counseling staff to engage in diagnostic activity for its own sake; and if diagnosis provides no obvious release or escape from their dilemmas as torture/trauma survivors during their temporary stay at Bandiana Safehaven, it is clear that the ecological niche supporting the assignation of the diagnosis did not exist until after the deadline set by the Australian government for eligibility for the Winter Reconstruction Allowance had passed. By November 1999 an ecological niche had formed which supported the diagnosis of post-traumatic stress, and on reflection, it helps to make sense of the shift to patient-hood among the survivors remaining in Australia. After this date, those who had elected to return home and rebuild had gone.

With the consolidation phase[10] of Operation Safehaven, new residents came to Bandiana from other Australian Safehaven camps that were closing or being made available to the East Timorese refugees. The Kosovar residents had rejected the inducement of the Winter Reconstruction Allowance. By this time many had learned basic English. Counseling staff were now asked whether some of the remaining residents were known to be suffering from post-traumatic stress conditions. Some were, and we said so, but in all likelihood we could have said the same thing about some of the survivors who had already returned to their homeland. The diagnosis of post-traumatic stress disorder now also acted as a justifiable release from the obligation to return home for some of these torture/trauma survivors. Evidence of families being known to our counseling service was considered a de facto diagnosis of post-traumatic stress, and we advised the Immigration Department accordingly. No doubt this strengthened their case for remaining in Australia. Many of those remaining wanted to seek permanent residency when they were legally able to do so.

In developing the notion of the ecological niche, Hacking (1991) identified a period of 15 years or so at the turn of the 19th and 20th centuries when the mental illness fugue circulated and flourished. He then described the ecological niche that made this possible. In reflecting on our work with the survivors of torture/trauma during Operation Safehaven we can see a similar ecological niche making its appearance as the Safehavens across Australian began to close and the camp consolidation process gathered apace. However, at the time all we could see was that the phase characterized by the first stage in Herman's (1992) model of recovery from trauma as *Safety* had passed and had been supplanted by a phase of managing a patient caseload.[11]

Eighth point: Transient mental illnesses are those mental illnesses appearing in an ecological niche, characterized by a particular set of social vectors. With a lineage traceable to railway spine, war neurosis, and shell shock, post-traumatic stress disorder may well prove to be another transient mental illness diagnosis like its predecessors.

Post-traumatic What?

The assumption of widespread post-traumatic stress among refugee populations has come under challenge (Steel, 2001). The interesting finding of practitioners in this field of work is that a majority of torture/trauma survivors do not fit the post-traumatic stress disorder criteria. Although almost all of the torture/trauma survivors had been exposed to events described in the criteria, two-thirds of the survivors passing through Bandiana Safehaven were not identified as suffering from post-traumatic stress. Furthermore, in the work I did with refugee and humanitarian entrants to Canberra, this proportion of the designated population not seeking treatment or help for post-traumatic symptomatology was maintained.[12] There is little evidence to support the objection that there are large numbers of undetected sufferers of post-trau-matic stress in these populations, or that some systematic underreporting is taking place. More fruitful explanations are offered in the concepts of social vectors in Hacking's theory of ecological niches for transient mental illness, outlined earlier.

So we need to take stock of the diagnostic criteria themselves. In summary, we have noted that the aim of the architects of the *DSM* (and post-traumatic stress disorder) has been to standardize symptom lists so that communication between treating professionals is made efficient (Pressman, 1993); to strip the contextual, cultural, and local features of the distressing experiences which are treated as outside the particular focus of scientific interest; and to then investigate the treatment of sufferers diagnosed by the disorder. However, in the enthusiasm for establishing a family of complaints or readily communi-cable symptom lists, there is little focus on theories of causation.

Ninth point: A minimum requirement for multicultural counseling with survivors of torture/trauma is a theory of how they react to, and recover from, their distress.

Our focus needs to move from the diagnosis of post-traumatic stress to building theories of causation and recovery in relation to the torture/trauma experience. It is not enough to tick a symptom checklist to determine whether survivors are "in" or "out." We must examine the key features of the human response to torture/trauma with an eye on both the manner in which the human spirit is diminished and its manner of rising again. Traumatic mem-ory is a key notion in this theory building recognized in the post-traumatic stress formulations. However, the formulations in their present form need to be extended.

The idea of traumatic memory can be traced from Freud's work on melancholy.

> "Mourning is regularly the reaction to the loss of a loved person, or to the loss of some abstraction which has taken the place of one, such as one's country, liberty, an ideal or so on" (Freud SE 14, p. 243). An open-ing is thus made from the outset in the direction we shall take below. And the first question that ... [Freud] poses is to know why, in the case of certain patients, "the same influences produce melancholia instead of mourning." (Ricoeur, 2004, p. 72)

One of my Mon refugee clients talked about the importance of remember-ing his close male friend who had died in his arms in the jungles on the bor-der of Thailand and Myanmar. My client had not wanted his friend to die, and as the (homeopathic) paramedic in their unit he had done his utmost to preserve his friend's life. But what he wanted from his counselors here in Australia was a suitable commemoration and celebration of his friend's life. We gathered one morning with him, and took part in a simple commemoration service in our office. There was little more than a statue of Buddha on a corner table, and some statements by the Mon man in memory of his fallen comrade and some acknowledgment by us (male and female counselor) of the significance of this relationship for our client. This commemoration was part of a mourning process for the client. Mourning is not a passive process.

> But why then is mourning not melancholia? And what is it that makes mourning tend toward melancholia? What makes mourning a normal, albeit painful, phenomenon is that "when the work of mourning is completed the ego becomes free and uninhibited again." It is from this angle that the work of mourning can be compared to the work of remembering... it is as a work of remembering that the work of mourning proves to be liberating, although at a certain cost, and that this relation is reciprocal. The work of mourning is the cost of the work of remembering, but the work of remembering is the benefit of the work of mourning. (Ricoeur, 2004, p. 72)

This theory of mourning and melancholia takes us beyond a categorization of symptoms and encourages us to notice the acts by which mourning is promoted. Here we recognize the intentions of survivors toward wellness and wholeness and a response by the counselor to that intention.

Tenth point: Knowledge of mourning practices in the survivor's homeland is a first step in developing helpful multicultural counseling interventions that promote mourning as a healthy and necessary step toward recovery.

The groundwork for what follows comes from Ricoeur's (2004) monumental investigation of memory and forgetting. Ricoeur was a hermeneutic philosopher who made an enormous contribution to the work of philosophy and theology, and had a long association with the University of Chicago. Ricoeur outlines two very useful polarities regarding memory for our consideration of post-traumatic stress, focused as it is on problematic or painful memory.

The first of these distinguishes between *memory-as-habit* on the one hand, and *memory-as-distinct-recollection* on the other, following Bergson (1950). Ricoeur explains that underlying this polarity is a relation with time. In memory-as-habit, what has been acquired is incorporated into the living present (e.g., some Kosovar children singing a tune with the words "they killed my brother and they killed my sister"[13] as heard by service workers at Bandiana is a poignant example). The other end of this polarity carries reference to anteriority. Thus, in relation to the time of the initial experience the former is unmarked, and the latter is marked. One of the survivors telling me about a beating he had suffered at the hands of the Serbian paramilitary could serve as an example of memory-as-distinct-recollection.

We need to be aware that post-traumatic stress disorder specifies suffering in terms of the patient's recollection of traumatic events and a recollection of her or his individual reaction to trauma. Ricoeur reminds us that there is another side of the traumatic memory coin—the side imprinted memory-as-habit which carries a reference to past events by asserting a kind of timelessness in the present. In memorizing a song or a piece of verse, memory is asserted in an active and collective way. I will never forget my witnessing of the singing and dancing that took place not long after the establishment of Bandiana Safehaven, when the residents came together one night to celebrate their survival. It was an energetic display of dancing by the menfolk supported by the playing of the *ciftelia*[14] and much hand clapping. It was clearly a highly emotionally charged occasion in the context of commemoration and can be recognized as memory-as-habit expressed in collective form. We can imagine something similar in our own collective singing of our national anthem in times of trouble, commemoration, or challenge (e.g., international sporting contests).

Memory-as-habit in these examples of the children's song and the community's celebration in dance constitutes an assertion of resilience. As a collective and cultural response to genocide there is both an acknowledgment of what happened and an expression of defiance in relation to the intentions of the persecutors. In effect, these performances say, "See, we are still here and we will endure, despite our suffering."

Eleventh point: Traumatic memories can be addressed as individual problems of personal recollection of specified autobiographical events, and they can be addressed commemoratively, and collectively as memory-as-habit. Whereas the former expression lays emphasis on individual psychopathology, the latter expression is essentially a collective response and creates a shared experience of past events.[15]

Ricoeur's second polarity poses *evocation* on the one hand and *searching for* on the other. Aristotle's terms were *mneme* and *anamnesis,* respectively, with the latter indicating a recalling and the former associated with *pathos* (in psychology's terms, *affect*). *Searching for,* the second term, also suggests the problem of forgetting as an inconclusive or failed search.

For some survivors, the aftermath of torture/trauma consists of haunting memories of past events. Survivors have told me of beatings, of rapes and murders they witnessed, and of torture. There are times when these events are triggered by watching a movie, or simply occur in nightmares. In this sense they are evoked and often produce associated affect, so well summarized in the *DSM–IV* criteria for post-traumatic stress. However, the *DSM* articulation of the diagnostic criteria provides us with only half the picture of the response to calamitous events. Ricoeur (2004) alerts us to the occluded side of the post-traumatic aftermath.

Many survivors make determined efforts to gather together an account of past events and to have these made into some form of permanent record of what happened. A Kosovar survivor I shall call Amir ended up producing (with my assistance) this account of his experiences:

> We lived in a state of constant fear. The Serbian paramilitary had us under constant surveillance. My wife now suffers from a heart condition. It is because of them. They would come and choose a child from a family and take the child away. They would say to the family: "If you want to see the child again you must pay us money." In a family group they always chose the youngest child.
>
> We had meetings among ourselves and pooled our valuables and our monies. We made sure that each child had at least 100 deutschmarks for the next day. They wanted more. They said "this is not enough." If they did not get enough money they shot the children. They asked: "Would you like them to be shot in the leg or in the head?" They were laughing. They used [exploding bullets] so that people would die even if they were shot in the leg. (statement by Amir, October 21, 1999)

Amir believed it important that statements like his be recorded and preserved. He was hopeful that these statements would contribute to something like a Truth and Justice Commission, as established in South Africa following the collapse of the apartheid policy. For him, statements such as his were not simply to be understood as important for the speaker in a therapeutic sense, but important for the future of his country, in a justice sense. Amir did not have a legacy of unwanted and intrusive memories; he rather sought to harness his memory of events with a determined purpose in mind. It was evident in our encounters that this was an active searching.

Twelfth point: In working with survivors of torture/trauma, it is important for multicultural counselors to respond to the prompt, "Post-traumatic what?"

My formulations in this chapter are a response to the prompt, "Post-traumatic what?" *Recovery* is my response and the guiding idea in my work with the survivors of torture/trauma. We know that recovery in the early stages requires the establishment of safety (Herman, 1992) as a condition for later work, and the reestablishment of the familiar routines of everyday life, insofar as these are possible. We also know that there are individual and collective reactions by survivors of torture/trauma in the aftermath of trauma. Here I have attempted to build on, and extend the formulations on, post-traumatic stress in the *DSM-IV* by laying emphasis not on medicalizing the experiences of distress and suffering, but on drawing attention to the resourcefulness one finds in such populations of survivors, and building on that base. Furthermore, I have attempted to articulate theory that might advance our knowledge and understanding of multicultural counseling in such difficult contexts of work, and form a basis for continued research.

Notes

1. From the 1990s to the present, Australia has continued to accept approximately 12,000 refugee and humanitarian entrants annually.

2. For Albanian speakers the place is referred to as Kosova, not Kosovo.

3. Bandiana is the name of the army base that was made available to the Kosovars for the duration of their stay (June 1999 to April 2000) in Albury/ Wodonga, a town of 90,000 people located on the state borders of New South Wales and Victoria, in Australia.

4. Refugees are defined by the United Nations High Commissioner for Refugees as persons who are residing outside their countries and cannot return due to a well-founded fear of persecution because of their race, religion, nationality, political opinion, or membership of a particular social group (UNHCR, 1999).

5. Bandiana Safehaven opened on the site of an army camp in Bandiana North in June 1999 and closed in April 2000. It initially housed almost 400 residents, and probably had twice that number of residents stay there during its operation as a transit camp.

6. In the life of the camp, the East Timorese humanitarian crises occurred with large numbers of displaced Timorese being housed in army bases. On November 1, 1999, there were 305 East Timorese refugees at East Hills camp in Sydney and a further 860 intended for Puckapunyal camp in Victoria. In July 1999 the Australian government was drafting new legislation establishing a temporary protection visa that would allow holders to work up to 20 hours per week but impose a two-and-a-half-year period of noneligibility for making application for permanent residency.

7. The then Minister for Immigration, Phillip Ruddock, announced the Winter Reconstruction Allowance on August 21, 1999, in a press release. All residents in the camp were asked to nominate the day of their return on a form issued to residents at Bandiana Safehaven on September 8.

8. A very respectful question was put to the administrators at a Residents' Meeting on July 16 (in the first month of the camp): "If we do end up staying 3 months or longer, do we prepare our own food or do we have it provided?"

9. Although this describes the experience of exposure to a traumatic event, application of the diagnosis requires further criteria to be met: in summary, some persistent reexperiencing of the event and some continuing avoidance of stimuli associated with the event together with some difficulties in impulse control, concentration, hypervigilance, and/or exaggerated startle response, persisting longer than a month. The formal auditing of symptoms, which the diagnostic criteria of post-traumatic stress requires, tells us little about etiology or cause that is not already embedded in the diagnostic description. Frequently discussed in the literature are the issues of predisposition to the syndrome, comorbidity, and the uncertain trajectory of the disorder across cultural boundaries (see McFarlane in Wilson & Drozdek, 2004).

10. The consolidation phase was the name given to this period in Operation Safehaven by immigration officials. The first influx of Kosovars from other safehavens arrived on September 16, 1999, with 140 from Puckapunyal, Victoria, followed by 85 from Singleton, NSW, on October, 14, 1999, and 53 from Portsea, Victoria, on October 30. During this time, there were frequent departures of Kosovars returning home and so a community in constant flux.

11. It was during this second phase of the work that my time working with the survivors of torture/trauma came to an end. I left Bandiana Safehaven 4 months before its closure in April 2004 to take up an academic post.

12. Torture Rehabilitation and Network Service, ACT (now Companion House, ACT). The criteria used here are admittedly pragmatic. Persons do not suffer from post-traumatic stress if they don't present themselves, or get referred to the counseling program. In other words, they don't submit to the implicit diagnosis.

13. The children's rhyme "Ring a ring a rosie / A pocket full of posies / A tisket, a tasket / We all fall down" as a response to the Black Plague in London provides a similar example, from an earlier time. Shocking though it seemed at the time in the manner of offending our cherished ideas of protected and

sheltered childhood, the singing of the song by the children performed and celebrated resilience and survival.

14. A stringed instrument that would appear to belong to the lute family.

15. In Australia, Anzac Day services are held on April 25 each year, to commemorate the suffering and sacrifices made by those who served in the armed services for their country. They provide another example of memory-as-habit.

References

Author. (1999, July 9). *Kosovo emergency update*. Geneva: United Nations Human Commission on Refugees (UNHCR).

Bergson, H. (1950). *Matter and memory* (N. M. Paul & W. S. Palmer, Trans.). London: Allen & Unwin.

Denham, G. W. (2002). Trauma and counseling in a cross-cultural context: Bandiana safehaven. *Australian Journal of Counseling Psychology, 3*(2), 43–50.

Hacking, I. (1991). *Mad travelers: Reflections on the reality of transient mental illness*. Cambridge, MA: Harvard University Press.

Herman, J. (1992). *Trauma and recovery*. New York: Basic Books.

Kemp, T. P., & Rasmussen, D. M. (Eds.). (1989). *The narrative path: The later works of Paul Ricoeur*. Cambridge, MA: MIT Press.

Kleinman, A., Das, V., & Lock, M. (Eds.). (1997). *Social suffering*. Los Angeles: University of California Press.

Mertus, J. A. (1999). *Kosovo: How myths and truths started a war*. Berkeley: University of California Press.

Mezzich, J. E., Kirmayer, L. J., Kleinman, A., Fabrega, H., Parron, D. L., Good, B., et al. (1999). The place of culture in DSM-IV. *Journal of Nervous and Mental Disease, 187*(8), 457–464.

Pressman, J. D. (1993). Concepts of mental illness in the West. In K. F. Kipler (Ed.), *The cambridge world history of human diseases* (pp. 59–85) New York: Cambridge University Press.

Ricoeur, P. (1984). *Time and narrative* (K. McLaughlin & D. Pellauer, Trans. Vol. 1). Chicago: University of Chicago Press.

Ricoeur, P. (2004). *Memory, history, forgetting* (K. Blamey & D. Pellauer, Trans.). Chicago: University of Chicago Press.

Rosaldo, R. (1989). *Culture and truth: The remaking of social analysis*. Boston: Beacon Press.

Steel, Z. (2001). Beyond PTSD: Towards a more adequate understanding of the multiple effects of complex trauma. In C. Moser, D. Nyfeler, & M. Verwey (Eds.), *Traumatisierungen von Flüchtlingen und Asyl Suchenden: Einfluss des politischen, sozialen und medizinischen Kontextes* (pp. 66–84). Zurich: Seismo.

Wilson, J. P., & Drozdek, B. (Eds.). (2004). *Broken spirits: The treatment of traumatized asylum seekers, refugees, war and torture victims*. New York: Brunner-Routledge.

Zimmerman, M. (1994). *Interview guide for evaluating DSM-IV psychiatric disorders and the mental status examination*. East Greenwich, RI: Psych Products Press.

Suggested Readings

Judith Herman (1992) provides an account of the pathway to recovery from trauma and abuse. Her work has been used as a guiding schema by Australian nongovernmental agencies providing services for survivors of torture/trauma.

Paul Ricoeur can be relied on to provoke one's thinking through his hermeneutic philosophy. He has influenced me in profound ways through his work on mimesis or representation (Ricoeur, 1984). His last publication (Ricoeur, 2004) provided me with important distinctions regarding traumatic memory. Kemp and Rasmussen (1989) provide a thin volume introducing Ricoeur's main ideas.

Ian Hacking (1991) writes in a stimulating fashion on the vicissitudes of mental illness categories, an issue he captures in his use of the phrase *transient mental illness*. His work opens up the issue of local definitions of mental illness and poses unsettling questions in the light of uneven geographical distribution of some mental illness diagnoses.

Arthur Kleinman (1997) argues against an indiscriminant application of Western psychiatric nosologies to non-Western patients, and he contributed to an exposé of the process of constructing Western psychiatric nosological systems revealing its political dimensions (see Mezzich, et al., 1999).

Renato Rosaldo (1989) is an anthropologist who writes revealingly about his very personal experiences as a self-identified Chicano and incorporates them into his formulations and thinking about his discipline.

Part IV

Psychological Healing and Counseling: Indigenous, Western, or Both?

14

Interventions by Traditional Healers
Their Impact and Relevance Within Their Cultures and Beyond

Wolfgang G. Jilek and Juris G. Draguns

Contents

Introductory Comments

The theme of this chapter concerns the practices of traditional, indigenous healing, especially as they are applied to the alleviation of psychic distress, reduction of anxiety, and restoration and enhancement of personal well-being and self-efficacy. Our concern is with the modes of intervention that are based on oral tradition rather than on a historic, codified body of knowledge. As such, the indigenous modes of treatment stand in contrast not only to the modern empirically based and scientifically derived corpus of information but also to the historic Western healing systems going back to the contributions of Hippocrates and Galen. Similarly, traditions of Indian, Chinese, and Arabic ethnomedicine, embodied as they are in written texts, will remain outside of the scope of our consideration.

Following a brief historic overview, we shall report on the healing practices observed by one of us (WGJ) and on their incorporation into comprehensive, culturally sensitive programs of treatment. We shall also raise questions about the mechanisms of effectiveness of such interventions and shall attempt to discern the common ground between current and modern techniques of psychotherapy and the ministrations of healers. The current status of evidence concerning the indications and contraindications of indigenous treatments will be surveyed. The major question, tackled at the end of this chapter, is the relevance and applicability of these techniques beyond the milieus of their origin. Is our understanding of psychotherapy enriched by the accumulated information on traditional healing, and is the range of effective modes of intervention broadened?

Traditional Healers: Changing Conceptions and Images

As explorers, missionaries, and conquerors ventured forth beyond the confines of postmedieval Europe by land and sea, they were confronted with healing rituals well outside the range of their experience or knowledge. An abrupt encounter with the unfamiliar often provokes a negative reaction. Human beings dread what they do not understand and tend to attribute malevolent meaning to phenomena they cannot readily explain. Thus, the notion of the demonic, powerful, magic healer was born, more or less simultaneously in Mexico and Peru and in the northern reaches of European

Russia and Siberia (Jilek, 2005; Krippner, 2002). As religious fervor declined, a secular variant of the same conception gained ascendancy. No longer were the effects of healing practices and rituals traced to the devil or evil spirits; instead the emotional arousal and the apparently bizarre actions of the healers were accepted as proof positive of their derangement or madness (cf. Jilek, 2005; Krippner, 2002; Walsh, 1990). By this time, copious evidence exists that is contrary to this notion (e.g., Boyer, 1962; Fabrega & Silver, 1973; Heinze, 1982; Murphy, 1964; Walsh, 1990). Such data have been obtained by a variety of methods, from observations and interviews as well as projective tests. They converge in demonstrating that healers, and particularly those in the shamanic tradition that capitalizes on the induction and experience of altered states of consciousness, do not exhibit psychiatric impairment or symptoms. One of us (WGJ) has come to know a great many shamanic practitioners among the North American Coast Salish (Jilek, 1982; Jilek & Jilek-Aall, 1978); the Amerindians of Ecuador and Peru (Jilek-Aall & Jilek, 1983); and the Hmong of Southeast Asia (Jilek & Jilek-Aall, 2002). The conclusion from these observations over several decades of transcultural work is unequivocal: Healers are capable and intelligent practitioners who are free of personal instability or psychiatric impairment (Walsh, 1990). In Hoppal's (1992) words: "The shaman is rather a psychotherapist than a psychopath" (p. 123). It is true that behaviors akin to psychotic and dissociative symptoms occur, principally at three points in the shamanic healers' lives: during the initial crisis and in the course of the journey when the healer's calling and identity are confirmed and solidified, and during the actual healing ceremonies. In all three cases, however, these states are temporary and reversible and are not accompanied by any increase of dysfunction or distress over any extended period of time (Walsh, 1990). "In fact, the shaman may end up as one of the most psychologically healthy members of the tribe" (Walsh, 1990, p. 86).

Along somewhat similar lines, Opler (1959), a cultural anthropologist, was impressed with the sensitivity of dream interpretation by the Ute Indian healers and referred to them as intuitive psychoanalysts. Systematic collaboration between psychiatrists and healers began in the second half of the 20th century. Leighton et al., (1963) observed the modus operandi of the Yoruba healers in Nigeria. A prominent Nigerian psychiatrist, T. Lambo, became the principal mediator between the Yoruba and the Western systems of mental health treatment. His efforts led to the integration of healers into service delivery at the Aro Psychiatric Hospital in Nigeria. At about the same time, Prince (2004) reported on the ineffectiveness of transplanted psychotherapy techniques, such as reflection of feelings, in his work with Nigerian psychiatric patients. By contrast, direct and authoritative suggestions, similar to the local healers' ministrations', seemed to work. In the decades since then, the idea of collaboration with healers has been frequently proposed, but less often implemented. Later in this chapter, we shall present an account of pooling the resources of traditional healers and modern psychiatric practitioners.

One possible obstacle to the more widespread joint utilization of traditional and local resources is the holistic and amorphous function of the healer as compared with the crystallized and sharply delimited role of the psychotherapist. As has been pointed out in several sources (Draguns, 1975; Graham, 2005; Jilek, 1993; Krippner, 2002; Vontress, 2005) several traditions of shamanistic and other healers distinctively and explicitly minister to the spirit, mind, and body as an integrated whole. In the West, spiritual concerns were separated and made the exclusive province of religion a long time ago, and René Descartes drew a sharp line between body and mind. In many traditional cultures, however, the tripartite unity continues to hold sway. Thus, the local healer may be a psychotherapist, but is never just that. The role and function of the healer is invariably multifaceted and often ambiguous. Krippner (2002) described shamans as precursors of psychotherapists in traditional societies who, at the same time, are also the magicians, physicians, performers, and storytellers of their respective communities. In the present context, however, it is their psychotherapeutic function that is of principal interest, and we now turn to it.

Salish Spirit Dance Ceremonial: Therapeutic Rebirth

The home of the Coast Salish Indian nation is located in the southwestern part of British Columbia and northwestern Washington State. In traditional Coast Salish society, adolescents and young adults of both genders were encouraged to demonstrate endurance on an ascetic quest for a guardian spirit, which, after lengthy wanderings and rigorous ordeals, was expected to appear in a vision and to bestow on the seeker an individual song with protective powers, talents, and benefits. Each winter, the advent of the ceremonial Salish winter season ushered a nostalgic despondency in those who had acquired spirit powers, together with various physical symptoms that coalesced into the *spirit power illness*. In the traditional Salish culture, experiencing this state was regarded as a sign that the person truly experienced initiation. The illness was then alleviated by ritual singing and dancing that expressed the person's distinctive, individualized style.

Canadian and U.S. authorities suppressed the Salish guardian spirit ceremonial by the end of the 19th century. At the same time, most Salish children were sent to boarding schools, designed to bring about a thorough and complete assimilation, with attendant loss of indigenous language and customs. Yet, the ceremonial never completely disappeared, and, in the context of the native renaissance of the 1970s, it reemerged with a fresh force. This revitalization coincided with the growing awareness of multiple social and psychiatric problems that beset the Salish Indian community, such as alcohol and/or drug abuse, depression, suicide, and intrafamily violence.

Young men were particularly affected by this constellation of symptoms, thought to be associated with the breakdown of social bonds and norms and termed *anomic depression* by Jilek (1982). It is in response to the recognition of these problems that local elders and ritualists changed the revived guardian spirit dance ceremonial so that it would more explicitly serve its socio- and psychotherapeutic purpose. In their view, the anomic depression that a great many Salish young adults experienced was a manifestation of spirit power illness, brought about by the alienation from Indian spirituality and its replacement by the hedonism and materialism prevalent in modern North America. The remedy that the Salish Indian ritualists envisaged was designed to enable distraught and alienated young men and women to reidentify with their ancestral culture. The traditional spirit dance initiation was therefore compressed into a fixed time frame and transformed into a therapeutic process in the course of which the initiate would acquire the healing power of the guardian spirit. This objective would be attained through the experience of a vision in an altered state of consciousness.

The process culminates in the expression of newly acquired spirit power through dance and song and is completed in the course of one winter season. In the course of his collaboration with Salish Indian healers, one of us (WGJ) had the opportunity to observe the spirit dance ritual and obtain extensive information from the local leaders and ritualists. Material based on these experiences is woven into the present account.

The prerequisites for maintaining the initiate's status include continued active participation in the annual winter spirit dances as well as always abiding by the rules of traditional behavior: showing respect for the guardian spirit ceremonial and for the elders, feeling responsible for needy members of family and tribe, and living in accordance with the "old Indian ways." This last requirement centrally features refraining from alcohol and drug use, and especially so during the ceremonial season.

Observing these rules is believed to promote both physical and mental health and to bring other benefits. Whoever breaks these rules is thought to lose the guardian spirit's power, and he or she is considered to be at risk for grave and even lethal calamities.

The central theme of spirit dance initiation enacts the archetypal myth of death and rebirth. First, the former personality with its negative behaviors, rooted in alienation from the traditional culture, is killed off. In its place, a new person comes into being, a proud North American Indian imbued with the guardian spirit power and with its attendant virtues. In the first stage, the initiate to be is subjected to "de-patterning" and induction of an altered state of consciousness. Stress is imposed, more intensely upon males than females. The candidates are "grabbed" and symbolically "clubbed to death" by the chief ritualist's staff. They then undergo periods of immobilization under sensory and sleep deprivation, alternating with sensory overload and excitation by kinetic, tactile, temperature, and acoustic stimulation. The initiates are confined to the ceremonial house where they lie blindfolded in a screened-off area, intentionally made to feel as helpless as babies. Deprived of food or drink and made to sweat under heavy blankets, they are then chased around through snow and cold brooks. Intense auditory stimulation is produced by loud singing, rattling, and rhythmic drumbeat. This drumming was recorded, and the predominant frequencies were found to be above 3.0 cycles per second, within the range that has been demonstrated (e.g., by Neher, 1961, 1962) to elicit in the EEG auditory driving with theta waves, facilitating the induction of trance states. The impact of all of these intense stimuli brings about the eventual alteration in the initiate's state of consciousness. Its induction is further enhanced by collective expectations and direct suggestion. As a result, the initiates "find their song." Their distinctive style of song and dance is then demonstrated in the ceremonial house, as the initiates typically experience a sense of exhilaration and receive massive support from the audience in the form of chanting and clapping, accompanied by dozens of drums and deer-hoof rattles. For the first time, initiates are attired in the traditional Salish garb and are provided with the distinctive paraphernalia for the new spirit dancers. Special significance is attached to the new dancer's staff that is bestowed on the initiate for the dance, but it is then hidden at the end of the initiation season, to be preserved and reissued to its holder at the start of the following year's winter season.

Throughout the initiation ceremonial, the new dancers are physically hardened and culturally indoctrinated with ceremonial lore, rules of behavior, and Indian beliefs. In recent decades, ritualized and updated pan-Indian ideology has in part supplanted the traditional Salish mythology. The initiation process ends with a disrobing ceremony whereby the new dancers divest themselves of all traces of their former selves. They are publicly presented in the ceremonial house as witnesses to the regenerating power of the guardian spirit. After 4 years of participation in guardian spirit rituals, a distinctive human-hair headdress and a rattle stick are awarded in recognition of the status of a mature dancer. Even experienced spirit dancers have been observed to hold on to the rattle stick after completing their dance round, overcome by emotion, crying, and reliving the death and rebirth of their original initiation.

Components of psychotherapeutic experience are readily recognizable in the ritual we have described. Spirit dancers receive massive social support from the ritualists and from the audience. Self-esteem is bolstered and expressed as possession by the guardian spirit takes hold; drummers adjust to the individual dancer's rhythm, and spectators rise as the new dancer passes by. "Of each new dancer the ritualist would proclaim: 'Now everybody knows him, before nobody knew him'" (Jilek, 1982, p. 94). At the same time, the intended effect of the ceremony is to supplant self-centered preoccupations with the pursuit of collective goals; alienation is thereby overcome, and integration into society restored. An important by-product is the acquisition of skill for inducing an altered state of consciousness, which is highly prized by the culture and enhances the new initiate's self-esteem.

Through subsequent participation in annual spirit dances, this skill is further refined, providing more social recognition and admiration. Through the intense physical and psychological stress inflicted in the early phases of the spirit dance ceremonial, the process of personal and behavioral change is accelerated and intensified. Cathartic relief is achieved following the experience of transformation in the final stages of the ceremony, akin to the sympathy and abreaction in living through a play or undergoing group therapy or psychoanalysis (Barrucand, 1970).

What components of psychotherapy that are featured in the mainstream Euro-American culture are absent from these ritualized interventions? Two that immediately come to mind are nondirective techniques and those focused on unique, individual experience. The outside observer is immediately struck by the directiveness and even regimentation by the ritualists and their staff. Similarly, we do not find out much about the biographies of the individual participants, their fears, hopes, goals, and aversions. Induction of alternative states of consciousness proceeds at the group level. There is no hint of direct give and take on an emotional level and no experience or communication of individual empathy. Paradoxically, however, the initiate ends up finding his or her own voice, in the literal as well as figurative sense of the term. The product of initiation is highly individual and personal—a unique way of singing and dancing. It is, however, achieved for the purpose of reintegrating the person into the traditional social group and internalizing its values. Enculturation prevails over individuation, but individuation constitutes an essential stepping stone in acquiring a true Salish Indian identity.

Another remarkable aspect of the Salish Spirit Dance ceremony is its adaptability to the exigencies of time and place. Traditionally, these experiences served to strengthen tribal identity and coherence. In the face of massive penetration of goods, services, and entertainment from the dominant North American society, Salish ritualists and elders modified, updated, and streamlined the winter spirit dance ritual so as to focus it on restoring social solidarity and counteracting alienation, meaninglessness, distress, and despair. In this way, a culturally indigenous sophisticated antidote has been created against external threats that threaten this small tribal society and so many others.

Converging Evidence From Another Part of the World: Lao Hmong Shamanic Healing Ceremonials for Opium Addicts

The Lao Hmong, displaced from their ancestral lands and housed in refugee camps in Northern Thailand, have experienced an exacerbation of opium smoking in their midst. Standard Western detoxification programs have proved to be ineffective. One of us (WGJ) has participated in the development of a pilot program that has combined modern medical services by an international health staff with the traditional healing rituals of local shamans (Jilek & Jilek-Aall, 1990, 2004). To that end, the Lao myth of the Opium Goddess was revived and enacted. Opium Goddess is believed to ensnare men by her sexual charms in the course of narcotic dreams so as to make them addicted. Her allure and that of opium was counteracted in two ways. A miniature palace was built for the Opium Goddess so as to entice her to take up residence in it. At the same time, opium addicts were assembled by the shaman and made to swear a solemn oath never to use opium again. The patients were then exorcised. A series of rituals followed as the patients were literally tied together with a live pig that was to be sacrificed in order to act as messenger to the spirit world and to negotiate for the liberation of the addicts' souls held in heaven. A shaman in a trance state then embarked on the elaborate enactment of a journey to heaven in order to help bring about the release of addicts' souls, a process that takes several hours. Omens were consulted, and a propitious time was chosen to first bury and then burn the palace of the Opium Goddess. The rising smoke was considered indicative of Opium Goddess's return to her celestial abode. The charred remains of the palace were buried underneath the earth, together with the paraphernalia for smoking opium, so as to remove them from the world of the living. The ceremony ended with a communal meal, and the sacrificial pig was consumed by the shamans, patients, and health staff. Compared with standard detoxification, the program just described showed surprisingly high completion rates, amounting to between 80 and 90 percent of the participants.

Despite specific cultural trappings, several themes first encountered among the Salish Indians are discernible among the Lao. Thus, burning, followed by liberation, is akin to a death and rebirth experience. Addicts, however, are cast in a passive role, and the dramatic and emotional activity in a trance is performed by the shaman. In both locations, states of alternate consciousness are central to the healing procedure. Among the Salish Indians, however, the candidates for initiation have to expend prodigious effort and endure uncommon stress in order to experience a vision and receive their spirit song. The Lao Hmong opium addicts remained spectators while the drama of luring and expelling the Opium Goddess unfolded. The shaman with his power of inducing his own trance was the central figure and hero of the morality play that pitted good against evil and enslavement against liberation. Addicts emerged as its beneficiaries, provided that they succeeded in keeping the solemn oath that they had taken.

Effects of Traditional Healing:
Its Indications and Limitations

Do traditional healing methods "work"? Under what conditions are they effective, ineffective, or harmful? These are fundamental questions that, so far, have been exceedingly difficult to answer unequivocally and directly.

Traditional healing encompasses a multitude of approaches practiced in virtually all regions of the world and applied to a host of conditions of psychic distress, disability, and impairment. Moreover, for a long time a virtual chasm has existed between modern mental health professionals and their counterparts in traditional, often small-scale, isolated cultures. The term "witch doctor" did not disappear from the professional literature until recently, and the ministrations of indigenous healers were often denigrated and dismissed on an a priori basis as being useless or worse. Practitioners of traditional healing arts are well aware of these attitudes, and they remember the suppression and persecution of healers by colonial and other Western as well as Soviet authorities. Understandably, such experiences have predisposed healers to caution, defensiveness, and secrecy. Moreover, many of the healing categories are regarded as sacred or arcane. For these reasons, healers' professional acumen and skill are considered secrets to be jealously guarded, lest they be exploited by competitors and healers' livelihood be threatened. As ceremonies and rituals take place in specific cultural contexts, introduction of extraneous observers and of their instruments and methods may so thoroughly alter the situation as to distort and invalidate any results to be obtained. It is therefore no surprise that opportunities for firsthand observation, let alone for systematic, objective, and independent evaluation, have been slow to appear. Even now, it is hard to initiate dialogues and collaborations with native healers and to communicate credibly an attitude of respect for and interest in healers' operations and their effects. Thus, a tangle of political, interpersonal, conceptual, and methodological issues must be resolved before the customary standards of objective treatment evaluation can be conclusively and realistically applied to indigenous healing.

It is therefore not surprising that most of the information extant on the effects of healers' procedures is based on descriptive qualitative accounts by clinicians and/or anthropologists, as exemplified by the two reports recapitulated in the foregoing sections of this chapter. Attempts to design actual comparative studies of several treatment methods or to include appropriate no treatment or placebo control groups have apparently not yet been reported. Jilek (1993) surveyed the relevant evidence spanning over half a century, coming from all parts of the globe, and encompassing a plethora of techniques. Three generalizations have received substantial empirical support, as follows:

1. In general, tradition-based practices provide effective therapeutic management for neurotic disorders (especially with dissociation and conversion symptoms), for psychosomatic and somatoform disorders, for psychosocial problems, and for reactive depressions, including self-destructive behavior (Jilek, 1993, p. 363).

2. Traditional medicine practices, ritual procedures, and sedative herbal remedies are effective in the treatment of reactive and transient psychoses and psychosis-like, culture-bound syndromes. Traditional intervention by protective measures and by reassuring, anxiety-alleviating ceremonies involving kinspeople often avoids segregation of the patient from the family. This may prevent chronic psychotic developments, which are known to be less common in tradition-directed than in modern industrialized societies (Jilek, 1993, p. 363).

3. In the treatment, rehabilitation, and prevention of alcohol and drug dependence, therapeutic practices based on indigenous cultural and religious traditions have, in many instances, been as successful and sometimes more successful than "official" treatment and rehabilitation programs (Jilek, 1993, p. 364).

In the case of schizophrenia and epilepsy, traditional treatment practices, however, appear to be of limited usefulness at best, perhaps as auxiliary procedures to modern chemotherapy. There is, moreover, a major cause for concern lest demonstrably effective modern treatments be delayed, thereby compromising their effectiveness and benefit. A limited number of interventions in traditional societies are abusive and harmful. Prolonged physical restraint is a case in point, and various mythical and other cultural beliefs about epilepsy, schizophrenia, and other disorders may foster rejection, mistreatment, and avoidance (cf. Jilek, 1993).

Study of psychotherapeutic interventions in other cultures is an enterprise in progress, and questions about their consequences and effects have not as yet been definitively answered. Still, a great deal of information

has accrued, and we now know that techniques for the effective alleviation of psychological distress and disability are not the monopoly of
modern technologically advanced and economically prosperous civilizations. As for the cultures in which these folk interventions originated,
the challenge is not to discard the old and import the new, but rather to
blend and eventually to integrate the preserved and accumulated heritage with the best that the scientifically oriented therapies have to offer.
As Sartorius (1979) pointed out, traditional forms of mental health care
have not yet been fully utilized. Therefore, they must continue to be
intensively investigated. At the same time, steps should be taken to incorporate the skills and services of traditional healers into mental health
programs. The World Health Organization adopted a joint declaration
with UNESCO in 1978 in Alma Ata, Kazakhstan, that provided official
recognition to traditional indigenous healers in primary mental health
care (Jilek, 1993; Tseng, 2001). This objective, however, still remains to
be fully implemented.

Active Ingredients of Traditional Healing

Beneath their visible, culturally specific trappings, what are the effective
components of the therapies we have reviewed? Several specific features recur
in descriptions of healers' modus operandi.

First among them is the compatibility of the techniques to the culture
in which they are practiced. They do not need to be introduced, justified,
or explained. Instead, such interventions intuitively make sense and are
not likely to arouse resistance or skepticism. Second, healers combine psychological, medical, and spiritual functions, an advantage that permits to
relieve distress for the entire person. Third, to a greater extent than most
modern therapists, healers tend to capitalize on their confidence and cha-
risma, even to the point of employing tricks and sleights of hand (Fischer,
1995; Krippner, 2002; Walsh, 1990). Thus, the healer's social and personal
impact is increased, and positive expectations are aroused on the part of
the recipient of such services. Inducing altered states of consciousness
and/or promoting emotional arousal by other means is part and parcel of
the armamentarium of a great many, though not all, cultural systems of
healing. Fourth, traditional healing is typically not an exclusive matter
between the therapist and the patient. Instead, it concerns the patient's
in-group, including members of the patient's family, clan, and community

who join forces with the healer in defining the problem and deciding on the remedial course of action (cf. Nathan, 1995). Fifth, as illustrated in the previous sections of this chapter, therapeutic intent is often incorporated into established and well-known ceremonies or rituals. Sixth, instead of assuming a detached and impersonal stance, healers do not refrain from giving authoritative advice and directly or indirectly manipulating the client's social environment.

More specifically, the techniques of traditional healing involve naming and explaining the person's affliction in culturally meaningful and readily understandable terms. Divination may be used as a quasi-diagnostic procedure, and an appeal is made to supernatural powers. Divination methods, however, also rely on social network information, experience, and practiced intuitive judgment. Suggestion is widely utilized, implicitly and explicitly, both to strengthen expectations of favorable outcome and to confirm the success of treatment upon its completion. These components of therapy may be supplemented by sacrificial rites in order to placate any spirits that may have been offended and bolstered by culturally validated symbols, such as charms, amulets, and talismans. Under the impact of all of these elements, affective release is often triggered that is akin to psychodramatic abreaction, and this response is further increased by an accepting and empathetic audience.

It is easy to imagine that some of the trappings of indigenous healing may appear both alien and alienating to many contemporary Western psychotherapists, immersed as they are in the scientific ethos of their professions. Tobie Nathan (1995), a prominent Parisian ethnopsychiatrist, has been outspoken in admonishing psychotherapists who work across culture lines not to dismiss or explain away their clients' or native healers' beliefs. According to Nathan, an empathetic and receptive attitude toward these beliefs is indispensable for therapeutic impact and effectiveness. Specifically, Nathan exhorted Western therapists to respect the gods, rituals, healers, and artifacts of their clients' traditional cultures. Only in this way can a healing influence be achieved, compounded as it is of social impact achieved in a culturally plausible manner. Nathan's radical proposals have been embodied in a descriptive account of Yoruba healers' operations and rationale that is intentionally free of analysis and interpretation (Nathan & Hounkpatin, 1998). Without saying it in so many words, Nathan and Hounkpatin invite the reader to learn about healers' outlook on their own terms and not to rush to impose a presumably superior and more scientific framework upon it.

However, the issue of quality control needs to be addressed. Both traditional healers and modern psychotherapists have the potential of doing good, but also of inflicting harm. Skeptical observers of the traditional healing enterprise have raised the question of relevance of these services in rapidly modernizing societies (Scharfetter, 1985) and have pointed to instances of invervention that were not just irrelevant and ineffective, but pathogenic (Claver, 1976). Working with Cambodian refugees in Tahiland, Hiegel (1994) was able to observe the contrast between the operations of experienced and genuine healers and those of quacks and charlatans whom he described as unscrupulous, untrained, or self-trained people solely motivated by fame and money. They employed violent, dramatic, and protentially dangerous methods to tackle tasks, such as curing psychosis, from which legitimate healers generally refrain.

Blending Traditional Healing Into Counseling and Psychotherapy: Initial Steps Toward Eventual Integration

A recent compendium of accounts of non-Western therapies and healing (Moodley & West, 2005) is consonant with Nathan's orientation. It endeavors to provide as much factual information as possible about prominent approaches to therapeutic intervention in Africa and Asia as well as within the native cultures of the Americas and of Australia.

The intent of the volume has been to examine what within these traditions of healing may be useful to psychotherapy and counseling in Euro-American settings. To this end, Sima and West (2005) in Tanzania have embarked on a dialogue between modern counselors and traditional healers in order to share information and remove misgivings and mistrust on both sides so as to facilitate cooperation and coordination of therapeutic efforts. These efforts are based on the recognition that "the existence of traditional and cultural problems necessitates the support of traditional healers, whereas, particularly in the urban metropolitan areas, modern and postmodern stresses require the help of counselors and psychotherapists" (Sima & West, 2005, p. 324) Vontress (2005) has pointed to potential coalescence between the holistic emphasis of healers in Africa and the current rediscovery of the importance of spiritual aspects of experience by North American therapists and counselors (e.g., Fukuyama & Sevig, 2002; West, 2005). Moreover, emphasis upon organismic unity is in keeping with recent advances (Grawe, 2007) toward neuropsychotherapy that have the potential of eventually spanning the arc within the person between the brain and culture.

Fischer (1995) has emphasized that "shamans can teach social and behavioral scientists ways how individuals as well as societies can regulate their well-being. They can teach psychotherapists the importance of shifting attention, that change is possible by self-healing mechanisms, the capability of which is within oneself; or that by using mental imagery one can stimulate well-being by reconstructing and transforming experience" (p. 142).

Traditional healing has been slanted toward fitting suffering individuals into their social group, whereas therapists in Europe and North America have tended to capitalize upon their clients' unique and autonomous selves (Draguns, 2002). A closer scrutiny of healers' activities may help psychotherapists redress the balance and attend more to the issues of estrangement, loneliness, isolation, and anomie that, to varying degrees, affect modern societies and communities. As Laungani (2005) put it, "the multiplicity of healing strategies should not be seen as a disadvantage. In fact, they provide different cultures with exciting opportunities to learn valuable lessons from one another. It is hoped that such a course of action will not only lead to a better understanding of different healing strategies, but may also bring cultures together" (p. 147).

Conclusions

Psychotherapy has been construed as "a procedure that is sociocultural in its ends and interpersonal in its means" (Draguns, 1975, p. 273). Moreover, "it is embedded in a broader, less visible, but no less real cultural context of shared social learning, store of meanings, symbols, and implicit assumptions concerning the nature of social living" (Ibid, p. 273). This characterization applies par excellence to the procedures surveyed in this chapter. The provisional conclusion is that by and large the indigenous treatment techniques do make a difference in the milieus in which they are practiced and that this difference tends to be beneficial. It is dependent for its effectiveness on the sociocultural context, and as yet we do not have a complete understanding of the links between interventions and cultural features. In the meantime, some misconceptions have been dispelled. Thus, there is no longer any justification for believing that a psychological disturbance is an intrinsic characteristic of effective healers or that healers' operations are inapplicable and irrelevant in modern settings. Instead there are reasons to believe that traditional healing and modern psychotherapies will coexist for a long time to come. If that is so, a modus vivendi for these two broad approaches of helping people in psychic distress should be worked out. Equally urgent, flexible research designs combining quantitative and qualitative methods should be systematically applied in order to sort out fact and fiction in this vitally important area of inquiry.

References

Barrucand, D. (1970). *La catharsis dans le theatre, la psychoanalyse et la psychotherapie de groupe* [Catharsis in the theatre, in psychoanalysis and in group psychotherapy]. Paris: Editeurs EPI.

Boyer, L. B. (1962). Remarks on the personality of shamans, with special reference to the Apache of the Mescalero Indian reservation. In W. Muensterberger & S. Axelrad (Eds.), *The psychoanalytic study of society, 2,* 233–235.

Claver, B.-G. (1976). Problèmes de guérissage en Côte d'Ivoire, *Annales Médico-Psychologiques, 134*(1), 23–30.

Draguns, J. G. (1975). Resocialization into culture: The complexities of taking a worldwide view of psychotherapy. In R. W. Brislin, S. Bochner, & W. J. Lonner (Eds.), *Cross-cultural perspectives on learning* (pp. 273–279). Beverly Hills, CA: Sage.

Draguns, J. G. (2002). From empirically supported treatments around the world to psychotherapy as a mirror of culture: Tasks and challenges for international research on psychotherapy. *International Clinical Psychology, 4*(3), 7–9.

Draguns, J. G. (2004). From speculation through description toward investigation: A prospective glimpse at cultural research in psychotherapy. In U. P. Gielen, J. M. Fish, & J. G. Draguns (Eds.), *Handbook of culture, therapy, and healing* (pp. 369–388). Mahwah, NJ: Lawrence Erlbaum Associates.

Fabrega, H., Jr., & Silver, D. B. (1973). *Illness and shamanistic curing in Zinacantan.* Stanford, CA: Stanford University Press.

Fischer, M. (1995). Shamanism in Alaska. In L. L. Adler & B. R. Mukherji (Eds.), *Spirit versus scalpel: Traditional healing and modern psychotherapy* (pp. 137–144). Westport, CT: Bergin & Garvey.

Fukuyama, M. A., & Sevig, T. D. (2002). Spirituality in counseling across cultures: Many rivers to the sea. In P. B. Pedersen, J. G. Draguns, W. J. Lonner, & J. E. Trimble (Eds.), *Counseling across cultures* (5th ed., pp. 273–296). Thousand Oaks, CA: Sage.

Graham, M. (2005). *Maat*: An African-centered paradigm for psychological and spiritual healing. In R. Moodley & W. West (Eds.), *Integrating traditional healing practices into counseling and psychotherapy* (pp. 210–220). Thousand Oaks, CA: Sage.

Grawe, K. (2007). *Neuropsychotherapy: How the neurosciences inform effective psychotherapy.* Mahwah, NJ: Lawrence Erlbaum Associates.

Heinze, R. I. (1982). Shamans as mediums: Toward a definition of different states of consciousness. *Phoenix Journal of Transpersonal Anthropology, 6,* 25–44.

Hiegel, J. P. (1994). Use of indigenous concepts and healers in the care of refugees: Some experiences from the Thai border camps. In A. J. Marsella, T. Bornemann,

S. Ekblad, & J. Orley (Eds.) (1994), *Amidst peril and pain. The mental health and well-being of world's refugees* (pp. 293–310). Washington, D.C.: American Psychological Association.

Hoppal, M. (1992). Shamanism: An archaic and/or recent system of beliefs. In A. I. Siikala & M. Hoppal (Eds.), *Studies on shamanism* (pp. 117–131). Helsinki, Finland: Finnish Anthropological Society.

Jilek, W. G. (1982). *Indian healing—Shamanic ceremonialism in the Pacific Northwest today.* Surrey, BC: Hancock House.

Jilek, W. G. (1993). Traditional medicine relevant to psychiatry. In N. Sartorius, G. de Giralomo, G. Andrews, G. A. German, & L. Eisenberg (Eds.), *Treatment of mental disorders* (pp. 341–383). Washington, DC: American Psychiatric Press (published on behalf of the World Health Organization).

Jilek, W. G. (2005). Transforming the shaman: Changing Western views of shamanism and altered states of consciousness. *Investigacion en Salud, 7,* 8–15.

Jilek. W. G., & Jilek-Aall, L. (1978). The psychiatrist and his shaman colleague: Cross-cultural collaboration with traditional Amerindian therapists. *Journal of Operational Psychiatry, 9*(2), 32–39.

Jilek, W. G., & Jilek-Aall, L. (1990). The mental health relevance of traditional medicine shamanism in refugee camps of northern Thailand. *Curare, 13,* 217–224.

Jilek, W. G. & Jilek-Aall, L. (2002). Shamanic beliefs, practices, and messianic movements among the Hmong people of Southeast Asia. *Shaman, 10,* 83–112.

Jilek, W. G., & Jilek-Aall, L. (2004). Lao Hmong healing ceremonial for opium addicts. *Viennese Ethnomedicine Newsletter, 7,* 15–20.

Jilek-Aall, L., & Jilek, W. G. (1983). *Therapeutischer Synkretismus in latein-amerikanischen Heilkulten* [Therapeutic syncretism in Latin American healing cults]. In J. Sterly (Ed.), *Ethnomedizin und Medizingeschichte* (pp. 297–310). Berlin: Verlag Mensch und Leben.

Krippner, R. (2002). Conflicting perspectives on shamans and shamanism: Points and counterpoints. *American Psychologist, 57,* 962–978.

Laungani, P. (2005). Hindu spirituality and healing practices. In R. Moodley & W. West (Eds.), *Integrating traditional healing practices into counseling and psychotherapy* (pp. 138–147). Thousand Oaks, CA: Sage.

Leighton, A. H., Lambo, T. H., Hughes, C. C., Leighton, D. C., Murphy, J. M., & Macklin, D. B. (1963). *Psychiatric disorders among the Yoruba.* Ithaca, NY: Cornell University Press.

Moodley, R., & West, W. (Eds.). (2005). *Integrating traditional healing practices into counseling and psychotherapy.* Thousand Oaks, CA: Sage.

Murphy, J. M. (1964). Psychotherapeutic aspects of shamanism on St. Lawrence Island, Alaska. In A. Kiev (Ed.), *Magic, faith, and healing: Studies in primitive psychiatry today* (pp. 53–83). New York: Free Press.

Nathan, T. (1995). *L'influence qui guérit* [The healing influence]. Paris: Odile Jacob.

Nathan, T., & Hounkpatin, L. (1998). *La guérison Yoruba* [Yoruba healing]. Paris: Odile Jacob.

Neher, A. (1961). Auditory driving observed with scalp electrodes in normal subjects. *EEG and Clinical Neurophysiology, 13,* 449–451.

Neher, A. (1962). A physiological explanation of unusual behavior involving drums. *Human Biology, 34,* 151–160.

Opler, M. (1959). Dream analysis in Ute Indian therapy. In M. Opler (Ed.), *Culture and mental health—Cross-cultural studies* (pp. 97–117). New York: Macmillan.

Prince, R. (2004). Western psychotherapy and the Yoruba: Problems of insight and nondirective technique. In U. P. Gielen, J. M. Fish, & J. G. Draguns (Eds.), *Handbook of culture, therapy, and healing* (pp. 311–320). Mahwah, NJ: Lawrence Erlbaum Associates.

Sartorius, N. (1979). Cross-cultural psychiatry. In K. P. Kisker (Ed.), *Psychiatrie der Gegenwart. Volume I: Grundlagen und Methoden der Psychiatrie* (pp. 711–737). Berlin: Springer.

Scharfetter, C. (1985). Schamane: Zeuge alter Kultur – wieder belebbar? (Shaman as a witness to an old culture. Can he be revived?) *Schweizerische Zeitschrift für Neurologie, Neurochirurgie and Psychiatrie, 136,* 81–95.

Sima, R. G., & West, W. (2005). Sharing healing secrets. Counselors and traditional healers in conversation. In R. Moodley & W. West (Eds.), *Integrating tradtional practices into counseling and psychotherapy* (pp. 316–325). Thousand Oaks, CA: Sage Publications.

Tseng, W.-S. (2001). *Handbook of cultural psychiatry.* San Diego: Academic Press.

Vontress, C. (2005). Animism: Foundation of traditional healing in sub-Saharan Africa. In R. Moodley & W. West (Eds.), *Integrating traditional healing practices into counseling and psychotherapy* (pp. 124–137). Thousand Oaks, CA: Sage.

Walsh, R. N. (1990). *The spirit of shamanism.* Los Angeles: Jeremy R. Tarcher.

West, W. (2005). Crossing the line between talking therapies and spiritual healing. In R. Moodley & W. West (Eds.), *Integrating traditional healing practices into counseling and psychotherapy* (pp. 316–325). Thousand Oaks, CA: Sage.

Suggested Readings

Adler, L. L., & Mukherrji, B. R. (Eds.). (1995). *Spirit versus scalpel. Traditional healing and modern psychotherapy.* Westport, CT: Bergin & Garvey.

This compendium includes chapters on traditional non-Western healing practices and on contemporary Western approaches to psychotherapy and their sometimes implicit and hidden premises.

Jilek, W. G. (2000). Traditional non-Western folk healing as relevant to psychiatry. In M. G. Gelder, J. Lopez-Ibor, J. J., & N. Andreasen (Eds.), *New Oxford textbook of psychiatry* (Vol. 2, pp. 1509–1513). New York: Oxford University Press.

A concentrated overview of healing practices and their applicability in providing clinical services.

Laungani, P. (2004). *Asian perspectives in counseling and psychotherapy.* New York: Brunner-Routledge.

A highly personal integration of Eastern and Western traditions of making people whole by an erudite, bicultural psychotherapist and counselor.

Marsella, A. J., & White, G. (Eds.). (1982). *Cultural conceptions of mental health and therapy.* Dordrecht, The Netherlands: Reidel.
A classical account of the fundamental assumptions on which all therapies, from folk healing to modern interventions, rest.

Moodley, R., & West, W. (Eds.). (2005). *Integrating traditional healing practices into counseling and psychotherapy.* Thousand Oaks.
An attempt to broaden and enrich the armamentarium of techniques and outlooks of contemporary counselors on the basis of the experiences with traditional approaches from around the world.

Tseng, W.-S., & Streltzer, J. (Eds.). (2001). *Culture & psychotherapy. A guide to clinical practice.* Washington, DC: American Psychiatric Press.
A collection of case studies of culturally rooted presenting problems counteracted by culturally sensitive means, including traditional healing approaches.

Walsh, R. N. (1990). *The spirit of shamanism.* Los Angeles: Jeremy R. Tarcher.
A detailed account of the training techniques, experiences, states of mind, and healing practices of the traditional shaman.

15

Deepening Listening
The Marriage of Buddha and Freud

Jeffrey B. Rubin

Contents

"My, the lights are bright in here," a client said to me in her first session many years ago.

Where are lights bright? I wondered to myself.

As she discussed what brought her to therapy and what she was struggling with in her life—a feeling of self-contempt and never being "good enough"—I listened on two channels, focusing on what she was *consciously* saying *and* on her suggestive image.

Lights are bright in a police station, I eventually thought to myself. When I asked her if coming to therapy made her feel "grilled under the lights by the cops," she smiled nervously and told me about her fears of being judged in therapy. Because she always judged herself, she assumed that a stranger would have to judge her. After my question, she noticeably relaxed and spoke more freely and openly.

Listening is an essential component of the psychotherapeutic process. It is indispensable to all that the therapist does, whether she is a client-centered Rogerian or a psychoanalyst. In either case, careful listening aids the therapist in decoding the client's unconscious communications and empathetically understanding his or her life. An equally important aspect of listening is the therapist's awareness of his or her own internal emotional and physical reactions to the client. In addition, therapeutic listening is infinitely enhanced when the therapist can access his or her own imaginative capacities.

"In all our vast [therapeutic] literature," notes Coltart (1992), "very little attention has been paid to attention" (p. 180). Psychotherapeutic listening, like Poe's "purloined letter," may be neglected because it is right in front of us.

Freud (1912) delineated the ideal state of mind for therapists to listen, what he called "evenly hovering" or "evenly suspended attention." This is a state in which the therapist is alert and receptive and attentive to both what the client is saying and his or her own reactions. It aids the therapist in being both grounded and flexible. Without evenly hovering attention, the therapist, writes Freud (1912), "is in danger of never finding anything but what he already knows" (pp. 111–112).

No one in the therapeutic literature has critiqued, amended, or revised Freud's seminal recommendations. Yet, neither Freud nor his contemporaries or successors who explored this territory (e.g., Ferenczi, Horney, Fromm, Bion, and Langs) offered positive recommendations for *how* to cultivate this elusive yet *eminently trainable* state of mind. Freud and Bion, for example, focused on the *obstructions* to facilitating it—what *not* to do (Rubin, 1996). The former indicated that the analyst should neither try too hard to prematurely figure out the meaning of the patient's communications—a state of mind he called "reflection"—nor should the analyst attempt to formulate or write about a case prematurely. Bion encouraged therapists to listen "without memory, desire or understanding"—that is, without preconceptions about who the client is or expectations for what should happen in the treatment.

The fact that no one in the psychotherapeutic literature has formulated how one actually cultivates "evenly hovering attention" leaves an important gap in therapy training and technique. If therapists were trained to really listen in this way to each client, not only would the clinical data more readily challenge and expand their own most cherished formulations, but they would find it more difficult to maintain allegiance to single schools of psychotherapeutic thought. And our understanding of our own *countertransference*—those emotional factors that interfere with our capacity to understand and help our clients—would be enhanced. Misunderstandings in multicultural therapy or counseling have many sources, including differences between therapist or counselor and client due to lack of familiarity with different value systems and ways of life, misreading of nonverbal signals, and culturally based misunderstandings of symbols and metaphors. In quieting the mind and illuminating our hidden assumptions and deepening our attunement to other people, meditation can improve the listening skills of therapists and counselors in multicultural situations. In terms of cross-cultural therapy, not only would we be more attuned to tone of voice and subtle, nonverbal communications, we would have a heightened awareness of the hidden cultural assumptions, beliefs, and projections that can create misunderstandings. And the therapist would also have greater access to her own creativity and capacity for inner wisdom.

What Buddhism terms *meditation*—nonjudgmental attention to what is happening moment-to-moment—cultivates exactly the extraordinary, yet accessible, state of mind Freud was depicting.

Meditation fosters heightened attentiveness and equanimity, self-awareness, and tolerance of feeling. In training one's capacity to notice ordinarily obscure phenomena—ranging from fleeting somatic sensations to subliminal thoughts, feelings and fantasies, to emergent and inchoate, creative images and insights—meditation offers user-friendly techniques for accessing "evenly hovering attention," which could facilitate psychotherapeutic listening. Not only does meditation short-circuit the deeply ingrained tendency of most of us to excessively criticize ourselves, but it increases access to our capacity for empathy, creativity, and intuition. This is an extraordinary—and relatively untapped—resource for therapists, providing the foundation for genuine psychotherapeutic listening.

But genuine psychotherapeutic listening—listening to the *latent* and metaphoric as well as the *manifest* and literal meaning—requires one other quality: the capacity to *decode* or translate what we hear on various channels or levels at once—which meditation does not do.

A college student tells me of a conversation with her Buddhist teacher during which they talk about her wish to deepen her study of Buddhism by going to a monastery in Asia for a retreat.

She doesn't sound very enthusiastic. And I'm not sure why.

"Tell me more about what you both actually said," I say.

"It's funny you ask that," she says, shifting on my couch. "I told him 'I *don't* want to go, I mean I want to go.' She pauses. "Is that a Freudian slip?" she asks, with a look suggesting she doesn't need an answer.

"What comes to mind about *not* wanting to go?" I ask. "I'm not sure," she says. "I may be pushing myself, doing it for the wrong reasons—because my boyfriend wants me to. And he may have other motives beside my well-being. Like wanting to justify what he's into. And my teacher didn't ask me if I had any hesitation—he just assumed that I wanted to go."

It is tempting to hear only the surface of what the student said to her Buddhist teacher, just as the teacher did. But then we might miss what is underneath.

"Don't get me wrong—I love Buddhism, and it's changed my life," she continues. "But it is not a panacea and I sense certain problems with it. It can be too detached, antiemotional, and as I've told you—I have had quite enough of that with my intellectual parents to last several lifetimes."

"I hope that Freud and his pupils will push their ideas to their utmost limits, so that we may learn what they are," writes William James in a letter of September 28, 1909, to Théodore Flournoy. "Obviously 'symbolism' is a most dangerous method" (James, 1920, pp. 327–328).

Why is it so *dangerous*? Because it reveals that we often *say* more than we *know*.

Without attention to the *symbolic* aspect of listening, my client's ambivalence about studying Buddhism abroad would go unnoticed.

In this chapter I will draw on the best of the Western psychotherapeutic and Eastern meditative traditions to delineate the two ingredients of optimal listening. I will attempt to illuminate how therapists could use meditation to cultivate "evenly hovering attention" and deepen their ability to understand themselves and their clients. I will also suggest how to deepen one's practice of meditation. Then I will examine how a Western psychotherapeutic understanding of the *language* and *logic* of the *unconscious* complements and enriches meditative attention. Although I will focus on perspectives and insights gleaned from classical and post-Freudian psychoanalysis, my remarks are applicable, with the appropriate changes, to other schools of psychotherapeutic thought, including Rogerian therapy.

Coltart (1992) claims that the practice of paying attention is the same whether taught by a Buddhist meditation master or an experienced analyst. But they are actually very different. Psychoanalysis lacks an appreciation for cultivating two qualities that meditation fosters, namely *concentration* and *equanimity.* These are heightened states of focus and acceptance that are not even mapped in Western psychologies. Explaining the meditative process in some detail—what it is and how to do it—will illuminate this.

Misunderstandings about meditation abound. It has been viewed as everything from a "self-improvement technique" to a "passive withdrawal from the world" (Welwood, 2000, p. 75).

"Meditation" is not one thing, such as a technique to lower stress or blood pressure or quiet the mind. In the classical Buddhist *Visudhimagga: The Path of Purification,* for example, there are at least 40 potential objects of meditation (Buddhaghosa, 1976, p. 99).

There are many kinds of meditation ranging from classical Theravadin Buddhist techniques of concentrating and focusing the mind and deconstructing take-for-granted conceptions of self, to the emphasis in Zen on being-this-moment, to Tibetan Buddhist strategies for transforming emotions. In this chapter I will focus on Vipassana meditation, a core technique of classical Buddhism. *Vipassana* is a Pali word meaning separating things into their component parts, seeing into them and gaining insight.

Take several moments to "turn your eyes inward" and look into your own depths and observe your mind ... perhaps the first thing you notice is how difficult it is to pay attention in any sustained way. Your mind is probably filled with endless chatter: wandering thoughts, fleeting images and fantasies, transient somatic sensations. You invariably lose track of what is occurring and wander off and are emotionally hijacked by such things as criticisms of yourself, anticipations of the future, or regrets from the past. Close inspection of your actual experience reveals that your typical mode of perception is, to an unrecognized extent, selective, distorted, and outside voluntary control. You often operate on automatic pilot, reacting to a conscious and unconscious blend of fallacious associations, anticipatory fantasies, and habitual fears that make you unaware of the actual texture of your experience. Your mind is often foggy, seldom clear and serene. Buddhism likens the mind to a monkey endlessly jumping from branch to branch. It is difficult to see or think clearly when monkey mind prevails.

Because ordinary consciousness is usually too turbulent, preoccupied, and constricted to be attentive and focused, the mind must be trained to focus. Meditation[1] is one deeply powerful way of doing that. Meditation is the training of moment-to-moment attentiveness—awareness without judgment of what actually happens to us instant-by-instant. Meditation involves greeting life—here and now—with focus, care, and respect. In a meditative state we perform each task with wholeheartedness.

The *Mahāsatipatthāna Sutra: The Greater Discourse on the Foundations of Mindfulness* (Buddha, 1987) is the core Buddhist text on the meditative process. There are four "foundations to mindfulness," according to the Buddha:

1. Awareness of the body in four positions (walking, standing, sitting, and lying down)
2. Awareness of "feelings" (*vedanā*)—which refers to physical (or emotional) sensations of pleasantness, unpleasantness, or neutrality rather than what we call emotions
3. Awareness of states of mind—for example, whether we are clear or distracted, angry or calm, contracted or spacious
4. Awareness of "mind-objects"—which ranges from Buddhist notions about the hindrances to meditation (sense desire, ill will, sloth and torpor, worry, and doubt) to the five "aggregates" or elements that make up every moment of experience (form, feeling, perception, mental formation, and consciousness) to the Seven Factors of Enlightenment (mindfulness, investigation, energy, delight, tranquillity, concentration, and equanimity) to the Four Noble Truths (the reality and pervasiveness of suffering, the cause of it, the solution, and the path to end it)

The meditative process, according to classical Buddhism, consists of two steps or stages: *concentration* and *insight*. In concentrative meditation we focus on a single object, such as the breath at the nostrils or abdomen with whole-hearted attentiveness. It is an *exclusive* state of mind—it excludes everything but the single object we are focusing on. We sit physically still either in a lotus (or half lotus or an upright) position and pay attention to the immediate flow of moment-to-moment experience—attending to the breathing process, silently noting the experience of inhalation and exhalation at the nostrils or abdomen. The effort is not to control the breathing but to be attentive to it. Concentrative meditation cultivates mental focus. In traditional Buddhist practice developed by the Buddha, we often begin with concentrative meditation. When attentiveness is developed and stabilized, then *insight* meditation is practiced.

Insight meditation involves an *inclusive* state of mind in which we attend to the changing objects of our experience—nonjudgmentally noting and then silently labeling whatever thoughts, feelings, fantasies, or somatic sensations that we experience moment-by-moment such as "planning," "judging," "regretting," and so forth. If we feel lost or confused, unable to label the thoughts, feelings, sensation, or fantasies that arise, then that experience is labeled "confusion." If we judge our inattentiveness or thinking, we label that "judging."

As attentiveness increases and becomes more refined, we can use the developing capacity to focus the mind to observe the nature of our consciousness. Like a movie that is slowed down, we can see how one frame of our consciousness leads to another—how particular feelings condition specific reactions. We might become aware, for example, that we are making expansive plans after feeling diminished. Or we might realize that we get angry at a loved one when we feel scared about his or her safety.

As our awareness becomes clearer and more focused, we experience a sense of psychological spaciousness: We do not become as entangled in reactive patterns of feeling and thinking. When praised, we might allow ourselves to bask in a warm glow instead of automatically devaluing the person who praised us. *Psychological resilience* is cultivated: When we are unsettled or distracted, we regain clarity more quickly. We can begin to notice within the first few seconds that we are unthinkingly attacking ourselves—thus avoiding getting emotionally hijacked and caught in a downward spiral of self-contempt and self-destructive behavior.

Shinzen Young (2006a), a contemporary teacher of Buddhist meditation, suggests that meditation cultivates two predominant traits: *clarity* and *equanimity*. *Clarity* regards the components of your sensory experience—physical sensations or emotions in the body, visual thinking or internal images, and verbal thinking or internal talk—as they emerge moment-after-moment alone or in various combinations. *Equanimity* is an acceptance of whatever happens—the ability to meet whatever life brings—from strife to joyfulness—with calm acceptance.

Meditation lessens distractedness, quiets the inner pandemonium, reduces self-criticism, and cultivates the capacity to tolerate a greater range of emotions. It also helps you appreciate your life and miss less life. And it enables you to respond to pain without suffering and to fully experience and derive fulfillment from emotional and physical pleasure (Young, 2006b, p. 1).

There are several ways of deepening one's practice of meditation. First, one needs to learn the fundamentals and then practice them regularly over time. Having a regular practice is enormously helpful in doing this. It is helpful to *build* this into one's life, rather than *fit* it in. Whatever is built in—say, the hygienic routines you do in the morning—always get done. Much of what is "fitted in" doesn't. I have witnessed two sorts of traps when therapists try to develop a personal practice: doing meditation irregularly because one has no structure and rebelling because of having too rigid a structure.

What is helpful is a *flexible structure*, a set of guidelines about practicing that is realistic and based on one's interest and time availability and emotional capacity.

One also needs a nonjudgmental attitude—sometimes your best-laid plans of meditating will not come to fruition—and you need to remember that doing *some* meditation is better than not meditating at all. If you fail, begin again.

Seek ways of bringing meditation into your life outside formal periods of meditating. Mindfulness can be practiced washing the dishes, shaving, or eating a meal, as well as sitting quietly and observing your breath. Take one activity a week and do it mindfully, that is, with focus and clarity. Therapists can also meditate in between sessions. That way, they let go of the previous session and train themselves to be optimally receptive to the next person.

Daily practice—learning the fundamentals and then practicing them regularly over time—can be supplemented and deepened by periodic intensive, longer retreats. Retreats are a second powerful means of deepening one's practice. One can participate in retreats ranging from all-day sittings to 7- to 10-day residential retreats. *The Complete Guide to Buddhist America* (Morreale, 1998) and http://www.dharma.org and http://www.shinzen.org, among many other sites online, offer further information about meditation centers, teachers, and retreats.

Integrating Meditation and the Psychoanalytic Unconscious

Meditation provides an operationalizable technique for cultivating evenly hovering attention and thus deepening psychoanalytic listening. But one additional element is indispensable for ideal listening: understanding the *language*—and *logic*—of the unconscious, which Buddhism neglects and doesn't understand. Without an understanding of the complexity and richness of *unconscious communication*, one is hampered in one's understanding, as I mentioned earlier.

Two aspects of the meditative method interfere with listening in this way. Meditation focuses on *deconstructing* experience into its component parts, rather than decoding its *meaning*. And meditators without exposure to psychotherapy lack an understanding of the *language*—and *logic*—of the *unconscious*, the unknown as it lives and moves in us and through us, as Jung described it.

The Buddhist tradition contains a *conception* of the unconscious.[2] It is alert, in other words, to the way traces of old experiences and feelings shape—and sometimes limit—one in the present. But the *psychoanalytic* understanding of the unconscious—particularly the notion of the *primary process*—offers something more: namely a fertile and revolutionary conception of unconscious *communication*. This Buddhism lacks.

The Interpretation of Dreams, Freud wrote in 1931, "contains the most valuable of all the discoveries it has been my good fortune to make. Insights such as this falls to one's lot but once in a lifetime."[3] One of the most revolutionary ideas in *The Interpretation of Dreams* was that the mind is capable of thinking in two different ways or logics. There are, to use the title of one of Freud's papers, "two principles of mental functioning," which he called the *primary and secondary processes.* The *secondary process,* which Freud claimed was characteristic of conscious thought in waking life, is adapted to the realities of the external world. It is our ordinary rational and conventionally accepted way of thinking and speaking. You are using it as you think about and reflect on what you are now reading. The secondary process obeys the laws of grammar and formal logic, respects the differences between images, and acknowledges opposites and the categories (i.e., ordering principles) of space and time. My client's conscious wish to study meditation illustrates this type of thinking.

The *primary process,* on the other hand, is characteristic of *unconscious* mental activity and emerges in dreaming, artistic creations, neurotic symptom-formation, slips of the tongue (like my client made), and schizophrenic thinking. Opposites can—and often do—coexist in primary process communications. One can, for example, love *and* hate the same person or wish for *and* fear the same thing—like my client did. The primary process is oblivious to the categories of time and space—significant facets of our psychological past are, for example, very much "alive" in the present. The primary process is governed by processes Freud called *condensation* and *displacement.* In the former, one image in a dream or work of art or a patient's communications may stand for several different things, whereas in the latter, a person or image of lesser emotional significance can replace and symbolize another one of greater importance.

Let me illustrate both processes. A client dreams that she is sitting at the end of her bed, which is on the roof of a building. She sees her dog, who is her pal, jump from the building and plunge to the ground. As her dog plummets, she doesn't look like a dog—she resembles a blob. My client feels powerless and is devastated. We explore her associations to the images in the dream. Sitting on the edge of her bed on a roof has three meanings to her:

1. She feels that her personal life is "on edge"—in a precarious state;
2. She fears her bed will soon be "empty" if her husband takes a job abroad;
3. She is "falling" at work—losing the secure ground she used to have.

The presence of multiple meanings concentrated within one image illustrates the process of *condensation*. *Displacement*—the process of putting something of greater emotional meaning and intensity in a less important place—is illustrated in her associations to the dog plummeting. As she described this horrific sight, she said that as the dog fell toward the ground it no longer resembled itself. She sheepishly indicated that she felt that *she* was changing shape and feeling like a "blob"—aging and losing something vital, particularly an athleticism that was an important part of her former identity.

Even a meditatively trained mind that is highly concentrated, attentive, and focused is greatly handicapped in deciphering the dense and fertile texture of what it is attempting to understand without comprehending the *language and logic of the unconscious*. In a letter/poem to Thomas Butts on November 22, 1802, William Blake writes: "And a double vision is always with me/With my inward Eye 'tis an old Man grey/With my outward a Thistle across my way/ ... May God us keep/From Single vision and Newton's sleep" (quoted in Bentley, 2001, pp. 219–220). Blake was not only challenging an exclusively rationalistic view of the universe, he was pointing toward a more *inclusive* kind of perception. To truly understand what Freud called the "overdetermination" of internal and interpersonal experiences—the way the "same" thought, feeling, fantasy, or action may be motivated by various unconscious factors and have multiple unconscious meanings and functions—we need to have "double vision," to listen *stereophonically*, on at least two channels at once, to the manifest and the hidden meaning.

The Thirty-Seventh Zen Patriarch, Ling-yu of the Mazu lineage, lived in the ninth century. He was sitting up in bed with his eyes wide open one morning when his secretary entered the room and asked him why he had such a strange look on his face.

"I've just had a dream," the Master said. "Why don't you try to interpret it?"

The secretary bowed respectfully and left the room. Moments later, Ling-yu's assistant came in and was asked the same question. The assistant bowed and walked out.

The secretary soon returned with a tub of hot water for the Master's bath, and the assistant brought a cup of tea. Seeing that neither disciple was lured into the world of dreams, Ling-yu praised them (Taylor, 1999).

One way of interpreting this story is that the secretary and the assistant were devoted to what Zen might call life-as-it-is and were not "sidetracked" by phantoms or dreams.[4] "Dreams, in Buddhism, can refer to deluded thoughts ... especially becoming ensnared in the trance of everyday self-absorbed thinking" (Bobrow, personal communication, January 15, 2007).[5] I suspect many centuries of Buddhists might agree.

"All things at all times teach," says the Buddhist *Avantamsaka Sutra* (Tongxuan, 1989).

"A dream unanalyzed is like a letter unopened," it says in the Talmud.

If everything is real[6]—if dreams teach—then perhaps the secretary and the assistant, like the Master, missed an opportunity to learn when they listened on one channel instead of two.

***

Freud presented the primary and secondary processes as inherently antithetical to each other. He believed that the primary process was developmentally more archaic and maladaptive than the secondary process, and that in healthy development it would be outgrown or mastered.

Although Freud's *bilingual logic of the mind* is a profound contribution to human self-understanding, there are several serious defects with it—especially the fact that it is underwritten by an increasingly beleaguered mechanistic model of the mind as a mental apparatus within which impersonal and unruly instinctual drives circulate, press for discharge, get dammed up, and assault the besieged individual. Fewer contemporary analysts find this a compelling view of the mind, because it has been devastatingly critiqued over the last several decades by Schafer (1976), Stolorow and Atwood (1979), and Greenberg and Mitchell (1983), among many others.

Freud's theory also pathologizes the primary process and makes it more primitive than the secondary process. Later analysts such as Rycroft (1956, 1962) and Loewald (1980) did not believe that primary process and secondary process were mutually antagonistic or that the primary process was inevitably neurotic. In fact, they viewed them as mutually enriching.

Aware of both the breathtaking insights and the difficulties in Freud's conceptualizations, both Rycroft and Loewald attempt to reformulate the primary and secondary process in such a way as to throw out the bathwater of the theoretical problems without eliminating the baby of the seminal insights.[7]

The philosopher Suzanne Langer (1942) describes two modes of communication, what she termed *discursive* and *nondiscursive* symbolism—or conscious, rational thought in words presented successively in accordance with accepted rules of grammar and logic and visual or auditory images appearing in a single instance rather than in a successive sequence. Drawing on this distinction, Rycroft unlinks the theory of the primary and secondary processes from the mechanistic assumptions of Freud's defective drive model, while retaining the wisdom embedded in Freud's two principles of mental functioning. Rycroft then uses Langer to synthesize the two facets of mental functioning that Freud's theory depicts, suggesting that they are potentially cross-pollinating. In other words, we need to operate in both modes to lead a full and rich life.

Loewald (1980) reconceptualizes primary and secondary processes while also disconnecting them from their original usage as modes of energetic regulation. Instead of dichotomizing these aspects of experience and privileging one over the other, he recommends integration, balance, and cross-pollination. If one lives too much in the primary process mode, then one drowns in a dysfunctional, phantasmagorical world of metaphors and images. If one resides too exclusively in a hyper-rational world of the secondary process, then one lives a more emotionally shallow and impoverished life devoid of the creative and vitalizing aspects of the primary process.

Training attentiveness and psychoanalytic listening has, it seems to me, six stages:

1. First you need to quiet your mind;
2. Then you must attend to whatever it is you want to perceive;
3. Next you must focus in and deepen your concentration on it;
4. Then you become one with it—perceiving its actual texture;
5. Then you must decode or translate what it means;
6. And finally you need to respond.

Optimal psychoanalytic listening, in my view, involves quieting and focusing the mind through meditation and then examining and investigating whatever arises with a sensitivity to the *language*—and *logic*—of the *unconscious*. Inner concentration and quietude increases our capacity for self-awareness and tolerance of feeling. When we still the normally turbulent waters of our minds, we have greater access to our emotional depths. We can literally notice more of what is occurring as well as sit through a greater range of feelings without the need to identify with them, act on them, or push them away. Comfort with the primary process encourages us to stay with and eventually translate or decode the meaning of unconscious communication. We literally have more access to it and greater adeptness in handling it.

Attempting to listen to someone without developing heightened attentiveness is like taking a photograph with a wonderful lens held by an unsteady hand—the picture will be blurred. Psychoanalytic therapy falls into this trap. The "meditative photographer" holds the camera completely still but uses a narrower lens and doesn't develop the picture. The picture will be clear, but restricted—neglecting various aspects of unconscious communication such as dreams and slips of the tongue. For optimal psychotherapeutic listening we need to hold the camera steady—concentrate the mind—and use a wide-angle lens. Then the picture will be both clear and more comprehensive.[8]

Notes

1. There are many kinds of meditation including Christian, Catholic, Jewish, Sufi, Taoist, Yogic, Hindu, and Buddhist types. In this chapter I will be focusing on Buddhist meditation. Dan Goleman's (1988) *The Meditative Mind* offers a clear and comprehensive overview of the main kinds of meditation.

2. There actually seem to be at least three conceptions of the unconscious in Buddhism—the classical Buddhist *skandhas*, or subconscious aggregate of previous conditioning (Narada, 1975, pp. 349, 351); the *alaya-vijnana* or "storehouse" consciousness of Mahayana Buddhism—the "subjectless flow of mutually conditioning events that momentarily constitute at the surface level of consciousness something akin to an ego that experiences and reflects" (Unno, 2006, p. 7); and "mushin," that state of complete un-self-consciousness and optimal responsiveness that Zen terms "no mind" (Suzuki, 1959, pp. 110–111).

3. Freud (1932), "Preface to the Third (Revised) English Edition of *The Interpretation of Dreams*" in the Standard Edition, Vol. 4, p. 32.

4. "Reality," for Freud, referred to internal psychic experience such as dreams and the external world—with the former taking precedence over the latter. Buddhism, on the other hand, argues that our ordinary conception of reality—including what Freud termed "secondary process" as well as the taken-for-granted assumption of an autonomous, isolated, solid me "in here" and a separate you "out there"—is an illusion. "The fundamental delusion of

humanity," Zen master Yasutani Roshi once said, "is to suppose that I am here and you are out there" (cf. http://www.cise.ufl.edu).

5. "There's another view of dream in Zen, the evanescence of each moment and every phenomenon (in the Diamond Sutra): a source of delusion if we attach blindly to it, a source of play and liberation if we do not (row row row your boat)" (Bobrow, personal communication, January 15, 2007).

6. Zen master Dogen is the exception that suggests the generalization—treating everything (including dreams)—as real (cf. Cook, 1978; Kim, 2004).

7. One can appreciate the profound value of the primary process as an exquisite means of unconscious communication without subscribing to—or endorsing—every aspect of Freud's immense body of work. One can, for example, challenge his mechanistic model of the mind (or his pessimistic model of health) without eliminating his stunning insights about the way we often communicate more than we know.

8. The feedback of Joe Bobrow, Jefferson Fish, Uwe Gielen, Ellen Luborsky, Mitsunen Lou Nordstrom, Erika Strauss, Mary Traina, and Gail White was helpful in the completion of this chapter.

References

Bentley, G. E. (2001). *The stranger from paradise: A biography of William Blake*. New Haven, CT: Yale University Press.
Bion, W. (1994). Notes on memory and desire. In *Cogitations* (ext. ed.). London, UK: Karnac.
Buddha. (1987). *Mahāsatipatthāna Sutra: The greater discourse on the foundations of mindfulness*. In *Thus have I heard: The long discourses of the Buddha* (pp. 335–350). London: Wisdom Publications.
Buddhaghosa, B. (1976). *Visudhimagga: The path of purification*. Berkeley, CA: Shambhala.
Coltart, N. (1992). The practice of psychoanalysis and Buddhism. In *Slouching toward Bethlehem* (pp. 164–175). New York: Guilford Press.
Cook, F. (1978). *How to raise an ox: Zen practice as taught in Zen master Dogen's Shobogenzo*. Los Angeles: Center Publications.
Freud, S. (1900). The dream work and the primary and secondary process. In *Interpretation of dreams* (standard ed., Vol. 5, pp. 599–609, 277–281, 305–309). London: Hogarth Press.
Freud, S. (1912). *Recommendations to physicians on practicing psycho-analysis* (standard ed., Vol. 12, pp. 111–120).
Freud, S. (1932). Preface to the third (revised) English edition of *The interpretation of dreams* (standard ed., Vol. 4).

Germer, C., Siegel, R., & Fulton, P. (Eds.). (2005). *Mindfulness and psychotherapy.* New York: Guilford Press.

Goleman, D. (1988). *The meditative mind: Varieties of the meditative experience.* Los Angeles: Jeremy Tarcher.

Greenberg, J., & Mitchell, S. (1983). *Object relations in psychoanalytic theory.* Cambridge, MA: Harvard University Press.

James, W. (1920). *The letters of William James* (Henry James, Ed.). Boston: Atlantic Monthly Press.

Jung, C. G. (1928/1953). The synthetic or constructive method. In *Two essays on analytical psychology* (pp. 79–87). Collected Works: 7. Princeton, NJ: Princeton University Press.

Kim, H.-J. (2004). *Eihei Dogen: Mystical realist.* Boston: Wisdom Publications.

Langer, S. (1942). Discursive and presentational forms. In *Philosophy in a new key* (pp. 75–94). Cambridge, MA: Harvard University Press.

Langs, R. (1978). *The listening process.* New York: Jason Aronson.

Loewald, H. (1980). Primary process, secondary process and language. In *Papers on psychoanalysis* (pp. 178–206). New Haven: Yale University Press.

Morreale, D. (1998). *The complete guide to Buddhist America.* Boston: Shambhala.

Narada. (1975). *A manual of Abhidhamma: An outline of Buddhist philosophy.* Kandy, Sri Lanka: Buddhist Publication Society.

Ricoeur, P. (1970). Hermeneutics: The approaches to symbols. In *Freud and philosophy* (pp. 494–524). New Haven, CT: Yale University Press.

Rubin, J. B. (1996). *Psychotherapy and Buddhism: Toward an integration.* New York: Plenum Press.

Rycroft, C. (1956). Symbolism and its relation to the primary and secondary process. In *Imagination and reality: Psycho-analytical essays 1951–1961* (pp. 42–60). London: Hogarth Press.

Rycroft, C. (1962). Beyond the reality principle. In *Imagination and reality: Psycho-analytical essays 1951–1961* (pp. 102–113). London: Hogarth Press.

Schafer, R. (1976). *A new language for psychoanalysis.* New Haven, CT: Yale University Press.

Stolorow, R., & Atwood, G. (1979). *Faces in a cloud: Subjectivity in personality theory.* New York: Jason Aronson.

Suzuki, D. T. (1959). Zen swordsmanship. In *Zen and Japanese culture* (pp. 87–136). Princeton, NJ: Princeton University Press.

Taylor, J. P. (1999, Spring). Koans of silence: The teaching not taught. *Parabola: Myth, Tradition and the Search for Meaning,* 6–11.

Tongxuan, L. (1989). *Entry into the realm of reality, the Guide: A commentary on the Gandavyuha, the final book of the Avatansaka Sutra* (T. Cleary, Trans.). Boston: Shambhala.

Unno, M. (2006). Introduction. In M. Unno (Ed.), *Buddhism and psychotherapy: Essays on theories and practices* (pp. 87–104). Boston: Wisdom Publications.

Welwood, J. (2000). *Toward a psychology of awakening: Buddhism, psychotherapy, and the path of personal and spiritual transformation.* Boston: Shambhala.

Young, S. (2004). *Break through pain.* Boulder, CO: Sounds True.

Young, S. (2006a). *What is mindfulness?* Retrieved from http://www.shinzen.org

Young, S. (2006b). *Why practice mindfulness?* Retrieved from http://www.shinzen.org

Suggested Readings and Resources

Buddha. (1987). Mahāsatipatthāna Sutra: The greater discourse on the foundations of mindfulness. In *Thus have I heard: The long discourses of the Buddha* (pp. 335–350). London: Wisdom Publications.

The classic description of how to meditate.

Freud, S. (1900). The dream work and the primary and secondary process. In *Interpretation of dreams* (standard ed., Vol. 5, pp. 599–609, 277–281, 305–309). London: Hogarth Press.

The classical—and still the most suggestive—description of the primary and secondary processes.

Freud, S. (1912). *Recommendations to physicians on practicing psycho-analysis* (standard ed., Vol. 12, 111–120).

The best account of the ideal therapist's state of mind—"evenly hovering attention."

Goleman, D. (1988). *The meditative mind: Varieties of the meditative experience.* Los Angeles: Jeremy Tarcher.

A lucid and comprehensive overview of the main types of meditation.

Rubin, J. B. (1996). *Psychotherapy and Buddhism: Toward an integration.* New York: Plenum Press.

Describes how psychotherapy and meditation can enrich each other and offers clinical examples of how to integrate them.

Young, S. (2004). *Break through pain.* Boulder, CO: Sounds True.

A clear and valuable exploration of how to use meditation for physical and emotional pain.

Young, S. (2006a). *What is meditation?* Retrieved from http://www.shinzen.org

A lucid and substantive description of what meditation is.

Young, S. (2006b). *Why practice mindfulness?* Retrieved from http://www.shinzen.org.

A clear and thoughtful account of the value of meditation.

Web Sites Offering Relevant Information on Meditation

Audiovisual materials of all kinds: http://www.soundstrue.com
Talks by teachers of mindfulness: http://www.dharmaseed.org
Journal for mindfulness practitioners: http://www.inquiringmind.com

Meditation Training Centers

Vipassana:

Insight Meditation Society, 1230 Pleasant Street, Barre, MA 01005; http://www
.dharma.org

Spirit Rock Meditation Center, P.O. Box 909, Woodacre, CA 94973; http://www
.spiritrock.org

New York Insight, P.O. Box 1790, Murray Hill Station, New York, NY 10156; http://
www.imc.org

Tibetan:

Naropa University, 2130 Arapahoe Avenue, Boulder, CO 80302; http://www.naropa
.edu

Shambhala Mountain Center, 4921 Country Road 68-C, Red Feather Lakes, CO
80545; http://www.shambhalamountain.org

Zen:

Brevard Zen Center—1261 N. Range Road, Cocoa, FL 32926; http://www.brevard
.zen; (321) 795-6570

San Francisco Zen Center, 300 Page Street, San Francisco, CA 94102; http://www
.sfzc.com

Zen Center of San Diego, 20407 Felspar Street, San Diego, CA 92109; Tel. 858-
270-5363

Part V

Academic Findings
and Resources for
Multicultural Counseling

16

What Have We Learned About the Interplay of Culture With Counseling and Psychotherapy?

Juris G. Draguns

Contents

Counseling and Psychotherapy as Cultural Interventions

In an early statement (Draguns, 1975), psychotherapy was construed "as a series of reinitiation techniques for reentry into a fuller, more efficient participation in society. Psychotherapy then is always a procedure that is sociocultural in its ends and interpersonal in its means; it occurs between two or more individuals, and is embedded in a broader, less visible, but no less real cultural context of shared social learning, store of meanings, symbols and implicit assumptions concerning the nature of social living" (p. 273). This characterization is also applicable to the related and overlapping operations of counseling. In fact, culture can be conceived as a third, invisible yet essential component in a counseling psychotherapy encounter (Draguns, 1975).

These assertions, daring and controversial when they were first proposed, are now more widely accepted, and multicultural counseling and psychotherapy has moved from the periphery toward the center of the helping human services. As the field has expanded, questions have begun to be raised about the relevance, effectiveness, and nature of culturally shaped or adapted interventions in counseling and psychotherapy and, more broadly, about the role of culture in the delivery of mental health and counseling services. These questions, however, are not easy to answer on a factual and empirical basis. Until recently, cultural variables were rarely included in the research design of studies on the effectiveness of psychotherapy or counseling services. Hall (2001) discovered the disjunction between empirically supported (EST) and culturally sensitive (CST) therapies. To simplify, ESTs were often designed with no reference to cultural considerations, and CSTs not infrequently lacked rigorous empirical validation. Moreover, Rehm (2002) has noted that ESTs rest on research in the United States and other English-speaking countries. As Draguns (2006) has pointed out, over much of the past century developments and innovations in psychotherapy have radiated asymmetrically. New theories and techniques originating in North America tend to be eagerly and promptly adopted by the rest of the world. Yet only a few of the many original and worthwhile contributions from other parts of the world penetrate the cultural and language barrier to gain recognition and acceptance in the United States.

Thus, there is a lot of ambiguity and uncertainty about the current state and applicability of conceptualizations and interventions in multicultural contexts, both within the United States and Canada and beyond North America. In this, the final chapter of this volume, an attempt will be undertaken to contribute toward clarification. The objective is to convey sound, practically applicable information for the readers of this book and for cross-cultural psychotherapists and counselors. To this end, three bodies of findings will be surveyed: the writings of influential, for the most part recent, contributors to the development and application of human services in a variety of cultural contexts; research approaches, both already implemented or only planned; and the cutting edge of new thinking about culture in the counseling and therapy transactions.

The chapter will conclude with a list of needed topics of investigation.

Pioneers and Innovators: Clinical Contributions

Kraepelin: A Forgotten Forerunner of Cultural Psychotherapy Research

Emil Kraepelin (1856–1926), a prominent German psychiatrist, is generally credited with inaugurating scientific, biomedical psychiatry (Jilek, 1995). An indefatigable systematizer, he identified schizophrenia and bipolar mood disorder, although under different names. What is less widely known is that Kraepelin pioneered the exploration of mental disorder outside of Europe and that he traveled to Algeria and Indonesia to observe the symptoms of hospitalized mental patients. His report of these observations (Kraepelin, 1904) continues to be cited to this day, although it may be more often invoked than read. Sections of this classical article sound remarkably prescient:

> If the characteristics of a people are manifested in its religion and its customs, in its intellectual artistic achievements, in its political acts and its historical development, then they will also find expression in the frequency and clinical formation of its mental disorders, especially those that emerge from internal conditions. Just as the knowledge of morbid psychic phenomena has opened up for us deep insights into the working of our psychic life, so we may also hope that the psychiatric characteristics of a people can further our understanding of its entire psychic character. In this sense comparative psychiatry may be destined to one day become an important auxiliary science to comparative ethnopsychology ("Völkerpsychologie"). (as cited by Jilek, 1995, p. 231)

Relating culturally dominant values, attitudes, and outlooks to symptoms of mental disorder was novel in 1904. By now this notion is widely, though not universally, accepted, and research is being pursued on the intertwining of culture and expressions of psychological disturbance. Although Kraepelin did not explicitly refer to psychotherapy, his statement can be extrapolated to it. If psychopathology is influenced by culture, the techniques to counteract or alleviate it are also likely to be culturally shaped. What remains to be pinpointed is the specific role that the culture plays in psychotherapy. To elucidate this putative link, the chapter proceeds to the contributions of contemporary psychotherapists, counselors, and researchers who have taken special steps to adapt their services to their clients of very different cultural backgrounds and outlooks.

Contemporary Innovators: Their Experiences and Conclusions

Expectations of Therapists and Clients: Cultural Divergence

Wolfgang Pfeiffer, a German psychiatrist with extensive international clinical and research experience (Pfeiffer, 1994), endeavored to provide culturally fitting psychotherapeutic services to Turkish guest workers in Germany (Pfeiffer, 1996). On the basis of this experience, he identified five obstacles in implementing psychotherapy in dyads of Turkish clients and German therapists:

1. The client comes seeking advice and direction; the therapist expects the client both to seek and find his/her own solution to the presenting problem.

2. The client turns to the members of his or her family for help and advice in decision making; the therapist encourages individuality and autonomy and promotes personal and private choices and decisions.

3. The client solicits advice, suggestions, and solutions from the elders within her or his family; the therapist emphasizes technical expertise as opposed to social status based on reputation and seniority.

4. The client often expresses his or her distress in somatic terms; the therapist is focused on the client's thoughts and feelings.

5. The client embarks on therapy with the expectations of expeditious, or even instantaneous, relief; the therapist knows that gradual and uneven improvement is the rule and that a sudden cure is an exception rather than a rule.

The cogency of these contrasts extends beyond the specific cross-cultural encounter between German professionals and Turkish help-seekers. Highly similar incompatibilities may be observed in other cross-cultural encounters between traditional clients coming from more collectivistic cultures and their modern therapists. Conceptions of what is helpful, necessary, and effective for relieving distress differ across cultures, especially along the modern versus traditional divide. To accommodate culturally based expectations in meeting client needs and alleviating their distress remains an urgent task in a variety of settings.

Taking Cultural Beliefs and Practices Seriously

Tobie Nathan (1994), a psychoanalyst in Paris, has pioneered in devising culturally appropriate and effective therapeutic services for distressed migrants and sojourners from northern and western Africa. Nathan observed that conventional Western interventions failed to help clients whose cultural background was markedly different. To respond to African clients, Nathan developed a radically different approach. It emphasizes the discovery of the meaning of symptoms within the framework of cultural symbols and beliefs. Verbal communication is deemphasized in favor of manipulation of artifacts and objects. Psychoanalytic interpretations are replaced by metaphors, proverbs, and sayings. Instead of isolating the client in the culturally alien office, clinic, or hospital setting, Nathan actively involves family members who participate with the client in the search for understanding and solution of his and her problems or dilemmas. Insight in the traditional Western psychodynamic sense is deemphasized. Instead, prompt reduction of somatopsychic distress is sought. As a distillate of these experiences, Nathan has proposed several recommendations. Specifically, he exhorts prospective therapists to: respect their clients' religious beliefs, even if they appear to be strange and bizarre; accept the traditional ways of doing things and the customary modes of decision making within their clients' cultures; respect the cultural artifacts and take seriously the powers attributed to them; honor the cultural rules of hospitality and act in accordance with them in the therapy setting; recognize the distress that their clients experience as a result of feeling uprooted from their homes and separated from their families and communities; and convey this recognition empathetically, in a culturally meaningful manner. Nathan recognizes that social influence is indispensable for therapeutic change to occur. However, for social influence to take effect, it must be compatible with the person's sociocultural belief system.

In most therapy encounters in the United States and Canada, the cultural gulf is not as wide as that which Nathan had to bridge. However, his recommendations are still relevant in working with recent immigrants from Asia and Africa whose traditional beliefs survive resettlement and transplantation into the United States. In the past decades, such beliefs were encountered among the traumatized survivors of the killing fields of Cambodia (Kinzie, Fredericksen, Ben, Fleck, & Karls, 1984; Mollica, Wyshak, & Lavelle, 1987) and, more recently, among immigrants from sub-Saharan Africa (Vontress, 2005).

Discovering the Subjective Reflection of Culture in Therapy

Bin Kimura (1995), a Japanese psychiatrist steeped in the German tradition of phenomenological analysis, has pooled his lifelong knowledge of Japanese culture, his theoretical outlook, and his therapeutic sensitivity in capturing the interpersonal nature of Japanese subjectivity. In Kimura's view, the Japanese self is interpersonally and not intrapsychically experienced, as the internalization of that which happens between two interacting human beings. The self is not harbored within the individual. Rather, it is expressed in the course of the social give-and-take between persons. Thus, guilt may be keenly felt, but as a result of letting down or disappointing specific persons. Similarly, Kimura traces morbid shyness or avoidance of people to social hypersensitivity and the fear of giving offense to another person. Kimura's formulations highlight the potential of looking at psychotherapy as a reflection of subjective culture while at the same time making psychotherapeutic operations more personally sensitive and culturally appropriate. Thus, therapy can be considered a mirror through which a culture's subtle and implicit features are reflected, as anticipated by several authors (Draguns, 1981; Kakar, 1978; Roland, 1988; Vassiliou & Vassiliou, 1973). Kimura, however, has gone further than anybody else in using phenomeno-logical psychotherapy as the source for the identification and description of the rarely articulated, yet fundamental, notions that guide social interaction and personal conduct in a culture. Emblematic of this orientation in the Japanese language is the word *ki*, which ties together affect, cognition, and volition and does so invariably in relation to another person. The meaning of *ki* overlaps with *self* in English except that experiencing *ki* in isolation, intrapsychically, is a semantic impossibility. Kimura's approach is worthy of emulation and extension as an avenue of exploring culturally shaped experience through elucidating concepts that are shared but implicit and are elicited and put into words in psychotherapy that is attuned to the subtleties of subjective experience.

Developing and Applying Mental Health Services Across Cultures: Blending Approaches From Within and Outside of Culture

Karl Peltzer (1995), a German clinical psychologist, has described his unique experiences in developing mental health services in several African countries, from Ghana to Malawi, by blending guided imagery and other standard Western intervention techniques with a variety of culturally specific treatment approaches that are embodied in traditional healing rituals. Dreams were utilized by integrating Western principles of interpretation with African symbols. Euro-American approaches had to be adapted in order to respond more sensitively to a specifically or uniquely local problem, such as depressive reactions and post-traumatic stress disorders in Malawi following incarceration and torture by an oppressive, and eventually overthrown, regime (Peltzer, 1996). On the basis of his experiences, Peltzer offered the following advice to therapists faced with similar challenges:

> Detect indigenous coping strategies and culturally mediated protective factors. This includes operational research on the cultural dimension of the psychosocial mechanisms that determine how people cope with trauma. The objective of this research is threefold: a) formulate guidelines for a community-based mental health care approach and for the counselling of victims which takes the context of the local culture in account, b) formulate guidelines for preventive actions both on community and individual level, and c) involve local healers in the programme and achieve that they work side by side with health workers. (Peltzer, 1996, p. 18)

According to Peltzer, three distinct components coexist within the present-day African population: (a) traditional persons who continue to live within the framework of their respective cultures, little affected by modernization; (b) transitional persons, shuttling between the modern and traditional worlds; and (c) modern persons fully participating in the worldwide sweep toward modernization and globalization. Therapy needs and outlooks of these three categories diverge, and, in designing and implementing services, differences must be accommodated. Therapeutic interactions between a healer and his traditional patient tend to be shorter than those between a modern therapist and patient, and direction prevails over inquiry.

The outlooks and expectations of transitional patients pose the greatest challenge to therapists to come up with creative and individually fitting syntheses of the old and the new. Vontress (2005) estimated that 80% of the population in sub-Saharan Africa consults traditional healers, although they may not rely upon them consistently or exclusively. Thus, Peltzer's pragmatic and flexible orientation is worthy of large-scale emulation throughout the continent and beyond.

Modifying Psychotherapy to Fit Cultural Reality

Alba Nyda Rivera-Ramos (1984), a Puerto Rican clinical psychologist trained in the mainland United States, has been impressed by the disparity between her training and the clinical and social realities in Puerto Rico. One of these discrepancies pertains to the social and familistic emphasis characteristic of Puerto Ricans. According to Rivera-Ramos, shame is more prominent than guilt as a source of distress. A sharp line is drawn between the host of relatives within the extended family and other persons. Distrust of strangers must be overcome before trust is established and self-disclosure ensues. Social ties, especially within the family, are more important than the cultivation of unique individuality. Moreover, Puerto Ricans of working-class backgrounds, and especially those who are poor, may perceive standard psychotherapy not only as irrelevant but condescending. A person's respect is based more on his or her age and family reputation than on wealth or success. These considerations may be glossed over by the often youthful therapists trained on the U.S. mainland and eager to intervene in the most efficient and expeditious fashion. Their unintentional disregard of the subtleties of cultural sensitivity may be perceived as offensive to the client's sense of dignity, a key value in Puerto Rican and other Latin American cultures. Instead, Rivera-Ramos advocates a model of psychotherapy based on mutuality between the therapist and client and free of paternalism and protectionism. Both parties to the therapy transaction cooperate in working for the attainment of the mutually agreed therapy objectives. Rivera-Ramos objects to referring to the help-seeker as client and prefers to look upon her or him as a companion in a shared task or an "interacter" (*interactuante*). Her collaborative orientation, problem-solving focus, and social emphasis merge in construing the person as "an integral, necessary, and indispensable component of society, that is, as a social being who cannot attain his or her goals in isolation. This position stands in diametric contrast to the traditional view of psychotherapy, in older as well as in more recent models, which consider the individual as responsible for and capable of everything" (Rivera-Ramos, 1984, p. 71). This formulation converges with and anticipates an important trend in theory, research, and practice of therapy in culture (for a culture-sensitive intervention program targeted at Mexican American and Mexican adolescents, see Koss-Chioino, Baca, & Vargas, this volume).

Ethnographic Observations of Intercultural Therapy Dyads

Karen Seeley (2000), an American psychotherapist with an interdisciplinary background, applied anthropological techniques to investigate therapy transactions between American therapists and their clients who were born abroad and/or were socialized in a cultural and language community other than that of mainstream of the United States. Seeley's interviews explored the intertwining of therapy and culture. To study these encounters, she explicitly adopted the ethnographer's modus operandi. Clients became informants on their experiences in therapy, much like the indigenous resource persons who are asked to elucidate the practices of their culture to an anthropologist in the field. Client's perceptions in therapy have rarely been given a voice; Seeley's research is unique in that she went out of her way to interview other therapists' patients in order to observe their inside therapy experience from an outsider's perspective. A total of six therapy clients were intensively investigated in this manner by means of systematic qualitative methods. Four of them came from south or east Asia; two were brought up in Spanish-speaking families and communities.

The most general, and striking, finding to emerge from this project was the pervasiveness and subtlety of culture's effects upon the subjective experience of therapy, even though the six persons studied were thoroughly acculturated and were competent and experienced participants in the contemporary American culture. Yet, their cultures of origin were found to affect the therapy relationship, self-disclosure, self-concept, emotional expression, structuring and reconstructing of formative experience, and the mode of expressing distress. Converging with other observers, Seeley emphasized the centrality of self-experience. In particular, she concluded that her informants' selves were both bounded and individuated differently from Western selves. In Seeley's words: "Often their self-other boundaries were indistinct, so that self, family, and community representations, identifications, and interests were fused… . Further, the subjects described selves that devalued the independent action, self-expression, and self-assertion that Western selves commonly prize" (Seeley, 2000, p. 221). Thus, therapy is a valuable source of information about the distinctive features of subjective culture. Conversely, such information may be useful and even indispensable for avoiding misunderstandings and enhancing cultural and personal sensitivity.

Shifting Cultural Perspectives

Pittu Laungani (2004), a counseling psychologist born and socialized in India and steeped in the culture of contemporary England where he lived and worked for several decades, delved into his bicultural experience in formulating the following guidelines for culturally sensitive and effective counseling:

1. Take into account the culturally significant experience of a socially diverse clientele and, instead of using culture as a wastebasket category for whatever aspects of clients' experience are baffling and unexplained, pay heed to the distinctive features of family life, socialization, gender differences, and identity;
2. Do not assume uniformity or homogeneity within a culture, but address the client's individual structuring of his unicultural or multicultural experience;
3. Be prepared for unexpected and surprising developments, which are more frequent whenever counseling is done across culture lines;
4. Do not be overcommitted to a theoretical model of intervention, even if it is highly popular, and keep in mind that its popularity is not synonymous with validity, especially if it is applied across culture lines;
5. Do not attempt to squeeze cultural sensitivity into a tight rule structure and steer clear of uniform protocols designed for an entire ethnocultural group;
6. Accept beliefs and practices originating in clients' cultures and integrate them into counseling interventions;

7. Be receptive to clients' expectations for counseling interventions that are rooted in their cultural background instead of rushing to apply techniques developed elsewhere.

In addition to these admonitions, applicable across space and time, Laungani addressed some of the contrasts between the two cultures that he knew so well: individualism, cognitivism, free will, and materialism in England, juxtaposed to communalism, emotionalism, determinism, and spiritualism prevalent in India. British counselors emphasize neutrality or objectivity, cognitive control, and empathy. Indian clients expect, and Indian counselors strive toward, wisdom, spirituality, and decisiveness. The ethos of counseling in Europe or America tends toward horizontal or egalitarian relationships; in India and elsewhere in Asia the counselor–counselee interactions are more likely to be vertical, based on the acceptance of the counselor's superior qualities and powers. Even more to the point, Western clients, according to Laungani, seek freedom *to* achieve goals or develop their potential whereas Asian clients strive to attain freedom *from* distress, disruption, and turmoil in order to experience harmony and serenity.

Cultural Assumptions and Therapeutic Intervention

Alan Roland (1988, 1996, 2006), a psychoanalyst in New York, went further than most Western psychotherapists to investigate the subtle and hidden features of the experience of Japanese and Indian analysands. He concluded that Western psychoanalysts are unaware of how deeply ingrained their individualistic assumptions are. Therefore, divergence in expectations and outlooks may go undetected for long periods of time and may complicate and obstruct the therapeutic process. As Roland (2006) indicated, "psychoanalytic norms of development and functioning are more Western-centric than most analysts realize" (p. 456). Thus, there is the danger of misconstruing what is normal in an Asian culture as pathological in light of Western standards. At the same time, pathology within the culture may be missed by a therapist from outside the culture. Therapy relationships tend to be construed hierarchically by Asian patients, with the patient showing deference and expressing respect. The hidden aspect of the hierarchical relationship is the patient's expectation of nurturance and protection by the therapist, which is alien to the Western psychotherapists' implicit ethos and explicit training. Anger may be aroused by the violation of these culturally based expectations, but is unlikely to be expressed readily and openly. Direct anger is more likely to appear in the late stages of psychoanalytic psychotherapy, and the patient may storm out of therapy rather than confront the therapist. Moreover, nonverbal communication plays a more prominent role in therapeutic work with Asians than it does with Americans, and the spiritual, cosmic, and mystical aspects of the self are much more central and salient, especially among Indian patients.

Interim Conclusions

What are some of the recurrent themes in the contributions of these eight innovators? First, all of them advocate and practice flexibility. It is safe to conclude that tactics of intervention are less universal than general treatment goals. Second, an open and receptive attitude on the part of the therapist is endorsed. Third, the services that are offered must be meaningful in the cultural context in which they are applied. Preexisting beliefs and attitudes do not have to be overcome as a condition for instituting therapy; rather, if at all possible, they should be accepted at the point of departure. Fourth, need assessment should precede intervention, on both individual and community levels. Fifth, traditional treatment services should not be dismissed nor rejected; instead, attempts to utilize these resources should be undertaken whenever possible. Sixth, empathy for the help-seeking members of a different culture must be felt and should be communicated in a fashion that makes sense in the given cultural milieu. Seventh, subtle but potentially significant features of the cultures in which psychotherapy and counseling are studied are likely to be revealed in their complexity in the course of the therapy encounter, and these opportunities should not be missed. Eighth, and finally, cross-cultural therapists should be on guard, as these eight pioneers have been, against construing cultural differences in terms of deficits and disorders. Different, unusual, deviant, or even bizarre behaviors may stem from a multiplicity of sources, and they should not be attributed to disturbance automatically, unthinkingly, or easily (cf. Draguns, 2008).

Toward Research on Psychotherapy Within and Across Cultures

The trappings of psychotherapy are dazzlingly different across cultures. Clinical and qualitative observation of psychotherapy in action, as provided by the master innovators in the foregoing section, is valuable in the early and exploratory stages of investigation. Eventually it must be supplemented by more elaborate and sophisticated methods in order to disentangle the threads that connect causes and effects. What, if anything, about psychotherapy remains constant across cultures and effective regardless of its locale? How do the various features of psychotherapy vary with the characteristics of culture? The results of major worldwide studies of personality and social behavior may provide the foundation for initiating large-scale research on variation of psychotherapy across cultures.

Hofstede's Cultural Dimensions

In the 1970s, Geert Hofstede (1980), an organizational psychologist in the Netherlands employed by a major multinational corporation, embarked on a worldwide project of an unprecedented magnitude. The sheer number of participants set world records: At the several stages of this investigation, a total of 116,000 IBM employees in more than 50 countries filled out questionnaires pertaining to work-related attitudes. Complex multivariate statistical techniques were applied, and eventually four factors were extracted from the accumulated data. In the ensuing decades these four statistically independent dimensions have been extensively and intensively compared across national cultures, in industrial-organizational settings and beyond them, in family, school, community, and clinical contexts (Draguns, 2007; Hofstede, 2001).

Of these four factorially based dimensions, individualism-collectivism has received the greatest amount of research scrutiny (Hofstede, 1980, 2001; Hofstede & Hofstede, 2005, Triandis, 1995). At the individualist end of the continuum, persons experience themselves as self-contained and autonomous human beings; collectivists perceive themselves primarily in reference to groups, as members of a family, community, or nation. In Hofstede's worldwide comparison, Americans emerged as the most individualistic nation, consonant with the importance that Katz (1985) independently assigned to individualism as the pivotal value that guides the rationale and practice of American counseling.

The other three factors are: power distance, which refers to the degree to which disparities in income, status, and influence are tolerated and accepted within a culture; uncertainty avoidance, which describes the unease or discomfort that is experienced in situations that are ambiguous, unstructured, or unpredictable; and masculinity-femininity that spans the gamut from emphasizing performance and efficiency to prizing care and tenderness. An additional dimension, long-term versus short-term orientation, was derived somewhat later and on the basis of a very different methodology (Chinese

Culture Connection, 1987). This construct was explicitly formulated in advance, as a measure of Chinese cultural Confucian values, characterized at the high end by perseverance, thrift, and hard work, all at the service of the group, and not for the sake of personal advancement. As anticipated, countries around the Western Pacific Rim, China, Hong Kong, Taiwan, Japan, and South Korea, yielded the highest scores on this dimension.

From the Culture to the Self

Several authors (e.g., Chang, 1998; Markus & Kitayama, 1991) have articulated a number of connections between individualism-collectivism and the nature and quality of self-experience. At the individualistic extreme, as represented by the national cultures of North America and Western Europe, the self is experienced as the core of individual being: central, separate, and unique. At the opposite, collectivistic, end of the continuum, the self is expressed through the person's characteristic interactions and relationships with other persons. Chang (1988) has gone so far as to liken the individualistic self to a wall that separates the person's private world from others, and the collectivistic self to a bridge that connects the individual to other human beings. Hofstede (2001), Triandis (1995), and Draguns (2007) have postulated positive relationships between individualism and an autonomous self, and between collectivism and an interdependent self.

Beyond individualism-collectivism, Draguns and Tanaka-Matsumi (2003) have extrapolated the following hypothetical relationships from Hofstede's (2001) writings: (a) between high power distance and an encapsulated self, and between low power distance and a permeable self; (b) between high uncertainty avoidance and consistency and explicitness of self-experience, and between inconsistencies within the self and its amorphous and/or nonverbal nature and low uncertainty avoidance; (c) between masculinity and a pragmatic and action-oriented self, and between femininity and an altruistic and feeling-oriented self; (d) between long-term orientation and self-restraint, modesty, and humility, and between short-range orientation and self-assertion and self-promotion.

From the Self to Therapy Preferences

Proceeding from the relationships proposed above, several predictions can be made about links between Hofstede's cultural dimensions and the preferred modalities and styles of therapy. The entire set of these predictions is incorporated into Table 16.1.

TABLE 16.1
Five Cultural Dimensions in Psychotherapy

Individualism:	**Collectivism:**
Insight, self-understanding	Alleviation of suffering
Guilt, alienation, loneliness	Relationship problems, shame
Therapist as father figure	Therapist as nurturant mother
Development of individuality	Social integration
Development of responsibility	Acceptance of controls
Conflict and resolution	Harmonious relationships
Feelings more important than relationships	Relationships more important than feelings
Individual expression through behavior	Role determines behavior
High Power Distance:	**Low Power Distance:**
Directive psychotherapy	Person-centered psychotherapy
Therapist as expert	Therapist as sensitive person
Conformity and social effectiveness	Self discovery and actualization
Differentiation of therapist and client roles	Dedifferentiation of therapist and client roles
Emphasis upon professional credentials	Promotion of self-improvement
Expertise through interpretation and direction	
High Uncertainty Avoidance:	**Low Uncertainty Avoidance:**
Biological explanations	Psychological explanations
Behavioral techniques	Experiential psychotherapy
Medical orientation	Multiprofessional orientation
Few schools of therapy	Many schools of therapy
Tightly regulated therapy practice	Loosely regulated therapy practice
Technique adhered to	Spontaneity promoted
Masculinity:	**Femininity:**
Society's needs paramount	Person's goals paramount
Responsibility, conformity, adjustment	Expressiveness, creativity, empathy
Guilt	Anxiety
Enabling	Caring
Competition	Cooperation
Long-Term Orientation:	**Short-Term Orientation:**
Interpersonal therapy	Intrapsychic or behavioral therapy
Somatic interventions	Psychological interventions
Self-control	Self-assertion
Self-subordination	Self-actualization
Limited and slow change expected	Rapid and general change expected

The assumption on which these predictions rest is that culturally characteristic values and preferences, especially as they apply to the self, are reflected in the experience of psychotherapy, in its goals, techniques, and patterns of interaction and communication. Specific hypotheses pertaining to Hofstede's dimensions have been tested in schools (Hofstede, 1986), intercultural contacts (Triandis, Brislin, & Hui, 1998), relationships within the family (Hofstede & Hofstede, 2005), economic decisions and political behavior (Hofstede, 2001), subjective well-being (Arrindell et al., 1997), and psychiatric symptoms (Draguns, 1990). In relation to individualism-collectivism, Snider (2003) explicitly examined the hypotheses proposed here in three samples of university students: Chinese who were studying in Australia, and Australians and Americans in their respective countries. Snider found that collectivistically oriented individuals preferred interventions that were direct, practical, and based on professional expertise. Snider also discovered that collectivism-individualism was a stronger predictor of preferences for counselors' intervention than the counselee's ethnicity. More generally, Snider reported that the dominant influence upon counseling preference was verticalism or power distance among the Chinese, egalitarianism among the Australians, and individualism among the Americans. It is worth noting that these findings are consonant with Roland's (2006) and Laungani's (2004) observations on the importance that Asian clients accord to hierarchical relationships in therapy and counseling.

Snider's findings strengthen the expectation that Hofstede's dimensions are relevant to therapeutic services. With this in mind, the specific points in Table 16.1 can be further elaborated as follows. Individualism fosters independent self-exploration and search for insight; collectivism promotes quest for harmony within the family and the community as well as lifelong integration into these groups. High power distance favors expertise in intervention, whereas low power distance puts a premium on human sensitivity. High uncertainty avoidance promotes reliance upon goal-oriented interventions of demonstrated scientific merit; low uncertainty avoidance stimulates a search for novel approaches to psychotherapy, even if their value has not yet been demonstrated. In masculine cultures, therapists tend to be regarded as agents of their society, and their principal objective is to restore their clients' social and economic competence. In feminine cultures, therapists and counselors are viewed as helpers whose interventions are the expression of a caring attitude. Long-term orientation is associated with the promotion of self-control and self-subordination, whereas the focus in short-range orientation cultures is placed on self-assertion and self-actualization.

Other Research Approaches and Findings

For a long time, the need for cultural sensitivity and accommodation has been a plausible belief not yet supported by systematic evidence. A recent meta-analytic review of culturally adapted treatments for multiethnic populations in North America (Griner & Smith, 2006) provides substantial data on the value of such interventions. Across the 76 studies examined, the resulting weighted average random effect size amounted to a *d* of .45, indicative of a moderately strong benefit of culturally adapted treatments. The effects were substantially greater if they were targeted to a homogeneous ethnocultural group, and interventions conducted in the clients' first language were twice as effective as those that were conducted in English. Ethnic matching of therapists and clients, however, did not produce conclusive results.

Shifting from interventions to therapists, a major international comparison by Orlinsky and Ronnestad (2005) yielded a complex pattern of findings on psychotherapists' professional development in 20 countries. The overriding result that emerged from this project was that the therapists viewed themselves as participants in a meaningful and complex interpersonal encounter rather than as technicians dispensing uniform and standardized interventions. Across nations, three second-order factors emerged from multivariate analysis: healing involvement, stressful involvement, and controlling involvement. Relevant in this connection is also the finding by Beutler, Mohr, Grawe, Engle, and McDonald (1991) that independent clients find nondirective therapy congenial whereas less independent persons seek therapists' guidance and counsel. This result has points of contact with Snider's (2003) conclusions in his interethnic comparison in Australia and has cross-cultural implications that remain to be explored.

Beyond Categorization: Toward Integrative, Individualized, and Culturally Sensitive Human Services

For several decades, innovative and venturesome psychotherapists and counselors have striven to enhance the cultural relevance of psychological services. This chapter is based on their combined efforts, which have borne fruit. Thus, the guidelines of the American Psychological Association (2003) mandate and provide standards for culturally appropriate and sensitive counseling and therapy. There has been a proliferation of resources that purport to provide useful information on the needs and services for culturally distinct groups within the North American population (e.g., McGoldrick, Giordano, & Garcia-Preto, 2005; Pedersen, Draguns, Lonner, & Trimble, 2008; Sue & Sue, 2003). Helpful as these compilations are, they are subject to a potential limitation, that of reifying group differences and possibly promoting stereotypes. In fact, categorizing cultural groups and imputing specifying characteristics to them and riding roughshod over the cultural distinctness of counselees and patients have been referred to as the Scylla and Charybdis of counseling across cultures: the twin opposite, although concurrent, dangers that should be avoided at all costs (Draguns, 1976).

Several recent developments may help lessen these perils. Lopez (1997) has introduced the Shifting Cultural Lens model. In Lopez's view, cultural competence entails "moving between two cultural perspectives, that of the therapist and that of the client" (Lopez, 1997, p. 571). Both participants in psychotherapy communicate their conceptions of culture and, optimally, integrate them. Culture then is not an immutable extraneous entity, but a personal interpretation of cultural experience by two unique and interacting individuals. Along somewhat similar lines, Leong (1996) has applied the classical dictum by Kluckhohn and Murray (1950) to the cultural counseling context: "Every man is in certain respects (a) like all other men; (b) like some other men, and (c) like no other man" (p. 35). The implication of this statement is that no intervention in therapy is ever exclusively cultural and that cultural aspects are relevant to all psychotherapy and counseling contacts, albeit to widely differing degrees (Gielen, Draguns, & Fish, this volume). Similarly, the universal components of psychotherapy or counseling experience should in no case be overlooked. The ideal is the integration of these three threads of personal experience as they are intertwined in a specific person's ideation, perception, motivation, and action. Pedersen (1999) has asserted that cultural issues and components are the rule rather than the exception in the therapy and counseling encounters in diverse, multicultural settings that are typical throughout much of the contemporary United States and Canada. The Cultural Accommodation model proposed by Leong (1996) and by Leong and Lee (2006) aims to increase the counselor's or therapist's sensitivity and flexibility in developing awareness of the cultural ("like some other persons") dimension of his or her clients' experience and of its dynamic shifting nature. At the same time, this model is designed to sensitize the counselor to his or her cultural sensitivities and blind spots in order to constructively make use of them in providing services and not to be mislead by them.

What Else Do We Need to Know: Toward Exploration and Investigation

Although a lot has been learned about culture in relation to counseling and psychotherapy, the need for continued research by a multitude of approaches remains acute. Below are some suggestions waiting to be implemented.

At the least ambitious level, the gap between rendering counseling and therapy services should be narrowed. There is both need and merit in providing accounts of culturally distinctive services in the multicultural settings of North America and elsewhere. The more detailed, factual, and quantified such reports are, the greater is their falsifiability and hence their value as documentation of empirical data.

Kimura's (1994), Seeley's (2000), and Roland's (1988) research approaches are rooted in phenomenological psychiatry, anthropological fieldwork, and psychoanalytic practice, respectively. All of these three methods are qualitative and provide access for information that is not otherwise accessible, such as the culturally distinctive subjective experience of self and personhood. Such approaches are worth emulating and extending, in order to open new and as yet unexplored vistas on psychotherapeutic experience.

Scrutiny of culturally characteristic critical incidents, initiated by Brislin, Cushner, Cherrie, and Young (1986), should be extended to therapist-client interactions in various cultures. The illustrations so amply provided by Laungani (2004), Nathan (1994), and Peltzer (1995) could be used as "raw materials" for open-ended vignettes. Culturally variable expectations (e.g., for therapist's directive interventions; Folensbee, Draguns, & Danish, 1986), his or her sensitivity to nonverbal clues (e.g., Roland, 1988), or the client's quest for interpersonal harmony and conflict avoidance (Joo, 1998) could be incorporated into the construction of culturally characteristic and differentiating critical incidents. Eventually, the responses by clients and therapists obtained in this manner could be studied more intensively in relation to culturally shaped self-experience as well as social values and attitudes.

In a more direct fashion, studies may be conducted of both clients and therapists across cultural or ethnic lines to investigate the role of culture upon attitudes toward various aspects of therapy or counseling. Specifically, what kinds of experiences did the clients consider decisive in producing therapy benefits? These questions could be posed before the initiation, in the course of, and upon the conclusion of therapy.

A remarkable natural experiment has so far gone unutilized. In the bilingual and bicultural city of Montreal, French-speaking and English-speaking therapy dyads work side by side. Are there any detectable differences across the cultural and linguistic divide? The same question could be scrutinized in the course of therapist-client interaction on the two banks of the Rio Grande, in such border cities as Nogales, Arizona, and Nogales, Sonora, and in Europe, in Fribourg/Freiburg, Switzerland, where the French–German language boundary cuts right through the town as well as in Helsinki, Finland, where therapy is transacted in Finnish and in Swedish.

To break new ground in worldwide investigation of the traditional proto-types of psychotherapy, Human Research Area Files (HRAF; Barry, 1980) should be searched and coded for healing practices in order to relate them to other relevant and available cultural indicators. Eventually, subsamples within HRAF may even be coded for some or all of the Hofstede dimensions in order to link them to healing methods and styles.

Finally, meta-analyses of psychotherapy outcome, exemplified by Smith, Glass, and Miller (1980) in the United States and by Wittmann and Matt (1986) in Germany, may be compared as a first step toward instituting an eventual global meta-analysis or meta-analyses. In fact, Matt (1993) has already initiated such a procedure. The implementation of such a global project would be a fitting culmination of the continuing effort to disentangle the multiple putative cultural threads in psychotherapy.

Parting Comment

Over a century ago, Kraepelin (1904) daringly alluded to the possibility that psychotherapy and culture might be related. Even though there has been a spurt in the accumulation of factual information in the last three decades, we are not even close to an empirically based understanding of the nature and extent of the connections between culture and/or counseling and psychotherapy in all of their facets. There is, however, the prospect that, in the foreseeable future, pertinent questions will be asked, appropriate and multiple methods will be applied, and definitive answers will finally be forthcoming. Many observers have semi-intuitively concluded that culture permeates psychotherapy and that psychotherapy illuminates culture. If so, we should be able to infer the characteristics of therapy from the knowledge of culture, and to predict cultural features from the knowledge of psychotherapy. As research on psychotherapy and counseling within and across cultures comes of age, we shall learn whether this expectation is utopian or realistic.

References

American Psychological Association. (2003). Guidelines on multicultural education, training, research, practice, and organizational change for psychologists. *American Psychologist, 58,* 377–402.

Arrindell, W. A., Hatzichristou, C., Wensink, J., Rosenberg, E., van Twillert, B., Stedema, J., et al. (1997). Dimensions of national culture as predictors of cross-national differences in subjective well-being. *Personality and Individual Differences, 23,* 37–53.

Barry, H. (1980). Description and uses of the Human Research Area Files. In H. C. Triandis & J. W. Berry (Eds.), *Handbook of cross-cultural psychology. Volume 2: Methodology* (pp. 445–478). Boston: Allyn & Bacon.

Beutler, L. E., Mohr, D. C., Grawe, K., Engle, D., & MacDonald, R. (1991). Looking for differential treatment effects: Cross-cultural predictors of psychotherapy efficacy. *Journal of Psychotherapy Integration, 1,* 121–142.

Brislin, R. W., Cushner, K., Cherrie, S., & Young, M. (1986). *Intercultural interactions: A practical guide.* Beverly Hills, CA: Sage.

Chang, S. C. (1988). The nature of self: A transcultural view. Part I: Theoretical aspects. *Transcultural Psychiatric Research Review, 25*(3), 169–204.

Chinese Culture Connection (1987). Chinese values and the search for culture-free dimensions of culture. *Journal of Cross-Cultural Psychology, 18,* 143–164.

Draguns, J. G. (1975). Resocialization into culture: The complexities of taking a worldwide view of psychotherapy. In R. W. Brislin, S. Bochner, & W. J. Lonner (Eds.), *Cross-cultural perspectives on learning* (pp. 273–289). Beverly Hills, CA: Sage.

Draguns, J. G. (1976). Counseling across cultures: Common themes and distinct approaches. In P. B. Pedersen, J. G. Draguns, & W. J. Lonner (Eds.), *Counseling across cultures* (pp. 1–17). Honolulu: University of Hawaii Press.

Draguns, J. G. (1981). Cross-cultural counseling and psychotherapy: History, issues, current status. In A. J. Marsella & P. B. Pedersen (Eds.), *Cross-cultural counseling and psychotherapy* (pp. 3–27). Elmsford, NJ: Pergamon.

Draguns, J. G. (1990). Normal and abnormal behavior in cross-cultural perspective: Toward specifying the nature of their relationship. In J. J. Berman (Ed.), *Nebraska symposium on motivation 1989* (pp. 236–277). Lincoln: University of Nebraska Press.

Draguns, J. G. (1998). Transcultural psychology and the delivery of clinical psychological services. In S. Cullari (Ed.), *Foundations of clinical psychology* (pp. 375–402). Boston: Allyn & Bacon.

Draguns, J. G. (2006). Psychotherapeutic and related interventions for a global psychology. In M. J. Stevens & U. P. Gielen (Eds.), *Toward a global psychology: Theory, research, intervention, and pedagogy* (pp. 233–267). Mahwah, NJ: Erlbaum.

Draguns, J. G. (2007). Culture's impact at the workplace and beyond. *Reviews in Anthropology, 36,* 43–58.

Draguns, J. G. (2008). Universal and cultural threads in cross-cultural counseling. In P. B. Pedersen, J. G. Draguns, W. J. Lonner, & W. E. Trimble (Eds.), *Counseling across cultures* (6th ed.,). Thousand Oaks, CA: Sage.

Draguns, J. G., & Tanaka-Matsumi, J. (2003). Assessment of psychopathology across and within cultures. *Behaviour Research and Therapy, 41,* 755–776.

Folensbee, R. W., Jr., Draguns, J. G., & Danish, S. J. (1986). Impact of two types of counselor intervention on Black American, Puerto Rican, and Anglo-American analogue clients. *Journal of Counseling Psychology, 33,* 446–458.

Griner, D., & Smith, T. B. (2006). Culturally adapted mental health intervention: A meta-analytic review. *Psychotherapy: Theory, Research, Practice, Training, 43,* 531–549.

Hall, G. C. N. (2001). Psychotherapy research with ethnic minorities: Empirical, ethical, and conceptual issues. *Journal of Consulting and Clinical Psychology, 69,* 502–510.

Hofstede, G. (1980). *Culture's consequences: International differences in work related values.* Beverly Hills, CA: Sage.

Hofstede, G. (1986). Cultural differences in teaching and learning. *International Journal of Intercultural Relations, 10,* 301–320.

Hofstede, G. (2001). *Culture's consequences: Comparing values, behaviors, institutions, and organizations across nations* (2nd ed.). Thousand Oaks, CA: Sage Publications.

Hofstede, G., & Hofstede, G. J. (2005). *Cultures and organizations: Software of the mind. Intercultural cooperation and its importance for survival* (rev. ed.). New York: McGraw-Hill.

Jilek, W. G. (1995). Emil Kraepelin and comparative sociocultural psychiatry. *European Archives of Psychiatry and Clinical Neuroscience, 245,* 231–238.

Joo, E. (1998). The psychotherapeutic relationship in Korea compared to Western countries. *Korean Journal of Clinical Psychology, 17,* 39–56.

Kakar, S. (1978). *The inner world: A psychoanalytic study of childhood and society in India.* Delhi: Oxford University Press.

Katz, J. H. (1985). The sociopolitical nature of counseling. *The Counseling Psychologist, 13*(4), 615–624.

Kimura, B. (1995). *Zwischen Mensch und Mensch* [Between one human being and another] (H. Weinhendl, Trans.). Darmstadt, Germany: Akademische Verlaganstalt.

Kinzie, J. D., Fredericksen, R. H., Ben, R., Fleck, J., & Karls, W. (1984). Posttraumatic stress disorder among survivors of Cambodian concentration camps. *American Journal of Psychiatry, 141,* 145–150.

Kluckhohn, C., & Murray, H. A. (1950). Personality formation: The determinants. In C. Kluckhohn & H. A. Murray (Eds.), *Personality in nature, society, and culture* (pp. 35–38). New York: Knopf.

Kraepelin, E. (1904). Vergleichende Psychiatrie [Comparative psychiatry]. *Zentralblatt für Nervenheilkunde und Psychiatrie, 27,* 433–437.

Laungani, P. (2004). *Asian perspectives in counseling and psychotherapy.* Hove, Sussex: Brunner-Routledge.

Leong, F. T. L. (1996). Toward an integrative model for cross-cultural counseling and psychotherapy. *Applied and Preventive Psychology, 5,* 189–209.

Leong, F. T. L., & Lee, S.-H. (2006). A cultural accommodation model for cross-cultural psychotherapy: Illustrated with the case of Asian Americans. *Psychotherapy: Theory, Research, Practice, Training, 43,* 410–423.

Lopez, S. R. (1997). Cultural competence in psychopathology. A guide for clinicians and their supervisors. In C. E. Watkins (Ed.), *Handbook of psychotherapy supervision* (pp. 570–588). New York: Wiley.

Markus, H. R., & Kitayama, S. (1991). Culture and the self: Implications for cognition, emotion, and motivation. *Psychological Review, 98*(2), 224–253.

Matt, G. E. (1993). Comparing classes of psychotherapeutic interventions. A review and reanalysis of English- and German-language meta-analyses. *Journal of Cross-Cultural Psychology, 24,* 5–25.

McGoldrick, M., Giordano, J., & Garcia-Preto, N. (Eds.). (2005). *Ethnicity and family therapy* (3rd ed.). New York: Guilford.

Mollica, R. F., Wyshak, G., & Lavelle, J. (1987). The psychosocial impact of war trauma and torture on Southeast Asian refugees. *American Journal of Psychiatry, 144,* 1567–1572.

Nathan, T. (1994). *L'influence qui guérit* [The healing influence]. Paris: Odile Jacob.

Orlinsky, D. (2002). Disorder-specific, person-specific, and culture-specific psychotherapy: Evidence from psychotherapy and social science. *Der Psychotherapeut, 49,* 88–100.

Orlinsky, D. E., & Ronnestad, M. H. (2005). *Therapeutic work and professional development: The psychotherapist's perspective.* Washington, DC: APA Books.

Pedersen, P. (1999). Culture-centered interventions as a fourth dimension in psychology. In P. Pedersen (Ed.), *Multiculturalism as a fourth force* (pp. 3–18). Philadelphia: Brunner/Mazel.

Pedersen, P. B., Draguns, J. G., Lonner. W. F., & Trimble, J. E. (Ed.). (2007). *Counseling across cultures* (6th ed.). Thousand Oaks, CA: Sage.

Peltzer, K. (1995). *Psychology and health in African cultures: Examples of ethnopsychotherapeutic practice.* Frankfurt/Main: IKO-Verlag für Interkulturelle Kommunikation.

Peltzer, K. (1996). *Counseling and psychotherapy of victims of organized violence in sociocultural context.* Frankfurt/Main: IKO-Verlag für Interkulturelle Kommunikation.

Pfeiffer, W. M. (1994). *Transkulturelle Psychiatrie* [Transcultural psychiatry] (2nd ed.). Stuttgart: Thieme.

Pfeiffer, W. M. (1996). Kulturpsychiatrische Aspekte der Migration [Cultural psychiatric aspects of migration]. In E. Koch, M. Özek, & W. M. Pfeiffer (Eds.), *Psychologie und Pathologie der Migration* (pp. 17–30). Freiburg/Breisgau: Lambertus.

Rehm, L. P. (2002). Empirically supported treatments: Are they supported elsewhere? *International Clinical Psychologist, 4*(2), 1.

Rivera-Ramos, A. N. (1984). *Hacia una psicoterapia para el puertorriqueño* [Toward psychotherapy for Puerto Ricans]. San Juan: Centro para el Estudio y Desarollo de la Personalidad Puertorriqueña.

Roland, A. (1988). *In search of self in India and Japan.* Princeton, NJ: Princeton University Press.

Roland, A. (1996). *Cultural pluralism and psychoanalysis: The Asian and North American experience.* New York: Routledge.

Roland, A. (2006). Across civilizations: Psychoanalytic therapy with Asians and Asian Americans. *Psychotherapy: Theory, Research, Practice, Training, 43,* 454–463.

Seeley, K. L. (2000). *Cultural psychotherapy: Working with culture in the clinical encounter.* Northvale, NJ: Jason Aronson.

Smith, M. L., Glass, G. V., & Miller, T. I. (1980). *The benefits of psychotherapy.* Baltimore: Johns Hopkins University Press.

Snider, P. D. (2003). *Exploring the relationship between individualism and collectivism and attitudes towards counseling among ethnic Chinese, Australian, and American university students.* Unpublished doctoral dissertation, Murdoch University, Perth, Australia.

Sue, D. W., & Sue, D. (2003). *Counseling the culturally different: Theory and practice* (4th ed.). New York: Wiley.

Triandis, H. C. (1995). *Individualism and collectivism.* Boulder, CO: Westview.

Triandis, H. C., Brislin, R. W., & Hui, C. H. (1988). Cross-cultural training across the individualism-collectivism divide. *International Journal of Intercultural Relations, 15,* 65–84.

Vassiliou, G., & Vassiliou, V. G. (1973). Subjective culture and psychotherapy. *American Journal of Psychotherapy, 27,* 42–51.

Vontress, C. E. (2005). Animism: Foundation of traditional healing in sub-Saharan Africa. In R. Moodley & W. West (Eds.), *Integrating traditional healing practices into counseling and psychotherapy* (pp. 124–137). Thousand Oaks, CA: Sage.

Wachtel, P. L. (1977). *Psychoanalysis and behavior therapy: Toward an integration.* New York: Basic Books.

Wittmann, W. W., & Matt, G. E. (1986). Meta-Analyse als Integration von Forschungsergebnissen am Beispiel deutschsprachiger Arbeiten zur Effektivität von Psychotherapie [Meta-analysis as integration of research findings as exemplified by German-language studies on the effectiveness of psychotherapy]. *Psychologische Rundschau, 37,* 20–40.

Suggested Readings

Fish, J. (1996). *Culture and therapy: An integrative approach.* Northvale, NJ: Jacob Aronson.

A vivid and personal account of an American psychotherapist's experience in practicing and adapting psychotherapy in Brazil and in deriving general and practically applicable principles in the process.

McGoldrick, M., Giordano, J., & Garcia-Preto, N. (Eds.). (2005). *Ethnicity and family therapy* (3rd ed.). New York: Guilford.

The fifty chapters of this edited volume present clinically valuable information on family dynamics of various ethnically distinctive components of the United States. Focused on family therapy, it is useful to all therapists and counselors practicing in the culturally diverse settings of North America.

Pedersen, P. B., Draguns, J. G., Lonner. W. J., & Trimble, J. E. (Eds.). (2007). *Counseling across cultures* (6th ed.). Thousand Oaks, CA: Sage Publications.

One of the first books to deal with multicultural counseling when it was first published in 1976, it presents general principles of counseling and culture as well as information on several of the major ethnocultural components of the U.S. population. It also addresses counseling in emergencies and disasters, drug and alcohol problems, services to school-age and geriatric populations, spiritual concerns, and gender-related issues.

Sue, D.W., & Sue D. (Eds.). (2008). *Counseling the culturally diverse: Theory and practice* (5th ed.). New York: Wiley.

The editors of this book were among the pioneers who identified the unmet needs of ethnoculturally distinctive segments of the American population. The volume examines the sociopolitical context in which multicultural counseling occurs and invites its practitioners to scrutinize their own attitudes and possible prejudices in order to optimize the sensitivity and relevance of counseling services.

Tseng, W.-S. (2001). *Handbook of cultural psychiatry.* San Diego: Academic Press.

A virtually encyclopedic resource on all aspects of the interface between human distress and disturbance and the cultural context in which it occurs, it includes a systematic treatment of the role of culture in rendering therapy services to children, adolescents, families, the elderly, and the physically ill.

17

Principles of Multicultural Counseling and Therapy
A Selective Bibliography

Uwe P. Gielen, Juris G. Draguns, Jefferson M. Fish

Contents

This selective bibliography includes volumes, a few chapters, and some journals grouped under the following 19 headings: introductions to multicultural therapy and counseling; handbooks; works related to multicultural interventions; multicultural therapy and counseling; special populations and issues; multicultural therapy with children and adolescents; multicultural and international family therapy; the care of refugees and immigrants; the history of psychological healing in the West; psychopathology and mental health across cultures; transcultural psychiatry; culture and assessment; shamanism; altered states of consciousness; indigenous North American healing traditions; indigenous healing traditions in Latin America and the Caribbean; Asian and Oceanic healing traditions; Western psychology and Asian traditions; African and Islamic healing traditions, psychotherapy, and counseling; and selected journals. A variety of disciplines and traditions of inquiry (and fields) are represented, including medical anthropology, psychological and cultural anthropology, cross-cultural psychology, clinical psychology, counseling psychology, abnormal psychology, health psychology, family psychology, transcultural psychiatry, alternative medicine, the history of medicine, religious studies, and area studies. Readers may also wish to consult the extensive bibliography included in U. P. Gielen, J. M. Fish, & J. G. Draguns (Eds.). (2004). *Handbook of culture, therapy, and healing* (pp. 389–400). Mahwah, NJ: Lawrence Erlbaum Associates.

Introductions to Multicultural Therapy and Counseling

Abel, T., Metraux, R., & Roll, S. (1987). *Psychotherapy and culture* (rev. ed.). Albuquerque: University of New Mexico Press.
Aponte, J. R., & Wohl, J. (Eds.). (2000). *Psychological intervention and cultural diversity* (2nd ed.). Boston: Allyn & Bacon.
Atkinson, D. R. (2003). *Counseling American minorities: A cross-cultural perspective* (6th ed.). Boston: McGraw-Hill.

Costantine, M. G. (Ed.). (2007). *Clinical practice with people of color.* New York: Teachers College Press.

Costantine, M. G., & Sue, D. W. (2005). *Strategies for building multicultural competence in mental health and educational settings.* Hoboken, NJ: Wiley.

Dana, R. H. (2000). *Multicultural intervention perspectives for professional psychology.* Upper Saddle River, NJ: Prentice Hall.

Fouad, N. A., & Arredondo, P. (2007). *Becoming culturally oriented: Practical advice for psychologists and educators.* Washington, DC: American Psychological Association.

Harper, F. D., & McFadden, J. (Eds.). (2003). *Culture and counseling: New approaches.* Boston: Allyn & Bacon.

Hays, P. A. (2001). *Addressing cultural complexities in practice: A framework for clinicians and counselors.* Washington, DC: American Psychological Association.

Hoshmand, L. T. (Ed.). (2006). *Culture, psychotherapy, and counseling: Critical and integrative perspectives.* Thousand Oaks, CA: Sage.

Kazarian, S. S., & Evans, D. R. (1997). *Cultural clinical psychology: Theory, research, and practice.* New York: Oxford University Press.

Lee, C. C. (Ed.). (2006). *Multicultural issues in counseling: New approaches to diversity* (3rd ed.). Alexandria, VA: American Counseling Association.

McAuliffe, G., & Associates. (2008). *Culturally alert counseling: A comprehensive introduction.* Thousand Oaks, CA: Sage.

Palmer, S., & Laungani, P. (Eds.). (1999). *Counseling in a multicultural society.* London: Sage.

Paniagua, F. (2005). *Assessing and treating culturally diverse clients: A practical guide* (3rd ed.). Thousand Oaks, CA: Sage.

Pedersen, P. B., Draguns, J. G., Lonner, W. J., & Trimble, J. E. (Eds.). (2007). *Counseling across cultures* (6th ed.). Thousand Oaks, CA: Sage.

Seeley, K. M. (2000). *Cultural psychotherapy: Working with culture in the clinical encounter.* Northvale, NJ: Jason Aronson.

Sue, D. W., & Sue, D. (2008). *Counseling the culturally diverse: Theory and practice* (5th ed.). New York: Wiley.

Tseng, W.-S., & Streltzer, J. (Eds.). (2001). *Culture and psychotherapy: A guide to clinical practice.* Washington, DC: American Psychiatric Press.

Handbooks

Bergin, A. E., & Richards, P. S. (Eds.). (2000). *Handbook of psychotherapy and religious diversity.* Washington, DC: American Psychological Association.

Carter, R. T. (Ed.). (2004). *Handbook of racial-cultural psychology and counseling: Theory and research.* New York: Wiley.

Coleman, H. L. K., & Yeh, C. (Eds.). (2007). *Handbook of school counseling.* Philadelphia: Taylor & Francis.

Cuellar, I., & Paniagna, F. A. (Eds.). (1999). *Handbook of multicultural mental health: Assessment and treatment of diverse populations.* San Diego: Academic Press.

Gielen, U. P., Fish, J. M., & Draguns, J. G. (Eds.). (2004). *Handbook of culture, therapy, and healing.* Mahwah, NJ: Lawrence Erlbaum Associates.

Jimerson, S. R., Oakland, T. O., & Farrell, P. T. (Eds.). (2007). *The handbook of international school psychology.* Thousand Oaks, CA: Sage.

Kazarian, S. S., & Evans, D. R. (2001). *Handbook of cultural health psychology.* New York: Academic Press.

Kitayama, S., & Cohen, D. (Eds.). (2007). *Handbook of cultural psychology.* New York: Guilford.

Koenig, H. G. (Ed.). (1998). *Handbook of religion and mental health.* San Diego, CA: Academic Press.

Pedersen, P. B. (2000). *Handbook for developing multicultural awareness* (3rd ed.). Alexandria, VA: American Counseling Association.

Pedersen, P. B., & Carey, J. C. (2002). *Multicultural counseling in schools: A practical handbook* (2nd ed.). Boston: Allyn & Bacon.

Ponterotto, J. G., Casas, J. M., Suzuki, L. A., & Alexander, C. M. (Eds.). (2001). *Handbook of multicultural counseling* (2nd ed.). Thousand Oaks, CA: Sage.

Pope-Davis, D. B., Coleman, H. L. K., Liu, W. M., & Toporek, R. L. (Eds.). (2003). *Handbook of multicultural competencies in counseling and psychology.* Thousand Oaks, CA: Sage.

Prince, R. (1980). Variations in psychotherapeutic procedures. In H. C. Triandis & J. G. Draguns (Eds.), *Handbook of cross-cultural psychology: Vol. 6: Psychopathology* (pp. 291–309). Boston: Allyn & Bacon.

Sue, S., Zane, N., & Young, K. (1994). Research on psychotherapy with culturally diverse populations. In A. Bergin & S. Garfield (Eds.), *Handbook of psychotherapy and behavior change* (4th ed., pp. 783–817). New York: Wiley.

Wong, P. T. P., & Wong, L. C. J. (Eds.). (2005). *Handbook of multicultural perspectives on stress and coping.* New York: Springer.

Works Related to Multicultural Interventions

Adler, L. L., & Mukherji, B. R. (Eds.). (1995). *Spirit versus scalpel: Traditional healing and modern psychotherapy.* Westport, CT: Bergin & Garvey.

Andrews, M. M., & Boyle, J. S. (2003). *Transcultural concepts in nursing care* (4th ed.). Philadelphia: Lippincott Williams & Wilkins.

Brody, H. (1992). *The healer's power.* New Haven, CT: Yale University Press.

Corey, G., Corey, M. S., & Callanan, P. (2007). *Issues and ethics in the helping professions* (7th ed.). Belmont, CA: Thomson Brooks Cole.

Csordas, T. (1994). *The sacred self: A cultural phenomenology of charismatic healing.* Berkeley: University of California Press.

Dwairy, M. (2006). *Counseling and psychotherapy with Arabs and Muslims: A culturally sensitive approach.* New York: Teachers College Press.

Eisenberg, D. (Ed.). (2002). *Complementary and alternative medicine: State of the science and clinical applications.* Cambridge, MA: Harvard Medical School.

Fish, J. M. (1973). *Placebo therapy: A practical guide to social influence in psychotherapy.* San Francisco, CA: Jossey-Bass.

Fish, J. M. (1996). *Culture and therapy: An integrative approach.* Northvale, NJ: Jason Aronson.

Frank, J. D., & Frank, J. B. (1991). *Persuasion and healing: A comparative study of psychotherapy* (3rd rev. ed.). Baltimore: John Hopkins University Press.

Gurung, R. A. R. (2006). *Health psychology: A cultural approach.* Belmont, CA: Thomson Wadsworth.

Kiev, A. (Ed.). (1974). *Magic, faith, and healing: Studies in primitive psychology today.* New York: Free Press.

Kinsley, D. (1996). *Health, healing and religion: A cross-cultural perspective.* Upper Saddle River, NJ: Prentice Hall.

Kirsch, I. (Ed.). (1999). *How expectancies shape experience.* Washington, DC: American Psychological Association.

McCalin, C. S. (Ed.). (1989). *Women as healers: Cross-cultural perspectives.* New Brunswick, NJ: Rutgers University Press.

Moodley, R. (2006). *Race, culture, and psychotherapy: Critical perspectives in multicultural practice.* New York: Routledge.

Moodley, R., & West, W. (Eds.). (2005). *Integrating traditional healing practice into counseling and psychotherapy.* Thousand Oaks, CA: Sage.

Moyers, B. (1993). *Healing and the mind.* New York: Doubleday.

Romanucci-Ross, L., Moerman, E. E., Moerman, D. R., & Tancredi, L. R. (Eds.). (1997). *The anthropology of medicine: From culture to method* (3rd ed.). Westport, CT: Greenwood.

Sargent, C. F., & Johnson, T. M. (Eds.). (1996). *Medical anthropology: Contemporary theory and method* (rev. ed.). Westport, CT: Praeger.

Scheff, T. (1979). *Catharsis in healing, ritual, and drama.* Berkeley: University of California Press.

Ukasha, A., Arboleda-Florez, J., & Sartorius, N. (Eds.). (2000). *Ethics, culture, and psychiatry: International perspectives.* Arlington, VA: American Psychiatric Publishing.

Wampold, B. E. (2001). *The great psychotherapy debate: Models, methods, and findings.* Mahwah, NJ: Lawrence Erlbaum Associates.

Multicultural Therapy and Counseling: Special Populations and Issues

Boyd-Franklin, N. (2006). *Black families in therapy: Understanding the African American experience* (2nd ed.). New York: Guilford.

Comas-Díaz, L., & Greene, B. (Eds.). (1994). *Women of color: Integrating ethnic and gender identities in psychotherapy.* New York: Guilford Press.

Fukuyama, M. A., & Sevig, T. D. (1999). *Integrating spirituality into multicultural counseling.* Thousand Oaks, CA: Sage.

Garcia, J. C., & Zea, M. C. (Eds.). (1997). *Psychological interventions and research with Latino populations.* Needham Heights, MA: Allyn & Bacon.

Hays, P. A., & Iwamasa, G. Y. (Eds.). (2006). *Culturally responsive cognitive-behavioral therapy.* Washington, DC: American Psychological Association.

Laungani, P. (2004). *Asian perspectives in counseling and psychotherapy.* Hove, UK: Brunner-Routledge.

Lee, E. (Ed.). (1997). *Working with Asian Americans. A guideline for clinicians.* New York: Guilford.
Leong, T. L., & Savickas, M. L. (Eds.) (2007, January). Special Issue on International Perspectives on Counseling Psychology. *Applied Psychology, 56*(1).
Marsella, A. J., Friedman, M. J., Gerrity, E. T., & Scurfield, R. M. (Eds.). (1996). *Ethnocultural aspects of posttraumatic stress disorder: Issues, research, and clinical applications.* Washington, DC: American Psychological Association.
Nathan, T. (1994). *L'influence qui guérit* [The healing influence]. Paris: Odile Jacob.
Velasquez, R. J., Arellano, L. M., & McNeill, B. W. (Eds.). (2004). *The handbook of Chicano psychology and mental health.* Mahwah, NJ: Lawrence Erlbaum Associates.

Multicultural Therapy With Children and Adolescents

Canino, I. A., & Spurlock, J. (2000). *Culturally diverse children and adolescents: Assessment, diagnosis, and treatment.* New York: Guilford.
Cramer-Azima, F. J., & Grizenko, N. (Eds.). (2002). *Immigrant and refugee children and their families: Clinical, research, and training issues.* Madison, CT: International Universities Press.
Fadiman, A. (1998). *The spirit catches you and you fall down. A Hmong child, her American doctors and the collision of two cultures.* Farrar, Straus & Giroux.
Ho, M. K. (1992). *Minority children and adolescents in therapy.* Newbury Park, CA: Sage.
Koss-Chioino, J. D., & Vargas, A. (1999). *Working with Latino youth: Culture, context, and development.* San Francisco: Jossey-Bass.
Ungar, M. (Ed.). (2005). *Handbook for working with children and youth: Pathways to resilience across cultures and contexts.* Thousand Oaks, CA: Sage.
Vargas, L. A., & Koss-Chioino, J. D. (Eds.). (1992). *Working with culture: Psychotherapeutic interventions with ethnic minority children and adolescents.* San Francisco: Jossey-Bass.

Multicultural and International Family Therapy

Falicov, C. J. (1998). *Hispanic families in therapy.* New York: Guilford.
Gielen, U. P., & Comunian, A. L. (Eds.). (1998). *The family and family therapy in international perspective.* Trieste, Italy: Lint.
Gielen, U. P., & Comunian, A. L. (Eds.). (1999). *International approaches to the family and family therapy.* Padua, Italy: UNIPRESS.
Gopaul-McNicol, S. A. (1994). *Working with West Indian families.* New York: Guilford.
Ho, M. K. (1987). *Family therapy with ethnic minorities.* Newbury Park, CA: Sage.
Lee, E. (1998). *American Asian families: A clinical guide to working with families.* New York: Guilford.

Lefley, H. P., & Johnson, D. L. (Eds.). (2002). *Family interventions in mental illness: International perspectives.* Westport, CT: Praeger.

McGoldrick, M. (Ed.). (2002). *Re-visioning family therapy: Race, culture, and gender in clinical practice.* New York: Guilford.

McGoldrick, M., Giordano, J., & Garcia-Preto, N. (Eds.). (2005). *Ethnicity and family therapy* (3rd ed.). New York: Guilford.

Minuchin, P., Colapinto, J., & Minuchin, S. (2007). *Working with families of the poor* (2nd ed.). New York: Guilford.

Ng, K. S. (2003). *Global perspectives in family therapy.* New York: Brunner-Routledge.

Nichols, W. C. (Ed.). (2004). *Family therapy around the world: A Festschrift for Florence W. Kaslow.* Binghamton, NY: Haworth Press.

Wehrly, B., Kenney, K. R., & Kenney, M. E. (1999). *Counseling multiracial families.* Thousand Oaks, CA: Sage.

Zimmerman, T. S. (Ed.). (2001). *Integrating gender and culture in family therapy training.* Binghamton, NY: Haworth Press.

The Care of Refugees and Immigrants

Bemak, F., Chung, C-Y., & Pedersen, P. B. (2003). *Counseling refugees: A psychosocial approach to innovative multicultural counseling interventions.* Westport, CT: Greenwood Press.

Ingleby, D. (2005). *Forced migration and mental health: Rethinking the care of refugees and displaced persons.* New York: Springer.

Kemp, C., & Rasbridge, L. A. (2004). *Refugee and immigrant health: A handbook for health professionals.* Cambridge, UK: Cambridge University Press.

Marsella, A. J., Bornemann, T., Ekblad, S., & Orley, J. (Eds.). (1994). *Amidst peril and pain: The mental health and well-being of the world's refugees.* Washington, DC: American Psychological Association.

Peltzer, K., Aycha, A., & Bittenbinder, E. (Eds.). (1995). *Gewalt und Trauma. Psychopathologie und Behandlung im Kontext von Flüchtlingen und Opfern organisierter Gewalt* [Violence and trauma: Psychopathology and treatment in the context of refugees and victims of organized violence]. Frankfurt/M., Germany: IKO-Verlag für Interkulturelle Kommunikation.

Westermeyer, J. (1989). *Psychiatric care of migrants: A clinical guide.* Washington, DC: American Psychiatric Press.

Wilson, J., & Drozdek, B. (Eds.). (2004). *Broken spirits: The treatment of traumatized asylum seekers, refugees, war and torture victims.* New York: Brunner-Routledge.

The History of Psychological Healing in the West

Crabtree, A. (1993). *From Mesmer to Freud: Magnetic sleep and the roots of psychological healing.* New Haven, CT: Yale University Press.

Davies, S. (1995). *Jesus the healer: Possession, trance, and the origins of Christianity.* New York: Continuum International.

Edelstein, E., & Edelstein, L. (1945). *Asclepius* (Vols. 1–2). Baltimore: John Hopkins University Press.

Ellenberger, H. F. (1970). *The discovery of the unconscious: The history and evolution of dynamic psychiatry*. New York: Basic Books.

Entralgo, P. L. (1970). *The therapy of the word in classical antiquity* (L. J. Rather & J. H. Sharp, Trans.). New Haven, CT: Yale University Press.

Freedheim, D. K. (Ed.). (1992). *History of psychotherapy: A century of change*. Washington, DC: American Psychological Association.

Grawe, K., Donati, R., & Bernauer, F. (1994). *Psychotherapie im Wandel—Von der Konfession zur Profession* [Psychotherapy in transition: From confession to profession], (3rd ed.), CT Goettingen, Germany: Hogrefe.

Jackson, S. W. (1999). *Care of the psyche: A history of psychological healing*. New Haven: Yale University Press.

McNeill, J. T. (1965). *A history of the cure of souls*. New York: Harper Torchbooks.

Meier, C. A. (1967). *Ancient incubation and modern psychotherapy*. Evanston, IL: Evanston.

Pilch, J. J. (2000). *Healing in the New Testament: Insights from medical and Mediterranean anthropology*. Minneapolis, MN: Fortress Press.

Plotkin, M. (2001). *Freud in the Pampas: The formation of a psychoanalytical culture in Argentina*. Palo Alto, CA: Stanford University Press.

Zilboorg, G., & Henry, G. W. (1941). *A history of medical psychology*. New York: Norton.

Psychopathology and Mental Health Across Cultures

Al-Issa, I. (Ed.). (1995). *Handbook of culture and mental illness: An international perspective*. Madison, WI: International Universities Press.

Desjarlais, R., Eisenberg, L., Good, B., & Kleinman, A. (1995). *World mental health: Problems and priorities in low-income countries*. New York: Oxford University Press.

Gaw, A. C. (Ed.). (1993). *Culture, ethnicity, and mental illness*. Washington, DC: American Psychiatry Press.

Kleinman, A. M., & Good, B. (Eds.). (1985). *Culture and depression: Studies in the anthropology and cross-cultural psychiatry of affect and disorder*. Berkeley: University of California Press.

Marsella, A. J., Friedman, M. J., Gerrity, E. T., & Scurfield, R. M. (Eds.). (1996). *Ethnocultural aspects of posttraumatic stress disorder: Issues, research, and clinical applications*. Washington, DC: American Psychological Association.

Schumaker, J. F., & Ward, T. (Eds.). (2001). *Cultural cognition and psychopathology*. Westport, CT: Praeger.

Tanaka-Matsumi, J. (2001). Abnormal psychology and culture. In D. Matsumoto (Ed.), *The handbook of culture and psychology* (pp. 265–286). New York: Oxford University Press.

Tanaka-Matsumi, J., & Draguns, J. (1997). Culture and psychopathology. In J. W. Berry, M. H. Segall, & Ç. Kagitçibasi (Eds.), *Handbook of cross-cultural psychology, Vol. 3: Social behavior and applications* (pp. 449–491). Boston: Allyn & Bacon.

Transcultural Psychiatry

Gaines, A. (Ed.). (1992). *Ethnopsychiatry: The cultural construction of professional and folk psychiatries.* Albany, NY: State University of New York Press.
Gaw, A. C. (Ed.). *Culture, ethnicity, and mental health.* Washington, DC: American Psychiatric Press.
Higginbotham, H. N. (1984). *Third World challenge to psychiatry: Culture accommodation and mental health care.* Honolulu: University of Hawaii Press.
Kiev, A. (1972). *Transcultural psychiatry.* New York: Free Press.
Kleinman, A. (1980). *Patients and healers in the context of culture: An exploration of the borderland between anthropology, medicine, and psychiatry.* Berkeley: University of California Press.
Kleinman, A. (1988a). *The illness narratives: Suffering, healing and the human condition.* New York: Free Press.
Kleinman, A. (1988b). *Rethinking psychiatry: From cultural category to personal experience.* New York: Free Press.
Lim, R. F. (Ed.). (2006). *Clinical manual of cultural psychiatry.* Arlington, VA: American Psychiatric Publishing.
Murphy, H. B. M. (1992). *Comparative psychiatry.* Berlin: Springer-Verlag.
Pfeiffer, W. M. (1994). *Transkulturelle Psychiatrie: Ergebnisse und Probleme* [Transcultural psychiatry: Results and problems] (2nd ed.). Stuttgart: Thieme.
Skultans, V., & Cox, J. (Eds.). (2000). *Anthropological approaches to psychological medicine: Crossing bridges.* London: Jessica Kingsley.
Torrey, E. F. (1986). *Witchdoctors and psychiatrists: The common roots of psychotherapy and its future.* New York: Harper & Row.
Tseng, W.-S. (Ed.). (2001). *Handbook of cultural psychiatry.* San Diego, CA: Academic Press.

Culture and Assessment

Dana, R. H. (Ed.). (1998). *Handbook of cross-cultural and multicultural personality assessment.* Mahwah, NJ: Erlbaum.
Dana, R. H. (2005). *Multicultural assessment: Principles, applications, and examples.* Mahwah, NJ: Lawrence Erlbaum Associates.
Mezzich, J. E., Kleinman, A., Fabrega, H., Jr. & Parron, D. L. (Eds.). (1996). *Culture and psychiatric diagnosis: A DSM-IV perspective.* Washington, DC: American Psychiatric Press.
Suzuki, L. A., Meller, P. J., & Ponterotto, J. G. (Eds.). (1996). *Handbook of multicultural assessment: Clinical, psychological, and educational applications.* San Francisco: Jossey-Bass.

Shamanism

Atkinson, J. M. (1992). Shamanisms today. *Annual Review of Anthropology, 21,* 307–330.

Eliade, M. (1964). *Shamanism: Archaic techniques of ecstasy.* New York: Pantheon.

Harner, M. (1984/1990). *The way of the shaman.* San Francisco: Harper.

Kalweit, H. (1992). *Shamans, healers, and medicine men* (M. Kohn, Trans.). London: Shambhala.

Pratt, V. (Ed.). (2007). *An encyclopedia of shamanism: A comprehensive guide to the field of shamanism* (Vols. 1–2). New York: Rosen Publishing Group.

Vitebsky, P. (1995). *The shaman. Voyages of the soul, trance, ecstasy, and healing from Siberia to the Amazon.* Boston: Little, Brown.

Walter, M. N., & Fridman, E. J. (Eds.). (2004). *Shamanism: An encyclopedia of world beliefs, practices, and culture* (Vol. 1). Santa Barbara, CA: ABC-CLIO.

Winckelman, M. (2000). *Shamanism: The neural ecology of consciousness and healing.* Westpoint, CT: Bergin and Garvey.

Altered States of Consciousness

Bourguignon, E. (1976). *Possession.* San Francisco: Chandler & Sharp.

Dobkin de Rios, M. (1984). *Hallucinogens: A cross-cultural perspective.* Albuquerque: University of New Mexico Press.

Eliade, M. (1958). *Yoga: Immortality and freedom.* Princeton, NJ: Bollington Foundation.

Goldman, D. (1977). *The varieties of meditative experience.* New York: Irvington.

Lewis, I. M. (1989). *Ecstatic religion: An anthropological study of spirit possession and shamanism* (2nd ed.). New York: Routledge.

Prince, R. (Ed.). (1968). *Trance and possession states.* Montreal: Buck Memorial Society.

Schultes, R. E., Hoffman, A., & Ratsch, C. (2001). *Plants of the gods: Their sacred healing and hallucinogenic powers.* Rochester, VT: Healing Arts Press.

Stoler Miller, B. (Trans.). (1998). *Yoga: Discipline of freedom: The Yoga Sutra attributed to Pantanjali.* New York: Bantam.

Suryani, L. K., & Jensen, G. D. (1993). *Trance and possession in Bali.* Kuala Lumpur, Malaysia: Oxford University Press.

Ward, C. A. (Ed.). (1989). *Altered states of consciousness: A cross-cultural perspective.* Newbury Park, CA: Sage.

Indigenous North American Healing Traditions

Devereux, G. (1969). *Mohave ethnopsychiatry: The psychic disturbances of an Indian tribe.* Washington, DC: Smithsonian Institute Press. (Original work published 1961)

Farris, J. C. (1990). *The Nightway: A history and a history of documentation of a Navajo ceremonial.* Albuquerque: University of New Mexico Press.

Hultkranz, A. (1992). *Shamanic healing and ritual drama: Health and medicine in native North American religions.* New York: Crossroad.

Jilek, W. G. (1974). *Salish Indian mental health and culture change. Psychohygienic and therapeutic aspects of the guardian spirit ceremonial.* Toronto: Holt, Rinehart & Winston.

Jilek, W. G. (1982). *Indian healing: Shamanic ceremonialism in the Pacific Northwest today.* Blaine, WA: Hancock House.

Keeney, B. (Ed.). (2001). *Walking Thunder: Diné medicine woman.* Stony Creek, CT: Leete's Island Books.

Lame Deer, J., & Erdoes, R. (1972). *Lame Deer, seeker of visions.* New York: Simon & Schuster.

Lyon, W. S. (1996). *Encyclopedia of Native American healing.* Santa Barbara, CA: ABC-CLIO.

Neihardt, J. G. (1932/1973). *Black Elk speaks.* New York: Washington Square Press.

Perrone, B., Stockel, H., & Krueger, V. (1989). *Medicine women, curanderas, and women doctors.* Norman: University of Oklahoma Press.

Rasmussen, K. (1952). *Intellectual culture of the Hudson Bay Eskimos. Report of the Fifth Thule Expedition, 1921–1924, Vol. 7* (W. E. Calvent, Trans.). Copenhagen: Gyldenval.

St. Pierre, M., & Soldier, T. L. (1995). *Walking in the sacred manner: Healers, dreamers, and pipe carriers—Medicine women of the Plains Indians.* New York: Touchstone.

Wolfson, E. (1992). *From the earth to beyond the sky: Native American medicine.* Boston: Houghton Mifflin.

Indigenous Healing Traditions in Latin America and the Caribbean

Brodwin, P. (1996). *Medicine and morality in Haiti: The contest for healing power.* New York: Cambridge University Press.

Brown, K. M. (1991). *Mama Lola: A Voodoo priestess in Brooklyn.* Berkeley: University of California Press.

Dobkin de Rios, M. (1972/1984). *Visionary vine: Hallucinogenic healing in the Peruvian Amazon.* Prospect Heights, IL: Waveland.

Dobkin de Rios, M. (1992). *Amazon healer: The life and times of an urban shaman.* Bridgeport, UK: Arism Press.

Fabrega, Jr., H., & Silver, D. B. (1973). *Illness and shamanistic curing in Zinacantan.* Stanford, CA: Stanford University Press.

Finkler, K. (1985). *Spiritualist healers in Mexico: Successes and failures in alternative therapeutics.* South Hadley, MA: Bergin & Garvey.

Keeney, B. (Ed.). (2003). *Hands of faith: Healers of Brazil.* Stony Creek, CT: Leete's Island Books.

Kiev, A. (1968). *Curanderismo.* New York: Free Press.

Koss-Chioino, J. D. (1992). *Women as healers, women as patients: Mental health care and traditional healing in Puerto Rico.* Boulder, CO: Westview Press.

Langdon, J. M., & Baer, G. (1992). *Portals of power: Shamanism in South America.* Albuquerque: University of New Mexico Press.

Reichel-Dolmatoff, G. (1975). *The shaman and the jaguar: A study of narcotic drugs among the Indians of Colombia.* Philadelphia: Temple University Press.

Rubel, A. J., O'Neill, C. W., & Collado, A. R. (1984). *Susto: A folk illness.* Berkeley: University of California Press.

Trotter, R. T., & Chavira, J. A. (1981). *Curanderismo: Mexican American folk healing.* Athens: University of Georgia Press.

Asian and Oceanic Healing Traditions

Clifford, T. (1984). *Tibetan Buddhist medicine and psychiatry: The diamond healing.* York Beach, ME: Samuel Weiser.

Cohen, K. S. (1997). *The way of qigong: The art and science of Chinese energy healing.* New York: Ballantine.

Desjarlais, R. R. (1992). *Body and emotion. The aesthetics of illness and healing in the Nepal Himalayas.* Philadelphia: University of Pennsylvania Press.

Dioszégi, V., & Hoppál, M. (Eds.). (1978). *Shamanism in Siberia.* Budapest: Akadémiai Kiadó.

Doi, L. T. (1973). *Anatomy of dependence.* Tokyo: Kodansha International.

Kakar, S. (1982). *Shamans, mystics, and doctors: A psychological inquiry into India and its healing traditions.* New York: Alfred A. Knopf.

Keeney, B., & Osumi, I. (Eds.). (2000). *Ikuko Osumi, Japanese master of Seiki Jutsu.* Stony Creek, CT: Leete's Island Books.

Lei, T. (2004). Indigenous Chinese healing: Theories and methods. In U. P. Gielen, J. M. Fish, & J. G. Draguns (Eds.), *Handbook of culture, therapy, and healing* (pp. 191–212). Mahwah, NJ: Lawrence Erlbaum Associates.

Reynolds, D. (1980). *The quiet therapies: Japanese pathways to personal growth.* Honolulu: University of Hawai'i Press.

Reynolds, D. K. (1983). *Naikan psychotherapy: Meditation for self-development.* Chicago: University of Chicago Press.

Western Psychology and Asian Traditions

Epstein, M. (1995). *Thoughts without a thinker. Psychotherapy from a Buddhist perspective.* New York: Basic Books.

Goleman, D. (2003). *Healing emotions: Conversations with the Dalai Lama on mindfulness, emotions, and health* (new ed.). Boston: Shambala.

Roland, A. (1988). *In search of self in India and Japan: Toward a cross-cultural psychology.* Princeton, NJ: Princeton University Press.

Roland, A. (1996). *Cultural pluralism and psychoanalysis: The Asian and North American experience.* New York: Routledge.

Rubin, J. B. (1996). *Psychotherapy and Buddhism: Toward an integration.* New York: Plenum.

Segal, S. (Ed.). (2003). *Encountering Buddhism: Western psychology and Buddhist teachings.* Albany: State University of New York.

Uno, M. (Ed.). (2006). *Buddhism and psychotherapy across cultures: Essays on theories and practices.* Somerville, MA: Wisdom Publishing.

African and Islamic Healing Traditions, Psychotherapy, and Counseling

Ahmed, R. A., & Gielen, U. P. (1998). *Psychology in the Arab countries.* Menoufia, Egypt: Menoufia University Press.

Al-Issa, I. (Ed.). (2000). *Al-Junun: Mental illness in the Islamic world.* Madison, CT: International Universities Press.

Al-Issa, I., & Al-Subaie, A. (2004). Native healing in Arab-Islamic societies. In U. P. Gielen, J. M. Fish, & J. G. Draguns (Eds.), *Handbook of culture, therapy, and healing* (pp. 343–365). Mahwah, NJ: Lawrence Erlbaum Associates.

Boddy, J. (1989). *Wombs and alien spirits: Women, men, and the Zar Cult in Northern Sudan.* Madison: University of Wisconsin Press.

Crapanzano, V. (1973). *The Hamadsha: A study in Moroccan ethnopsychiatry.* Berkeley: University of California Press.

Janzen, J. M. (1992). *Ngoma: Discourses of healing in central and southern Africa.* Berkeley: University of California Press.

Katz, R. (1982). *Boiling energy: Community healing among the Kalahari !Kung.* Cambridge, MA: Harvard University Press.

Katz, R., Biesele, M., & St. Denis, V. (1997). *Healing makes our hearts happy.* Rochester, VT: Inner Traditions.

Leighton, A. H., Lambo, C. G., Hughes, C. G., Murphy, J. M., & Macklin, D. B. (1963). *Psychiatric disorder among the Yoruba.* Ithaca, NY: Cornell University Press.

Lewis, I. M., Al-Safi, A., & Hurreiz, S. (Eds.). (1991). *Women's medicine. The Zari-Bori cult in Africa and beyond.* Edinburgh: Edinburgh University Press for the International African Institute.

Nathan, T., & Hounkpatin, L. (1996). *La guérison Yoruba* [Yoruba healing]. Paris: Odile Jacob.

Peltzer, K. ((1995). *Psychology and health in African cultures: Examples of ethnopsychotherapeutic practice.* Frankfurt/M.: IKO-Verlag für Interkulturelle Kommunikation.

Peltzer, K., & Ebigbo, P. O. (1989). *Clinical psychology in Africa.* Enugu, Nigeria: Work Group for African Psychology.

Turner, E. (1992). *Experiencing ritual: A new interpretation of African healing.* Philadelphia: University of Pennsylvania Press.

Selected Journals

American Journal of Community Psychology
Anthropologia Medica

Counseling Psychologist
Cultural Diversity and Ethnic Minority Psychology (previously *Cultural Diversity and Mental Health* [1995–98])
Culture, Medicine and Psychiatry
Curare
International Journal of Social Psychiatry
Journal for the Psychoanalysis of Culture and Society
Journal of Counseling Psychology
Journal of Multicultural Counseling and Development
Journal of Transcultural Nursing
Medical Anthropology
Medical Anthropology Quarterly
Multicultural Journal of Social Work
Nouvelle Revue d'Ethnopsychiatrie
Shaman's Drum
Social Psychiatry
Social Science and Medicine
Transcultural Psychiatry (previously *Transcultural Psychiatry Research Review* [1963–99])
Zeitschrift für Ethnomedizin und transkulturelle Psychiatrie [Journal for Ethnomedicine and Transcultural Psychiatry]

About the Editors

Uwe P. Gielen, PhD, is professor of psychology and director of the Institute for International and Cross-Cultural Psychology at St. Francis College, where he served previously as chair of the Psychology Department. He received his PhD in social psychology from Harvard University. His work has centered on cross-cultural and international psychology, Tibetan studies, international family psychology and therapy, and moral development. Dr. Gielen is the senior editor or coeditor of 18 volumes, including two volumes on international family therapy that were published in Italy. He is a former president of both the International Council of Psychologists (ICP) and the Society for Cross-Cultural Research (SCCR) as well as president of APA's International Psychology Division (2008). He has done fieldwork in the Himalayas and conducted research in North America, the Caribbean, Europe, Asia, and the Arab world. His recent edited volumes include *Handbook of Culture, Therapy, and Healing* (2004), *Childhood and Adolescence: Cross-Cultural Perspectives and Applications* (2004), *Families in Global Perspective* (2005), and *Toward a Global Psychology: Theory, Research, Intervention, and Pedagogy* (2007). For more information, go to http://www.iiccp.freeservers.com.

Juris G. Draguns, PhD, Dhc, is professor emeritus of clinical psychology at Pennsylvania State University. He has coauthored and coedited several books on cross-cultural psychology—predominantly psychopathology, personality, and counseling—including six editions of *Counseling Across Cultures,* Volume 6: *Psychopathology* in the six-volume *Handbook of Cross-Cultural Psychology, Personality and Person Perception Across Cultures,* and *Handbook of Culture, Therapy, and Healing.* He is author or coauthor of 160 publications on microgenesis, cognitive style, models of psychopathology, and culture and personality. Dr. Draguns has held visiting appointments in Germany, Australia, Taiwan, Latvia, and Hawaii and is the recipient of the 2001 Award for Distinguished Contributions to the International Advancement of Psychology by the American Psychological Association.

Jefferson M. Fish, PhD, is professor emeritus of psychology at St. John's University, where he previously served as chair of the Department of Psychology and as director of the PhD program in clinical psychology. He is the author, editor, or coeditor of nine books; is the author of more than 100 journal articles, book chapters, and other works; and was a Fulbright scholar in Brazil and China. Dr. Fish, who spent 2 years as a visiting professor in Brazil and who lived for a month with the Krikati Indians, speaks English, Portuguese, French, and Spanish, as well as some German. He is a fellow of the American Psychological Association and of the Association for Psychological Science and is an American Board of Professional Psychology Diplomate in both clinical psychology and family psychology. He has served on the editorial boards of eight journals in the United States, Brazil, and India and has been a consulting editor or invited reviewer for nine others.

About the Contributors

Jasem Mohammed A. Al-Khawajah, PhD, was born in Kuwait in 1954. He studied psychology at Kuwait University where he obtained his B.S. He then went on to attain his master's degree at the University of Wisconsin–Milwaukee, USA, and his PhD at the University of Surrey in the United Kingdom. He is the past chairman of the Psychology Department at Kuwait University, where he teaches counseling psychology. In addition, he has also worked as a counselor at the Mental Hospital in Kuwait, Kuwait's Social Development Office, and at the family courts to help families overcome their problems before seeking divorce. Furthermore, he has served part-time as a supervisory counselor for a crisis hotline. The cognitive-behavioral therapy has been his main approach to counseling, and he has been especially interested in family counseling.

Louise Baca, PhD, earned her degree in clinical psychology from Arizona State University (ASU) and has worked in a range of clinical settings, including Community Mental Health and Prevention Centers and ASU's Counseling and Consultation Center. She has also served as director of ASU's Multicultural Advancement Program. After teaching at ASU for 12 years she joined the faculty of the Arizona School of Professional Psychology/Argosy University in 1999. She currently works with all aspects of diversity training and group psychotherapy and teaches and publishes primarily within this area. Her current work pertains to the use of Native American/Latino spirituality in the healing process.

Hardin Coleman, PhD, is a professor of counseling psychology and associate dean of Continuing Studies and Diversity Initiatives in the School of Education at the University of Wisconsin–Madison. Professor Coleman joined the faculty in 1991. His primary teaching and training focus is on the development of school counselors. He also teaches family therapy, supervision, advanced clinical courses, spirituality in counseling, and multicultural competence. He provides a wide range of professional development training in multicultural competence for teachers. His clinical focus is with lower-income African American families, with a particular interest in adolescents. His current research focus is on the noncognitive factors that affect minority student achievement in K–12 educational settings and interventions that enhance cultural identity development. His other research interests include the development of cultural identity, strategies for effectively coping with cultural diversity, and bicultural competence. He is a graduate of Germantown Friends School, Williams College, University of Vermont, and Stanford University.

Geoff Denham, PhD, is director of postgraduate studies in psychology at the Auckland University of Technology, New Zealand. He is past chair of the Australian Psychological Society's Counseling College and coordinating editor of the *Australian Journal of Counseling Psychology*. He has worked as a counseling psychologist in both government and nongovernment sectors and has also worked in private practice. Prior to taking up an academic post in 2000 he coordinated the counseling service to Kosovars in Australia under the government-funded Operation Safehaven that brought almost 4,000 refugees to Australia in the second half of 1999 following government-sponsored ethnic cleansing in Serbia. His published work is on the potency of representation and discourse in psychotherapy and counseling, the medicalizing of human suffering and distress (and its consequences), transcultural mental health, and (virtual) community through e-culture and its consequences for modern personal identity.

Michele S. Hirsch, PhD, is a professor of psychology and director of the Women's Center at St. Francis College in Brooklyn Heights, New York. Her interests lie in the area of health psychology, specifically pain, trauma, the mind/body connection, psychoneuroimmunology, and healing. She authored a chapter on a biopsychosocial perspective on cross-cultural healing that appears in the *Handbook of Culture, Therapy, and Healing* (2004). Additionally, she has published in the journals *Pain* and *Clinical Infectious Diseases* and has presented at regional, national, and international conferences.

Wolfgang G. Jilek, MD, MSc, MA, Dipl Psych, FRCP(C), was born in 1930 of Austrian parentage. He is clinical professor emeritus of psychiatry, University of British Columbia, Vancouver, Canada; affiliate professor, Department of Psychiatry and Behavioral Sciences, University of Washington, Seattle, USA; and guest professor in transcultural and ethno-psychiatry, University of Vienna, Austria. Trained in Germany, Austria, Switzerland, the United States, and Canada, he holds in degrees in medicine, general and social psychiatry, and social anthropology. He served the World Health Organization as mental health consultant in Papua New Guinea and the South Pacific, the UN High Commissioner for Refugees as refugee mental health coordinator in Thailand, and the World Psychiatric Association as long-term chairman of its Transcultural Psychiatry Section. His primary research interests include comparative cultural psychiatry, ethnopsychology, and ethnomedicine, in which fields he conducted investigations in east Africa, the Caribbean, South America, southeast Asia, Papua New Guinea, and South Pacific islands and among North American indigenous and ethnic populations. Dr. Jilek has published three books and 125 articles and chapters in scientific journals and books.

Joan D. Koss-Chioino, PhD, is professor emerita in anthropology at Arizona State University, currently research professor at George Washington University, and adjunct professor in the Department of Psychiatry and Neurology, Tulane Medical Center. She is a board member of the Metanexus Institute in Philadelphia, Pennsylvania. Koss-Chioino focuses her current interests on cultural psychology, cultural psychiatry, medical anthropology, and art and ritual. She has carried out research in Puerto Rico, Mexico, New Mexico, and Bali, Indonesia, as well as among Puerto Ricans, Mexican Americans, Mexican immigrant families and adolescents, and African Americans in clinical settings in the United States. This work has resulted in 70 articles and chapters and five books. *Working With Latino Youth: Culture, Development and Context* with Luis A. Vargas (Jossey-Bass, 1999) is relevant for readers of this book on counseling. The most recent book, coedited with Philip Hefner (Altamira Press, 2006), is *Spiritual Transformation and Healing: Anthropological, Theological, Neuroscience and Clinical Perspectives.*

Judy Kuriansky, PhD, is a licensed clinical psychologist on the adjunct faculty of the Department of Counseling and Clinical psychology at Columbia University Teachers College and Columbia Medical Center's Department of Psychiatry, and honorary professor at Peking University Health Science Center and the Department of Psychiatry at the University of Hong Kong. A representative at the United Nations for the International Association of Applied Psychology and the World Council of Psychotherapy, she has done disaster relief after 9/11 in the United States, the Asian tsunami, SARS in China, bombings in Israel, and earthquakes around the world. A journalist, award-winning TV news reporter and radio talk show host for 22 years, she is columnist for the *New York Daily News, China Trends Health Magazine,* and others, and author of books including *The Complete Idiot's Guide to a Healthy Relationship* (2nd ed.), *Terror in the Holy Land: Inside the Anguish of the Israeli-Palestinian*

Conflict, and *Beyond Bullets and Bombs: Grassroots peacemaking between Israelis and Palestinians.*

Pittu Laungani, PhD, was a senior research fellow at Manchester University, United Kingdom, at the time of his death in 2007. Prior to this appointment he spent many years teaching counseling psychology at South Bank University, London. A specialist in cross-cultural counseling and death and bereavement studies, he is the author of numerous articles, chapters, and books. They include four volumes on *Death and Bereavement Around the World* (2002–2006), *Asian Perspectives in Counseling and Psychotherapy* (2004), and *Understanding Cross-Cultural Psychology: Eastern and Western Perspectives* (2007).

Jennifer J. Lindwall, MS, is a doctoral student at the University of Wisconsin–Madison in the Department of Counseling Psychology. Upon receiving her master's in counseling, she became licensed as a school counselor and worked with elementary and middle school students before pursuing her doctorate. Additionally, she has worked as a teacher, mentor, and counselor for youth and families in a variety of settings, including precollege programs, an after-school program, a community counseling agency, and primary care settings. Her clinical and research interests include school counseling, school psychology, prevention science, and the creation of effective interventions for culturally diverse youth. She also assists in the development and delivery of courses for K–12 educators that focus on addressing the cultural factors that impact the educational experiences of diverse youth.

Jeffrey B. Rubin, PhD, practices psychoanalysis and psychoanalytically oriented psychotherapy in New York City and Bedford Hills, New York. He is a Dharma Holder in the White Plum Sangha and Red Thread Zen Circle. The author of *Psychotherapy and Buddhism, The Good Life,* and *A Psychoanalysis for Our Time,* he is considered one of the leading integrators of the Western psychotherapeutic and Eastern meditative traditions. The creator of *meditative psychotherapy,* Dr. Rubin has taught at various universities and psychoanalytic institutes including Union Theological Seminary, the Postgraduate Center for Mental Health, the C. G. Jung Foundation of New York, and Yeshiva University. He is a training and supervising analyst at the Westchester Institute for Training in Psychoanalysis and Psychotherapy. Dr. Rubin can be contacted through his Web site (http://www.drjeffreyrubin.com).

Michael J. Stevens, PhD, DHC, is a professor of psychology at Illinois State University and a licensed clinical psychologist. He served as president of the Division of International Psychology of the American Psychological Association in 2007, having previously chaired its Curriculum and Training, Information

Clearinghouse, and International Liaisons committees, and cochaired its Program Committee. He is a fellow of the division and received its Outstanding Mentor Award and Recognition Award twice, as well as a Presidential Citation. He is an honorary professor at the Lucian Blaga University in Romania, where he completed a Fulbright grant and received the Doctor Honoris Causa degree. He has been invited to lecture in Argentina, China, Cyprus, Guatemala, Finland, Pakistan, Tajikistan, Uruguay, and Vietnam. Dr. Stevens has published 100 articles and book chapters and presented over 100 papers, symposia, and invited talks. Recent scholarship related to global psychology includes the *Handbook of International Psychology* (2004), *Psychology: IUPsyS Global Resource* (2005–2009), and *Toward a Global Psychology: Theory, Research, Intervention, and Pedagogy* (2007).

Linda Sussman, PhD, is a research associate, Department of Anthropology, Washington University. She received her doctorate in sociology at Washington University, held a postdoctoral fellowship in psychiatric epidemiology, and has been a faculty member at the Washington University School of Medicine. She has also served as associate editor of the *American Anthropologist*. Her research has focused on lay medical beliefs, practices, and treatment seeking; traditional healers and ethnobotany; risk factors and treatment seeking for depression; and the design of culturally appropriate and responsive community programs for chronic diseases. She has conducted fieldwork in Madagascar, Mauritius, and the United States.

Junko Tanaka-Matsumi, PhD, is professor of psychology at Kwansei Gakuin University, Japan, and professor emeritus at Hofstra University, Hempstead, New York, where she taught clinical psychology for 20 years until 2000. She obtained her PhD in clinical psychology from the University of Hawaii at Manoa on an East-West Center scholarship. She is a fellow of American Psychological Association (Divisions 12 and 52) and has published on culture and psychopathology, functional analytic approaches to cross-cultural assessment and therapy, and school-based behavioral assessment. She is an associate editor of the *Journal of Cross-Cultural Psychology* and on the editorial board of *Multicultural Aspects in Counseling Series* of Sage Publications.

Luis A. Vargas, PhD, is an associate professor in the Department of Psychiatry at the University of New Mexico. He was previously the director of the psychology internship program for 14 years. Dr. Vargas' clinical and scholarly work has focused on providing culturally responsive services to diverse children and adolescents, particularly in Latino communities. He is coeditor (with Joan D. Koss-Chioino) of *Working With Culture: Psychotherapeutic Interventions With Ethnic Minority Children and Adolescent* and a coauthor (with Joan D. Koss-Chioino) of *Working With Latino Youth: Culture, Development, and Context*, both published by Jossey-Bass.

Danny Wedding, PhD, MPH, trained as a clinical psychologist at the University of Hawaii and the University of Mississippi Medical Center. He later spent 2 years working as a health policy fellow and science policy fellow for the U.S. Congress. He joined the University of Missouri–Columbia School of Medicine in 1991 as professor of psychiatry and director of the Missouri Institute of Mental Health, a research and policy center serving the mental health community. His research interests include international health, the portrayal of mental illness and addictions in films, and ways to alter attitudes about mental illness and substance abuse.

Author Index

Katz, R., 122
Kay, P., 77
Kazdin, A.E., 175, 182, 184
Keefe, S., 249
Keener, R., 242
Kelley, J.E., 128
Kelly, C., 208, 211, 223
Kelly, J.A., 246, 247
Kemp, T.P., 348
Kessler, R.C., 116, 124
Keys, S., 204, 206, 210, 211, 213, 214, 215, 216,
    217, 223
Keys, S.G., 214
Khantzian, E.J., 238, 243
Kiecolt-Glaser, J., 127
Kiecolt-Glaser, J.K., 122, 124, 125, 127
Kim, B.S.K., 218, 224
Kim, H.-J., 386
Kim, S.C., 218, 224
Kim, U., 265
Kimura, B., 398, 399, 411
King-Sears, M.E., 214
Kinzie, J.D., 398
Kirmayer, L.J., 338
Kirsch, I., 77, 85, 87, 123, 124
Kitayama, S., 406
Kleinman, A., 39, 41, 45, 47, 124, 131, 332,
    335, 337, 338
Kleinman, A.M., 180, 189
Kluckhohn, C., 3, 7, 410
Kocet, M.M., 140, 149, 155
Kohn, L., 174, 177, 184
Koss-Chioino, J., 231, 233
Koss-Chioino, J.D., 231, (231–252), 237, 239,
    246, 249
Kraepelin, E., 393, 395, 396, 412
Krantz, D.S., 120
Krasner, M., 126
Krippner, R., 355, 356
Krippner, S., 76
Kroeber, A.L., 3
Krohne, H.W., 125
Krug, S., 140, 151, 152, 153
Kujac, H., 312
Kulik, J.A., 125
Kumanyika, S.K., 61
Kuriansky, J., (295–330), 297, 305, 312, 321
Kurtines, W., 247
Kurtines, W.M., 235

L

LaFromboise, T., 174, 177, 184
LaFromboise, T.M., 220

Lam, K., 180, 185, 186
Lambert, M.J., 88, 174, 177, 185
Lambo, T.H., 355
Lang, G.C., 47, 62, 63
Langer, S., 384
Langs, R., 374
LaPerriere, A., 235
Larsen, E., 312
Lasker, J., 125
Lau, A., 174, 177, 184
Laungani, P., 255, (255–276), 257, 265, 367,
    402, 403, 408, 411
Lavelle, J., 398
Leach, M.M., 170
Lee, C., 204, 206, 210, 211, 212, 214, 216, 217,
    222
Lee, C.C., 204
Lee, S.-H., 410
Lee, S.M., 204
Lefebvre, R.C., 124
Lehrer, T., 82
Leighton, A.H., 355
Leighton, D.C., 355
Leisen, J.C.C., 128
Leong, F.T.L., 170, 410
Levenstein, S., 129
Lewis, J., 247
Li, L.C., 181
Lindner, E.tG., 305
Lindwall, J.J., (199–229), 209, 224
Linton, R., 176
Lipchik, E., 82
Lipsey, M.W., 174
Lock, M., 332, 335, 337, 338
Lockhart, E.J., 215, 216
Loewald, H., 383, 384
Loftus, M., 246
Lonner, W.J., 170, 171, 297
Lonner.W.F., 410
Lopez, S.J., 124
Lopez, S.R., 110, 410
Low, C.A., 128
Luecke, R., 47
Lumley, M.A., 131
Lunt, I., 170
Lynn, T.N., 125

M

MacCullum, R.C., 122, 127
MacDonald, R., 409
Machado, P., 88
Macklin, D.B., 355
MacNaughton, J., 156

Subject Index